C for COBOL Programmers

A Business Approach

D1605162

To my parents, Phil and Byrdie

C For COBOL Programmers

A Business Approach

Jim Gearing

Gearing Associates

Addison-Wesley Publishing Company, Inc.

Menlo Park, California • Reading, Massachusetts
New York • Don Mills, Ontario • Wokingham, U.K. • Amsterdam
Bonn • Paris • Milan • Madrid • Sydney • Singapore • Tokyo
Seoul • Taipei • Mexico City • San Juan, Puerto Rico

Acquisitions Editor: J. Carter Shanklin
Executive Editor: Dan Joraanstad
Projects Manager: Ray Kanarr
Editorial Assistant: Christine Kulke
Administrative Assistant: Debbie Bravo
Cover Design: Annabelle Ison
Text Design: Richard Kharibian
Copy Editing: Barbara Conway
Proofreader: Holly Aldis
Composition Services: Syarikat Seng Teik Sdn. Bhd.
Senior Manufacturing Coordinator: Janet Weaver

Instructional Material Disclaimer
The examples presented in this book have been included for their instructional value. They have been tested with care but are not guaranteed for any particular purpose. The publisher does not offer any warranties or representations, nor does it accept any liabilities with respect to the programs or examples.

Library of Congress Cataloging-in-Publication Data
Gearing, Jim.
    C for COBOL programmers / Jim Gearing
        p.   cm.
    Includes bibliographical references and index.
    1. C (Computer program language) I. Title.
QA76.73.C15G39   1995   95-25182
005.13'3—dc20   CIP

ISBN 0-8053-1660-4

1 2 3 4 5 6 7 8 9 10—CRS—99 98 97 96 95

Addison-Wesley Publishing Company, Inc.
2725 Sand Hill Road
Menlo Park, CA 94025-7092

Quick Guide to Chapters

Contents

Preface

This book was born of rage.

When I first tried to learn the C language in 1985, I could not find a book that made sense to me. I had been designing business systems and programming COBOL for more than 15 years. All the books on C that I found were "self-referential." That is to say, the authors had been writing C for so long that they had forgotten what it was like not to know it. I gave up after a few months. I was enraged that nobody had written a readable and useful book.

One day in 1988 my client, Rob Gillette, dropped 20 C programs on my desk and said, "Here, Jim, learn C and finish this subsystem." I went back to the bookstore and found the books to be a little better than three years before, but still not very good. I learned C, but it was a painful experience.

In 1991 I began working on business systems being developed in C. It was at this time I realized that I could write the book I had been looking for: *C for COBOL Programmers*.

C is just another language. Much of it works like COBOL, but with symbols instead of words. Parts of C have assumptions different from COBOL, and parts have rules different from COBOL. The purpose of this book is to use your knowledge of COBOL to teach you C. The book shows you where C works the same way as COBOL and shows you where it's different. It also focuses on the parts of C used most often in business systems.

C has some very nice features and some that are a real pain in the neck, just like COBOL.

Come on, jump in! The water's not *that* cold!

Acknowledgements

First and foremost I acknowledge and thank my wife and love, Beverly. Bev is the unsung hero of this book. The author has the glamorous job, writing, and the spouse has the un-glamorous, but more important, job: keeping the family functioning and together. We're still happily married, but I won't be writing any more books at night and on weekends.

Many thanks to many people. Thanks to Rob Gillette for kick starting me on C; to Wally Knapp for creating an environment where it was possible to get the work done; to Barry Miller for hours of discussion about whether C or COBOL was the worse language, and also for illuminating C++ discussions.

My reviewers volunteered to review the manuscript without quite realizing how much work they had taken on. I am grateful for their effort and grateful for the improvements they contributed. A big round of applause, please, for Jim Beard, James DeRocher, Tom Enns, Dave Feigin, Dave Gasque, Kathleen Harkin, Joanna Manthos, Anne O'Donnell, Tom Raymond, and Rusty Romaine. I would also like to acknowledge the contributions of Dr. Mark W. Smith and Michael Payne of Purdue University, Gerald Tatar of Dusquesne University and E. Gladys Norman of Linn-Benton CC.

Thanks to Arnold Bosserman for reviews and suggestions when the manuscript was a toddler.

I also want to thank Vasan Ramaswamy for his grace during my unyielding insistence that my project (this book) had a higher priority than his project.

The reviewers caught a number of errors while doing their work. Remaining errors in the book are the sole property of the author.

How to Use This Book

I believe that there are only a few people who ever read a computer language book from beginning to end: the author, the copy editor, and kind reviewers.

We programmers are generally impatient and want to get to the heart of the matter immediately. We usually read the first 20 or 30 pages of a computer language book and begin our work. Then we come back to the book for new topics, further explanation, or to figure out problems. The problem for the author is how to combine teaching and reference material in the same book.

With that in mind, I have designed this book to work on several different levels. These levels are:

1. Give me an introduction.
2. Give me the syntax.
3. Give me the detail.
4. What's wrong with my program?

Here's how they work:

1. Give me an introduction.

The first two chapters of the book are a general introduction to the C language. Chapter 1 compares and contrasts C with COBOL. Chapter 2 covers compiling, formatting, and comments. This is the only part of the book I expect you will read straight through.

In addition, each chapter begins with an introduction, in English, to the programming topic of that chapter.

2. Give me the syntax.

The next level of use occurs when you want to use or learn about a C keyword (reserved word) or function (subprogram) and want the basic syntax. This is addressed on the first page of each section about a C operator or function. The C language uses functions to do a lot of the work of the language. When you see the word function, think "subprogram."

The first page contains the syntax, a code sample, any include file (copy member) needed, a short description of the operator or function, how parameters must be defined, and what is contained in the return value (RETURN-CODE) of a function call. This is generally enough for people who need to refresh their memories or have been programming in C long enough to not need a detailed explanation.

3. Give me the detail.

When you want a more detailed explanation of the syntax and more discussion of the operator or function, you can continue to read the detailed examination of the parts of the statement (anatomy) and a general discussion. After each discussion there is a short section on common errors for the topic discussed.

You may also continue reading the next two parts, which are the example program and a set of comments about the example program.

The example program and comments are designed to work on two levels. Within the example program there are comments on the right side of the significant statements, which give a capsule description of the action taking place in the statement. This is followed by a comments section where there is more detail on each significant statement in the example program.

The example program typically contains several of the common errors made for that C operator or function. This is especially important for people coming from COBOL, because several underlying assumptions in the C language are different from or opposite to the corresponding assumptions in COBOL.

4. What's wrong with my program?

When a program does not work the way you think it should, you may want to review the syntax at the beginning of the section, review the parameter definitions, review the common errors, and then look at the example program and its comments to get clues about your problem.

This is why the detailed comments are often longer than the example program. These comments not only explain how things work, but why certain techniques should be used and why other techniques should not be used.

A Few Comments on Repetition

Those of you valiant enough to read this book cover-to-cover will find a lot of repetition in it. As the famous software saying goes, "That's not a defect, it's a feature!"

The repetition is here for two reasons. My observation is that most people read between three paragraphs and two pages when they look at a computer book. Repeating topics and tips increases the likelihood that important material will be found when "dipping." And for people who read whole chapters, the repetition reinforces the learning process.

Condensed List of Functions

Inside the front and back covers of this book is a list of all the functions and operators discussed in the book. After you acquire a degree of familiarity with C, you often only need the syntax for a given operator or function. Instead of having to search the index or table of contents to find the page, you can look inside the covers and find the basic syntax. The page number where the operator/function is discussed is also shown.

Quick Guide to Chapters

This book has been designed with a block on the outer edge of the first page of each chapter. The Quick Guide to Chapters page has all the chapters of the book listed, with blocks that match the ones in the chapters. This is another feature to help you find things quickly.

Table of Contents

I have written the Table of Contents using (mostly) English or COBOL terms, which is unusual for a book on C. You should be able to recognize almost every topic. This is the way natural language books are structured: syntax and grammar of the known language are used to teach the new language.

Additionally, C keywords and operators are shown to the right of page numbers where they are discussed. This is provided as another cross-reference.

Summary

I have written the book I wanted to find when I learned C. I use language books in several different ways, so I have tried to make this one useful in several different ways. If this book makes the C language seem understandable and accessible to you, then I have succeeded.

Jim Gearing

CHAPTER 1

From COBOL to C

Introduction

You already know a lot more about C than you think; C just expresses things differently. It uses fewer words and more punctuation symbols than COBOL, so it doesn't look like the "English" we're used to in COBOL.

This book is not a comprehensive book on C. In business applications there is a core of the C language that should be used to produce maintainable systems. The same thing is true for COBOL. In the business environment the working set for both COBOL and C is considerably smaller than the whole of either language. This book addresses the business working set of the C language. This should cover most, if not all, the problems you are likely to encounter in your first year or two using C.

Which C? Which COBOL? Which Computer?

There are literally hundreds of C compilers and dozens of COBOL compilers in existence. The following sections discuss which versions of C and COBOL are discussed in this book.

Which C?

C existed for about a dozen years before the American National Standards Institute (ANSI) published the ANSI C standard in 1989. The purpose of the standard was to promote portability, reliability, and maintainability of C programs on a variety of machines. Although C was already supposed to be portable, there were many variations between C compilers that would cause the same program to give different results on different compilers.

This book uses and discusses only ANSI C. Most contemporary compilers implement the ANSI standard.

Which COBOL?

Although there are now several dozen COBOL compilers in existence, the majority of COBOL programmers are familiar with IBM COBOL. This book uses OS/VS COBOL as a base. Some IBM extensions are mentioned, but readers who know other COBOLs should find most, if not all, of the COBOL examples understandable.

IBM announced that it would stop supporting the OS/VS COBOL compiler after 1994. It did this in order to encourage conversion to COBOL II. COBOL II is based on the 1985 ANSI COBOL standard. Many of the new features of COBOL II are closer to the equivalent C features than those of OS/VS COBOL.

This chapter is primarily an overview of basic COBOL compared to ANSI C. COBOL II is discussed in later chapters where appropriate. Where there is a comparison of COBOL and C, there is a discussion of the COBOL II feature when it is different from OS/VS COBOL.

Which Computer?

C probably runs on more operating systems than any language in the world. The ANSI C standard helps keep the language coherent because it defines a standard C. Although ANSI C syntax may be the same across computers and operating systems, compiling programs is at least slightly different on every operating system.

C compilers can now be found on every kind of personal computer, all workstations, and even IBM mainframes. Because of this I have chosen not to go into specifics on how to compile programs or organize disk files; there are simply too many variations. For that information you must consult either someone who knows the operating system you're using or your compiler documentation.

Sample Programs: Free On-line or Cheap by Mail

This book makes extensive use of sample programs to illustrate concepts and techniques of C. Over 40 complete programs are presented. These programs were compiled and tested before they were placed in the book. Also, several more business utility programs are presented in Appendix F. These programs are all available free from Benjamin/Cummings through the Internet. If you have access to America Online, CompuServe, Prodigy, or other popular on-line services, you have access to Internet.

Alternatively, you can order a diskette with these programs by using the coupon in the back of the book.

In addition to sample programs, Chapter 13, which covers C standards for a business environment, is available in three formats: Microsoft Word, WordPerfect, and ASCII text. This could be useful as a base from which to create your own standards.

A more detailed discussion on downloading these files is presented in Appendix H.

Evolution of C

In the beginning, there was COBOL—the COmmon Business Oriented Language—which was created to provide self-documenting programs in English-like statements for the business world.

C was developed to write the operating system Unix. An operating system works at very low levels within the computer. A language capable of writing an operating system must be able to perform low-level tasks. C has this ability.

From the point of view of assembly programmers who write operating systems, C is a high-level language. This is because a single C statement can do the work of several assembler statements. From the point of view of COBOL programmers, however, C is a low-level language. Many things that COBOL handles with a single statement require several lines or even a subprogram in C. On the other hand, there are many things you can do in C more compactly than in COBOL.

C is, in a sense, like a genetic experiment that escaped from the lab. It has mutated in the field, sometimes far from its original design. Flexibility and features have been added, sometimes at the cost of consistency.

While C is not particularly well suited for solving business problems, it is increasingly becoming the tool we have to use as Unix, VMS, and MS-DOS platforms become more common in business data processing. IBM also now offers a C compiler on a mainframe. While we may enjoy complaining about C, the fact remains that we need to master it.

A Quick Survey of C Compared to COBOL

The premise of this book is that C is more similar to COBOL than it seems. The reason the two languages don't seem similar is that most C books are not oriented to either COBOL programmers or to business data processing problems. C uses punctuation and symbols more than COBOL does, but basically these are both computer languages that have the same jobs to do.

The following sections show COBOL and equivalent C code fragments side by side. After each sample there is a brief discussion of similarities and differences.

The rest of the book covers these same topics, plus additional ones, in more detail.

Data Names

COBOL	C
CUST-NAME	cust_name
LINE-COUNT	line_count
SUB-TOTAL-2	sub_total_2
TOTAL-AMORTIZATION-AMOUNT	total_amortization_amount

The most obvious feature of C data names is they are in lowercase. C allows both upper- and lowercase to be used both in data names and in function (subprogram) names. The common and sensible usage is lowercase. Also, the underscore is the connector in a data name, not the dash. C uses the dash exclusively as the subtraction operator. In ANSI C you are allowed 31 characters for data names.

Data names are covered in detail in Chapter 3, "Defining Data In C."

Data Definition—Alphanumeric

COBOL		C
MIDDLE-INIT	PIC X.	char middle_init;
LAST-NAME	PIC X(30).	char last_name [31];

In COBOL a statement ends with a period. In C a statement ends with a semicolon.

Where COBOL uses PIC X or PIC X(30), C uses the *data type* char or char [31]. C doesn't have an equivalent to the PIC clause—it just jumps straight to the data type. The C definition for last_name is larger than in COBOL because in C there is an extra character used to end alphanumerics. This character is called the *null terminator*. Alphanumerics of more than one character are called strings in C. Strings are inherently variable in length. C uses the null terminator to tell when it has reached the end of a string. The null terminator is a character with a value of hex zeroes; in COBOL it is called LOW-VALUE.

Alphanumeric data definition is discussed further in Chapter 3, "Defining Data In C."

Data Definition—Numeric

COBOL			C	
SUB-1	PIC S9(4)	COMP.	int	sub_1;
REC-COUNT	PIC 9(5).		int	rec_count;
SUB-2	PIC S9(8)	COMP.	long	sub_2;
VOTE-COUNT	PIC 9(8).		long	vote_count;
YTD-SALES-AMT	PIC S9(8)V99.		double	ytd_sales_amt;
OVERHEAD-PCT	PIC V9(3).		double	overhead_pct;
GROSS-SALARY	PIC S9(5)V99	COMP-3.	double	gross_salary;

Numeric data item definition in C is simpler than in COBOL. You just declare a data type and a data name. Notice that `int`, `long`, and `double` have no digits. When you declare a numeric data type, you automatically get the maximum number of digits that go along with it.

PIC S9 *without* a V translates to `int` or `long`. These are two integer data types; they have no decimal places. Typically an `int` is a two-byte signed binary integer, and a `long` is a four-byte signed binary integer. A two-byte `int` can go up to 32,767, which makes it easy to overflow. A `long` will go over 2 billion before it overflows. If your compiler has a two-byte `int`, save yourself grief and always use `long`. Strictly speaking, PIC 9 translates to `unsigned int` or `unsigned long`, which are unsigned numbers. However, they are not used much in business data processing; rather, integer variables are declared simply as `int` or `long`.

PIC S9 *with* a V translates to a `double`. A `double` is a floating point number, which has decimal places. A `double` has an accuracy of about 15 significant digits, meaning that the number starts getting flaky around the 15th least significant position. This is well beyond the bounds of the average business system. Another consequence of a `double` is that you always get a lot of decimal places, whether you want them or not. If you are keeping track of dollars and cents, you will need to do your own rounding in C.

Numeric data definition is discussed further in Chapter 3, "Defining Data In C."

Moving Data

COBOL		C		
MOVE 1	TO SUB-1.	sub_1	= 1;	
MOVE DEPT-NO	TO PREV-DEPT-NO.	prev_dept_no	= dept_no;	
MOVE MID-INIT	TO HOLD-INIT.	hold_init	= mid_init;	
MOVE PAY-REC	TO PAY-REC-OUT.	pay_rec_out	= pay_rec;	
(*record* or *group item* in COBOL)		(*structure* in C)		

Most often, moving data in C means using the equal sign. A single equal sign in C always means copy (move) the data element on the right to the data element on the left. If you try to read the C statements as MOVE statements, they are hard to read. If instead you look at them as COMPUTE statements without the COMPUTE word, you see something much more familiar.

COBOL	C
MOVE LAST-NAME TO PREV-LAST-NAME.	strcpy (prev_last_name, last_name);

This line of code shows a big difference between COBOL and C. COBOL uses the MOVE statement for all data types, including alphanumerics (called *strings* in C). In C most operations with strings require calls to functions (subprograms). There is a standard set of functions, called *library functions*, that come with the compiler. You will call a lot of functions in C to do things that use reserved words in COBOL.

"strcpy()" is discussed further in Chapter 7, "Moving Data."

Screen Input/Output

Just as no one in the IBM COBOL world would try to write a substitute for CICS for the new accounting system, no one using C should write his or her own screen manager.

Buy a package. It won't be perfect, but it will work, probably better than anything you could write. And when industry or vendor standards change, you won't have to rewrite it, the vendor will.

This said, there is still a requirement for screen I/O in C business data processing. In the world of PCs and workstations, production systems now run from users' desks, not from a centralized machine room. It is common in these distributed systems to prompt the user for parameters when they aren't supplied and to display status messages on the screen. These tasks are accomplished by calling library functions (subprograms) in C programs.

Screen I/O is covered in detail in Chapter 5, "Terminal Input/Output."

Sequential File Input/Output

Sequential file I/O is very different in C compared to COBOL. Everything having to do with sequential file I/O in C is done through calls to library functions (supplied subprograms). A short line-by-line comparison between COBOL and C on this subject is not feasible.

The good news is that if you're using C in business, you shouldn't be doing very much sequential file I/O. You should be using a database or file manager package for data storage and retrieval. If you are writing your own version of this major area, you're doing something wrong. Vendors can supply the solution more cleanly and in the long run (even the medium run) more cheaply than you can do it yourself. There is no acceptable rationale for a "home-grown" data manager as we approach the end of the first half-century of computing.

There is still a requirement for sequential file handling in C for things such as interface files to other systems. Chapter 6, "File Input/Output," covers the useful parts of C sequential file I/O.

Arithmetic

COBOL	C
COMPUTE NET-AMT = GROSS-AMT - TAX-AMT.	net_amt = gross_amt - tax_amt;
COMPUTE SALE-AMT = UNITS * COST-AMT.	sale_amt = units * cost_amt;
COMPUTE EST-WEEKS = EST-DAYS / 5.	est_weeks = est_days / 5;
ADD 1 TO SUB-1.	sub_1 += 1;
SUBTRACT 1 FROM SUB-2.	sub_2 -= 1;

COBOL's COMPUTE statement translates very directly to C—just drop the word COMPUTE.

COBOL's ADD TO and SUBTRACT FROM also translate directly, if not obviously. First of all, the C statements read from right to left. This is fairly characteristic of C. The detailed discussions in the rest of the book emphasize the direction of each operator or function call.

The += and -= are examples of a *compound assignment operator*, which uses the right operand to do an arithmetic operation on the left operand. The result is then stored in the left operand. It is the same operation as ADD TO and SUBTRACT FROM, but in C it reads from right to left.

Arithmetic is discussed in detail in Chapter 8, "Arithmetic."

If Statements

COBOL	C
IF HOURS = 40	if (hours == 40)
IF HOURS > 40	if (hours > 40)
IF HOURS NOT GREATER THAN 40	if (hours <= 40)
IF HOURS NOT = 40	if (hours != 40)

C if statements are easily recognizable. The quirk is that the equality comparison is *two* equal signs, ==, not one. A single equal sign **always** means assign (move) the right value to the left operand. The intended comparison does not occur. This will trip you up 10 or 20 times in your first year of writing C programs. The other oddity is the use of the exclamation point for NOT.

== means IF EQUAL.

!= means IF NOT EQUAL.

C also has "less than or equal to" and "greater than or equal to" operators: <= and >=.

COBOL	C

`IF HOURS > 40`
`    COMPUTE OVERTIME = HOURS - 40.`
	`if (hours > 40 )`
	`{`
	`        overtime = hours - 40;`
	`}`

If the if is true, then what? COBOL has one or more statements after its IF, terminated by a period or an ELSE. C has one or more statements after its if, but termination is trickier. In C the true statement or statements are terminated by either

- a closing brace, }
- an else
- the end of the first statement after the if when there are no braces and no else

Termination can be confusing and is best handled by always using braces to delimit the statements for both the true and false conditions in if statements, as shown in the preceding and following samples.

COBOL	C

`IF HOURS > 40`
`    COMPUTE OVERTIME = HOURS - 40`
`ELSE`
`    MOVE 0 TO OVERTIME.`
	`if (hours > 40 )`
	`{`
	`        overtime = hours - 40;`
	`}`
	`else`
	`{`
	`        overtime = 0;`
	`{`

The `else` condition in C statements is handled in the same way as the true condition. Always use braces to delimit both the true and the false conditional statements, and your life will be simpler. It will also benefit the person who has to work on the program in the future. Who knows, it could be you.

If statements are covered in more depth in Chapter 9, "If, Case (`EVALUATE`), and Class Test."

PERFORM-type Statements

COBOL	C

`01  PAGE-NUMBER   PIC 999.`
`01  LINE-COUNT    PIC 999.`
 	
`PROCEDURE DIVISION.`
 	
`    PERFORM 1000-INITIALIZE`
 	
`    GOBACK.`
 	
`1000-INITIALIZE.`
 	
`    MOVE 0 TO PAGE-NUMBER.`
`    MOVE 0 TO LINE-COUNT.`
	`int  page_number;`
	`int  line_count;`
	
	`main()`
	`{`
	`    a1000_initialize();`
	
	`    return (0);`
	`}`
	
	`a1000_initialize()`
	`{`
	`    page_number = 0;`
	`    line_count  = 0;`
	`}`

COBOL arranges programs by paragraphs and sections, while C arranges programs by functions. The difference is that in C a function can be written to act like either a COBOL paragraph or a COBOL subprogram. This example shows how to write a function as a paragraph.

Data items are declared at the top of both programs and are therefore available throughout both programs. Instead of `PROCEDURE DIVISION`, C has `main()`. C delimits functions, including `main()`, by the opening and closing braces, `{   }`.

Whereas in COBOL, `PERFORM` is followed by a paragraph name, in C you just give the function name. Function calls always have parentheses, which is where parameters are placed. When you're treating C functions like paragraphs, there are no parameters because the function is using global memory, just as a COBOL paragraph does.

A function name (and a data name) in C cannot begin with a number. If you want to number your functions as you do paragraphs in COBOL, you must put a letter before the number in the C function name.

The `return (0)` statement in `main()` returns control to the operating system and hands back a condition code, zero in this case. The script (JCL equivalent) that executes the program can evaluate the `return code` and take appropriate action. `return` is like `RETURN-CODE`, except that the concept is considerably broader in C.

The `a1000_initialize` function is functionally identical to the `1000-INITIALIZE` paragraph. The syntax is about the same except the function name has parentheses after it and it has braces to delimit its statements.

PERFORM-type statements are discussed in greater detail in Chapter 10, "Flow of Control Statements."

Calling Subprograms

COBOL	C

CALL 'COMPFICA' USING EMP-SSNO,
                 HOURLY-WAGE,
                 HOURS-WORKED.
	compute_fica (emp_ssno,
	            hourly_wage,
	            hours_worked);

In C you can write a function that works like a subprogram in COBOL. Such a function in C has parameters, just as a COBOL subprogram does. The C call statement is recognizable compared to COBOL: You drop `CALL`, `USING`, and the single quotes around the subprogram name and put parentheses around the parameter list. That's it.

Calling subprograms is discussed further in Chapter 4, "Instructions, Keywords, and Function Calls" and in Chapter 11, "Calling Functions (Subprograms)."

LINKAGE SECTION

COBOL	C

IDENTIFICATION DIVISION.
PROGRAM-ID. COMPFICA.
  ...
LINKAGE SECTION.
01 EMP-SSNO   PIC 9(9).
01 HOURLY-WAGE PIC 99V99.
01 HOURS-WORKED PIC 999V9.
PROCEDURE DIVISION USING EMP-SSNO,
                 HOURLY-WAGE,
                 HOURS-WORKED.
	compute_fica (long emp_ssno,
	            double hourly_wage,
	            double hours_worked)

This code is an obvious example of the compactness of C. Every significant item in the COBOL example on the left is found in the three lines of C at the right: subprogram name, parameter list, and parameter definition.

ANSI C combines `LINKAGE SECTION` and `PROCEDURE DIVISION USING`. In ANSI C you put the data type of the parameter in the parameter list, in front of the parameter name.

This topic is covered in detail in Chapter 11, "Calling Functions (Subprograms)."

Tables (Arrays)

COBOL Table Definition	C Array Definition
| ```
01  DIV-SUB      PIC S9(4) COMP.
01  SALES-TOTALS.
    05  DIV-TOTAL  OCCURS 12 TIMES.
               PIC S9(7)V99.
``` | ```
int    div_sub;
double div_total [12];
``` |

Tables are called *arrays* in C. Since C does not have the concept of levels in data definition, you can define an elementary item as an array, as in the preceding code. Square brackets enclosing a number are the equivalent of OCCURS n TIMES. When you have multiple totals that need to be in an array, you can define an array with a structure, C's equivalent of the COBOL group item.

C arrays are accessed using subscripts. Subscripts must be defined separately, as in COBOL. The INDEXED BY clause in COBOL has no equivalent in C.

In C you can define multidimensional arrays. There is effectively no limit to the number of dimensions in a C array.

COBOL Table Use	C Array Use
| ```
MOVE 0 TO DIV-TOTAL (DIV-SUB).
...
ADD SALES-AMT TO DIV-TOTAL (DIV-SUB).
``` | ```
div_total [div_sub] = 0;
...
div_total [div_sub] += sales_amt;
``` |

Using an array in C is similar to using a table in COBOL: The data name is followed by a subscript. C's subscript notation uses square brackets, where COBOL uses parentheses. The real differences in the preceding statements are due to C's use of symbol operators instead of reserved words. C uses the single equal sign as the equivalent of the COBOL MOVE statement. The += symbol is equivalent to ADD TO, except the order is reversed compared to COBOL.

C allows *relative subscripting*, which is equivalent to COBOL's relative indexing.

```
div_total [ div_sub + 1 ]
```

is legal in C.

Table definition and use are covered in depth in Chapter 12, "Table Handling."

Fundamental Concepts of COBOL and C Compared

This section compares some of the fundamental concepts of the two languages and finds they are not so different. Comparisons cover syntax, reserved words, symbols, subprograms, and program hierarchy.

COBOL Language Syntax

The COBOL language was originally designed to have an English-like syntax and to use symbols as little as possible. It was created to solve problems in the business environment. Previous languages were oriented to mathematical or scientific problem solving.

COBOL statements generally follow the imperative mood of English grammar, which tells someone (or some computer) to perform some action on some object. The form is *verb-object-subject*. For example, the English sentence *Subtract the deductions from the gross giving net amount* in COBOL would be

```
SUBTRACT DEDUCTIONS FROM GROSS GIVING NET-AMOUNT.
```

COBOL drops the articles (a, an, the), but the result is still recognizable as an English sentence.

C Language Syntax

C was developed with little regard for English and to write the Unix operating system. It was designed to be a high-level language capable of manipulating a computer at a low level. Its original audience was assembler programmers, and its syntax is based on the structure of machine language.

C syntax generally consists of *object-verb-subject*—generally the reverse of both English and COBOL. For example, the COBOL statement

```
SUBTRACT DEDUCTIONS FROM GROSS GIVING NET-AMOUNT.
```

is equivalent to the C statement

```
net_amount = gross - deductions;
```

However, this C statement looks suspiciously like the COBOL statement

```
COMPUTE NET-AMOUNT = GROSS - DEDUCTIONS.
```

So there's more similarity than may appear at first.

Another common construct in C is *function call (object parameter, subject parameter)*. A function in C is equivalent to a subprogram in COBOL. C uses function calls to do a lot of the work of the language. For example, the COBOL statement

```
MOVE LAST_NAME TO SAVE_LAST_NAME.
```

is equivalent to the C statement

```
strcpy (save_last_name, last_name);
```

The string copy function is typical in that it takes the right parameter and uses it to do something to the left parameter. This is machine-friendly rather than user-friendly. Most C statements operate from right to left. The detailed discussions later in the book show the direction in which each statement operates.

Much of C uses syntax different from COBOL, and it takes a while to get used to it.

Reserved Words and Keywords

The term *reserved word* is used for any word known to the COBOL compiler, while the term *keyword* is used in C.

ANSI COBOL has over 300 reserved words.

ANSI C has only 32 keywords.

COBOL does its work with reserved words, while C has only a few keywords and does much of its work with functions and symbols.

Subprograms

One of the big differences between COBOL and C is subprograms.

COBOL has none bundled with mainframe compilers.

C has several hundred functions (subprograms) bundled with each compiler.

COBOL has a big list of reserved words and no bundled subprograms, while C has only a few keywords and a lot of bundled functions. In C these bundled functions are called library functions, and they are essential to writing programs in C. All file I/O operations in C are handled by calls to I/O functions, such as `fopen()`, `fprintf()`, and `fclose()`. These functions are equivalent to the COBOL reserved words `OPEN`, `WRITE`, and `CLOSE`, respectively. Whereas in COBOL you code

```
OPEN INPUT TRAN-FILE.
```

in C you code

```
tran_file = fopen ( tran_file_dsn, 'i' );
```

The reason C uses so many library functions is to remove machine-specific and operating-system-specific features from the language. Therefore, the process of writing a C compiler for a new machine is easier. The machine-specific language is contained in the library functions, so application programs do not contain machine-specific instructions. This means C programs are relatively easy to move from compiler to compiler. It also means that instead of coding print or read statements, you code calls to print or read functions.

Punctuation and Symbols

If you're developing a computer language and you want to have a minimal list of reserved words, you use punctuation and symbols to do what other languages do with reserved words.

COBOL has little punctuation and few symbols.

C has a lot of punctuation and a lot of symbols.

C is therefore somewhat harder to read than COBOL, since many of C's symbols are reserved words in COBOL.

Program Hierarchy in COBOL and C

COBOL Program Hierarchy		C Program Hierarchy	
Main program	equals	. . . .	main()
Subprogram	can equal	. . . .	function
Paragraph	can equal	. . . .	function

COBOL has main programs, subprograms, paragraphs (sections), and executables. C has main() functions, functions, and executables. In C there are two kinds of functions: main() and all the rest. Everything in C is a function, including main().

The main program in COBOL is what is executed by JCL; it is the "executable." The main() function in C is what is executed by a script (JCL equivalent) or from the operating system prompt; it is the "executable."

A function in C can look like either a subprogram or a paragraph in COBOL, depending on how you write it. Therefore, in the preceding table a function is listed as equivalent to either a subprogram or a paragraph.

These concepts are discussed further in Chapter 11, "Calling Functions (Subprograms)."

Program Organization in COBOL and C

COBOL programs have this organization:

```
IDENTIFICATION DIVISION.
...
ENVIRONMENT DIVISION.
...
DATA DIVISION.
...
FILE SECTION.
...
WORKING-STORAGE SECTION.
...
REPORT SECTION.
...
LINKAGE SECTION.
...
PROCEDURE DIVISION.
...
```
Program Instructions ...

To use COBOL terms for how C programs are arranged, C programs have this organization:

```
WORKING-STORAGE SECTION.        (global data declarations)
...
PROCEDURE DIVISION.
...
LINKAGE SECTION.                (Optional)
...
WORKING-STORAGE SECTION.        (Local data declarations)
...
```
Program Instructions ...

The IDENTIFICATION and ENVIRONMENT divisions in COBOL programs are basically documentation, with the exception of the PROGRAM-ID. C does not have any language constructs for the items in these two divisions. C programmers generally create a set of comments at the beginning of C programs, such as program name, author, and remarks, which do many of the same things as the two COBOL divisions. The difference is that C does not require this type of documentation.

In COBOL the file name and the PROGRAM-ID name are usually the same. The equivalent of PROGRAM-ID in C is the file name of the program for main programs. A main program in C is one executed by a script, from the command line, or by JCL.

Most of the concepts of DATA DIVISION do not exist inside the C language. In COBOL all files must be defined in the FILE SECTION, but in C there is no required internal file size and layout definition. In C you define a file name to be an address (pointer) for the file.

This is equivalent to a COBOL FD name, which is not called a pointer or address but in fact is one.

After you define the file name, you then define the data elements. In C you can define the equivalent of a record, called a structure. A structure is a lot like a COBOL record: a collection of data elements of various types that can be referenced as a group or individually. Alternatively, you can define individual fields and call a different function to load individual fields. This is a choice you don't have in COBOL (see Chapter 6, "File Input/Output").

C has a real equivalent to the WORKING-STORAGE SECTION, but it doesn't have a label in the program. Data elements are declared at the top of C functions. However, in C you can choose between local and global data declarations. Let's look at memory in COBOL first.

COBOL memory is global to the file—all paragraphs can use WORKING-STORAGE—but local with respect to the linked object module. COBOL WORKING-STORAGE items in a main program are not available to subprograms that are called by it except through parameters.

In C there are three ways to set up program memory:

1. Same as in COBOL. You can define data elements that are available to all the functions (paragraphs) in the same file.

2. Local to a function. This is equivalent to defining data elements inside a paragraph, except that you can't do that in COBOL. Data elements defined inside a function are invisible outside that function.

3. Global to the file and known to all functions that are linked together. This is true global memory, which is available in COBOL II, but not in traditional COBOL.

See Chapter 11, "Calling Functions (Subprograms)," for further discussion of functions and global and local memory.

File vs. Program

C allows multiple functions to exist in one file. Traditional COBOL does not allow multiple subprograms in one file.

A medium or large C program can have a dozen or more functions in three or more files. Each file is compiled separately and creates an object module. Each function in each file is visible to the link editor.

After all the files are compiled, the link editor is invoked. There will be a list of object modules for the link editor to link. The editor will resolve all calls to functions, regardless of which object module contains them. If any functions are called that are not in the object module, the link editor will complain and fail, as in COBOL.

The only real difference between this and the COBOL link editor is that in COBOL each subprogram will create a separate object module. In C there can be multiple functions in one object module.

This page is left intentionally blank so that an easy comparison can be made between the two code listings found on the following facing pages.

A Minimal COBOL Program (Two Versions)

Traditional COBOL Minimal Program

```
000001    IDENTIFICATION DIVISION.
000002    PROGRAM-ID. TINYPROG.
000003    ENVIRONMENT DIVISION.
000004    CONFIGURATION SECTION.
000005    INPUT-OUTPUT SECTION.
000006    FILE-CONTROL.
000007    DATA DIVISION.
000008    FILE SECTION.
000009    PROCEDURE DIVISION.
000010    DISPLAY 'C IS NOT HARD, JUST DIFFERENT!'.
000011    STOP RUN.
```

COBOL II Minimal Program

```
000001    IDENTIFICATION DIVISION.
000002    PROGRAM-ID. TINYPROG.
000003    PROCEDURE DIVISION.
000004    DISPLAY 'C IS NOT HARD. JUST DIFFERENT!'
000005    GOBACK.
```

The minimal COBOL programs are here as a comparison to the minimal C program found on the facing page. This C program, which is included in practically every C book in the world, shows how little it takes to create a C program.

The traditional COBOL minimal program requires 11 lines to put one line on the console. In COBOL II this can be done in five lines. COBOL II has many fewer required items than traditional COBOL.

Each minimal COBOL program displays C IS NOT HARD, JUST DIFFERENT! on the system console. This is classified somewhere between bad practice and a capital offense in the mainframe world.

The C program displays C is not hard, just different! on the terminal from which the program has been run. In the C world it is normal to write to the terminal from which a program has been run. However, production programs in the C environment usually also write their program messages to a file, which is printed after the program has run. Messages written to the terminal are usually lost.

A Minimal C Program

```
#include <stdio.h>                              /* line 1 */
main()                                          /* line 2 */
{                                               /* line 3 */
  printf ("C is not hard, just different!\n");  /* line 4 */

  return (0);                                   /* line 5 */
}                                               /* line 6 */
```

The minimal C program displays the phrase C is not hard, just different! on the terminal from which it was run. But what are these strange statements?

First, a note about comments in C. A comment begins anywhere in the program that a slash-star (/*) combination occurs. That comment ends when a star-slash (*/) combination occurs. The /* and the */ can appear anywhere in a C program, even in the middle of a statement. Bye bye column 7. . . . This C program has a comment at the end of each line which shows the line number, as in:

```
#include <stdio.h>                              /* line 1 */
```

Line 1 has what is called an *include statement*. The #include part of this statement is equivalent to COPY ... SUPPRESS in COBOL. It brings into the program the file that is named inside the angle brackets. The file name stdio.h means "standard input/output header file." It contains definitions necessary for input and output subroutines, like reading and printing. There is neither a read statement nor a write statement in C. You call a function that performs a read and another function that performs a write. These functions are defined in the file stdio.h.

```
main()                                          /* line 2 */
```

The main() statement is the *function name declaration*. It is analogous to the PROCEDURE DIVISION statement in a COBOL main program (the one executed by the JCL). No instructions can precede it. The parentheses allow parameters to be passed at run time, as in PROCEDURE DIVISION USING statement. The parentheses are required after the function name even if there are no parameters.

One odd thing about C is this thing called main(). There is no program identifier, per se. In C the program ID of the main is usually the file name of the program that contains the main() statement. Every C program that can be executed by the operating system has a function called main() somewhere in it. By their file names shall ye know them.

Every other function name in a linked C program must have a name other than main().

```
{ (left brace)                                  /* line 3 */
```

The left brace on the line after main() marks where instructions can begin. C generally uses paired braces to define sets of statements. This brace is related to the right brace on line 6.

```
    printf ("C is not hard, just different!\n");        /* line 4 */
```

> **NOTE:** COBOL statements end with periods and C statements end with semicolons.

This statement calls a function, printf(), and passes it a parameter—what you want to print. The printf() function is discussed more fully in Chapter 5, "Terminal Input/Output." Here's the COBOL equivalent (more or less) to printf():

```
01  PRINT-MESSAGE      PIC X(30) VALUE
                       'C IS NOT HARD, JUST DIFFERENT!'.
PROCEDURE DIVISION.
    ...
    CALL 'PRFUNCT' USING PRINT-MESSAGE.
```

In the printf() call, what is printed is what is inside the pair of double quotes. The characters \n inside the quotes tell the printf() function to perform a line feed.

The printf() function puts its output, C is not hard, just different!, on something called stdout, which stands for *standard output device*. This is normally defined as the terminal. stdout can be redefined as a file, but this is not the usual practice.

So then, you might ask, how do I get something on paper in this language? The usual practice in the C world is to "print" to a file and then print the file. The function you use is fprintf(), which stands for file print formatted. Again, see Chapter 6, "File Input/Output" for more detail.

```
    return (0);                                         /* line 5 */
```

This statement returns control to either the calling function or the operating system. If return is used in a main() function, as here, it returns control to the operating system. return is a keyword (reserved word) in C. The value in parentheses is called the *return value*. A return value can be evaluated by the operating system or by the calling function. This handy feature is similar to, but more powerful than, COBOL's RETURN-CODE.

```
    }  (right brace)                                    /* line 6 */
```

The right brace signifies the end of the main() function. Another function could begin after this brace.

How COBOL Translates to C

This section takes a quick look at how COBOL translates to C. Major sections of a COBOL program are compared to their equivalents (if there is one) in C.

IDENTIFICATION DIVISION

COBOL: IDENTIFICATION DIVISION.
           PROGRAM-ID.
           AUTHOR.
           INSTALLATION.
           DATE-WRITTEN.
           DATE-COMPILED.
           SECURITY.
           REMARKS.

C: `main()` or *function_name*()

With the exception of PROGRAM-ID, these statements are primarily documentation in COBOL. In C the equivalent of PROGRAM-ID is the function declaration statement, which is a combination of PROGRAM-ID, PROCEDURE DIVISION, and LINKAGE SECTION. This concept is discussed later in this chapter in the section on LINKAGE SECTION and also in Chapter 11, "Calling Functions (Subprograms)."

ENVIRONMENT DIVISION

COBOL: ENVIRONMENT DIVISION.

           CONFIGURATION SECTION.
           SOURCE-COMPUTER.
           OBJECT-COMPUTER.
           SPECIAL-NAMES.
           INPUT-OUTPUT SECTION.
           FILE-CONTROL.
           IO-CONTROL.

C: No equivalent.

The COBOL CONFIGURATION SECTION is documentation and has no equivalent in C.

The INPUT-OUTPUT SECTION does not translate to C either. C identifies files with something called a *file pointer*. A file pointer is equivalent to an FD without requiring a SELECT *file-name*. File pointers are discussed in the next section and in Chapter 6, "File Input/Output."

DATA DIVISION
FILE SECTION

COBOL: DATA DIVISION.
           FILE-SECTION.

           FD *file-name* RECORD MODE IS *mode*
               BLOCK CONTAINS ....
               RECORD CONTAINS ....
               LABEL RECORDS ....
               VALUE OF ID IS ....

```
                    DATA RECORD(S) IS/ARE ....
                    REPORT(S) IS/ARE ....
              01 RECORD-NAME ....
C:            FILE *file_name;
```

C has no equivalent of a file buffer section within the program where you read in a record. In C you always "read into WORKING-STORAGE." C requires you to define a data element to hold the memory address of the beginning of the file buffer. This is equivalent to a stripped-down version of the FD statement. In C it is called a file pointer and is in fact the file name. An asterisk before a data name means it is a pointer.

In C, instead of coding a read command, you code a call to a read function. Each time you call a C read function, you pass the file name as one of the parameters. This is essentially the same as using the FD *file-name* in a COBOL READ statement.

In C you have a choice between setting up fixed-length records or using variable-length records. C has a tendency to produce variable-length records because it stores alphanumerics (strings) as variable lengths. However, you can define a structure in C, which is equivalent to a fixed-length record in COBOL. There are separate read and write functions for fixed- or variable-length records. See Chapter 6, "File Input/Output" for more detail.

If you are using C in a business environment, you should not be doing much work with sequential files. You should be using a database or file manager package for the bulk of your data handling. It is not cost effective to write entire file-handling systems in C for business applications.

```
COBOL:     SD sort-file-name
              RECORDING MODE ....
              RECORD CONTAINS ....
              DATA RECORD(S) IS/ARE ....
C:            No equivalent.
```

C has no language support for sorting. You can either

- Have your database package do the sort
- Let the operating system or an operating system utility sort the data
- Purchase a function library with prewritten sort functions

Do not write your own. Sorting should be done by a package or the operating system.

WORKING-STORAGE SECTION

In COBOL you specify the level number of the data item, give its name, and then supply the PICTURE clause, which tells the compiler the characteristics of the field and how much space to reserve in memory. In C you specify a data type and a data name. The data type determines both the characteristics and the size of the data element. C data types have no levels, and you have fewer choices about how to define data. Data declaration statements in C end with a semicolon (;).

For numbers the main difference is that COBOL allows a wide range of size declarations, where C has only a few. In COBOL you can, indeed must, specify the number of digits for each numeric data item, where in C you specify the data type and *that* determines the size and maximum value.

For alphanumerics in C you give the type (which is somewhat equivalent to the `PIC` clause), then the name, and then the size. Alphanumerics in C need one additional character for the string termination character, as in the `last_name` example in the following table. The C compiler does not truncate long alphanumerics and does not space-fill short ones. See the section on `strcpy()` in Chapter 7, "Moving Data" for further discussion.

Level numbers do not translate to C, although there is an equivalent to a record or group item in C called structure. Structures are discussed in Chapter 3, "Defining Data in C."

Here are the basic C data types used in business and their COBOL equivalents:

C		COBOL		
Data Type	Data Name	Level	Data Name	Data Type
char	middle_init;	01	MIDDLE-INIT	PIC X.
char	last_name [31];	01	LAST-NAME	PIC X(30).
int	employee_count;	01	EMPLOYEE-COUNT	PIC S9(5).
long	population_count;	01	POPULATION-COUNT	PIC S9(10).
double	price;	01	PRICE	PIC 9(4)V99.
double	ytd_gross_sales_amt;	01	YTD-GROSS-SALES-AMT	PIC S(9)V99.
double	fed_tax_rate;	01	FED-TAX-RATE	PIC V999.

Notice that C does not specify digits or decimal places in numbers. The number of digits, which controls the maximum size, depends both on the data type and the compiler. As for decimal places, there are either none, for `int` and `long`, or more than 15 for `double`.

In C business applications you use the `double` data type for numbers with decimal places—money, percents, and so on. You cannot specify the number of decimal places in C. Since a `double` is a floating point number, there are a lot of decimal places. When you use a `double`, you automatically get "about" 15 significant digits. If you're keeping track of pennies, this means you can have 13 digits to the left of the decimal without worrying about losing digits. Thirteen digits is a trillion dollars, which is still large enough to handle U.S. federal government budget numbers.

COBOL lets you specify the number of decimal places and takes care of rounding. In C you get the number of decimal places that go with the data type and you must do your own rounding.

Rounding in C is done according to the Institute of Electrical and Electronics Engineers (IEEE) rounding standard, which is a scientific rounding convention. The IEEE rounding convention is *not* the same as the business rounding convention. IEEE rounding will round .5 *down* in some cases, where in business data processing .5 should always round *up*.

Business data processing in C requires a rounding function that uses the business rounding convention. The rounding function called **round()** is discussed in Appendix F. Further discussion of rounding is found at the beginning of Chapter 8, "Arithmetic."

LINKAGE SECTION

C has the equivalent of a LINKAGE SECTION. In each called function there is a list of parameter definitions, as in COBOL. Also, the **main()** function can have run-time parameters, as in COBOL. These are discussed in Chapter 11, "Calling Functions (Subprograms)."

In an ANSI C function, there is a function name declaration, the C equivalent of the PROCEDURE DIVISION statement, followed by call parameters and their data types. The functionality is identical to COBOL, but the format is different.

Example

COBOL:

```
    PROGRAM-ID. CALC-PAY.
    ...
    LINKAGE SECTION.

    01  SOC-SEC-NO       PIC 9(9).
    01  REG-HOURS        PIC 9(3).
    01  OVERTIME-HOURS   PIC 9(2).
    01  STATE-CODE       PIC XX.
    01  GROSS-PAY        PIC S9(5)V99.
    01  NET-PAY          PIC S9(5)V99.

    PROCEDURE DIVISION USING  SOC-SEC-NO,
                              REG-HOURS,
                              OVERTIME-HOURS,
                              STATE-CODE,
                              GROSS-PAY,
                              NET-PAY.
```

C:

Function name	Parameter Data Type	Parameter Name
calculate_pay	(long	soc_sec_no,
	int	reg_hours,
	int	overtime_hours,
	char[]	state_code,
	double	gross_pay,
	double	net_pay)

Note that the function name in C is not limited to 8 characters. With a maximum of 31 characters available, you can make your function names long and readable.

REPORT SECTION

Report Writer is fading away in the COBOL world. C has no equivalent of a report writer embedded in the language. In C, as in COBOL, the best advice is to purchase a report writer package which is designed for your file/database environment. You will probably still wind up writing 10 percent of your reports in C, because hardly any report writer will effectively produce all your reports.

PROCEDURE DIVISION in COBOL Structured Programs

In a main structured COBOL program (the one executed by JCL), the mainline is the first set of statements after the PROCEDURE DIVISION statement. The mainline basically contains PERFORM statements, which perform paragraphs or sections of the program or CALL statements that invoke other COBOL subprograms. (The term *paragraph* will be used in the remainder of the text to mean both paragraph and section). At the end of the mainline is a GOBACK or STOP RUN. Subprograms have this same structure except they should end only with a GOBACK.

Paragraphs do the detailed work of the program. They do not have parameters passed to them because every paragraph in a COBOL program has access to everything in the FILE SECTION, WORKING-STORAGE SECTION, and LINKAGE SECTION.

All data declarations in a COBOL program are global *within* the program. We tend to say that COBOL doesn't have global data declarations, but within one COBOL program all the data is global because every paragraph has access to everything declared in the FD, SD, WORKING-STORAGE, and LINKAGE sections.

In a COBOL linked executable consisting of a main program and one or more subprograms, data definition is local to each compiled program. Any data sharing in this case has to be done by parameter passing between programs. In this sense there is no global data declaration.

main() Function in C Structured Programs

The main() function of a C program is what is executed by invoking the linked executable name at the operating system prompt or by a script.

The mainline is the first set of statements after the main() statement. It consists basically of calls to other C functions. A function in C is a compiled piece of code that can be executed from the operating system prompt, executed by a script, or called by another function.

The main() function is the one that is run by a script (JCL equivalent) or from an operating system prompt. All other functions are called. The main() function in C is analogous to a main COBOL program. It is a program invoked by an operating system command and cannot be called by another program. A called function in C can be the equivalent of either a COBOL paragraph or a COBOL subprogram, depending on how it is written.

Functions can have parameters passed to them and/or they can use global data declarations.

You can write a C program so that its functions work like COBOL paragraphs, you can write a C program so that its functions work like COBOL subprograms, or you can do both in the same C program. C is flexible. However, when you link edit one or more C object modules, there can only be one function named main().

See Chapter 11, "Calling Functions (Subprograms)," for further discussion of functions.

Summary

C is not an alien language. Every major method in COBOL has a corresponding method in C. The difference is that in C there are few reserved words and many symbols that behave like reserved words. C also has library functions that behave like reserved words. Our task is to correlate these diverse pieces to a known whole: COBOL. We can do it.

CHAPTER **2**

Compiling, Preprocessor, Formatting, Comments

Introduction

This chapter covers several topics you should be familiar with before you start programming in C. Topics include the functions of the C compiler and preprocessor, statement formatting, and inserting comments in programs.

Compiling C Programs

You can package, compile, and link C programs the same way as COBOL programs. You can put all the functions in one source file and then compile and link that file. A better alternative is to break up a large program into several source files of related functions. You then compile each file to create an object module and link edit the object modules into an executable.

A C compiler makes two passes on a source file. The first pass is made by the *preprocessor*, and the second is made by the compiler. The preprocessor looks for statements that require substitution or insertion of code. These statements are called *preprocessor directives*. The COBOL equivalent is the `COPY` statement, which brings code into a COBOL program.

A preprocessor directive is identified by its first character, the pound sign (#). C business systems primarily use two preprocessor directives: `#include` and `#define`. An include statement brings code into a program and a `#define` statement causes substitution of code. These statements are discussed in the next section of this chapter.

The preprocessor writes a temporary output file. All the included files are in it, and all the substitutions have been made. The compiler then takes this file as input and compiles it. If there are no errors, an object module is created.

The link editor is invoked after the object module(s) are created. C's link editor works like the COBOL link editor: It links a list of object modules into an executable. If the link editor cannot find all the object modules, it fails, as it does in COBOL.

At this point the program can be run. During development you usually run the program from the command-line prompt of the operating system. Production programs are usually run by scripts, the C world's equivalent of JCL.

The next section discusses the `#include` and `#define` preprocessor directives.

Using Preprocessor Directives

A C statement that begins with a pound sign, #, is a preprocessor directive. As previously mentioned, preprocessor directives tell the C compiler to include a file or make substitutions in your program at compile time.

The two common preprocessor directives in business data processing are `#include` (called the include statement) and `#define` (called the define statement). The include statement brings a piece of code (a file) into the program. The define statement is used to create program constants.

Each is discussed below.

Copy code into a program.

C Keyword/Symbol/Function	`#include`

`#include` works the same way as COPY ... SUPPRESSING in a COBOL program. It tells the compiler to bring in a piece of code to be compiled but not to show it in the output listing. `#include` statements are found in almost every C program.

The first line of most C programs is

```
#include <stdio.h>
```

This tells the preprocessor to get the file named `stdio.h` and insert it in the program during compilation. Include files are expanded during compiles but are not expanded when you print a program. You have to print include files separately.

There are two formats for include statements:

Format 1

```
#include <stdio.h>        ← Use this format for standard include files.
```

Format 2

`#include "gl100.h"`   ← Use this format for project include files.

Each format tells the compiler to get a file, `stdio.h` or `gl100.h`, and include it in this program. The standard I/O include file, `stdio.h`, contains the code necessary for C read and write routines. Always include it in your programs because virtually every C program uses something from `stdio.h`.

Format 1 uses the angle brackets `<>` around the include file name. The angle brackets tell the preprocessor to go to a *standard directory* in the computer for include files. A standard directory is a directory that is available to every developer. `stdio.h` and other generally used include files are put in a well-known location which the preprocessor knows to look for by the presence of the angle brackets. Your systems person will take care of this.

Format 2 uses double quotes and tells the compiler that this include file is stored locally. *Locally* means either in the same directory as the program or in the list of directories defined in the script that compiles programs.

Using Standard Include Files

Standard include files, such as `stdio.h`, `stdlib.h`, `string.h`, and so on, primarily contain library *function prototypes*. A function prototype is a template of the call parameters and the return value for a function.

ANSI C uses function prototypes to check that your parameter lists for function calls are correct. This is a great service that does not exist in COBOL. ANSI C will catch short parameter lists or long parameter lists, which are a *huge* source of error in system development.

Using Project Include Files

In a project development environment, an include file is a place to put common data definitions, such as record definitions. This is the same thing you would do with `COPY` members in COBOL. These data definitions can be any of the C data definition types, most commonly structures (group item/record equivalents) and program constants (`#define`, which is discussed in the following pages).

Program constants.

C Keyword/Symbol/Function	`#define`

`#define` preprocessor directives allow literal definitions that can be referenced by name in the program. The virtue of this is that you can define a literal numeric value by name. You can then use the name throughout the program. If you have to change the value, you change it in one place only.

Example

COBOL:

```
01  PAGE-LENGTH          PIC 99   VALUE 66.
01  HEADER-LENGTH        PIC 9    VALUE 8.
01  DETAIL-SUBSCRIPT     PIC 99   VALUE 1.
01  COMMA                PIC X    VALUE ','.
01  PERIOD               PIC X    VALUE '.'.
```

C:

```
#define     PAGE_LENGTH         66
#define     HEADER_LENGTH       8
#define     DETAIL_SUBSCRIPT    1
#define     COMMA               ','
#define     PERIOD              '.'
```
    ← *Notice there are no semicolons*

Discussion

`#define` defines a value that is substituted for the `#define` name during the compile. For example, if you code

```
#define  HEADER_LENGTH  66
```

then the statement

```
if (line_count > HEADER_LENGTH )
```

is translated by the preprocessor to

```
if (line_count > 66 )
```

HEADER_LENGTH is not a data element, it gets no memory allocation in the program. It is a substitution token that is replaced by the preprocessor.

There are several differences between the define statement in C and defining constant values in COBOL:

1. The `#define` names are in uppercase, by convention. This makes them stand out in a program because C is usually written in lowercase.

2. There are no semicolons after the define statements. This is because they are food for the preprocessor, not C statements.

3. They reserve no memory in the program.

4. Any type of data can be substituted in the define statement. The examples show numbers, a comma, and a period being substituted. Setting up punctuation symbols as `#define` items can be helpful if you're doing a lot of string manipulation. C has too much punctuation to start with, so if you can substitute words your programs will be more readable.

5. `#define` statements are replaced by the preprocessor before the compiler gets the source code.

6. `#define` items can't be altered while the program is running. A `#define` is not a data element.

Statement Formatting

While COBOL has very specific rules about what can appear in what column, C is almost completely indifferent to where you put statements. COBOL's rules are based on an 80-column punched card. The C language was developed using terminals and is basically free-form.

COBOL reserves

columns 1–6	for the sequence number
column 7	for continuation or comment
columns 8–11	for Area A
columns 12–72	for Area B
columns 73–80	for program name

COBOL instructions run from columns 12 through 72. C has no restrictions on what columns instructions are in. In fact, you can get a clean compile of a C program that has no line feeds, although this is not recommended.

C compilers not only don't care what column you put statements in, they also don't care how wide your lines are. It is a good idea to use a line length, such as 80, that will not cause wrapping or truncation when you print programs or view them on a screen.

There are some general conventions for formatting statements in C. These have evolved from AT&T Bell Laboratories and from the Berkeley, California, Unix and C communities. Some of the "standard" ways of doing things do not make sense in the business environment. We'll take on the highly charged issue of standards in Chapter 13, "C Standards for a Business Environment."

Using White Space

In C the term *white space* refers to spaces, tabs, and line feeds. Unfortunately, perhaps, white space is optional almost all the time. About the only required line feeds in ANSI C are for `#include` and `#define` directives. As the following horrible example shows, you can format statements in C in ways you would not dream of in COBOL. This program compiles, links, and runs. It copies strings and displays them on the terminal.

```
/*crush.c06/27/94*/
#include<stdio.h>
#include<string.h>
char date_time[25]="Mar 11 1993 09:53 AM" ;char dept_name[9];char
prev_dept_name [9];char report_title[61];char run_date[12];char
time[9];main(){strcpy(dept_name ,"ABCDEFGH");printf("crush2:
dept_name = %s\n\n",dept_name);strcpy(dept_name,"Sales");
printf("crush3: dept_name = %s\n\n",dept_name);
strcpy(prev_dept_name, dept_name);printf("crush4: prev_dept_name =
%s\n\n",prev_dept_name);strcpy(time, &date_time[12]);
printf("crush5: time = %s\n\n",time);strcpy(&date_time[12],"04:\
27:00 PM");printf("crush6: date_time = %s\n\n",date_time);
strcpy(report_title, "GL100 General Ledger EOM Trial");
printf("crush7: report_title = %s\n\n", report_title);
strcpy(dept_name,"Int'l Product Support");printf("crush8: date_time
= %s\n",date_time);strcpy(run_date,date_time);printf("crush9:
run_date = %s\n",run_date);printf("crush10: time = %s\n",time);
return(0);}
```

This is obviously not the way to format a C program. C programs should be formatted the same way COBOL programs are, with generous use of double spacing, consistent indentation, and page breaks where functions begin. The example programs in this book are formatted this way, as are the author's programs in the work environment. Formatting is discussed further in Chapter 13, "C Standards for a Business Environment."

Inserting Comments

As in COBOL, comments should be placed in programs to help the reader understand business or technical reasons for non-trivial code. I have often found my own comments useful after being away from a program for several months.

Inserting comments.

C Keyword/Symbol/Function	/* */

C is quite flexible about where comments can go. Comments in C begin with the /* (slash-star) characters and end with the */ (star-slash) characters. C does not care in what column you begin a comment, and it doesn't care in what column you end one.

   Three common ways of formatting comments are as follows:

1. `/* One-line comment before code */`

   ```
   c_statement;
   c_statement;
   ```

   This shows a one-line comment on its own line.

2.  ```
    /*
    A multiline
    comment before a complicated piece of code
    */
    c_statement;
    c_statement;
    c_statement;
    ```

    This demonstrates a multiline comment with the comment delimiters and the comment indented to the same column as the code it goes with. C does not require the indentation, but it makes the program more readable.

3.  ```
    FILE *pay_master;    /* Payroll Monthly Master */
    ```

    This comment follows a C statement on the same line. This is fine with the compiler.

    ANSI C does not allow comments to be nested inside other comments. The following fragment shows the common error in nesting comments:

    ```
    /*
    commenting out the following for test purposes....
    counter = counter + 1;    /* keep the counter running */
    */
    ```

This will cause an error during compiling.

Summary

This chapter covered several miscellaneous elements that programmers need when they are beginning to program in C. The C preprocessor is used in business programming primarily to bring include files into the program and to define constants for the program. The compilation of C programs is similar in the hundreds of environments in existence. However, since there are so many variations, this book does not go into specifics of compiling programs in C. Check your local guru or documentation.

Formatting of statements in C programs is almost completely free-form as far as the compiler is concerned. But since humans still need to read the programs, we still need to format statements for readability. This primarily means generous use of white space and consistent indentation. Formatting is also discussed in Chapter 13, "C Standards for a Business Environment."

C also allows comments to be almost free-form, but there are several conventions which have evolved in the C community to provide a consistent look for them. Forms of comments are also discussed in Chapter 13, "C Standards for a Business Environment."

CHAPTER **3**

Defining Data in C

Introduction

Data definition in C is both simpler and less flexible than in COBOL. COBOL offers a rich set of options in defining numeric data elements, while C has few options. Character and alphanumeric data definition is roughly equivalent in both languages.

    Data names in C follow a set of rules similar to that of COBOL. C allows 31 characters (one more than COBOL) and uses underscores instead of dashes in data names. A *data type* is used in C to tell the compiler what kind of data element is being defined. Data types are keywords. The data types most commonly used in business programming are `int`, `long`, `double`, and `struct` (used for record definition).

Data Names in C

In C, data names must

- Begin with a letter.
- Contain from 1 to 31 characters.
- Contain only letters (upper- or lowercase), numbers, and underscores.

C data names cannot

- Be a keyword.

- Begin with a number (unlike COBOL).
- Contain dashes (unlike COBOL). The dash is always the subtraction operator in C.
- Contain special characters such as @, #, $, and so on.

Valid Data Names in C	
`total_amortization_amount`	`payment_amount`
`line_count`	`last_name`
`sub_total_2`	`middle_init`
`region_rev_total`	`first_name`

Although some C programmers tend to create cryptic data names, there is no reason to do so. In general, the same situation can occur with a C program as with a COBOL program: Someday someone who is not the author is going to have to maintain the program. This person is called the unborn programmer. Have mercy on the unborn programmer: Make it easy to read your programs. The more obvious a program is, the better it is for everyone involved. Who knows, you may even wind up maintaining it yourself. Therefore, create data names using whole words or obvious abbreviations. Use underscores as connectors the way you use dashes as connectors in COBOL. Make names obvious.

Invalid Data Names in C	
`1st_total`	You cannot use a number as the first character of a data name.
`first-total`	The dash in C is always a minus sign, and a minus sign always means subtract. The compiler will try to read this as "first minus total." It will be a compile error.
`deferred_cost_commission_amortization`	More than 31 characters for a data name will not compile.
`special_$file_name`	Only letters, numbers, and the underscore are allowed in data names.

Mixed Case in Data Names: Don't Do It

COBOL II allows lowercase letters to be used in data names and literals, and an argument can be made for using lowercase letters in literals in some cases. The following section makes the case for using all lowercase *data names* in C. The same reasoning applies to using all uppercase names in COBOL.

ANSI C allows upper- and lowercase letters in both data names and function names, as in the following:

```
Total_Amortization_Amount
Region_Rev_Total
Last_Name
TotalAmortizationAmount
RegionRevTotal
Lastname
```

These names are all valid. They will also drive you crazy. Even if you remember which letters to capitalize, you waste time looking for the Shift key in the middle of data names.

English doesn't work this way, COBOL doesn't work this way, and C does not have to work this way. The capitalization rule in English is that proper nouns are capitalized and common nouns are not. Almost all data names in programs are common nouns or words based on common nouns.

Mixed case in names causes a lot more grief than any benefit from a naming convention that allows or requires mixed case. This is true whether you are a touch typist or not.

Here are examples drawn from real life. Some of the names have been changed to protect the innocent.

```
accounting_period                    AccountingPeriod
cust_accrued_int_pay_bal             CustAccruedIntPayBal
cust_discount_adj_amt                CustDiscountAdjAmt
cust_discount_amt                    CustDiscountAmt
cust_eom_all_in_cost_pct             CustEomAllInCostPct
cust_hedge_gain_amrt_adj_amt         CustHedgeGainAmrtAdjAmt
cust_hedge_gain_amrt_amt             CustHedgeGainAmrtAmt
cust_hedge_loss_amrt_adj_amt         CustHedgeLossAmrtAdjAmt
cust_hedge_loss_amrt_amt             CustHedgeLossAmrtAmt
cust_imp_coupon_exp_adj_amt          CustImpCouponExpAdjAmt
cust_imp_coupon_exp_amt              CustImpCouponExpAmt
cust_int_exp_adj_amt                 CustIntExpAdjAmt
cust_int_exp_amt                     CustIntExpAmt
cust_int_income_adj_amt              CustIntIncomeAdjAmt
cust_int_income_amt                  CustIntIncomeAmt
```

Which column is easier to read?

Those incredibly ugly names in the second column came from the Pascal language. In Pascal there is no connector, such as the underscore or dash, for data names, so you are forced to use mixed case. What is a grim necessity in Pascal is completely unnecessary in C. Furthermore, it makes programs harder to read.

Therefore, to make your programs readable, use underscores in data names. To make your programs maintainable, use all lowercase letters in your data names. Looking for the Shift key in the middle of data names is a pain in the neck.

Data Types

Every data type in C has an exact equivalent and a functional equivalent in COBOL. However, COBOL has one data type that C does not have: internal decimal numbers. In C you always use floating point numbers to represent numbers with decimal places. The only real consequence of this is that you must take care of precision (the desired number of decimal places) and rounding yourself. See Chapter 8, "Arithmetic," for further discussion of precision and rounding.

Common C Data Types	
char	One alphanumeric character.
char [n]	More than one alphanumeric character. n stands for some number.
int	Integer. No decimal places.
long	Long integer. Bigger than int.
double	Big floating point number. Used for numbers with decimal places.
float	Floating point number. Inadequate for business requirements. The float data type should never be used in business systems because it is guaranteed to keep track of only six significant digits. This means you will lose data if you use it. Use double.
struct	Structure. C equivalent of a group item or record.

The following table lists the common COBOL data types and their equivalent expressions in C:

COBOL Data Types	Equivalent C Data Types	Comments
PIC X	char	One character alphanumeric.
PIC X(30)	char [31]	More than one character alphanumeric. C treats all alphanumerics as variable-length strings of characters. It therefore needs to know where the end is. The end is signified by a character called the *null terminator*. Its value is hex 00. It's represented in C programs by the literal '\0'. The compile translates this literal to hex zero. To accommodate the null terminator character, you have to define string variables one character larger than the data.
PIC S9(4) COMP	int	Two-byte binary integer when machine word is two bytes.

PIC S9(4)	int	Two-byte binary integer when machine word is two bytes.
PIC S9(8) COMP	long	Four-byte binary long integer.
PIC S9(8)	long	Four-byte binary long integer.
PIC S9(8)V99	double	Floating point number with large number of decimal places, whether you want them or not.
PIC V9(5)	double	Floating point number with large number of decimal places, whether you want them or not.
COMP-1	float	Short precision floating point number. float is too short for use in business applications.
COMP-2	double	Double-precision floating point number.
COMP-3	n/a	No equivalent in C. All numbers in C are stored as either binary numbers or floating point numbers. In effect, they are already packed. If you want decimal points in your number, use double.

The following sections discuss in detail the basic C data types.

Define a single character.

C Keyword/Symbol/Function	char

char, with no square brackets, defines a data item that is one alphanumeric character. This is the equivalent of COBOL PIC X. The treatment of a single character data item in C is in most ways the same as for numeric data items. A char data element can generally be manipulated directly with C language keywords. This is not true for strings.

Syntax	COBOL Equivalent
char data_name = 'A';	01 DATA-NAME PIC X VALUE 'A'.

NOTE: C always uses single quotes for single character literals.

Samples	COBOL Equivalents
char prev_code = ' ';	01 PREV-CODE PIC X VALUE ' '.
char curr_code;	01 CURR-CODE PIC X.
char middle_init = 'm';	01 MIDDLE-INIT PIC X VALUE 'M'.

Anatomy

```
char    data_name   = ‘c’      ;
 |          |          |        |
Required  Required  Optional  Required
```

char

Data element type. char means character. It says this data element can contain alphanumeric data. C allows any ASCII character to be in a char field.

data_name

Whatever data name you want to use, within C's bounds. The lack of square brackets with a number inside means that this data item contains one character.

=

If you want to create an initial value for the char, you can give it a value with the equal sign. The equal sign in C is called the *assignment operator*. It moves (assigns) the value on the right side of the equal sign to the left side. It's the same as a VALUE clause in a PIC.

‘c’

If you use the optional assignment operator, you must supply a value that is enclosed by single quotes. C uses single quotes for single characters and double quotes for multiple characters. ANSI C will generate an error on compiling if you mix them.

;

A semicolon ends all data declaration statements.

Discussion

C's handling of characters is quirky in that single character literals always use single quotes and string literals always use double quotes. This is in contrast with COBOL, in which most compilers are set to use single quotes with all alphanumerics of any size. The only saving grace is that ANSI compilers will catch any inappropriate use of quotes.

Common Error

Using double quotes on a single-character literal.

Using appropriate quotes will be confusing for a while, but fortunately ANSI compilers catch the error. On traditional C compilers this mismatch would be undetected until run time, when it would blow up the program. Use ANSI C.

Define alphanumerics of two or more characters (String).

C Keyword/Symbol/Function	char [n]

char [n], where n is the number of characters to reserve in memory, defines an alphanumeric data item of two or more characters. This is known in C as an *array of characters* or a *string*. This is equivalent in COBOL to a PIC X(n), where n is a number of characters greater than 1.

Syntax   COBOL Equivalent

char data_name [n] = "AA" ;   01 DATA-NAME PIC X(n) VALUE 'AA'.

> **NOTE:**   C always uses double quotes for string literals. A string literal is two or more alphanumeric characters.

Samples   COBOL Equivalents

```
char  last_name   [30] = "                              ";
                         01  LAST-NAME    PIC X(29) VALUE SPACES.
char  first_name  [25];  01  FIRST-NAME   PIC X(24).
char  source_code [7]  = "XJ5.11";  01  SOURCE_CODE  PIC X(6)  VALUE 'XJ5.11'.
char  name        [6]  = "O'Day";   01  SOURCE_CODE  PIC X(5)  VALUE 'O DAY'.
```

Anatomy

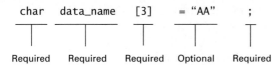

```
char    data_name    [3]    = "AA"      ;
```
Required   Required   Required   Optional   Required

char

Data element type. char means character. It says this data element can contain alphanumeric data. C allows any ASCII character to be in a char field.

data_name

Whatever data name you want to use, within C's bounds.

[3]

The square brackets with a number inside mean that this data item is a string of characters. The main thing to note here is that the number inside the square brackets tells C
only how many characters to reserve in memory.

You must supply a number that is one larger than your largest expected value. The extra
character is used for the null terminator, which is a character that signifies the end of a
string. The hexadecimal value of the null terminator is 00. It is represented in programs
by the literal '\0'. It's also called *backslash-zero*. The compiler translates '\0' to hex
zero.

=

If you want to create an initial value for the string, you can give it a value with the equal
sign. The equal sign in C is called the assignment operator. It moves (assigns) the value
on the right side of the equal sign to the left side. It's the same as the VALUE clause in a
PIC.

"AA"

If you use the optional assignment operator, you must supply a value that is enclosed
by double quotes. C uses double quotes for multiple characters and single quotes for
single characters. This is a significant difference from COBOL.

Single quotes within a string literal are acceptable:

    "O'Donnell"

Double quotes within a string literal must be preceded by a backslash character:

    "Year-to-date \"Actual\" Totals"

;

A semicolon ends all data declaration statements.

Discussion

A string in C is really an array (table) of single characters. The following definition

    char last_name [31];

can be referenced by last_name to pick up the whole string. It can also be referenced by
individual character by using C subscript notation, last_name [1].

If you could define this string in COBOL exactly the same way C does, you would code

    01 LAST-NAME   PIC X(30).
    01 LAST-NAME   REDEFINES LAST-NAME
                       PIC X
                       OCCURS 30.

This would obviously not compile in COBOL, but it does show the concept of using the
same name for a whole array and for individual characters within it.

In C, strings have to be manipulated by function calls (subprograms) rather than by language commands. This is strange but true. Comparing or moving strings is done by various function calls such as strcmp() (compare) and strcpy() (copy/move).

Strings in C are very different from alphanumerics in COBOL. Unlike COBOL, C inherently defines all strings to be variable in length. The number in the square brackets does not control the maximum length of the string. All that number does is allocate that number of bytes in program memory. C looks for a null terminator, hex zero, to identify the end of the string.

When you move one string to another, the last character moved is the null terminator. It actually takes up one character. Therefore, you need to make the size of the string one character larger than your largest expected value, so there's room for the null terminator.

To repeat: The length of the string depends on the position of the null terminator. A string is as long as the number of characters before the null terminator.

Single Quotes and Double Quotes in String Literals

String literals are enclosed by double quotes. There is no problem if you want to place a single quote inside a string literal, as in

```
char  last_name  [31] = "O'Donnell";
```

Placing a double quote inside a string literal requires a small trick, however. Precede the double quote with the backslash character, as in

```
char  title      [51] = "General Ledger \"Trial\" Run";
```

This will display as General Ledger "Trial" Run. The backslash is the escape character, which tells the compiler to "escape" the usual meaning of the following character. The escape character together with the one following it tell the compiler to do something special. In this case it is to place a double quote inside a string literal.

Escape sequences are also used for other special characters. See examples in the printf() section on page 88 and the fprintf() section on page 159.

Continuation of String Literals

ANSI C created a significant improvement in the handling of continuation of string literals to another line. The technique can be used when declaring a string or when using one in the strcpy(), strcat(), printf(), fprintf(), sprintf(), or other functions which use string literals.

The technique is to use double quotes at the break point of the literal. Resume the literal on the next line with another set of double quotes. It is easier to show than to explain:

```
char header_1 [133] = "GL101      General Ledger Trial     "
                      "                      Accounting Dept ";
```

This allows you to line up the literal. You do not have to wrap lines or use the old technique (not discussed in this book), which prevents you from aligning the literal. Here's an example in a printf() statement:

```
printf ("C is not hard, "
        "just different." );
```

This statement displays C is not hard, just different. on one line on the terminal. This string continuation technique is handy and can be used to help keep your programs readable by allowing you to control the alignment of string literals.

Common Errors

1. Corrupting memory.

   Let's define a string:

   ```
   char  company_name  [31];
   ```

   If you move "AA Auto" into company_name, C will automatically place a null terminator in the 8th position. If you move 50 characters into company_name, the copy function will continue right after the 31st character, corrupting memory. The null terminator will be at position 51. See the example for strcpy() in Chapter 7.

   In COBOL you don't have to worry about corrupting memory this way, because the destination item controls how many characters are moved. COBOL space fills short data items and truncates long ones. C puts a null terminator at the end of short data items and keeps copying long ones until it finds the end of the source item.

   This is a large source of error in C. You could even call it a defect in the language. I have yet to hear a valid business case for corrupting memory in a program.

2. Using single quotes on a string literal.

   This error is a more common error than using double quotes on a single character literal because single quotes are usually the default on COBOL compilers. ANSI compilers can catch this error. On traditional C compilers this mismatch would be undetected until run time, when it would blow up the program.

Define an integer—no decimal places.

C Keyword/Symbol/Function	int

int defines a data item that is a signed integer—whole numbers only. You can optionally give it a value when you define it. int is actually a signed binary number, equivalent to a COMP in COBOL.

Syntax	COBOL Equivalent
int data_name = 0;	01 DATA-NAME PIC S9(4) COMP VALUE 0.

Samples

```
int record_count;
int page_length  = 60;
int line_count   = 0;
int hours_taken  = -13;
```

COBOL Equivalents

```
01  RECORD-COUNT  PIC S9(4)  COMP.
01  PAGE-LENGTH   PIC S9(3)  VALUE 60.
01  LINE-COUNT    PIC 9(2)   VALUE 0.
01  HOURS-TAKEN   PIC S9(4)  VALUE -13.
```

Anatomy

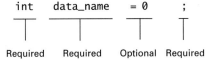

```
int     data_name     = 0       ;
```
Required   Required   Optional Required

`int`

Data element type. `int` means integer.

`data_name`

Whatever data name you want to use, within C's bounds.

`=`

If you want to create an initial value for the `int`, you can give it a value with the equal sign. The equal sign in C is called the assignment operator. It moves (assigns) the value on the right side of the equal sign to the left side. It's the same as `VALUE` in a `PIC` clause.

`0`   (zero)

If you use the optional assignment operator, the equal sign, you must supply an integer value. It can be any integer value within the size limit of `int` on your compiler.

`;`

A semicolon ends all data declaration statements.

Discussion

In C you do not specify the number of digits a numeric data item contains, it is determined by the size of the data type (`int` in this case) on your compiler. This book assumes a two-byte `int`, which is common. Many workstation compilers define `int` as four bytes. To find the size of `int` on your compiler, see your compiler documentation or the `sizeof()` discussion in Chapter 7.

The difference between `int` and COBOL `PIC S9(4) COMP` is that the COBOL number is limited to ±9,999 due to specifying `PIC S9(4)`. An int, whether two or four bytes, has a larger range than ±9,999.

The range of values for an `int` is based on the number of bits in it. If your compiler has a two-byte `int`, there are 16 bits. The high-order bit does double duty as both a number and a sign. Thus the range for a two-byte `int` is –32,768 through +32,767, due to a technique called *two's complement* arithmetic. Two's complement arithmetic is beyond the scope of this discussion, but we can see its effects.

The following example assumes the high-order binary digit is on the left, the same as the decimal and hexadecimal numbers. This is what certain critical values look like for a two-byte `int`:

Decimal	-32.768	-1	0	+1	+32,767
Hex (half bytes)	8000	ffff	0000	0001	7fff
Binary (bits)	1000 0000 0000 0000	1111 1111 1111 1111	0000 0000 0000 0000	0000 0000 0000 0001	0111 1111 1111 1111 +1
	↑				↓

The line above with arrows shows the result of adding 1 to 32,767:

```
  0111 1111 1111 1111      7fff      32,767
+ 0000 0000 0000 0001     +0001    +      1
  _____      _____    _____
  1000 0000 0000 0000  =   8000   = -32,768
        binary              hex     decimal
```

You can see in this example that if you add +1 to +32,767, binary arithmetic puts a 1 in the high-order bit and zeroes-out the rest. That makes the number 32,768, but since the high-order bit is turned on (its value is 1), the compiler interprets it as a negative number (two's complement rule).

The main effect is that your number is corrupted and the compiler does not tell you that an overflow occurred. Use `long` unless your compiler has a four-byte `int`.

If your compiler has a two-byte `int`, don't use it. It will only cause you heartburn. Use `long` for integer counters and totals that are not likely to exceed 2 billion. If they are likely to be larger than that, use `double`.

Common Errors

1. The number unexpectedly goes negative (or positive).

   This occurs when you exceed the maximum possible number for an `int`. See the preceding "Discussion" section.

Define a large integer—no decimal places.

C Keyword/Symbol/Function	`long`

long defines a data item that is a signed integer—whole numbers only. It's the same as int except bigger. You can optionally give it a value when you define it. Based on the assumption of a two-byte int, a long will take four bytes. Because of the way binary arithmetic works, the maximum value is much more than twice as large. Each additional bit doubles the maximum possible value.

Syntax:	COBOL Equivalent
`long data_name = 0;`	`01 DATA-NAME PIC S9(8) COMP  VALUE 0.`

Samples / COBOL Equivalents

```
long  vote_count  = 0;              01  VOTE-COUNT  PIC S9(8) COMP VALUE 0.
long  gl_period   = 199203;         01  GL-PERIOD   PIC 9(6)        VALUE 199203.
long  cust_no;                      01  CUST-NO     PIC 9(6).
long  soc_sec_no  = 262439921;      01  SOC-SEC-NO  PIC 9(10)       VALUE 262439921.
long  hours_taken = -13;            01  HOURS-TAKEN PIC S9(4)       VALUE -13.
```

Anatomy

```
long    data_name    = 0       ;
 |         |          |         |
 |         |          |         |
Required  Required  Optional  Required
```

long
: Data element type. long means long integer.

data_name
: Whatever data name you want to use, within C's bounds.

=
: If you want to create an initial value for the long, you can give it a value with the equal sign. The equal sign in C is called the assignment operator. It moves (assigns) the value on the right side of the equal sign to the left side. It's the same as a VALUE clause in a PIC.

0 (zero)
: If you use the optional assignment operator, the equal sign, you must supply a numeric value, without quotes, as in COBOL. No decimal points are allowed on int and long.

;
: A semicolon ends all data declaration statements.

Discussion

The range of values for a long is based on the number of bits in it. Since we are assuming a four-byte long, there will be 32 bits. However, as with int, the high-order bit does double duty as both a number and a sign. Two's complement arithmetic also applies to long. This causes the range for a four-byte long to be –2,147,483,648 through +2,147,483,647. The binary and hexadecimal values follow the same pattern as with int. For more discussion of what happens when you exceed the maximum, in either direction, see the end of the "Discussion" section for int.

Two billion is a reasonably large number. This is good enough for most counters. If 2 billion is not a large enough number for your program, use a double.

Common Errors

1. The number unexpectedly goes negative (or positive).

   This occurs when you exceed the maximum possible number for a long. See the end of the "Discussion" section for int.

Define a large decimal number.

C Keyword/Symbol/Function	double

double defines a floating point number with an accuracy of approximately 15 significant digits. It also stores a large number of decimal places. If you want only a few decimal places stored, such as pennies, you will have to round the number using the round() function, as discussed in Appendix F.

Syntax	COBOL Exact Equivalent
`double data_name = n.n;`	`01 DATA-NAME   COMP-2 VALUE n.n.`

Samples

COBOL Functional Equivalents

```
double total_tax = 0;

double min_wage  = 4.25;
double tax_rate;
double int_rate  = .0725;
double deficit   =
            -3222111444555.99
```

```
01 TOTAL-TAX PIC S9(6)V99  COMP-3
                           VALUE 0.
01 MIN-WAGE  PIC 99V99     VALUE 4.25.
01 TAX-RATE  PIC V9(3).
01 INT-RATE  PIC V9(5)     VALUE .0725.
01 DEFICIT   PIC S9(13)V99 VALUE
                      -3222111444555.99
```

Anatomy

```
double   data_name   = n.n       ;
```
Required   Required   Optional Required

double

Data element type. `double` means double-precision floating point decimal number.

data_name

Whatever data name you want to use, within C's bounds.

=

If you want to create an initial value for the `double`, you can give it a value with the equal sign. The equal sign in C is called the assignment operator. It moves (assigns) the value on the right side of the equal sign to the left side. It's the same as a VALUE clause in a PIC.

n.n

`n.n` stands for decimal point number. If you use the optional assignment operator, you must supply a numeric value, not enclosed in quotes. If you supply integer values (0 or 15, say), they will be converted to decimal numbers (0.0 or 15.0).

;

A semicolon ends all data declaration statements.

Discussion

COBOL has an exact equivalent of `double` in COMP-2, a double-precision floating point number. COMP-2 is not used much because in COBOL you can specify the number of decimal places you want a number to have. The functional equivalent of a `double` in COBOL is any PIC clause with a V in it: a number with a decimal portion.

A floating point number is internally separated into three areas: sign, exponent, and significant digits. These areas are not visible to the programmer. A `double` takes eight bytes and is divided as follows:

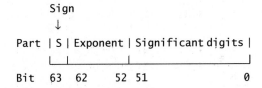

```
         Sign
          ↓
Part  | S | Exponent | Significant digits |

Bit   63  62      52 51                  0
```

The sign tells whether the number is positive or negative. The exponent stores the power of 10 needed to express the number. Significant digits store the number. This format is very useful for scientific computing, but it is also adequate for business use.

If we define a `double` and assign a value, as follows,

```
double sales_amt = 6543.21;
```

it is converted to $6.54321 * 10^3$ and then stored as follows:

Sign	0 (positive number)
Exponent	3 (represents 10^3)
Significant Digits	654321 (implied decimal after first digit)

Use `double` to store and manipulate any number with decimal places and do not worry about exponential notation.

When you use `double` for numbers with decimal portions, you need to be aware that C has no built-in rounding ability in its arithmetic statements. One consequence of all those decimal places is that you always get them, whether you want them or not. If you don't want fractions of pennies, you have to round the `double` yourself. In C you can use `sprintf()`, `fprintf()`, or `printf()` to round, but then you get the IEEE rounding method, which sometimes rounds .5 down. The business rounding function `round()` (discussed) in Appendix F solves this problem. For further discussion on rounding, see Chapter 8, "Arithmetic."

In most C compilers a `double` takes up eight bytes.

The range of values for a `double` is approximately 10^{-308} through 10^{+308}. This will definitely handle all business application numbers. Use it.

Why Precision Is Considered Approximate

A `double` has an approximate precision of 15 significant digits, which means the number can get flaky at around 15 decimal digits. This is due to the problem of binary representation of decimal fractions. For most business applications this is not a problem.

Decimal values for the `double` data type become "curiouser and curiouser" for the last decimal digits in a number with a lot of decimal places. The problem stems from trying to represent base 10 decimal fractions in a base 2 world. This is generally not a problem until you get past 15 decimal places.

COBOL solves this problem by doing all decimal arithmetic as Binary Coded Decimal (BCD). All numbers in a computation get multiplied by a power of 10 sufficient to make them all integers. Arithmetic then proceeds on an integer basis, which is no problem for binary hardware. At the end, the result is divided by the same power of 10, rounding is applied, and out pops the result.

Common Errors

1. Unwanted fractions.

    This is due to the fact that a `double` carries up to 15 decimal places, whether you need them or not. The typical case is a system requirement to carry dollars down to pennies, but not fractions of pennies. In COBOL you solve this problem by defining the destination field as V99. In C you have to round the number yourself. The round() function is discussed further in Appendix F.

2. Incorrect fractions.

    If you are calculating percentages or ratios, they may become inaccurate after 15 decimal places. This is due to inaccuracies inherent in floating point arithmetic. It is a system limitation and you need to gently convince your users that 15 decimal places is enough.

Define an inadequate decimal number.

C Keyword/Symbol/Function	float

float means death in business systems. float is a short-precision floating point number, which means that the number is stored internally in exponential form and in four bytes. A float can have up to six significant decimal digits. This is what makes it unsuitable for business systems.

Syntax	COBOL Equivalent
float data_name = n.n;	05 DATA-NAME COMP-1 VALUE n.n.

Discussion

The reason float is death has to do with a disparity between precision and range. *Range* is what the largest and smallest values can be. For a float, the range is approximately 10^{-38} through 10^{+38}, which is large enough for all business applications. The problem is precision: Approximately six significant digits are accurate. In practice the precision is usually nine or more digits, but a float will lose both dollars and pennies. Don't use float.

    Why did I put a section on float in this book? So I could tell you:

DON'T USE float

Use double (as discussed in the previous section) for all variables that need decimal places.

Common Errors

1. Using float.

    As previously mentioned, float is inappropriate in business systems. See the next error.

2. Losing digits.

    float has a precision of approximately six digits, which means you are subject to losing digits on any number over 1 million. While most compilers usually provide nine or more digits, you can still easily lose digits. Worse yet, it's a silent error that can take a long time to detect and a long time to fix. Use double.

Numeric Literals and Constants

The numeric values shown in the samples in this chapter are all base 10 numbers. This is typically all you ever need in business programming. However, C also allows numeric values to be assigned in base 8 (*octal*) and base 16 (*hexadecimal*).

Octal numbers are relics of an earlier age of computers. Base 8 numbers have a range of digits from 0 through 7. While they make it easy to translate binary numbers, they have no use in business systems. They are discussed here for completeness and because there is a way to inadvertently create octal numbers that you don't want.

Hexadecimal numbers are more familiar to people who have worked on mainframes. Base 16 digits have a range of 0 through F, with A through F (uppercase or lowercase) representing 10 through 15. Hexadecimal values conveniently represent half bytes because four bits have a range of values of 0 through 15.

When you assign a numeric literal which does not begin with zero, the compiler takes it as a decimal number. If a numeric literal begins with a 0 (for numbers other than 0), it is an octal number. If the literal starts with 0x or 0X, it is a hexadecimal number. A short example shows the effects:

```
/*                       literal.c      11/18/94              */
#include <stdio.h>
main()
{
    int  int_1 = 15;            /*                   decimal 15      */
    int  int_2 = 015;           /* octal       15 = decimal 13      */
    int  int_3 = 0x15;          /* hexadecimal 15 = decimal 21      */

    int  int_4 = 0;             /*                   decimal 0      */
    int  int_5 = 00;            /* octal        0 = decimal 0       */
    int  int_6 = 0x0;           /* hexadecimal  0 = decimal 0       */

    printf (" int_1 = %d  int_2 = %d  int_3 = %d \n",
        int_1,
        int_2,
        int_3 );
    printf (" int_4 = %d  int_5 = %d  int_6 = %d \n",
        int_4,
        int_5,
        int_6 );

    return (0);
}
```

The first `printf()` statement prints the values of the first three integers as decimal numbers. The result will be

    int_1 = 15 int_2 = 13 int_3 = 21

If you use `%x` instead of `%d` in the `printf()`, the result would be

    int_1 = f int_2 = d int_3 = 15

The numbers are the same. What is different is the base in which they are expressed.

Since 0 is the same in all bases, the second `printf()` statement produces

    int_4 = 0 int_5 = 0 int_6 = 0

You can forget about octal numbers forever, unless you create a numeric literal with a leading zero, as shown by `int_2` above. If you do that, you will get an octal number, which will not have the same value as the same digits in a decimal number (unless it is less than 8). Since you do not commonly begin numeric literals with leading zeroes, this problem will not occur often, if at all.

Hexadecimal literals are sometimes used to represent non-printable ASCII characters in `#define` statements, as in

    #define LINE_FEED 0xA

This is often done because many ASCII charts do not show decimal number equivalents for the ASCII codes. The compiler does not care whether you use a decimal or hexadecimal literal: they are both translated to a binary number. The following statements are equivalent:

    #define LINE_FEED 10
    #define LINE_FEED 0xA

For printable characters you can use the character itself, a decimal value, or a hexadecimal value. The following statements are equivalent:

    #define COMMA ','
    #define COMMA 0x2C
    #define COMMA 46

Using the character is the most obvious way to create the constant.

Define a record or group item.

C Keyword/Symbol/Function	`struct` (structure)

Structures are how you get fixed-length records in C. There are three main ways, and an alternate, to use structures to define records or group items:

1. Format 1 covers a basic group item with one level of elementary items. This is equivalent to a COBOL group item with an 01-level item and multiple 05-level items. Format 1 allocates memory, just as a COBOL group item does.

2. Format 2 shows how to define a template for a structure using the keyword typedef. This template can then be used multiple times for different occurrences of the same kind of data. This is similar to, but more flexible than, COBOL COPY members. In C the structure template definition does not allocate memory.

3. Format 3 shows how to create nested structures—group items within group items. These are equivalent to COBOL group items with multiple levels. Nested structures can use either Format 1, Format 2, or both. Using Format 3 will cause memory to be allocated.

4. Format 4 shows an alternative method for creating a structure template using a *tag name*. Its use is not recommended because the syntax is awkward, but you may encounter it in existing code.

Structure Format 1: Structure with Elementary Items

This format is the simple use of a structure: a name and a collection of fields attached to it. Memory is allocated in the program for the structure. Define a structure this way when you want to put a set of fields together. If you are likely to need the same layout multiple times, you should use Format 2 and create a template. Start here to see what the basic definition is.

Syntax (Format 1)

```
struct
{
   data_type   element_name = value;
   data_type   element_name = value;
   ...
   data_type   element_name = value;
} structure_name;
```

Sample (Format 1)

Structure in C   Equivalent Group Item in COBOL

```
struct
{                              01  PAY-REC.
   long    soc_sec_no;            05  SOC-SEC-NO     PIC 9(9).
   char    last_name    [31];    05  LAST-NAME      PIC X(30).
   char    middle_init;          05  MIDDLE-INIT    PIC X.
   char    first_name   [21];    05  FIRST-NAME     PIC X(20).
   long    pay_grade;            05  PAY-GRADE      PIC 9(4).
   double  hourly_rate;          05  HOURLY-RATE    PIC 99V99.
} pay_rec;
```

Anatomy (Format 1: Allocates Memory)

```
struct  ◄─────────────────────────  Required
    {   ◄─────────────────────────  Required
        data_type  element_name = value;  ┐
        data_type  element_name = value;  │  ◄── At least one item
        ...                               │       must be defined
        data_type  element_name = value;  ┘

    }  structure_name ;
```

Optional

Required

struct

Data element type of structure. `struct` means that a group of data items follows.

{

Denotes the beginning of the structure's member list.

data_type element_name = value;

You can put any legal C data element definitions inside a structure. They follow the same rules as data elements defined outside of structures. They can also be initialized when they are declared.

}

Denotes the end of the structure's member list.

structure_name

This is the equivalent of the `01`-level group item name in COBOL. The standard rules for C data names apply.

;

A semicolon ends all data declaration statements.

Discussion (Format 1)

Defining structures in C is similar to defining group items or records in COBOL. In C you declare that a group item is being defined with the `struct` keyword. The name of the structure is the last part of the definition.

In COBOL you can have group items within group items. You can do this with structures, too, as shown in the section on Format 3, nested structures. Here we show the equivalent of a COBOL group item that starts with an 01-level item and has only 05-level sub-elements.

One difference between C structures and COBOL group items is that element names in structures must always be qualified when they are used in the program, even if the element name is unique. In COBOL you have to qualify an element name only if it is not unique. The following table compares qualification of names:

C Structure Name Usage	COBOL Qualified Name Usage
structure_name.element_name	ELEMENT-NAME OF GROUP-NAME
pay_rec.soc_sec_no	SOC-SEC-NO OF PAY-REC

The period is the qualifier. It is called the *structure member operator* (a big name for a period).

Common Errors

1. Problems with data alignment.

   The size of a structure you define will either be an even number of bytes or an odd number of bytes. This can become significant depending on the compiler. One source of error in sequential file operations using structures comes from the structure having a length that is an odd number.

   If this is a problem on your system, check the compiler options. There should be one that will cause structures to be filled out to an even number of bytes.

2. Compiler says template name is undefined or unknown.

   If it's not a typographical error in the template name, it usually means the include files in your program do not contain the template definition. You are probably missing an include file.

Example (Format 1)

The example for Format 2 covers both Format 1 and Format 2.

Structure Format 2: Structure Template Using `typedef`

This format defines a *template* for a group item using the keyword `typedef`. Use it when you need multiple instances of the same data layout. Instead of coding two or more sets of identical data definitions, you can define a template, which gives the same elementary item names and definitions to all occurrences. Defining the template does not allocate memory, and you can do it in the same program you want to use it in, which you can't do with a COPY member.

The `typedef` keyword is used to create your own data type that the compiler will recognize. In business its purpose is primarily to create structure templates. By convention, template names are written in uppercase, which helps identify them.

When creating a structure template, use the keyword `typedef` followed by the keyword `struct`. This tells the compiler you are creating a structure template, and no memory will be allocated. The structure name at the end of the definition becomes the template name when you use the keyword `typedef`. The template name is also known as the *typedef name*. This text uses both terms.

The discussion of structures uses the term `instance_name` to represent the name you give a structure when you invoke a template for the definition. The template name is the data type and the `instance_name` is the data name. The syntax is

```
TEMPLATE_NAME  instance_name;
```

Examples are

```
CUST_REC    master_in;
CUST_REC    master_out;
```

Syntax (Format 2: Define a Template)

```
typedef  struct              Begin a structure template definition.
{                            This syntax does not allocate memory.
  data_type  element_name;
  data_type  element_name;
  ...                        It is a template for a structure
  ...                        and is used for multiple occurrences
  data_type  element_name;   of the same structure type.
} TEMPLATE_NAME;             Template name is used later to invoke template.
```

Sample (Format 2: Define a Template)

Structure in C   Equivalent Group Item in COBOL

```
typedef  struct
{                            No exact equivalent. The closest
  long    soc_sec_no;        thing in COBOL is a COPY member,
  char    last_name   [31];  which is a template. But in C you
  char    middle_init;       can define the template right in
  char    first_name  [21];  the program and then use it. In
  long    pay_grade;         COBOL, if you define a field or a
  double  hourly_rate;       record, memory is allocated. This
} PAY_DATA;                  is not always true in C.
```

Syntax (Format 2: Use a Template)

```
TEMPLATE_NAME   instance_name ;
```

Samples (Format 2: Use a Template)

```
PAY_DATA  rec_in;
PAY_DATA  rec_out;
```

Anatomy (Format 2: Template *Does Not* Allocate Memory)

```
typedef  struct ◄─────────────── Required
{        ◄─────────────── Required
    data_type  element_name; ┐
    data_type  element_name  │
    ...                      ├─◄─── At least one item must be defined
    ...                      │
    data_type  element_name; ┘

} TEMPLATE_NAME ;◄─────────────── Required
```

The differences between Format 1 (allocation of memory) and Format 2 (template) are that Format 1 has a structure name and does not use the `typedef` keyword. Format 2 uses the `typedef` keyword and its structure name is the template name. Otherwise the rules are the same.

TEMPLATE_NAME

> This is the programmer-chosen data name for the template. The general practice in C is to use uppercase letters to make templates (`typedefs`) stand out. When you want to use a structure for which you have created a template, use

```
TEMPLATE_NAME  group_item_name ;
```

> TEMPLATE_NAME is a data name of your choice, as is `group_item_name`. The standard rules for C data names apply. See the "Example" section that follows.

Discussion (Format 2)

The template name is often called the typedef name. The name itself is uppercase, by convention. The data name you assign to the template is in lowercase, as usual.

The compiler treats your `typedef` template as a data type, just like `int` or `double`. When you use a `typedef`, you give the data type, which is the template name and then a data name for that occurrence of it:

```
int       rec_count;
PAY_DATA rec_in;
PAY_DATA rec_out;
```

Whether you use a template or not, you must qualify every reference to an elementary item in the structure.

C Structure Name Usage	COBOL Qualified Name Usage
group_item_name.element_name	ELEMENT-NAME OF GROUP-NAME
pay_rec.soc_sec_no	SOC-SEC-NO OF PAY-REC

The other issue with `typedef` is where to put the definition. If you have gone to the effort to create a template, that implies you will have multiple uses for it. If all uses of it are restricted to one program, it makes sense to put the template definition in the program. However, if multiple programs or multiple files need to use the template, it should be placed in an include file.

In fact, the common practice is to put all the structure definitions (defined by `typedef`) for a system or subsystem into a single include file that can be used by any program that needs it.

Common Errors

See the "Common Errors" section for Format 1.

Example (Formats 1 and 2)

```
/*                    struct1.c           06/12/94                      */

#include <stdio.h>
#include <string.h>                      /* 1  for strcpy() prototype           */
struct                                   /* 2  no typedef; memory allocated     */
{
   long    soc_sec_no;                   /* 3  declaration of elements          */
   char    last_name    [31];
   char    middle_init;
   char    first_name   [21];
   long    pay_grade;
   double  hourly_rate;

} pay_rec;                               /* 4  name of struct is pay_rec        */

typedef struct                           /* 5  typedef used; NO memory allocated */
{
   long    cust_no;                      /* 6  declaration of elements          */
   char    cust_name    [31];
   double  current_bal;

} CUST_REC;                              /* 7  template name is CUST_REC        */

CUST_REC  master;                        /* 8  declare data of type CUST_REC    */
CUST_REC  tran;                          /* 9  declare data of type CUST_REC    */
```

```
main()
{
    /*
    assign values to elementary items in
    structure "pay_rec"
    */
    pay_rec.soc_sec_no  = 262473412;          /* 10 assign numeric values          */
    pay_rec.pay_grade   = 14;
    pay_rec.hourly_rate = 15.50;

    pay_rec.middle_init = 'C';                /* 11 assign single char value       */

    strcpy (pay_rec.last_name,  "Cashman" );  /* 12 assign string values           */
    strcpy (pay_rec.first_name, "John" );

    /*
    assign values to elementary items in
    structures of type "cust_rec"
    */

    master.cust_no      = 7943;               /* 13 assignments same as above      */
    master.current_bal  = 10000.0;
    strcpy (master.cust_name, "The TV Store" );

    tran.cust_no        = 6642;               /* 14 assignments same as above      */
    tran.current_bal    = 4530.0;

    strcpy (tran.cust_name, "AAA Auto Sales" );

    return (0);                               /* 15 return to O/S                  */
}
```

Comments on Example

Line 1   The include file `string.h` contains the function prototype for `strcpy()` (string copy), which is used later in the program. A function prototype contains a template of the call parameters for the function. ANSI C uses this during compiling to check your call parameters.

Line 2   Begins a structure declaration. Since the keyword `typedef` does not precede the keyword `struct`, this is a structure definition that allocates memory. It is not a template.

Line 3   Defines elements in the structure. The usual suspects are used: `char`, `char [n]`, `int`, `long`, `double`. Any valid data types can be used.

Line 4   `pay_rec` is the name of the structure/record/group item. In COBOL the record/group item name is first; in C it is last.

Line 5   Begins a structure template definition. We know this because the keyword `typedef` precedes the keyword `struct`. No memory is allocated. The template will be used later in one or more structure declarations that do allocate memory.

Line 6 Declaration of elements in a template is exactly the same as in a structure that allocates memory.

Line 7 In a structure template definition, the structure name is the template name. It is the last data name in the template definition. It is a C convention to make the `typedef` (template) name uppercase, as here.

Lines 8 and 9 Use the template, `CUST_REC`, to define two other structures, `master` and `tran`. Note that the syntax is

```
TEMPLATE_NAME        instance_name;
CUST_REC             master;
CUST_REC             tran;
```

Both `master` and `tran` allocate memory. When the code refers to either of these structures, it uses `master` or `tran`. `CUST_REC` is out of the picture after it is used to declare `master` and `tran`.

Line 10 These three lines assign numeric values to members in the structure `pay_rec`. The structure member operator, the period, is used. The COBOL equivalent of the first of these assignment statements is

```
MOVE 262473412 TO SOC-SEC-NO OF PAY-REC.
```

In C you must always qualify the member elements in a structure.

Line 11 Assigns a single character value to a member in `pay_rec`.

Line 12 Shows two statements that assign values to character strings. C requires using the string copy function, `strcpy()`, to do this. The first parameter is the destination field name, and the second parameter is the source literal or source field name. Member name qualification is the same as for the previous assign statements.

Line 13 Shows assignment statements to the structure `master`, which was defined using a structure template. Note that the use of member names is the same as in lines 9 through 11.

Line 14 Assigns values to `tran`, the other structure that was defined using a template.

Line 15 The `return(0)` statement ends the program and returns control to the operating system with a return value of zero.

Structure Format 3: Nested Structures

Use a nested structure (a group item within a group item) when you need multiple levels of group items. Basically, you define a structure that has other structures as members of it. These other structures are typically invocations of templates which have already been defined. You can optionally define a new structure inside a nested structure, but you cannot define a template within a nested structure.

Once you have defined a structure template using the `typedef` keyword, you can use it multiple times. It can be used inside another structure or on a stand-alone basis.

When you use a structure inside another structure, code the template name followed by the data name for the instance of the template.

Syntax (Format 3)

```
struct
{
    data_type      element_name;
    data_type      element_name;
    ...
    TEMPLATE_NAME  instance_name;   ← Nested structure
    ...
    TEMPLATE_NAME  instance_name;   ← Nested structure
    ...
    data_type      element_name;
} structure_name;
```

Sample (Format 3)

Nesting structures in C   Subgroups in a COBOL Group Item

```
typedef struct   ← typedef denotes template
{
    double  ytd_gross;
    double  tax_rate;
    double  tax_amt;

} TAX_DATA;   ← Template name
struct
{                                   01 PAY-REC.
    long       soc_sec_no;          05 SOC-SEC-NO        PIC 9(9).
    char       last_name  [31];        05 LAST-NAME      PIC X(30).
    char       middle_init;            05 MIDDLE-INIT    PIC X.
    char       first_name [21];     05 FIRST-NAME        PIC X(20).
    long       pay_grade;           05 PAY-GRADE         PIC 9(4).
    double     hourly_rate;         05 HOURLY-RATE       PIC 99V99.
    TAX_DATA   fed;                 05 FED-TAX-DATA.
    TAX_DATA   state;                  10 FED-YTD-GROSS  PIC 9(5)V99.
    TAX_DATA   local;                  10 FED-TAX-RATE   PIC 9(5)V99.
                                       10 FED-TAX-AMT    PIC V9(4).
} pay_rec;                          05 STATE-TAX-DATA.
                                       10 STATE-YTD-GROSS PIC 9(5)V99.
         name of                       10 STATE-TAX-RATE  PIC 9(5)V99.
         template                      10 STATE-TAX-AMT   PIC V9(4).
         to be used                 05 LOCAL-TAX-DATA.
              Instance names           10 LOCAL-YTD-GROSS PIC 9(5)V99.
              for template             10 LOCAL-TAX-RATE  PIC 9(5)V99.
              usage                    10 LOCAL-TAX-AMT   PIC V9(4).
```

Anatomy (Format 3)

```
struct
{
    data_type       element_name;
    data_type       element_name;
    ...
    TEMPLATE_NAME   instance_name; ⎤  Only these lines
    ...                            ⎥  are discussed
    TEMPLATE_NAME   instance_name; ⎦  in this section.
    ...
    ...
    data_type       element_name;

} structure_name;
```

This "Anatomy" section deals only with the new concept in this section: including a structure inside another structure. The rest of the structure definition remains the same.

`TEMPLATE_NAME`

This is the template name of the structure template you want to use inside the current structure. The template's name is the structure name of the template and should be in all caps.

`instance_name`

This is the data name you will use for the structure.

`;`

A semicolon ends all data declaration statements.

Discussion (Format 3)

It is common in C to define repeating groups as structures and then include, or nest, them in other structures. This is C's version of the COBOL `COPY` statement.

Each included structure requires another qualifier when accessing its member data items.

Use this form to access the members of an included structure:

```
struct_1_name.struct_2_name.member_name
```

```
pay_rec.fed.tax_amt
```

`struct_1_name` is the name of the highest level structure. `struct_2_name` is the name given to the template when it is included in another structure. `member_name` is the elementary item from the template. See the "Example" section that follows.

As previously mentioned, nesting structures is similar to creating multiple levels in a group item in COBOL. You can either invoke a template or define a new structure inside the first one.

Common Errors

See the "Common Errors" section for Format 1.

Example (Format 3)

```
/*                      struct2.c                    06/12/94               */
#include <stdio.h>
#include <string.h>                     /* 1   for strcpy() prototype     */

typedef struct                          /* 2   typedef = template definition */
{
    double    tax_rate;                 /* 3   declare elements of template */
    double    tax_amt;
} TAX_DATA;                             /* 4   template name for later use  */

struct                                  /* 5   NO typedef; allocate memory  */
{
    long      soc_sec_no;               /* 6   declare elements             */
    char      last_name   [31];
    char      middle_init;
    char      first_name  [21];
    long      pay_grade;
    double    hourly_rate;
    double    hours_worked;
    double    gross_pay;

    TAX_DATA  fed;                      /* 7   declare structs within a struct*/
    TAX_DATA  state;                    /*     data type is "TAX_DATA" from   */
    TAX_DATA  city;                     /*     template defined above         */
} pay_rec;                              /* 8   name of struct is pay_rec      */

main()
{
    /*
    assign values to elementary items
    in structure "pay_rec"
    */
    pay_rec.soc_sec_no   = 262473412;   /* 9   assign numeric values        */
    pay_rec.pay_grade    = 14;
    pay_rec.hourly_rate  = 15.50;
    pay_rec.hours_worked = 80.0;
    pay_rec.middle_init  = 'C';         /* 10  assign single char value     */

    strcpy (pay_rec.last_name,  "Cashman" );  /* 11  assign string values   */
    strcpy (pay_rec.first_name, "John"    );

    pay_rec.gross_pay    = pay_rec.hours_worked * /* 12 compute gross pay    */
                           pay_rec.hourly_rate;

    pay_rec.fed.tax_rate = .15;         /* 13  assign a numeric             */
    pay_rec.fed.tax_amt  = pay_rec.gross_pay *  /* 14  compute a value       */
                           pay_rec.fed.tax_rate;
```

```
    pay_rec.state.tax_rate = .035;              /* 15 same as 13 & 14      */
    pay_rec.state.tax_amt  = pay_rec.gross_pay *
            pay_rec.state.tax_rate;

    pay_rec.city.tax_rate  = .015;              /* 16 same as 13 & 14      */
    pay_rec.city.tax_amt   = pay_rec.gross_pay *
                             pay_rec.city.tax_rate;

    return (0);                                 /* 17 return to O/S        */
}
```

Comments on Example

Line 1   The include file `string.h` contains the function prototype for `strcpy()` (string copy), which will be used later in the program. A function prototype contains a template of the call parameters for the function. ANSI C uses this during compiling to check your call parameters.

Line 2   Begins a structure template definition. We know this because the keyword `typedef` precedes the keyword `struct`. No memory is allocated. The template will be used later in one or more structure definitions that do allocate memory.

Line 3   Defines members in the template. In this case we have two `double` data items, `tax_rate` and `tax_amt`. Use of the `double` data type means we expect values with decimal fractions, like percents or pennies.

Line 4   Gives the template name. It is in the same place as a structure name, but the use of the `typedef` keyword at the beginning makes `TAX_DATA` available to use as a data type. Using `TAX_DATA` as a data type causes the template to be invoked.

Line 5   Defines another structure. Since this one does not use the keyword `typedef`, it allocates memory. The structure gets named at its end.

Line 6   Basic structure member declaration for the next eight lines in the program. Several data types are used.

Line 7   Declares a structure as a member of a structure, that is, a group item within a group item. The data type is `TAX_DATA`, which the compiler knows is a structure template. After the data type is the instance name, `fed`, which the program uses to access this "sub" group item.

   Since we want to keep track of three sets of tax data, we invoke the template three times. The program uses only the instance names, `fed`, `state`, `city`. The word `TAX_DATA` is used for template definition and invocation but not afterward.

Line 8   `pay_rec` is the name assigned to the outermost structure. The name `pay_rec` must be used in every reference to every field in the structure.

Line 9   Assigns numeric values to the first level members in `pay_rec`. The structure member operator, formerly known as the period, is used to qualify the member names.

Line 10   Assigns a single character value to a member in `pay_rec`.

Line 11 Uses the string copy function, `strcpy()`, to assign values to structure members that are character strings. The first parameter is the destination field name and the second parameter is the source literal or field name. Member name qualification is the same as for numeric and single character data items.

Line 12 Is the equivalent of a COBOL `COMPUTE` statement, without the `COMPUTE` keyword. The receiving field, `pay_rec.gross_pay`, is qualified by the structure name.

Line 13 Assigns a value to the nested structure member, `tax_rate`, in `fed`. The only thing that really happens is that both the outer structure name and the nested structure name are used to qualify the member name. In COBOL this would read

```
MOVE .15 TO TAX-RATE OF FED OF PAY-REC.
```

Is this somewhat awkward? Yes. Is there an alternative notation? No.

Line 14 Assigns the result of a computation to the nested structure member, `tax_amt`, in `fed`. This is basically the same as the previous line, except that a number is computed and then assigned.

Line 15 Covers two lines that are the same as lines 13 and 14, except that the `state` nested structure is used.

Line 16 Covers two lines that are the same as lines 13 and 14, except that the `city` nested structure is used.

Line 17 The `return (0)` statement ends the program and returns control to the operating system with a return value of zero.

Structure Format 4: Structure Template Using Tag Name (Alternative Method)

Format 4 defines a template for a group item using a tag name. This is an alternative method of creating a structure template. I don't recommend it because the syntax is awkward compared to using `typedef`. It is included because you may encounter it in existing code.

Syntax (Format 4: Define a Template)

```
struct  tag_name                    This syntax does not allocate memory.
{
   data_type  element_name;         It does have a tag_name.
   data_type  element_name;         It has no structure_name.
 .
                                    It is a template for a structure
 .
   data_type  element_name;         and is used for multiple occurrences
                                    of the same structure type.
};
```

Sample (Format 4: Define a Template)

Structure in C   Equivalent Group Item in COBOL

```
struct pay_data
{
    long     soc_sec_no;
    char     last_name    [31];
    char     middle_init;
    char     first_name   [21];
    long     pay_grade;
    double   hourly_rate;
};
```

No exact equivalent.

Syntax (Format 4: Use a Template)

```
struct tag_name instance_name ;
```

Samples (Format 4: Use a Template)

```
struct pay_data rec_in;
struct pay_data rec_out;
```

Discussion (Format 4)

This structure format is just one example of C's ability to perform an identical task in several ways. Use of the tag name to create structure templates is essentially identical to using `typedef`. The real difference is in invoking the template. When you invoke a template defined by a tag name, you must code the data type as `struct`, followed by the tag name, followed by the name of the group item. If you use `typedef`, you just code the template name and the group item name:

```
struct pay_data rec_out;          Structure template using tag name
PAY_DATA rec_out;                 Structure template using typedef
```

Template definition using `typedef` is simpler, less awkward, and therefore recommended.

Common Errors

See the "Common Errors" section for Format 1.

Define a data type for "no value".

C Keyword/Symbol/Function   void

The data type `void` is used primarily in *function prototypes*, which are templates for call parameters for functions. (An ANSI compiler uses the function prototype to validate parameters in a call to the function.) C functions can optionally send a value back to the calling function through a feature called *return value*. Return value is, in effect, an additional parameter in a function call. If there is no return value for a function, the return value data type is defined as `void`.

Return value and `void` are discussed in Chapter 4, "Instructions, Keywords, Function Calls" and in Chapter 11, "Calling Functions (Subprograms)."

Declare a small integer.

C Keyword/Symbol/Function	short

`short` is a data type like `int`, except that it may take less memory in the machine. An ANSI compiler may allocate less memory for a `short` than an `int`, but it is not required to do so.

This is another part of C which is essentially obsolete for business systems in an era of multi-megabyte memories and gigabyte disks. It is not worth bothering with.

Where to Declare Data

In COBOL this is an academic question, since all data must be declared in the `DATA DIVISION`. In C it is a real question, since there are three choices. Variables have different scope, or visibility, depending on where and how you declare them.

In C a data element can be a local data element, a "program global" data element, or a "file global" data element. A local data element is one which is defined within a function and can only be used within that function. Its definition follows the function name, as in

```
#include <stdio.h>
main()
{
    int  rec_count = 0;
    ...
}
get_record()
{
    ...
}
```

The variable `rec_count` is only available within the `main()` function. Even though the `get_record()` function is in the same file as `main()`, it cannot reference `rec_count`, because `rec_count` is a local variable in `main()`. This is roughly equivalent to defining data within a paragraph in COBOL, which is why it looks odd.

Local data definition is preferred in C because it limits the use of the data element to code which is near it. This is the "need to know" approach: only the code which needs to know about the data element knows about it. Local data definition offers the most protection against inadvertent data corruption.

The general rule is to define variables within a function and to pass data through parameters if another function needs access to the data. Nearly all the program examples in this book define data locally, within the function which will use it.

There are occasional justifications for global data elements, which come in two flavors in C. "Program global" data elements are ones which are available to every function in the linked executable program. This is what is usually meant by global variables. You can create program global variables in COBOL II with the `GLOBAL` and `EXTERNAL` reserved words. "File global" variables are data elements which can be used by every function in a file, but not by any function outside the file. This is basically equivalent to normal COBOL practice. Variables defined in `WORKING-STORAGE` are available to every paragraph in the file, but not to any program in another file.

These types of global data declarations are discussed further below in the section "Storage Classes" and in Chapter 11, "Calling Functions (Subprograms)."

Data Type Modifiers

C provides two keywords which can modify the meaning of a data type. These keywords are `signed` and `unsigned`. Since all numeric data types are signed numbers by default, the `signed` keyword is redundant and is not used in business systems. The following two lines are exactly equivalent in usage, range, and the number of bytes allocated:

```
signed int line_count;
       int rec_count;
```

There is no point in typing the default modifier and no one does.

However, there is a difference when the `unsigned` keyword is used. The `unsigned` modifier changes an `int` or `long` from a signed number to an unsigned number. The number of bytes allocated for an `unsigned int` is the same as for an `int`. An `unsigned long` is also allocated the same number of bytes as a `long`.

The difference is that the high order bit is not used as a sign bit in an unsigned number. It is used as a digit. This doubles the positive maximum for the unsigned number. It also means there are no negative values for an unsigned number. The following lines compare the ranges of signed and unsigned for a two-byte `int` and a four-byte `long`:

Modifier	Data Type	Data Name	Range	
	int	line_count;	/* -32,768 through	+32,767 */
unsigned	int	rec_count;	/* 0 through	+65,535 */
	long	day_count;	/* -2,147,483,648 through	+2,147,483,647 */
unsigned	long	soc_sec_no;	/* 0 through	+4,294,967,295 */

The other thing that happens with unsigned numbers is that they roll over when you add 1 to the maximum value. If an `unsigned int` has a value of 65,535 and you add 1 to it, the result is 0. The same thing happens to an `unsigned long` with a value of 4,294,967,295.

Having said all this, the fact is that the `unsigned` modifier is seldom used in business, since you generally want to know if a number is negative.

Storage Classes

In addition to data type, every variable has another attribute called storage class. Storage class controls how the variable is stored. The four classes are automatic, static, external, and register, with the respective keywords `auto`, `static`, `extern`, and `register`. Storage class, if used, precedes the data type of a variable.

auto Storage Class

Automatic storage is the default. All the examples earlier in this chapter (and most of the ones in this book) are automatic variables. They are automatic because no storage class is coded, so the default is used. The following two variables have the same usage, range, number of bytes allocated, and behavior:

```
        int rec_count        = 0;
   auto int line_count        = 0;
```

As with `signed`, there is no need to code the default.

When a function (`main()` or other) is executed or called, memory is allocated to the automatic variables. When the function returns control, memory for automatic variables is released. This is intuitively obvious for the `main()` function, since the program is no longer running. But it works the same way for all called functions. When a called function returns control to the calling function, memory is released for all automatic variables. If you call that function again, memory is allocated again. Any initializations, such as

```
   int rec_count = 0;
```

are executed again. If you do not have an initialization, the variable can have garbage in it. This can cause problems and is the reason to always create initial values for all variables.

Releasing memory for variables is the opposite of what normally happens in COBOL programs. COBOL programs are commonly compiled and linked so that WORKING-STORAGE variables remain in memory when a subprogram returns control to the calling program. This is generally not a problem, since most functions do not (and should not) have to remember the values of variables from the previous call. If necessary, you can keep variables in memory in C with the `static` storage class, which is discussed next.

static Storage Class

There are three uses of the `static` storage class. The primary use in business programs is to keep variable values in memory between calls to a function. Recall that memory assigned to automatic variables is returned when a function finishes, and that automatic is the default. Thus, if you simply declare variables inside a C function, they lose their values when the function returns. Most of the time this is acceptable.

When you do need to maintain a value from one call to the next, use the `static` storage class when you declare the variable. Here's a short example:

```
void print_line  ( char line_to_print [] )
{
        int line_length;       /* value reset on every call      */
    static int  page_count;    /* value maintained across calls */
    ...
    return;
}
```

The second use of `static` is to create "file global" variables. These are variables which can be used by any function *in the same file* where the variable is declared. COBOL variables are global to the file where they are defined: all paragraphs can use any data element defined in the DATA DIVISION.

To get this effect in C, declare a `static` variable prior to the first function in a file. Then all functions in the file can use the variable, but no function in another file can reference that variable, even if the function uses the `extern` keyword. Here's how to create "file global" variables:

```
#include <stdio.h>
static   int      rec_count   = 0;
static   double   sales_total = 0;
void get_records (void)
{
...
}
void print_totals (void)
{
...
}
```

Both functions can use the two data elements declared as `static`. However, no function in another file can use `rec_count` or `sales_total`. This is discussed further in Chapter 11, "Calling Functions (Subprograms)."

The third use of `static` is similar to the second, but it is applied at the function level. If you use the `static` keyword prior to the function header (the first line of a function with the function name and its parameters), it makes the function callable only by functions *in the same file*. If you declare a function as

```
static void print_line ( char line_to_print [] )
{
    ...
    return;
}
```

the link editor will not resolve a call to print_line() if it comes from a function in another file. This is the way to keep functions private within a file. This also makes a function equivalent to a COBOL paragraph.

extern Storage Class

The extern storage class is used by a function to gain access to a global variable defined in another file. Global variables are automatic variables declared prior to the first function in a file. They are available to every function linked in the C executable. Global definitions, by convention, are placed above the main() statement. Any use of that variable in another file must have an extern declaration to use it. Here's an example:

File #1

```
#include <stdio.h>
int  rec_count = 0;

main()
{
   ...
}
```

File #2

```
#include <stdio.h>
extern int rec_count;

get_a_record()
{
   ...
}
```

Assuming these two files are linked together, both functions can use the rec_count variable. They will both be referring to the original definition above main() in File #1. Since rec_count is defined as an automatic variable prior to the first function in File #1, it is a global variable. When the compiler finds

```
extern int rec_count;
```

in File #2, it assumes it is a valid reference to a global variable defined somewhere else. The link editor resolves the reference or produces an error message if it cannot find the global variable.

You can get the exact same effect in COBOL II by using GLOBAL after the data name of the original data element and by using EXTERNAL after a data name in another program that needs to refer to the original element.

Global data elements should not be used much. They violate the principle that a data element should be known only to the functions which need it. They are also prone to corruption since every function can update them. It is often difficult to determine which function incorrectly updated a global variable. In short, use of extern should be minimal.

register Storage Class

The declaration

```
register int rec_count;  or  register rec_count;
```

advises the compiler to use a hardware register to store the variable `rec_count`. If the data type is omitted, `int` is assumed.

This is an archaic part of the language which dates from the era of 8-bit CPUs with cycle speeds of thousands of instructions per second, and 32,000 characters of memory. If the compiler does place the variable in a register (it does not have to), the time the program spends on CPU cycles will be reduced. It will not speed up I/O at all, which is where business applications spend the most time.

Today's CPUs have a 32-bit architecture, megabytes of memory, and perform tens of millions of operations per second. CPU time is seldom an issue in business applications. Since many compilers routinely ignore `register`, you should too.

Summary

In this chapter we learned how to define data in C and which data types are appropriate for business use. Data names in C can have up to 31 characters, use the underscore for a connector, and typically are in lowercase.

`char` defines a single character field. It is more like a number than an alphanumeric in that it can be operated on by most of the same keywords as numeric fields. `char [n]` defines a character array (string), or alphanumeric of two or more characters. Strings need to be defined one character larger than the expected data size to allow for the string terminator. Strings in C are manipulated by calls to library functions rather than by keywords. It is relatively easy to corrupt memory during string operations because the source string controls how many characters are copied. This is the opposite of COBOL, where the destination field controls how many characters are copied.

In C you do not control how many digits are in a number. It is determined by the data type. There are three numeric data types commonly used in business: `int`, `long`, and `double`. `int` and `long` are used to define integers, which have no decimal places. The maximum value for each is compiler-dependent. C provides floating point data types for numbers with decimal places. Use `double` when you need decimal places. The `float` data type is inappropriate for business use because it loses digits easily.

Group items are defined in C by using the `struct` keyword. It allows a collection of data elements to be grouped together. Elements in a structure are called members. When you reference members of a structure you must qualify the member name with the structure name. A structure can exist inside another structure, which is equivalent to a group item inside another group item.

Templates for structures can be created with the `typedef` keyword. This allows a single structure (record) definition to be created and then invoked by multiple programs. An alternate method of creating a template is to use a tag name. Tag names are not as straightforward as `typedef`s.

The `void` data type is used primarily in function prototypes, which are templates of call parameters for functions. `void` is coded in a function prototype when a function does not use return value.

C has more options than COBOL for where data is defined. A variable can be declared to be available only to the function where it is declared, available only to functions in the same file, or available to all functions in the linked program.

C provides the `signed` and `unsigned` keywords, which are modifiers for integer data types. `signed` causes an integer (`int` or `long`) to be a signed number. It is the default, so it is never coded. `unsigned` causes an integer to be an unsigned number. It is seldom used in business applications.

Storage classes affect how variables are stored in memory during program execution. The default is `auto` (automatic), which causes memory for variables to be released when a function returns control. Declaring a variable as `static` causes it to be retained in memory when a function returns control. This is the norm in COBOL. Two other uses for `static` are to create "file global" variables and to create functions which can only be called by other functions in the same file. Use `extern` when you want to refer to a global data element defined in another file. The `register` class advises the compiler to store a variable in a machine register and is obsolete.

CHAPTER 4

Instructions, Keywords, and Function Calls

Introduction

This chapter presents some key features of C that are different than any that COBOL offers. These differences primarily result from the fact that C does much of its work with function calls rather than keywords, and C functions work differently than COBOL subprograms.

The first part of the chapter discusses the use of C keywords, symbol operators, and function calls. The rest of the chapter explores features of functions and function calls that go beyond COBOL.

Why C Uses Few Keywords

C has a very short list of keywords—32 in ANSI C. Some compilers add a few more keywords. C also has a list of symbol operators, which act like keywords. This list includes +, −, *, and / (there are no keywords for add, subtract, multiply, or divide). See Appendices A and B for the lists of keywords and symbols.

In ANSI COBOL the list of reserved words is over 300 items and tells you just about everything you can do in the language. In the C language the keyword list, even with the symbol operator list, is not sufficient to solve any real-life problem in a program. All C compilers come with a set of subprograms, called *library functions*, that provide the rest of the tools necessary to make things happen in C programs.

Virtually every C program is a combination of keywords, symbol operators, and calls to library functions. C does not have the words *open, read, write,* or *close* in its keyword list. It does have functions called `fopen()`, `fscanf()`, `fprintf()`, and `fclose()` to perform those tasks.

In C, names followed by parentheses are function calls. Parameters may or may not be inside the parentheses. In this book discussion of the parameters are generally omitted for brevity. Thus, `fopen()` is the file open function in the library. `fopen()` has several parameters, but no parameters will be shown except in the section on `fopen()` in Chapter 6, "File Input/Output."

When to Use Keywords/Symbol Operators and When to Use Functions

COBOL has a large number of reserved words which do the work of the language. In C the work is divided between keywords and symbol operators (which act like keywords), and library functions. The list below gives the rules for when keywords/symbol operators are used and when library functions are used.

1. Most of the things you want to do with *numbers* in C you can do with keywords or symbol operators. (In C there is no move statement: the single equal sign means move). For example:

   ```
   tax_amt = gross_pay * tax_rate ;
   ```

2. Most of the things you want to do with *single character fields* in C you can also do with keywords or symbol operators. Single character data items act more like numeric data types than they act like strings (character fields with more than one character). For example:

   ```
   update_option = 'Y' ;
   ```

3. Almost everything you want to do with *strings* you must do with function calls. For example:

   ```
   strcpy (prev_dept_name, dept_name) ;
   ```

4. Everything you want to do with *files* and *printing* you must do with function calls. For example:

   ```
   in_file = fopen ( tran_file_in, 'r' ) ;
   ```

C Functions Compared to COBOL Subprograms

C function calls are somewhat similar to COBOL subprogram calls, as shown in the following examples:

A Function Call in C	Equivalent Call in COBOL

compute_fica (emp_ssno,
              hourly_wage,
              hours_worked);
	CALL 'COMPFICA' USING EMP-SSNO,
	                     HOURLY-WAGE,
	                     HOURS-WORKED.

First, notice that the function name is larger than 8 characters. Function names can be up to 31 characters. You can therefore make up function names that describe their activities. A function name does not have to be the same as its source file name. For instance, if your operating system limits file names to 8 characters with a 3-character extension, you can still have function names up of to 31 characters. Create descriptive function names.

To translate a COBOL call to C, drop CALL, USING, and the quotes. Put the parameters inside parentheses. It does look funny calling a function without a CALL verb, but you get used to it after awhile. Calls to library functions use the same format as calls to programmer-coded functions.

As you will see in the following chapters, many C operations are done via calls to library functions. Here's an example of how C and COBOL move an alphanumeric:

A Library Function Call in C	Equivalent Code in COBOL
strcpy (prev_cust_id, cust_id);	MOVE CUST-ID TO PREV-CUST-ID.

strcpy() is the string copy library function. Whenever you need to move or copy a string, you code a call to strcpy().

Return Value of a Function

This section introduces you to *return value*, which is discussed in subsequent chapters whenever a library function is described. Those discussions show how return value is used for each function.

Return value is a very handy feature that has only a limited correspondence in COBOL. In addition to the parameter list, every C function can return an invisible parameter, called return value. It is passed back by the return keyword. return is equivalent to GOBACK in COBOL, with an extra feature: return hands control back one level and can optionally pass a value of any data type.

In the typical case return is the last statement in the function. If you are returning a value, code

```
return (value_or_data_name);
```

If there is no value to return, code

```
return;
```

If you code `return` in a called function, control is given back to the calling function. If you code it in a `main()` function, control is given back to the operating system. Using `return` with a value is similar to setting RETURN-CODE and coding GOBACK in COBOL.

While RETURN-CODE is a two-byte integer, C's return value can be in the form of any valid C data type: `int`, `long`, `double`, a programmer-defined structure, and so on. Further, RETURN-CODE can only be used in programs to pass a value back to the operating system. It cannot be used to return a value from a called program to a calling program. Return value in C is more powerful.

In C a return value can contain

1. A useful single result from the called function, such as a numeric result. In the called function this would look like

   ```
   return (tax_amount);
   ```

2. A status of how the function performed, such as SUCCEED/FAIL or TRUE/FALSE (these names would be declared using `#define`). In the called function this would look like

   ```
   return (SUCCEED);
   ```

3. A result from the called function that is usually not used. Some functions may have a return value that is only interesting for certain coding techniques and not for the normal usage. This is common in C library functions that deal with strings. They often return the number of characters affected or the address of the destination string. Neither of these is usually interesting. In the called function this would look like

   ```
   return (byte_count);
   ```

4. Nothing, which is called `void`. This is equivalent to *not* using RETURN-CODE in COBOL. In the called function this would look like

   ```
   return;
   ```

A common use of return value in C is to return the result of a function, say `tax_amount`. This works fine when a function has only one result, such as `tax_amount`. However, in business data processing, it is common to use database packages to retrieve data. A correctly designed program must always check the status from a database call.

There are always at least two pieces of data coming back from a function that calls a database package: status and one or more data values. The result is that such functions typically use return value to indicate status, such as

```
return  (SUCCEED);
```

where SUCCEED is globally defined for a project or program. The data is then passed back through parameters, either as an element, several elements, or a structure.

The example that follows the "Function Prototypes" section shows the handling of both return value and function prototypes.

Function Prototypes

A *function prototype* is a template of the call parameter list and return value for a function. With a function prototype, the compiler can examine calls to that function to verify that the call parameter list and return value match the function prototype parameter list and return value. Prototypes are used for all functions except `main()` functions.

The compiler's task of checking is simple: Parameter lists that are short or long generate error messages, as do some data type mismatches. When possible, the compiler forces a data type conversion to give a parameter valid data type. A valid conversion is not necessarily a correct one. The compiler may or may not give a warning on type conversion. For further discussion on conversion, see the section entitled "Coercion and Conversion of Parameters" later in this chapter.

However, just checking the number of parameters saves a tremendous amount of time for programmers. The most common error is caused by adding a parameter to a function but not to all of the calls to that function. If you are using function prototypes and your parameter list is short, you are stopped at compile time. You don't have to wait until the program blows up before trying to find the error.

A function prototype must occur in the program prior to any call to that function. This is usually solved by putting prototypes in an include file and including that file in the program. Since include files are usually the first lines in a program, that puts prototypes in ahead of any calls.

So function prototypes are a valuable feature. All library functions have prototypes defined in the include files. Your job is to create function prototypes for each function you write. These are typically placed in an include file, grouped by main program or library.

> **NOTE:** ANSI C allows you to subvert function prototype checking by coding the prototype with no parameters (this kind of trapdoor is typical of C). This shortcut definitely does not pay. Full function prototypes save hundreds of hours on a project and a lot of aggravation. The function prototype is arguably the ANSI C feature that most contributes to productivity.

Syntax

```
return_value_data_type  function_name ( data_type  parm_name,
                                        data_type  parm_name,
                                             .
                                             .
                                        data_type parm_name );
```

Sample

```
int       abs              (int      some_integer );

void      print_error_msg  (long     err_nbr,
                            long      err_severity,
                            char []   err_msg );

double    get_tax_amount   (double   sales_amt );

CUST_REC  get_cust_rec     (long     cust_no );
```

Anatomy

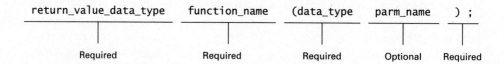

return_value_data_type	function_name	(data_type	parm_name	) ;
Required	Required	Required	Optional	Required

return_value_data_type

The *data type* of the return value. It can be any valid data type in C: int, long, double, and so on, or a programmer-defined structure template.

If the function returns an integer, the return value data type will be int, as in the abs() sample above. You can return a structure from a function. To do so you need to define a structure template using typedef and then use the typedef (template) name as the return value data type. This is shown in the get_cust_rec() prototype above, where CUST_REC is returned (assuming this is a structure).

function_name

The name of the function can be up to 31 characters long. Standard C naming rules apply. Make the name descriptive.

data_type

The data type for each parameter can be any valid C data type, such as int, long, double, or a programmer-defined structure template.

parm_name

The compiler says the parameter data name is optional, but your conscience requires it. The parameter name tells a reader what data is being passed to the function. Any valid data name will do, but make it descriptive.

Discussion

This discussion will cover both return value and function prototypes. These two topics are Siamese twins in C; you can't deal with one without dealing with the other.

Let's take several of the sample prototypes (and their return values) and see how they actually work in programs.

abs() is a library function. Its prototype is defined in the include file stdlib.h and looks like

```
int  abs (int some_integer );
```

abs() is passed one parameter, which is an int, and passes back the absolute value of that int in the return value. The return value is captured by the calling program:

```
positive_count = abs (count);
```

The capturing is done by assigning (moving) the result of abs() to positive_count. In C the single equal sign always means assign the right-hand value to the left-hand data element. At execution time, the call statement abs (count) is *replaced* by its return value. Here's what happens, assuming count contains –54:

```
positive_count = abs (count);
```

becomes

```
positive_count = abs (-54);
```

which becomes

```
positive_count = 54;
```

The syntax of using return value will look alien for awhile, because in COBOL you can't assign the result of a subprogram call, and in COBOL you use MOVE instead of = (assign).

The function print_error_msg() is an application error message printer. Its function prototype reads

```
void      print_error_msg (long     err_nbr,
                           long     err_severity,
                           char []  err_msg );
```

The parameters are a long that is the error number, another long that is the severity of the error, and a character array (string) that is the error message. (When you are receiving string parameters, you don't put a number between the square brackets.)

print_error_msg() does not return a value to the calling program, because all it does is print what is passed to it. Therefore, the data type for its return value is void; that is, it returns no value. A call to print_error_msg() looks like

```
if (database_status = DUPLICATE )
{
   print_error_msg ( ERR_INSERT,
                     ERR_FATAL,
                     duplicate_key_msg );
}
```

This looks more like a COBOL subprogram call. Since there is no return value, there is no assign statement (=) to capture it. Also, there is no replacement of the function call by its return value.

The following example shows a `main()` function and a called function, `get_abs_val()`. The prototype for `get_abs_val()` is coded in `main()`. In real life, prototypes are typically placed in an include file, and that file is included by the program. `get_abs_val()` returns its result through its return value, which has a data type of `double`.

Example

```
/*                      ret_val1.c                06/24/94                        */
#include <stdio.h>
double get_abs_val (double amount );         /* 1  function prototype            */
main()
{
   double gl_amt;                            /* 2  gl_amt must be positive       */
   double expense_amt = -65.37;              /* 3  amount which may be negative  */

   gl_amt = get_abs_val (expense_amt );      /* 4  call get_abs_val() function   */
                                             /*    and assign result to gl_amt   */

   return (0);                               /* 5  return to O/S                 */
}
double get_abs_val (double amount )          /* 6  function header               */
{
   double positive_amt;                      /* 7  work field                    */
   if (amount < 0.0 )                        /* 8  convert to positive if negative */
   {
      positive_amt = amount * -1;
   }
   else
   {
      positive_amt = amount;
   }
   return (positive_amt);                     /* 9  return a value as a double    */
}
```

Comments

Line 1 The function prototype for `get_abs_val()`, which will be called later. The first item in the prototype is the return value data type, `double`. That's followed by the function name. The parameter list is next. This function has only one parameter. The parameter data type `double`, comes first, followed by a somewhat descriptive name for the parameter, `amount`. The prototype has a semicolon at the end.

Function prototypes must occur in the code prior to any call to the function.

Line 2   An amount field that must always be positive. Most accounting systems only deal in positive numbers.

Line 3   Represents a detail field that can be negative.

Line 4   Calls `get_abs_val()` and assigns the return value to `gl_amt`. The compiler checks this call against the prototype to see that the parameters either match or can be forced to match.

Line 5   Returns control one level and returns a value of zero. Since this `return` statement is in the `main()` function, control is handed back to the operating system.

Line 6   Is the function header for `get_abs_val()`. The function header is the first line of a function. It is a combination of `LINKAGE SECTION` and `PROCEDURE DIVISION USING` statements. It has both parameter definitions and the calling sequence.

  The function header format is identical to that of the function prototype, except that the function header does not have a semicolon at the end. The compiler also checks the function header against the function prototype.

Line 7   Defines a result field, which is a `double`. This data element will be returned in line 9. Its data type is the same as the return value data type.

Line 8   Converts a negative number to a positive number, or moves in the parameter value if it's positive. Again, remember that the single equal sign in C always means assign (move). For equality comparisons, a double equal, `==`, is used.

Line 9   Returns control to the calling function and returns a value, `positive_amt`. The data type of the field inside the parentheses should match the return value data type in the function prototype. Both `positive_amt` and the return value data type are `doubles`.

Library Function Prototypes

When a library function is discussed in the following chapters, the include file that contains its prototype is named. If you don't include that include file, the ANSI compiler will give you a warning. If you do include it and have a short or long parameter list, the ANSI compiler will generate an error, so you can't link the program. This will save you a lot of time because it catches errors before they can blow up your program.

Coercion and Conversion of Parameters

As mentioned, if your parameter data type is not an exact match with the prototype parameter data type, the compiler will try to convert your data type to what the prototype expects. This is true for the return value too. This action by the compiler is called *conversion* or *coercion* of data.

In this text the term *conversion* is used for converting a smaller data type to a larger data type. The term *coercion* is used to describe converting a larger data type to a smaller data type. Strings are not converted (or coerced) to other data types and vice versa. If you pass a string and the prototype lists any other data type, the compiler will generate an error. Conversely, if the prototype shows a string and you pass any other data type, an error will be generated.

The hierarchy of sizes of nonstring data types used in business goes as follows:

Smaller   **Larger**

`char → int → long → double`

Conversion means changing to a data type to the right of where you are, for example, `int` to `long`. Coercion means changing to a data type to left of where you are, for example, `double` to `long`.

Conversion does not cause data corruption. Coercion *can* cause data corruption if the value of the data is larger than the capacity of the coerced type. An ANSI C compiler will issue a warning about coercing data. Pay attention to these warnings and change data types to eliminate them.

Two Ways of Passing Parameters

Parameter passing in C can be done in two ways, while in COBOL there traditionally was only one way. When you use the default method of passing parameters in COBOL, the called program has access to and can change the values of the data elements in the calling program. This is described as *call by reference*. Prior to COBOL II it was the only way to pass parameters in COBOL. In COBOL II you can pass a copy of the data by using the CALL BY CONTENT construct. This is described as *call by value*. When you pass a parameter by value the called program cannot change the parameter data in the calling program.

C has the same two options, with a twist. The default method in C is pass by value, which is opposite of the default in COBOL. C also has additional syntax when you use the call by reference technique, which is to pass the address of the data element when calling the function. For most data types this means using the *address operator* as a prefix to the data name. The address operator is the ampersand (&).

If you define a few basic data elements as

```
char      run_option;
char      account_name [31];
int       record_count;
double    gl_total_amt;
```

You can compare the following two function calls. The function on the left is called using the default parameter method, which is passing *by value*. The function on the right uses the pass *by reference* method, which requires the use of the address operator for most data elements.

```
check_gl_amount ( record_count,     update_gl_amount ( &record_count,
                  gl_total_amt,                         &gl_total_amt,
                  run_option,                           &run_option,
                  account_name );                        account_name );
```

The address operator is used as a prefix for all data types except arrays. This means both character arrays and any other kind of array, such as an array of numbers or an array of structures. An array cannot be passed by value in C. The called function can always change the contents of the array, whether it's a character string or 50 occurrences of a count. This is a quirk of C.

Later in the book you will find some library functions which change the contents of a parameter that you pass to it. When you call these functions you use the address operator for numeric and single character parameters so the function can change the data element. If you are passing a string, you simply use the string name since a string name is also its address.

Summary

This chapter introduced several key concepts in C:

1. Function prototype.

   A template of call parameters and return value for a function. It's used by the compiler to check the validity of your call.

2. Return value.

   The invisible parameter in a function call. The return value data type is the first item in a function prototype. If the function does not return a value, that data type is coded as void. Otherwise, it is coded as int, long, double, structure template name, and so on. A return value that is not void must be captured by the calling program if it is to be used.

3. A call to a function is replaced by its return value.

   When a function returns a value, the call to the function is replaced by the return value. If you want to use that value, you must assign it. This leads to the syntax of

   ```
   gl_amt = get_abs_val (expense_amt);
   ```

   You could code

   ```
   get_abs_val (expense_amt);
   ```

   by itself, but then the result would be lost. Some compilers generate a warning on this kind of statement.

4. Parameters can be passed by reference or by value.

COBOL II and C can pass copies of parameters or pass addresses for parameters which can be changed. The default is opposite in the two languages and C requires more syntax than COBOL.

Most of these concepts don't really exist in COBOL, and they are key concepts in C functions. If they don't seem clear yet, come back to this chapter when you find other references to return value, function prototypes, or passing parameters. These topics are also explored in more depth in Chapter 11, "Calling Functions (Subprograms)."

CHAPTER 5

Terminal Input/Output

Introduction

In the mainframe environment it is generally forbidden to write to the console. Because production jobs are often run overnight and operators generally are not familiar with the internal details of the programs, most shops want any input parameters to be in the JCL and any output messages to go to a file.

It's a brave new world in C. The computers are usually workstations or PCs. The end-users often run their own batch jobs and usually run their own reports. This means it is acceptable in most cases to send messages to the screen and request input from it.

C also allows a program to accept parameters at run time from an invoking script, just as COBOL can from JCL. You don't have to enter parameters through the screen. Run-time parameters are covered in Chapter 11, "Calling Functions (Subprograms)."

Terminal I/O covers writing messages to the terminal, getting data from the terminal in character form, and converting that character data into other forms. Single characters and character strings are the only data types that C gets from the terminal. You call a function to get a character or a string of characters. If you need that data in numeric form, you then call one of the numeric conversion functions. If you want to change characters to upper-case or lowercase, you call a case-conversion function.

The following table lists the common C library functions used for terminal I/O and conversion operations in business:

Desired Action	C Keyword/Symbol/Function
Terminal I/O	
Format and display field(s) on the terminal	`printf()`
Read a string of characters from the terminal	`gets()`
Read one character from the terminal	`getchar()`
Read and format field(s) from the terminal	`scanf()`
Converting Input	
Convert an alphanumeric to an integer	`atoi()`
Convert an alphanumeric to a long integer	`atol()`
Convert an alphanumeric to a decimal number	`atof()`
Convert a single character to lowercase	`tolower()`
Convert a single character to uppercase	`toupper()`

This chapter discusses each of these functions.

Format and display fields(s) on the terminal.

C Keyword/Symbol/Function   `printf()` (format and print on the terminal)

`printf()` displays literals and/or data values on the terminal. It defines a print line format, moves data into it, and displays it.

Syntax

```
printf ( "control string" [, arg_1, arg_2,...] );
```

Sample

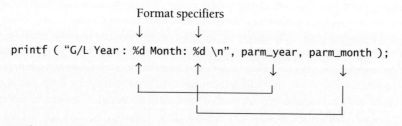

```
                    Format specifiers
                        ↓          ↓
printf ( "G/L Year : %d Month: %d \n", parm_year, parm_month );
```

Result: `G/L Year: 1994 Month: 10`

Include File

```
#include <stdio.h>
```
          (contains function prototype for `printf()`)

See Also

Parameter Definitions

"control string"

A literal within the `printf()` call statement where the formatting is defined. It is usually a combination of literal characters and format specifiers for the data items that follow.

`arg_1, arg_2...`

The data items to be moved into the format specifiers in "*control string*". They can be data elements or literals.

Return Value

The number of characters displayed. This is rarely used.

Direction

Arguments are substituted from left to right into the format specifiers in "*control string*".

Anatomy

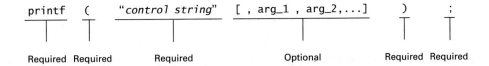

printf	(	*"control string"*	[, arg_1 , arg_2,...]	)	;
Required	Required	Required	Optional	Required	Required

`printf`

The function name for formatting and displaying data on *stdout* (standard output device), which is usually defined as the terminal. *stdout* can be defined as a file, but this is not common practice.

"control string"

String literal within the `printf()` call statement. It is enclosed by double quotes. It can contain literals as well as format specifiers into which variables can be substituted. After `printf()` fills in all the values, it displays everything between the double quotes on *stdout*.

Format specifiers are analogous to COBOL `PIC` clauses. A format specifier is identified by a percent sign (%) as the first character. Format specifiers are discussed in detail below.

"*control string*" does not need to have any format specifiers in it. If there are no format specifiers, the literal within the quotes is displayed as is.

Here are a few examples of control strings with some parameters and their results:

"Tax rate is %f", tax_rate	Tax rate is .28
"GL100 Final Run Page: %d", page_num	GL100 Final Run Page: 13
"Cust No Tran Date Order No"	Cust No Tran Date Order No

`[, arg_1, arg_2...]`   [brackets mean optional]

The optional data elements to be moved into "*control string*" where the format specifiers occur. If there are any data items to insert, a comma must follow the control string. After that comma the data names appear, separated by commas. Data elements are taken from left to right and inserted into the format specifiers from left to right. See the sample at the beginning of this section. The data items can be any of the following:

- Numeric data items.
- Single character data items.
- String data items
- Literals
- Expressions (computation results, return values of function calls)

`;`

A semicolon ends the statement.

Format Specifiers

Format specifiers are equivalent to the COBOL PIC clause. They give formatting directions to be applied to the data items in the argument list. Format specifiers are identified by a percent sign (%) as the first character. To move a percent sign into a string, put two together (%%). This is similar to the technique for putting a single quote in a VALUE clause in COBOL.

Format specifiers are coded as follows:

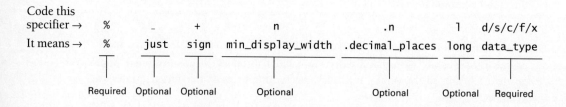

Code this specifier →	%	_	+	n	.n	l	d/s/c/f/x
It means →	%	just	sign	min_display_width	.decimal_places	long	data_type
	Required	Optional	Optional	Optional	Optional	Optional	Required

> **NOTE:** The only required items are the **%** and the data type.

%

A single percent symbol tells `printf()` that this is the beginning of a format specifier.

– (dash)

Produces **left** justification of the data item. The default is right justification for everything, which is good for numbers and bad for strings. You must code the dash to left-justify strings.

+

Tells `printf()` to put a plus sign with the number if it is positive. The plus always appears on the left. Minus signs are *always* inserted for negative numbers, whether or not you use +. The minus sign also appears to the left of the number.

n

Tells `printf()` the *minimum* width to format the data item. If, after formatting, the result string is wider than this value, printf() **will not** truncate, which is different from COBOL. Also, with `double` data elements this is the total display width, including integers, the decimal point, and the desired number of decimal places. Again, if the edited number comes out to be larger than the specified minimum width, `printf()` displays all of the characters. This could lead to a display that is wider than expected. On the other hand, data is not lost.

If you want leading zeroes, code a zero in front of the number, as in `%04d`. This tells `printf()` to format an integer for at least four digits, with leading zeroes. Here are some sample entries:

`%4`   Tells `printf()` to insert at least 4 characters
`%-20` Tells `printf()` to insert left-justified for a minimum of 20 characters
`%08`   Tells `printf()` to insert at least 8 characters with leading zeroes.

.n

Consists of a period and a number, which tells `printf()` how many decimal places to insert. For instance, `%10.6` tells `printf()` to display a number in a minimum of ten characters, with a decimal point and six decimal places. This leaves three characters for the integer value. If the integer value is larger than three characters, `printf()` displays as many characters as it takes to show it, leading to unexpected alignment. But, again, you don't lose data.

printf() rounds to the number of decimal places you tell it to show. However, C compilers do not use the business rounding convention of rounding up .5. ANSI C compilers use the IEEE standard that rounds .5 to the nearest round number. This affects printf(), sprintf(), and fprintf(). For business applications you must use your own rounding routine. Appendix F contains a round() function written by the author, which rounds according to business rules.

l

The letter l tells printf() that there is either a long or a double to be written. It is coded along with the data type, as in %ld or %lf. Most compilers now take care of this without explicit instruction.

d/s/c/f/x

Tells printf() the data type of the argument (parameter) for this format specifier. Common choices for business use include the following:

Format Specifier	Data Type	Output
%d	long/int	Signed decimal integer.
%c	char	A single character.
%s	char [n]	The string of characters until a \0 is found.
%s	string literal	The contents of the literal until the closing double quotes.
%f	double	Signed decimal number. If no precision is specified, the default format is to write all of the integer digits plus six decimal places.
%x	long/int	Unsigned hexadecimal.
%u	long/int	Unsigned decimal integer.
%o	long/int	Unsigned octal integer (seldom used in business).
%e	double	Exponential notation (seldom used in business).

Samples of Format Specifiers

These are a few samples of format specifiers for common data types. See the example program for more samples.

To Display	Use	Data	Result
A `long` or `int` in decimal form	%d	33	<u>33</u>
• With four digits	%4d	33	<u> 33</u>
• With leading zeroes	%04d	33	<u>0033</u>
• Left-justified	%-4d	33	<u>33</u>
A single character (`char`)	%c	M	<u>M</u>
A string (`char [n]`)	%s	Sirius	<u>Sirius</u>
• For 10 characters	%10s	Sirius	<u> Sirius</u>[1]
• 10 characters left-justified	%-10s	Sirius	<u>Sirius </u>
a `double`	%f	13.64	<u>13.640000</u>
• With 4 integers and 2 decimals	%7.2f	13.64	<u> 13.64</u>
• With 1 integer and 6 decimals	%8.6f	.654321	<u>0.654321</u>
A `long` or `int` in hexadecimal form	%x	47	<u>2f</u>

Carriage Control

To get line feeds/carriage returns, tabs, and page breaks to occur, put a backslash and a letter inside the format specification literal in the `printf()` call.

To get	Use	Example
Line feed/carriage return	\n	`printf ("Line feed after this: \n" );`
Tab	\t	`printf ("tab \t between \t words" );`
Page break	\f	`printf ("\f" );`

[1]Right-justified is the default format for strings; which is the opposite of both COBOL and English.

Printing "Special" Characters

Certain characters cannot be printed by themselves inside a `printf()` statement. To be displayed correctly, such characters require special character combinations such as the following:

To Get	Use	Example
Percent sign	%%	`printf ("Weighted average is %d%% ", average);`
Double quote	\"	`printf (" \"Best Guess\" Totals " );`
Backslash	\\	`printf ("Run-time directory is C:\\run " );`

Discussion

`printf()` is the workhorse of displaying data in C programs. It combines COBOL's DISPLAY and PRINT statements. `printf()` always sends its output to *stdout*. The normal definition for *stdout* is the terminal.

The most common use of `printf()` is for debugging programs. If your installation has a run-time debugger, it is worth learning how to use it for debugging purposes. Much of the time, however, programmers use `printf()` statements to display results while a program is running.

At the level you use C in business systems, C does not recognize the concept of a printer. To print a file you must write to the file and then use operating system commands to print it. There are two ways to do this:

1. Use `fprintf()` in your program for all print statements. `fprintf()` is like `printf()`, except it writes to a file rather than *stdout*. After the program runs, you can print the file. This is the preferred method because the program output is saved. If you need to print the results again, you print the output file rather than running the program again. In the PC and workstation environment, disk space is much cheaper than in the mainframe environment. Disk space for print files is typically not a major consideration.

2. Use `printf()` in your program for all your print statements, and then at run time, redirect the output to a file. After the program runs, print the file. This is much less desirable because you cannot define multiple print output files in the program.

Another advantage of using `fprintf()` is that if you want to write more than one print file, you can do it by simply opening two or more files and writing to whichever file is appropriate. `printf()` only writes to one file, *stdout*. If, for example, you want the program's error messages to come out on a separate printout from the basic results, open two files and use `fprintf()` to write to the appropriate file.

`fprintf()` should be used in production systems so that a print file is always produced.

Function prototype checking is not done on `printf()` calls because `printf()` has a variable-length parameter list. This seems to be a weak excuse, because all a compiler does is parse input. Nevertheless, there is no prototype checking, which gives rise to several of the common errors.

Common Errors

1. Bad value in the output, or the program blows up; more format specifiers than arguments.

   If you have three format specifiers in the format specification and two data elements, the value for the third symbol is unpredictable. You would think the compiler could count the format specifiers and the arguments, but it doesn't. This compiles cleanly.

2. Missing value in the output, or the program blows up; more arguments than format specifiers.

   This is the converse of the previous error. If you have two format specifiers and three arguments, the third data item does not get inserted into the control string. This also compiles cleanly.

3. Strange value in the output, or the program blows up; a mismatch of format specifier and argument.

   If the data type of the argument cannot be reasonably converted to the data type of the format specifier, either you get a strange result or the program blows up. Some compilers generate a warning on this, and some don't. The common sources of a mismatch are as follows:

Format Specifier	Supplied Data Type	Conversion Problem
%s	`int, long, double`	Numeric to string
%c	`char [n], double`	String or floating point to character
%d	`char [n], double`	String to integer; floating point to integer (decimal truncation)

As is often the case in C, you have to protect yourself because the compiler does not.

4. A number has rounded down.

   `printf()` rounds a `double` to fit the number of decimal places you specify. Since the IEEE rounding method is used, in some cases .5 rounds down. Don't depend on `printf()`, `sprintf()`, or `fprintf()` to round your numbers. Use the `round()` function, which is discussed in Appendix F.

   If you find this rounding problem hard to believe (and I still do), try these format specifiers and values:

Format Specifier	Data Value	Intent	Result
%.0f	2.5	Round to integer	2
%.2f	1.335	Round to 2 decimal places	1.33

Example

```
/*                      printf.c                 08/26/94                    */
#include <stdio.h>                      /* 1  for printf() prototype         */
main()
{
  int    day               = 7 ;
  char   first_name  [21] = "James" ;
  char   last_name   [31] = "Johnson" ;
  char   middle_init       = 'C' ;
  int    month             = 2 ;
  long   rec_count         = 12345 ;
  double sales_tot         = 11234.65 ;
  long   table_size        = 255 ;
  int    year              = 1993 ;

                                        /*     Result:                        */
  printf ( " '%s'      \n", "Totals" );  /* 2 'Totals'                        */
  printf ( " '%-10s'   \n", "Totals" );  /* 3 'Totals     '                   */
  printf ( " '%10s'    \n", "Totals" );  /* 4 '    Totals'                    */
  printf ( " '%4s'     \n", "Totals" );  /* 5 'Totals'        OVERFLOWS!      */

  printf ( " '%s %c %s'\n",              /* 6 'James C Johnson'               */
    first_name,
    middle_init,
    last_name );

  printf ( " '%d'      \n", rec_count  );  /* 7 '12345'                       */
  printf ( " '%d'      \n", -23456     );  /* 8 '-23456'                      */
  printf ( " '%8d'     \n", rec_count  );  /* 9 '   12345'                    */
  printf ( " '%+8d'    \n", rec_count  );  /* 10 ' +12345'                    */
  printf ( " '%08d'    \n", rec_count  );  /* 11 '00012345'                   */
  printf ( " '%-8d'    \n", rec_count  );  /* 12 '12345   '                   */
  printf ( " '%3d'     \n", rec_count  );  /* 13 '12345'        OVERFLOWS!    */

  printf ( " '%02d/%02d/%4d'  \n",         /* 14 '02/07/1993'                 */
    month,
    day,
    year );

  printf ( " '%f'      \n", sales_tot  );  /* 15 '11234.650000'               */
  printf ( " '$%.2f'   \n", sales_tot  );  /* 16 '$11234.65'                  */
  printf ( " '%.0f'    \n", sales_tot  );  /* 17 '   11235'                   */
  printf ( " '%11.2f'  \n", sales_tot  );  /* 18 '11234.65'                   */
```

```
    printf ( " '%011.2f' \n", sales_tot   );      /* 19  '00011234.65'                    */
    printf ( " '%6.2f'   \n", sales_tot   );      /* 20 '11234.65'       OVERFLOWS!       */

    printf ( " '%x'      \n", table_size  );      /* 21 'ff'                               */
    printf ( " '%4x'     \n", table_size  );      /* 22 '  ff'                             */
    printf ( " '%04x'    \n", table_size  );      /* 23 '00ff'                             */

    printf ( " '%x'      \n", middle_init );      /* 24 '43'          (ASCII value)        */

    return (0);
}
```

Comments on the Example

Line 1   Brings in the include file stdio.h, which contains the function prototype for the printf() function. A function prototype contains a template of the call parameters for the function. ANSI C uses this during compiling to check the call parameters, except when the function has a variable-length parameter list, which printf() has. With printf() you are on your own.

Lines 2–5   Show the effects of various format specifiers on a string literal. The results would be the same if a string variable name were used as the argument.

Line 2 is the minimal specification. The width will be the length of the string contents.

Line 3 shows how to get left-justified alphanumerics with a specified width.

Line 4 shows default justification for alphanumerics, which is right justification. This is obviously the opposite of what COBOL does.

Line 5 shows how printf() does not truncate if you specify a width smaller than the data element turns out to be. Four characters are specified and six characters are formatted. **Programmer beware!**

Line 6   Combines first name, middle initial, and last name in one field. Note that middle_init is a single-character field, char, and thus uses the %c format specifier.

Lines 7–13   Examples of various format specifiers for integer data types int and long.

Line 7 is the basic int/long specification. All the digits in the number will be formatted.

Line 8 shows the same thing, with a negative number. printf() automatically puts the negative sign on the left.

Line 9 directs printf() to use eight characters to format the number. The defaults in effect are right justification and no leading zeroes.

Line 10 shows how to get a plus sign to show up with a number. If the number is positive, the plus sign appears on the left side.

Line 11 uses a zero in front of the minimum width number to get leading zeroes to appear.

Line 12 uses the minus sign in the format specifier, which means left-justify. Since there are five digits and a minimum width of eight, there will be three spaces on the right.

Line 13 shows an overflow condition. `printf()` does not truncate numbers, or any other data type, if the data is wider than the specified minimum width. `printf()` just puts out the data. **Programmer beware!**

Line 14   Shows a common use of `printf()` to format dates into a normal form. The control string is hard to read. It says put in two integer digits with leading zeroes, a slash, two more integer digits with leading zeroes, another slash, and four integer digits. The arguments then supply `month`, `day`, and `year` to be inserted. The result is a date in a normal format for displaying or printing.

Lines 15–20   Show various format specifiers to handle a floating point number, a `double` in this case.

Line 15 uses the default formatting for a `double`, which will format to whatever width the `double` is and show six decimal places. Note that there are only two nonzero digits to the right of the decimal point, and C shows 6 anyway.

Line 16 puts a dollar sign in front of the number and limits it to two decimal places. The only problem is that C **never** puts commas in numbers. Also C does not float a dollar sign over to the first nonzero digit. If you want commas in your numbers, use the `dollar_comma()` and `double_comma()` functions, discussed in Appendix F.

Line 17 rounds the number and shows no decimal places. A potential problem is that the IEEE rounding method sometimes rounds down .5.

Line 18 right-justifies, suppresses leading zeroes, and shows two decimal places.

Line 19 right-justifies, shows leading zeroes, and shows two decimal places.

Line 20 specifies a minimum width (6), which is smaller than the data (8). `printf()` formats all the data and does not truncate. If you are expecting columns of data to line up, they won't if any of the numbers, after formatting, are larger than the minimum width specification. **Programmer beware!**

Lines 21–24   Show various effects of displaying numbers in hexadecimal form.

Line 21 is the basic hex format, with no minimum width specified.

Line 22 specifies a minimum width of four characters. Defaults of right justification and suppression of leading zeroes are in effect.

Line 23 specifies leading zeroes and a minimum width of four characters.

Line 24 shows how to get the hexadecimal value of a single character.

Read a string of characters from the terminal.

C Keyword/Symbol/Function	gets () (get a string)

gets () reads one or more characters from the terminal into a string variable. It puts a string terminator (hex zeroes) on the end of the string.

Syntax

```
gets ( string_from_terminal ) ;
```

Sample

```
gets ( first_name ) ;
```

Include File

```
#include <stdio.h>   (contains function prototype for gets ())
```

See Also

argc	— the number of run-time parameters
argv	— the data in the run-time parameters
getchar()	— get one character from the terminal
sscanf()	— extract numbers, characters, or strings from a string

Parameter Definitions

char string_from_terminal [n];

Character string to receive characters from the terminal. n is the maximum number of characters you're expecting, plus one for the string terminator.

Return Value

The address of string_from_terminal. Seldom used.

Direction

Left to right.

Anatomy

gets

The name of the function that reads a string of characters (an alphanumeric) from stdin, which is usually and properly defined as the terminal. It can be redefined as a file, but this is a somewhat advanced trick that is not addressed here. If you always think of stdin as the terminal, you will be safe almost all the time.

`string_from_terminal`

The data element that receives the string of characters entered from the terminal.

`;`

A semicolon ends the statement.

Discussion

When a program executes a gets() call, it pauses until the Enter key is pressed on the keyboard. The Enter key sends a hex 0A to the program, which tells the gets() function that it is finished. The hex 0A is not placed in the string variable in the program. In effect, the Enter key character is replaced by the null terminator.

If no characters are typed and the Enter key is pressed, the destination string has a null in the first character. This is intrepreted as an empty string.

You should use gets() in production programs only to get run-time parameters that were not submitted with the job.

If your program needs parameters at run time, you use argc and argv, as discussed in Chapter 11, "Calling Functions (Subprograms)." These variables allow you to submit parameters with the job.

However, it is typical in the C environment to design programs so they accept run-time parameters, if supplied, and prompt for them if they are not supplied. Use gets() to prompt the user for parameters.

Common Error

Memory corrupted.

If you or the user types in more characters than the size of the string you're assigning them to, memory will be corrupted. Results will be unpredictable. Make the destination string large.

Example

```
/*              gets.c                          07/23/94                    */
#include <stdio.h>                              /* 1  for gets() prototype   */
main()
{
    char  run_label [81];
    printf ( "Enter a description for the run:\n" );   /* 2  prompt user for   */
                                                       /*     input            */

    gets ( run_label ) ;                        /* 3  read a string          */
                                                /*     from the terminal     */

    printf ("Run description is: %s \n", run_label );  /* 4  display the input */

    return (0);
}
```

Comments on Example

Line 1   Brings in the include file stdio.h, which contains the function prototype for the gets() function. A function prototype contains a template of the call parameters for the function. ANSI C uses this during compiling to check the call parameters.

Line 2   A printf() call that prompts the user for the text to be read in as a string.

Line 3   The basic gets() call. Put your destination string name inside the parentheses. The program pauses until the Enter key is pressed. The Enter key character, hex 0A, is not placed in the destination string.

Line 4   Shows what was just read in. It substitutes the contents of run_label where the %s is in the format specification in the printf() call. This merely reflects to the user what was just read in. This is discussed fully in the section "Run-Time Parameters" in Chapter 11, "Calling Functions (Subprograms)."

Read one character from the terminal.

C Keyword/Symbol/Function	getchar() (get a character)

getchar() reads a single character from the terminal and puts it into a single character variable.

Syntax

```
character_from_terminal = getchar() ;
```

Sample

```
run_option = getchar() ;
```

Include File

```
#include <stdio.h>
```
(contains function prototype for `getchar()`)

See Also

`argc`	— the number of run-time parameters
`argv`	— the data in the run-time parameters
`fgetc()`	— read a single character from a file
`gets()`	— get a string of characters from the terminal

Parameter Definitions

`char character_from_terminal;`

Single-character field to receive the input from the terminal.

Return Value

The single character retrieved by `getchar()`.

Direction

Right to left.

Anatomy

```
character_from_terminal = getchar() ;
```
Required

`character_from_terminal`

The data element that receives the return value from `getchar()`. It will contain whatever character is typed in. If no character is typed and the Enter key is pressed, `getchar()` brings back the Enter key character (hex 0A), which is the character value of the Enter key.

`=`

The assignment statement that causes the character read by `getchar()` to be put into `character_from_terminal`.

`getchar`

The name of the function that reads a single character from `stdin`. `stdin` is usually defined as the terminal. It can be redefined to be a file, but this is a somewhat advanced trick that won't be addressed here. Think of `stdin` as the terminal.

`()`

Notice that `getchar()` has no parameters inside the parentheses. It always gets a single character from `stdin` and sends it back in the return value. In effect, `stdin` is the assumed parameter — the source of the single character to be retrieved.

`;`

A semicolon ends the statement.

Discussion

The only real use for `getchar()` in production programs is to get single-character runtime parameters from the user when the job is started and the parameters were not supplied. See Chapter 11, "Calling Functions (Subprograms)," for more discussion.

The only other common use is test programs in which programmers need to get single characters. If you want to get a number from the terminal, call `scanf()` or call `gets()` and then call `atoi()`, `atol()`, or `atof()` to put the number into a usable form.

Common Error

Getting no result when calling `getchar()`.

This is a result of not assigning the return value when calling `getchar()`. If you code

```
getchar();
```

without assigning the return value or using it in an `if` statement, the input character is lost. Most compilers will not generate a warning message on this, although they should.

Example

```
/*                getchar.c                          07/24/94                    */
#include <stdio.h>                          /* 1  for getchar() prototype       */
#include <ctype.h>                          /* 2  for tolower() prototype       */
main()
{
  char  run_option;

  printf ( "Enter 't' for Trial Run or 'f' for Final Run.\n" );
                                            /* 3  prompt for input             */

  run_option = getchar() ;                  /* 4  read one character           */
                                            /*    from the terminal            */

  run_option = tolower (run_option);        /* 5  make it lowercase            */
  if ( run_option == 'f' )                  /* 6  evaluate input               */
  {
      printf ( "G/L FINAL Run Begins\n" );  /* 7  display true case            */
  }
  else
  {
      printf ( "G/L Trial Run Begins\n" );  /* 8  display false case           */
  }

  return (0);
}
```

Comments on Example

Line 1   The include file stdio.h contains the function prototype for getchar(). A function prototype contains a template of the call parameters for the function. ANSI C uses this during compiling to check the call parameters.

Line 2   The include file ctype.h contains the function prototype for tolower() (lowercase conversion), which is used later in the program.

Line 3   Prompts the user for a single character to determine whether this run of the program is a trial run or a final run.

Line 4   Gets whatever character the user types. The typed character becomes the return value of getchar() and is assigned to run_option.

Line 5   Converts the entered character to lowercase so that the following if statement can check the lowercase value.

Line 6   Checks the entered character against a lowercase f. Both F and f will evaluate as true because of the tolower() conversion. The if statement then displays one of two messages.

Line 7   Displays the true case. A real program would use run_option later to determine other action.

Line 8   Displays the false case.

Read and format numbers and/or characters from the terminal.

C Keyword/Symbol/Function   scanf() (get and format fields from the terminal)

scanf() reads characters from the terminal, converts input to fields, and moves the fields into data items whose *addresses* are given by &arg_1, &arg_2, etc.

Syntax

```
scanf ( "control string", &arg_1 [, &arg_2, &arg_3...] ) ;
```

Sample

address operator for numeric and single character data elements

```
scanf ("%d", &employee_no ) ;
```

Include File

```
#include <stdio.h>
```
   (contains function prototype for scanf())

See Also

argc	— the number of run-time parameters
argv	— the data in the run-time parameters
getchar()	— get one character from the terminal
gets()	— get a string of characters from the terminal
sscanf()	— extract numbers, characters, or strings from a string

Parameter Definitions

"control string"

This is a literal within the scanf() call statement where the data conversion is specified. In order to maintain control of scanf(), the control string should contain a single format specifier.

&arg_1, &arg_2, etc.

These are addresses of the data items to be filled by the keyboard input. Again, to maintain control of scanf(), there should be only one argument per call. Use the address operator (&) for numbers and single characters. Use array name/string name without the address operator because an array name or string name also indicates its address.

Return Value

Is the number of fields successfully converted, or EOF if there was no input. This is rarely used.

Direction

Keyboard values are inserted from left to right into the data elements in the argument list.

Anatomy

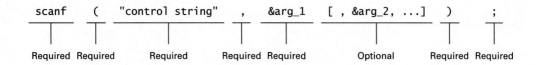

scanf

> is the function name for reading and converting data from stdin, which is usually defined as the terminal. stdin can be defined as a file, but this is not common.

"*control string*"

> This is a string literal within the scanf() call statement. It is enclosed by double quotes. It contains format specifiers for the data to be supplied by keyboard input.
>
> Format specifiers are analogous to COBOL PIC clauses. A format specifier is identified by a percent sign (%) as the first character. The only format specifiers that make sense for scanf() in a business environment are listed below.

Format Specifier	Data Type
%c	char
%d or %ld	int or long
%f or %lf	double

> The %ld format specifier may not be required to assign keyboard input to a long data element if your compiler has a four-byte int and a four-byte long. The %lf may, or may not, be required for a double, depending on the compiler.

, (comma)

> The comma after the control string is required because at least one parameter is required for scanf().

&arg_1 [, &arg_2...]   [brackets mean optional]

These are the addresses of the data elements to be filled by keyboard input. Addresses are passed because scanf() updates parameter fields. After the control string and comma, addresses of data elements appear, separated by commas. Fields from keyboard input are inserted into data elements from left to right. To be safe, specify only one data element per call to scanf().

;

A semicolon ends the statement.

Discussion

scanf() is a handy, but limited, way to get input from the keyboard and place it directly in numeric or single character data elements.

You pass the address of a field because you want the function to update the contents of that field.

scanf() discards leading spaces in keyboard input when taking in a number. It stops converting characters when it finds a non-digit, non-decimal point, non-sign character. scanf() leaves any trailing white-space characters and the Enter key character in the standard input stream (stdin). This can cause a problem, which is discussed below.

If you want to get a string from the terminal, it is simpler to use gets(). When you call scanf() to get a string from keyboard input, it stops at the first space it finds. If you have imbedded spaces in the string, only the beginning non-space characters are brought in. The remaining characters are left in stdin. In contrast, gets() brings in characters until it finds the Enter key character, which is more likely what you want.

The control string tells scanf() how many fields to read from keyboard input. The practical limit is one field per call. Although scanf() will read multiple fields in one call, the input is coming straight from the keyboard, unformatted and unedited. If you specify multiple fields, you are all but guaranteed that the program will get lost, sooner or later. This occurs because of keyboard input which does not match the number or type of format specifiers. In addition, more than a few compilers have trouble with scanf() calls with multiple fields. If you read one field at a time, you are better able to control and evaluate the input.

As mentioned above, when scanf() reads a number as the last or only field, it leaves any trailing non-numeric characters and the Enter key character in stdin. If this call is immediately followed by another call to scanf() for a single character field, what you get is the Enter key character from the preceding scanf() call, not the single character the user typed in. That character is still in stdin.

Each call to scanf() which reads a number or a single character needs to be followed by a call to fflush (stdin), which simply discards any characters remaining in stdin. The fflush() function is not discussed separately because of its limited use in business systems and its simplicity.

Using fflush (stdin) after scanf() is similar to always using braces in if statements: you may not always need it, but you are always protected. Proper use of fflush() is shown in the example program below.

Common Errors

1. The program blows up or abnormally terminates.

   This is the most common error and is usually due to using the name rather than the address of the target data element. The compiler should catch this, but does not. For numeric and single character data elements, precede the data name with the address operator (&).

2. Data input from the keyboard is unrecognizable.

   This commonly results from one of two sources: multiple fields requested in one call to scanf() for which the keyboard input does not match; or a compiler which has trouble with multiple input fields in one scanf() call.

   In both cases, the solution is simple: read only one field per call to scanf().

3. scanf() did not bring back the single character field entered.

   This happens when scanf() is called to get a number and the scanf() call is not followed by another scanf() or getchar() call to get rid of the Enter key character from the previous number input.

   Code an fflush (stdin) statement after each scanf() call.

4. A number has a different value than what was typed in.

   You can get an overflow condition using scanf() with numeric fields if the number which was input is larger than the maximum possible for the data type of the target field.

   If your compiler has a two-byte int, for example, any value keyed in which is larger than 32,767 will be corrupted when stored. Choose a data type which is large enough for any expected maximum value.

Example

```
/*                      scanf.c              11/11/94                    */
#include <stdio.h>                           /* 1  for scanf() prototype */
main()
{
    int     employee_no;
    double  percent;
    char    run_option;
    long    soc_sec_no;

    printf ( "Enter employee number: " );
    scanf ( "%d", &employee_no ) ;           /* 2  read an integer       */
    fflush (stdin);                          /* 3  flush stdin           */
```

```
    printf ( "Enter Soc Sec Number: " );
    scanf ( "%ld", &soc_sec_no ) ;              /* 4  read a long              */
    fflush (stdin);                             /* 5  flush stdin              */

    printf ( "Enter percent as NN.N: " );
    scanf ( "%lf", &percent ) ;                 /* 6  read a double            */
    fflush (stdin);                             /* 7  flush stdin              */

    printf ( "Enter Run Option as t or f: " );
    scanf ( "%c0, &run_option ) ;               /* 8  read a single character  */
    fflush (stdin);                             /* 9  flush stdin              */

    return (0);
}
```

Comments on Example

Line 1   Brings in the include file stdio.h, which contains the function prototype for the scanf() function. A function prototype contains a template of the call parameters for the function. ANSI C uses this during compiling to check your call parameters.

Line 2   calls scanf() to read input from the keyboard, format it as an int, and assign it to the field employee_no. Remember that since we are passing a numeric parameter that we want a function to update, we pass the address of the field, &employee_no. If a number is keyed which is larger than an int can handle, employee_no will have a corrupted value.

Recall that scanf() stops converting input to a number when it finds a nondigit, non-decimal point, nonsign character. This means that the Enter key character which follows the digits of employee_no is still in stdin, the keyboard buffer. This character can cause trouble and is the reason for the next statement.

Line 3   calls fflush() to discard *all* characters left in the keyboard buffer after the preceding scanf() call stopped reading input. This includes the Enter key character but could also include trailing spaces or other nondigit input.

Line 4   calls scanf() to get keyboard input, convert it to a long, and put it in soc_sec_no. The address operator is used because we want scanf() to update soc_sec_no. If your compiler has a four byte int and a four byte long, you can code %d instead of %ld.

Line 5   flushes stdin, the keyboard buffer.

Line 6   transforms keyboard input to a double and places the result in percent. The address operator is used so scanf() can change the value of percent. Depending on your compiler, you may be able to code %f here instead of %lf.

Line 7   flushes stdin, the keyboard buffer.

Line 8   shows how to get a single character from the keyboard into a field. We are still using the address operator, because we still want scanf() to update a field, run_option in this case.

If fflush() had not been called on line 7, this call to scanf() would bring in the Enter key character left behind by the scanf() call on line 6.

Line 9 flushes `stdin`, the keyboard buffer. It's a good habit to use `fflush()` after every call to `scanf()`, even after the final call.

Convert an alphanumeric to an integer.

C Keyword/Symbol/Function	`atoi()` (alpha to integer)

`atoi()` converts the contents of a string and creates an `int` (integer) from the characters 0–9, minus sign, and plus sign. It discards leading spaces. It converts digits until it finds the first nondigit, nonminus, nonplus character. The string terminator stops `atoi()`, as does any letter, space, or decimal point (no decimal places in an `int`). `atoi()` then hands the resulting integer back in the return value.

Syntax

```
result_integer = atoi ( string_to_convert ) ;
```

Sample

```
part_num = atoi (part_num_alpha);
```

Include File

```
#include <stdlib.h>
```
(contains function prototype for `atoi()`)

See Also

`argc`	— the number of run-time parameters
`argv`	— the data in the run-time parameters
`atol()`	— convert a character string to `long` (long integer)
`atof()`	— convert a character string to `double` (decimal number)

Parameter Definitions

`int  result_integer;`

Integer field to receive the return value of `atoi()`.

`char  string_to_convert [n];`

String you want to get the integer value of.

Return Value

`atoi()` returns the `int` value of `string_to_convert`. Since the return value is important in this function, you have to assign (move) it to another field.

Scope

Used on strings only.

Direction

Works from right to left.

Anatomy

```
result_integer = atoi (string_to_convert) ;
```
                              |
                          Required

`result_integer`

    The name of the integer data item that receives the return value of `atoi ()`.

`=`

    The assignment statement that moves the return value of `atoi ()` into `result_integer`.

`atoi`

    The name of the function to convert an ASCII string to an integer.

`string_to_convert`

    The name of the string data item that is to be converted to an integer.

`;`

    A semicolon ends the statement.

Discussion

There is no error checking in `atoi ()`. If it does not find a number in the string, it returns zero. You can check for zero as an error if zero is not a valid value.

Leading spaces are discarded, but an embedded space in a number causes `atoi ()` to stop converting the string.

The return value can be used "on the fly." See the following example program.

One good use of `atoi ()` is to convert run-time parameters from string to integer. C accepts all run-time parameters as character strings, so if any of them need to be `int`, they are converted with `atoi ()`.

Common Errors

1. Returned number is a strange number that doesn't match the input.

    If the string contains a number larger than an `int` can handle, the number will be corrupted. The same rule applies as when moving data. A two-byte `int` has a range of approximately ±32,760, and a four-byte `int` has a range of approximately ±2 billion.

2. Returned number is zero.

   There are several *almost* correct-looking numeric strings that cause atoi() to return a zero rather than the number in the string. Double signs, such as ++33 cause atoi() to return a zero. Another case is supplying a decimal fraction, such as .50. Since the return value is an int, which has no decimal places, .50 is converted to zero. If you have a decimal number to convert, use atof().

3. Nothing happens.

   If you don't capture the return value from atoi(), it appears that nothing happens. The following statement does nothing and does not generate a warning from most compilers:

   ```
   atoi (parm_from_screen);
   ```

   This statement converts the value of **parm_from_screen** to an integer, but since there is no assignment of the return value, the integer value is lost.

4. Decimal places are truncated.

   atoi() returns an int, which has no decimal places. If you pass it a number that has decimal places, they will be lost.

Example

```
/*                        atoi.c      8/26/94                      */
#include <stdio.h>
#include <stdlib.h>                   /* 1 for atoi() prototype    */

main()
{
    char date               [11] = "02/04/1993" ;
    char date_time          [31] = "Mar 11 1993 09:53 AM" ;
    int  dd;
    char input_value_1      [20] = " -3472 ";
    char input_value_2      [20] = " 112K54 ";
    char input_value_3      [20] = "333224444";
    int  mm;
    int  part_no;
    int  test_number;
    int  year;
    int  yyyy;

    test_number = atoi (input_value_1);     /* 2  convert -3472        */
                                            /*    stops at space after 2 */

    part_no = atoi (input_value_2);         /* 3  convert 112 - stops at K */

    year = atoi ( &date_time [7] );         /* 4  convert from middle  */
                                            /*    of string            */
```

```
   mm   = atoi ( date );            /* 5  convert month          */
   dd   = atoi ( &date [3] );       /* 6  convert day            */
   yyyy = atoi ( &date [6] );       /* 7  convert year           */

   if ( atoi (input_value_3) < 0 )  /* 8  use return value in if */
   {
      printf ("Value must be positive.\n" );
   }
   return (0);
}
```

Comments on Example

Line 1   The include file `stdlib.h` contains the function prototype for `atoi()`. A function prototype contains a template of the call parameters for the function. ANSI C uses this during compiling to check the call parameters.

Line 2   Converts an alphanumeric data element that has spaces both before and after a negative number. `atoi()` skips the leading spaces. When it finds a sign or a digit, it begins its conversion. It stops when it finds a space or other nonsign, nonnumeric character.

The value of `test_number` after this statement is –3,472.

Line 3   Shows a number being extracted from a string that mixes numbers and letters. The K in 112K54 stops `atoi()`.

The value of `part_no` after this statement is 112.

Line 4   Shows the technique of selecting from the middle of a string. In `date_time`, the year starts in offset 7. Use the address operator, **&**, and the offset [7] to pick up the year part of the date. `atoi()` stops when it finds the space after 1993. The value of `year` after this statement is 1993.

This technique is legal and morally acceptable. It does depend on well-behaved data. But, if you are using a database package you can rely on its date format.

Lines 5–7   Show a useful technique for turning an alphanumeric date into some `int` (integer) fields that can be used for computation and space compression. The relies on the fact that `atoi()` stops when it finds a nonnumeric, nonsign character, such as a slash. The address operator and the character offset pick out numeric parts in the middle of the string.

Line 5 picks up the month part of the date. Since we're starting at the beginning of the string, we don't need to use the address operator and an offset. In C the string name is implicitly the address of the first character, which is offset zero.

Line 6 gets the day from inside `date`. It begins at character 4, which is offset 3.

Line 7 finishes by extracting the year part of the date. Character 7 is offset 6.

After these statements,

mm	equals	2
dd	equals	4
yyyy	equals	1993

Line 8 Shows how to use the return value "on the fly." In this if statement the return value of the atoi() call is substituted into the comparison. The if statement

```
if ( atoi (input_value_3) < 0 )
```

becomes

```
if ( atoi (" -3472 " )    < 0 )
```

which becomes

```
if ( -3472              < 0 )
```

The atoi() function call is replaced by its return value, which is -3472. The if statement is then evaluated as

```
if ( -3472 < 0 )
```

The comparison is true, so the printf() statement following the if is executed.

Combining statements like this can lead to confusion. A simpler way to handle this condition is to call atoi() and assign the result. Follow this by an if statement, which uses the result:

```
input_num = atoi (input_value_3);
if ( input_num < 0 )
{
    printf ("Value must be positive.\n" );
}
```

Combining *one* other statement with an if statement is acceptable. More than one leads to trouble, especially in the wee hours when the unwelcome phone calls come. Make it easy on yourself and others: Keep it simple.

Convert an alphanumeric to a long integer.

C Keyword/Symbol/Function   atol() (alpha to long integer)

atol() converts the contents of a string and creates a long (long integer) from the characters 0–9, minus sign, and plus sign. It discards leading spaces. It converts digits until it finds the first nondigit, nonminus, nonplus character. The string terminator stops atol(), as does any letter, space, or decimal point (no decimal places in a long). atol() then hands the resulting long back in the return value.

Syntax

```
result_long = atol ( string_to_convert ) ;
```

Sample

```
soc_sec_no = atol (soc_sec_no_alpha);
```

Include File

```
#include <stdlib.h>
```
(contains function prototype for `atol()`)

See Also

`argc`	— the number of run-time parameters
`argv`	— the data in the run-time parameters
`atoi()`	— convert a character string to `int` (integer)
`atof()`	— convert a character string to `double` (decimal number)

Parameter Definitions

`long result_long;`

   Long integer field to receive the return value of `atol()`.

`char string_to_convert [n];`

   String you want to get the `long` integer value of.

Return Value

`atol()` returns the `long` value of `string_to_convert`. Since the return value is important in this function, you have to assign (move) it to another field.

Scope

Used on strings only.

Direction

Works from right to left.

Anatomy

```
result_long = atol (string_to_convert) ;
```
                      |
                   Required

`result_long`

   The name of the `long` data item that receives the return value of `atol()`.

`=`

   The assignment statement that moves the return value of `atol()` into `result_long`.

`atol`

   The name of the function to convert an ASCII string to a `long`.

string_to_convert

The name of the string data item that is to be converted to a long.

;

A semicolon ends the statement.

Discussion

The only difference between atol() and atoi() is that atol() returns a long instead of an int. The conversion rules are the same. If your compiler has a two-byte int and a four-byte long, there are different maximum values for int and long. If your compiler has a four-byte int and a four-byte long, there is no difference between atol() and atoi().

Common Errors

The common errors for atol() are the same as for atoi(), with one exception. If your compiler has a two-byte int and a four-byte long, it takes a larger number to create an overflow condition with atol().

Example

```
/*                     atol.c                        8/26/94              */
#include <stdio.h>
#include <stdlib.h>                       /* 1  for atol() prototype       */

main()
{
   char  date_time      [31] = "Mar 11 1993 09:53 AM" ;
   char  input_value_1 [20] = " -3472 " ;
   char  input_value_2 [20] = " 112K54 " ;
   char  input_value_3 [20] = "444113333" ;
   long  part_no;
   long  soc_sec_no;
   long  test_number;
   long  year;

   test_number = atol (input_value_1);          /* 2  convert -3472;              */
                                                 /*     stops at space after 2     */
   part_no = atol (input_value_2);              /* 3  convert 112; stops at K      */
   year = atol ( &date_time [7] );              /* 4  convert from middle          */
                                                 /*     of string                  */
   soc_sec_no = atol (input_value_3);          /* 5  convert a large number       */
   if ( atol (input_value_3) < 0 )             /* 6  use return value in if       */
   {
      printf ("Value must be positive.\n" );
   }

   return (0);
}
```

Comments on Example

Line 1   The include file `stdlib.h` contains the function prototype for `atol()`. A function prototype contains a template of the call parameters for the function. ANSI C uses this during compiling to check the call parameters.

Line 2   Converts an alphanumeric data element that has spaces both before and after a number. Also, the number is negative. `atol()` skips the leading spaces. When it finds a sign or a digit, it begins its conversion. It stops when it finds a space or other nonsign, non-numeric character.

The value of `test_number` after this statement is -3,472.

Line 3   Shows a number being extracted from a string which mixes numbers and letters. The K in 112K54 stops `atol()`.

The value of `part_no` after this statement is 112.

Line 4   Shows the technique of selecting from the middle of a string. In `date_time`, the year starts in offset 7. Use the address operator, &, and the offset [7] to pick up the year value. `atol()` stops when it finds the space after 1993.

The value of `year` after this statement is 1993.

Line 5   Shows that social security numbers will fit in data elements defined as `long`. The common four-byte `long` has a range of -2,147,483,648 to +2,147,483,647. The maximum possible value for a social security number is 999,999,999, or less than half the maximum for a four-byte `long`.

Line 6   Shows how to use the return value "on the fly." In this `if` statement the return value of the `atol()` call is substituted into the comparison. The `if` statement

```
if ( atol (input_value_3) < 0 )
```

becomes

```
if ( atol ("444113333" )  < 0 )
```

which becomes

```
if ( 444113333          < 0 )
```

The `atol()` function call is replaced by its return value, which is 444113333. The `if` statement is then evaluated as

```
if ( 444113333 < 0 )
```

The comparison is false, so the `printf()` statement following the `if` is not executed.

Convert an alphanumeric to a decimal number.

C Keyword/Symbol/Function	`atof()` (alpha to `double`)

atof() converts the contents of a string and creates a double (floating point number with a decimal portion) from the characters 0–9, decimal point, minus sign, or plus sign. It discards leading spaces. It converts digits until it finds the first nondigit, nonminus, nonplus character. The string terminator stops atof(), as does any letter or space. atof() then hands the resulting double back in the return value.

Syntax

```
result_double = atof ( string_to_convert ) ;
```

Sample

```
tax_rate = atof (input_tax_rate);
```

Include File

```
#include <stdlib.h>
```
(contains function prototype for atof())

See Also

argc	— the number of run-time parameters
argv	— the data in the run-time parameters
atoi()	— convert a character string to int (integer)
atol()	— convert a character string to long (long integer)

Parameter Definitions

```
double  result_double;
```
Double-precision floating point field to receive the return value of atof().

```
char  string_to_convert [n];
```
String you want to get the decimal number value of.

Return Value

atof() returns the value of string_to_convert as a double. Since the return value is important in this function, you have to assign (move) it to another field.

Scope

Used for strings only.

Direction

Works from right to left.

Anatomy

```
result_double = atof (string_to_convert) ;
```
———————————————————————————————————————
Required

`result_double`

The name of the `double` data item that receives the return value of `atof()`.

`=`

The assignment statement that moves the return value of `atof()` into `result_double`.

`atof`

The name of the function to convert an ASCII string to a `double`.

`string_to_convert`

The name of the string data item that is to be converted to a `double`.

`;`

A semicolon ends the statement.

Discussion

Why does the function to convert an alphanumeric to a `double` look like its name stands for alpha to `float`? Although it does convert the alphanumeric to a floating point number, that number is a `double`, not a `float`.

A typical use of `atof()` is to convert run-time parameters from string to `double` numbers. C accepts all run-time parameters as character strings, so if any of them need to be numbers with decimals, they must be converted with `atof()`.

Common Errors

1. Returned number is zero.

    There are several *almost* correct-looking numeric strings that cause `atof()` to return zero rather than the number in the string. Double signs, such as `++3.14` cause `atof()` to return a zero. Another case is double decimal points, such as `..75`. In both cases, the first sign or decimal point is valid, but the second one terminates the conversion.

2. Nothing happens.

    If you don't capture the return value from `atof()`, no conversion is recorded. The following statement does nothing and does not generate a warning from most compilers:

    ```
    atof (parm_from_screen);
    ```

This statement converts the value of `parm_from_screen` to a `double`, but since there is no assignment of the return value, the data value is lost.

3. Decimal places lost.

   How can you lose decimal places if you are using `atof()`? It returns a `double`, which has decimal places. If you assign the return value to an `int` or a `long`, however, decimal truncation occurs. You must assign the return value to a `double` to get the proper conversion.

Example

```
/*                     atof.c                    8/26/94                    */
#include <stdio.h>
#include <stdlib.h>                              /* 1 for atof() prototype   */

main()
{
    double   account_balance;
    double   federal_deficit;
    char     input_value_1  [30] = " 0.28 " ;
    char     input_value_2  [30] = "3.1415926535897932" ;
    char     input_value_3  [30] = " -65400.55 " ;
    char     input_value_4  [30] = "111222333444.55" ;
    double   pi;
    double   tax_rate;

    tax_rate = atof (input_value_1);        /* 2 convert decimal value  */
    pi = atof (input_value_2);              /* 3 convert up to 16       */
                                            /*   decimal places         */
    account_balance = atof (input_value_3); /* 4 negative numbers are OK */
    federal_deficit = atof (input_value_4); /* 5 convert a large number  */

    if ( atof (input_value_3) < 0 )         /* 6 use return value in if  */
    {
        printf ("GL amount must be positive.\n" );
    }

    return (0);
}
```

Comments on Example

Line 1   The include file `stdlib.h` contains the function prototype for `atof()`. A function prototype contains a template of the call parameters for the function. ANSI C uses this during compiling to check the call parameters.

Line 2   Converts an alphanumeric data element that has spaces both before and after a number that has a decimal point. `atof()` skips the leading spaces. When it finds a sign or a digit, it begins its conversion. It stops when it finds a space or other nonsign, nonnumeric character.

The value of `tax_rate` after this statement is `.28`.

Line 3 Shows a number (`pi`) that has a lot of decimal places being extracted from a string. This number of decimal places (16) challenges the accuracy of a double. Most C compilers start changing the digits of this number after the 16th significant digit. Since the basic definition of a double is accurate to about 15 significant digits, this is within the range of performance specified.

For most business applications this does not matter. If it does matter, take the user aside and explain that 16 significant digits really are enough.

The value of `pi` (using the author's compiler) after this statement is `3.141592653589793120`.

Line 4 An example of converting a negative number to a `double`.

The value of `account_balance` after this statement is `-65,400.55`.

Line 5 Demonstrates that a `double` can hold some truly large numbers, 111 billion in this case. This should take care of most, if not all, business applications.

The value of `federal_deficit` after this statement is `111,222,333,444.55`.

The actual limit for a `double` is literally astronomical: approximately 10^{-308} to 10^{+308} (10^{+308} is a 1 with 308 zeroes after it). However, only the first 15 digits are assured to be correct.

Line 6 Shows how to use the return value "on the fly." In this `if` statement, the return value of the `atof()` call is substituted into the comparison. The `if` statement

```
if ( atof (input_value_3) < 0 )
```

becomes

```
if ( atof (" -65400.55 ") < 0 )
```

which becomes

```
if ( -65400.55          < 0 )
```

The `atof()` function call is replaced by its return value, which is `-65400.55`. The `if` statement is then evaluated as

```
if ( -65400.55 < 0 )
```

The comparison is true, so the `printf()` statement following the `if` is executed.

Convert a single character to lowercase.

C Keyword/Symbol/Function	tolower() (to lower)

`tolower()` converts a single character from uppercase to lowercase. If the character is not a letter, that character is returned unchanged.

Syntax

```
lower_case_character = tolower ( some_character ) ;
```

Sample

```
run_option = tolower ( option_ind ) ;
```

Include File

```
#include <ctype.h>
```
(contains function prototype for `tolower()`)

See Also

`toupper()` — convert a single character to uppercase

Parameter Definitions

`char lower_case_character;`

Single-character field that receives the return value of `tolower()`.

`char some_character;`

Single-character field that you want to translate to lowercase.

Return Value

`tolower()` returns the lowercase letter of `some_character`, which must be assigned to a character field. If `some_character` is not an uppercase letter, it is returned unchanged.

Direction

Right to left.

Anatomy

```
lower_case_character = tolower (some_character);
```

Required

`lower_case_character`

The name of the character to receive the lowercase value of `some_character`. It can be the same field as `some_character`; you can assign the result to the source field.

`=`

The assignment statement that moves the return value of `tolower()` into `lower_case_character`.

`tolower`

The name of the function to convert a single alphabetic character to lowercase.

`some_character`

The name of the single character data item to be converted to lowercase.

`;`

A semicolon ends the statement.

Discussion

`tolower()` converts a single-character field to lowercase. If `some_character` is not a letter, its original value is returned with no conversion. The important thing to note is that the result comes back in the return value. If you don't assign the return value to some character field, it looks like nothing happens. You can assign the return value to the same character you're converting. See the example program below.

The typical use of `tolower()` is to convert run-time parameters that are single characters into lowercase. Converting a character to lowercase permits all if statements that refer to it to check only the lowercase value.

Some compilers offer a "string to lowercase" function. This is handy, but there should not be much need for it in the C business environment. The economical approach requires using a front-end package that can take care of converting input to lowercase or uppercase.

Common Error

Nothing happens

Nothing happens when the return value is not assigned. The statement

```
tolower ( run_option );
```

does not change the value of `run_option`. It converts whatever letter is in `run_option` to lowercase and hands it back in the return value. The subject field is not changed by `tolower()` unless the statement assigns the return value to the field, as in

```
run_option = tolower ( run_option );
```

Example

```
/*                    tolower.c              8/04/94                    */
#include <stdio.h>
#include <ctype.h>                        /* 1  for tolower() prototype    */

main()
{
   char  date_time  [31] = "TUE MAR 16 1993 09:53 AM" ;
   char  day_initial;
   char  input_value_1  = 'C' ;
   char  input_value_2  = 'B' ;
   char  input_value_3  = '9' ;
```

```
char  input_value_4  = 'x' ;
char  middle_init;
char  run_option     = 'F' ;
char  test_char_1;
char  test_char_2;

middle_init = tolower ( input_value_1 );      /* 2  convert single             */
                                              /*       character item          */
day_initial = tolower ( date_time [0] );      /* 3  convert a character in     */
                                              /*       a string                */
input_value_2 = tolower ( input_value_2 );    /* 4  convert "in place"         */
date_time [1] = tolower ( date_time [1] );    /* 5  convert "in place"         */
date_time [2] = tolower ( date_time [2] );    /*       in a string             */
date_time [5] = tolower ( date_time [5] );
date_time [6] = tolower ( date_time [6] );
test_char_1 = tolower ( input_value_3 );      /* 6  no effect on non-          */
                                              /*       alphabetic character    */
test_char_2 = tolower ( input_value_4 );      /* 7  no effect when already     */
                                              /*       lowercase               */
if ( tolower ( run_option ) == 'f' )          /* 8  evaluate return value      */
{                                             /*       in if statement         */
  printf ( "Run option is Final \n" );
}
else
{
  printf ( "Run option is Trial \n" );
}

return (0);
}
```

Comments on Example

Line 1   The include file `ctype.h` contains the function prototype for `tolower()`. A function prototype contains a template of the call parameters for the function. ANSI C uses this during compiling to check the call parameters.

Line 2   Shows the basic use of `tolower()`, which is to take some input value and guarantee that it winds up in lowercase. `tolower()` is called with `input_value_1` as a parameter and hands back the result in the return value. The return value is assigned to `middle_init`.

The value of `middle_init` after this statement is c.

Line 3   Converts a character inside a string to lowercase. When using `tolower()` inside a string, do not use the address operator, `&`, because you are dealing with a single character, not a substring. The offset still needs to be specified. Offset zero is the first character.

The value of `day_initial` after this statement is t.

Line 4   Uses `tolower()` to convert in place. You can assign the return value of `tolower()` to the field you are converting.

The value of `input_value_2` after this statement is b.

Line 5   Shows converting selected characters in a string, in place, to lowercase. Offsets 1, 2, 5, and 6 are used to convert the 2nd, 3rd, 6th, and 7th characters of `date_time` to lowercase.

The value of `date_time` after this statement is `Tue Mar 16 1993 09:53 AM`.

Line 6   Does nothing. If the character handed to `tolower()` is not alphabetic, that character is placed unchanged in the return value.

The value of `test_char_1` after this statement is `9`.

Line 7   Also does nothing. If the character is already lowercase, it is placed unchanged in the return value.

The value of `test_char_2` after this statement is `x`.

Line 8   Uses the return value of `tolower()` in an `if` statement. The compiler evaluates the `if` statement from the innermost set of parentheses to the outermost, as follows:

```
if ( tolower ( run_option ) == 'f' )
```

becomes

```
if ( tolower ( 'F' )        == 'f' )
```

which becomes

```
if ( 'f'                    == 'f' )
```

The `tolower()` function call is replaced by its return value, which is `f`. The `if` statement is then evaluated as

```
if ( 'f' == 'f' )
```

which is true (note the double equal signs). The statement in braces following the `if` is then executed. The statement in braces following the `else` is not executed.

The result of the `if` statement is `Run option is Final`.

Convert a single character to uppercase.

C Keyword/Symbol/Function	`toupper()` (to upper)

`toupper()` converts a single character from lowercase to uppercase. If `some_character` is not a lowercase letter, it is returned unchanged.

Syntax

```
upper_case_character = toupper ( some_character ) ;
```

Sample

```
middle_init = toupper ( middle_init_in ) ;
```

Include File

`#include <ctype.h>`   (contains function prototype for `toupper()`)

See Also

`tolower()`   — convert a single character to lowercase

Parameter Definitions

`char upper_case_character;`

Single-character field that receives the return value of `toupper()`.

`char some_character;`

Single-character field that you want to translate to uppercase.

Return Value

`toupper()` returns the uppercase value of `some_character`, which must be assigned to a character field. If `some_character` is not a lowercase letter, it is returned unchanged.

Direction

Right to left.

Anatomy

```
upper_case_character = toupper (some_character);
```
                            |
                        Required

`upper_case_character`

The name of the character to receive the uppercase value of `some_character`. It can be the same field as `some_character`; you can assign the result to the source field. See the following example program.

`=`

The assignment statement that moves the return value of `toupper()` into `upper_case_character`.

`toupper`

The name of the function to convert a single alphabetic character to uppercase.

`some_character`

The name of the single-character data item to be converted to uppercase.

;

A semicolon ends the statement.

Discussion

`toupper()` converts a single-character field to uppercase. If `some_character` is not a letter, its original value is returned with no conversion. The important thing to note is that
the result comes back in the return value. If you don't assign the return value to some character field, it looks like nothing happens. You can assign the return value to the same character you're converting. See the example below.

The typical use of `toupper()` is to convert run-time parameters that are single characters into uppercase. Converting a character to uppercase then permits all `if` statements
that refer to it to check only the uppercase value.

Some compilers offer a string to uppercase function. This is handy, but there should not
be much need for it in the C business environment. The economical approach requires
using a front-end package that can take care of converting input to uppercase or lowercase.

Common Error

Nothing happens.

Nothing happens when the return value is not assigned. The statement

```
toupper ( run_option );
```

does not change the value of `run_option`. It converts whatever letter is in `run_option`
to uppercase and hands it back in the return value. The subject field is not changed by
`toupper()` unless the statement assigns the return value to the field, as in

```
run_option = toupper ( run_option );
```

Example

```
/*                      toupper.c              8/04/94                    */
#include <stdio.h>
#include <ctype.h>                           /* 1  for toupper() prototype      */

main()
{
    char  date_time      [31] = "tue mar 16 1993 09:53 AM" ;
    char  input_value_1       = 'c' ;
    char  input_value_2       = 'b' ;
    char  input_value_3       = '9' ;
    char  input_value_4       = 'X' ;
    char  middle_init;
    char  month_initial;
    char  run_option          = 'f' ;
    char  test_char_1;
    char  test_char_2;
```

```
middle_init   = toupper ( input_value_1 );   /* 2  convert a single           */
                                             /*    character item             */
month_initial = toupper ( date_time [4] );   /* 3  convert a character in     */
                                             /*    a string                   */
input_value_2 = toupper ( input_value_2 );   /* 4  convert "in place"         */
date_time [0] = toupper ( date_time [0] );   /* 5  convert "in place" in      */
date_time [4] = toupper ( date_time [4] );   /*    a string                   */
test_char_1   = toupper ( input_value_3 );   /* 6  no effect on non-          */
                                             /*    alphabetic character       */
test_char_2   = toupper ( input_value_4 );   /* 7  no effect when already     */
                                             /*    upper case                 */
if ( toupper ( run_option ) == 'F' )         /* 8  evaluate return value      */
{                                            /*    in if statement            */
  printf ( "Run option is Final \n" );
}
else
{
  printf ( "Run option is Trial \n" );
}

return (0);
}
```

Comments on Example

Line 1   The include file `ctype.h` contains the function prototype for `toupper()`. A function prototype contains a template of the call parameters for the function. ANSI C uses this during compiling to check the call parameters.

Line 2   Shows the basic use of `toupper()`, which is to take some input value and guarantee that it winds up in upper case. `toupper()` is called with `input_value_1` as a parameter and hands back the result in the return value. The return value is assigned to `middle_init`.

The value of `middle_init` after this statement is C.

Line 3   Converts a character inside a string to uppercase. When using `toupper()` inside a string, do not use the address operator, &, because you are dealing with a single character, not a substring. The offset still needs to be specified. Offset zero is the first character.

The value of month_initial after this statement is M.

Line 4   Uses `toupper()` to convert in place. You can assign the return value of `toupper()` to the field you are converting.

The value of `input_value_2` after this statement is B.

Line 5   Shows converting selected characters in a string in place to uppercase. Offsets 0 and 4 are used to convert the 1st and 5th characters of `date_time` to uppercase. These are the first letters of day and month.

The value of `date_time` after this statement is Tue Mar 16 1993 09:53 AM.

Line 6   Does nothing. If the character handed to `toupper()` is not alphabetic, that character is placed unchanged in the return value.

The value of `test_char_1` after this statement is 9.

Line 7   Also does nothing. If the character is already uppercase, it is placed unchanged in the return value.

The value of `test_char_2` after this statement is X.

Line 8   Uses the return value of `toupper()` in an `if` statement. The compiler evaluates the `if` statement from the innermost set of parentheses to the outermost, as follows:

```
if ( toupper ( run_option ) == 'F' )
```

becomes

```
if ( toupper ( 'f'        ) == 'F' )
```

which becomes

```
if ( 'F'                  = 'F' )
```

The `toupper()` function call is replaced by its return value, which is F. The `if` statement is then evaluated as

```
if ( 'F' == 'F' )
```

which is true (note the double equal signs). The statement in braces following the if is then executed. The statement in braces following the `else` is not executed.

The result of the `if` statement is `Run option is Final`.

Summary

Terminal I/O is more common in the C world of PCs and workstations than in the mainframe world. It is acceptable in C programs to use the equivalent of `DISPLAY UPON CONSOLE`.

The `printf()` function is probably the most commonly used function in all of C. It is used to communicate with users and for debugging statements by programmers. It formats a line and displays it on the terminal from which the program has been run. `printf()` is a combination of defining a print line, moving data to it, and displaying the formatted line on the console. It uses format specifers to control how data will be displayed. These are equivalent to `PIC` clauses in print lines in COBOL.

Terminal input is also accomplished by function calls. `gets()` gets a string from keyboard input. `getchar()` gets a single character. `scanf()` gets keyboard input, converts to a data type, and moves it to a data element. `scanf()` has some quirks, such as leaving the Enter key character in the input stream when reading a number or single character. It is also easy for it to fail when retrieving multiple fields in one call. Use with care.

Two kinds of conversion functions were presented: string to numeric and upper/lower case conversion. The functions `atoi()`, `atol()`, and `atof()` are used to convert a string to, respectively, an `int`, a `long`, and a `double`. These functions are used when getting data with `gets()` and to convert run-time parameters.

Case conversion is performed by `toupper()` and `tolower()`. These functions operate on a single character at a time. Many compilers offer case conversion routines for strings. These can be handy, but there should not be much need for them if you are using a screen handling package, as this book recommends.

Terminal I/O in business systems is done through functions. You will write more `printf()` calls than any other kind. The terminal input functions are straightforward, with the exception of `scanf()`. The numeric conversion functions are easy to use, but you must be careful to use the one which matches the data type of your target field. The case conversion functions are simple.

6

File Input/Output

Introduction

File input/output (I/O) in C consists primarily of writing print files to disk and reading and writing sequential files. Print files are explicitly written to disk in the C environment and then printed using operating system utilities or commands. There is no direct high-level access to the printer in C. Sequential files are handled much the same way as in COBOL, except that in C they are more likely to be variable in length, due to the inherently variable length of strings.

In this chapter the C functions involved in file I/O are divided into three groups: opening and closing files, variable-length record processing, and fixed-length record processing. The discussion begins, however, with an overview of sequential files and their use in the C business environment.

Sequential Files

Sequential files are not used nearly as much in the C business environment as they are in the mainframe environment. Database packages should be the choice for storing, organizing, and retrieving data, whether a shop uses COBOL or C.

The multistep job with sequential files passing data along is not found often in the C environment. More often than not, temporary data stores are defined in a database. The main uses of sequential files in C are for interfaces to or from other systems, system conversions, test data files, and reports. This still leaves a significant requirement to read and write sequential files in C.

Another difference between the C and mainframe worlds is that disk space for workstations and PCs is almost as cheap as popcorn. Databases rather than sequential files are the primary consumers of disk space. Reports are typically written to disk and left there, to be overwritten the next time the report runs. As of this writing, a gigabyte disk (1000 billion bytes) for a workstation costs less than $3000.

File Handling in C

File handling in C is different from COBOL. There is much less structure to file handling in C and no JCL to speak of in the workstation and PC environments.

The concept of fixed fields and fixed-length records is basically foreign to C. In C the native mode is variable length. However, you can write and read fixed-length records in C if you set up structures and use `fwrite()` and `fread()`. This is discussed in the sections on `fwrite()` and `fread()` later in this chapter.

File allocation is much simpler in C than in COBOL, because most C environments run under MS-DOS, VMS, or a Unix variant. These operating systems have relatively simple methods for allocating files. You typically supply a file name and, optionally, a directory name to put it in. That's it. On workstations and PCs you do not run out of space until you fill up the entire disk drive you're writing to or exceed your quota of disk space.

C has three basic ways to handle sequential files in the business environment. They are listed below in the order of most to least common.

1. Writing a sequential file that will be input to another system. The file usually contains fixed-length fields and thus looks like a COBOL sequential file. This is the most common use of sequential files in the C business environment.

2. Reading a sequential file from another system or program. This mostly occurs for data feeds to your system or data conversions for a new system. Such a file can have many different forms, such as fixed-length fields, comma-separated fields, or any of the many PC file interchange formats. Some of these formats are a real pain in the neck to deal with and require parsing the input data, character by character, to find the fields.

3. Maintaining a sequential master file. This should be rare or nonexistent in C business data processing, because database packages offer the most cost effective and integrated method for storing, updating, and retrieving data. If you have to write your own sequential master file application, however, use structures and `fwrite()` and `fread()` to generate fixed-length records.

Variable-Length and Fixed-Length Records

C can deal with both variable-length and fixed-length records. In COBOL, fixed-length records are the norm. In C, variable-length records are the norm. Because variable-length records are much more common in C than in COBOL, they are discussed first in this chapter. The final two sections deal with writing and reading fixed-length records.

The following table lists the C library functions commonly used for sequential file operations in business:

Desired Action	C Keyword/Symbol/Function
Open a sequential file	`fopen()`
Close a sequential file	`fclose()`
Read a string of characters from a file	`fgets()`
Format and extract field(s) from a string (after you've read in a string)	`sscanf()`
Read one character from a file	`fgetc()`
Format and write fields to a file	`fprintf()`
Write a fixed-length record to a file	`fwrite()`
Read a fixed-length record from a file	`fread()`

Opening and Closing Files

Sequential files must be opened and closed in C, just as they are in COBOL. In C you call functions rather than using keywords. The `fopen()` (file open) and `fclose()` (file close) functions in C always pass back a status in the return value. A C program can trap a file-open or file-close error, while in COBOL the FILE STATUS IS clause in the SELECT statement does this.

Good programming practice in C, as in COBOL, checks the results of both the opening and closing of files. The program should print an error message and return an abnormal code to the operating system if either function returns an error.

Open a sequential file.

C Keyword/Symbol/Function	`fopen()` (file open)

fopen() opens a sequential file for reading, writing, or appending. C assigns an address to the FILE pointer file_name, just as COBOL assigns an address to the FD *file-name* in a COBOL OPEN. In both languages you just use the file name and do not worry about its being an address.

Syntax

```
FILE *file_name ;
file_name = fopen ( dataset_name, access_mode ) ;
```

Sample

```
FILE *in_file ;
in_file = fopen ( "conversion.data" , "r" ) ;    (double quotes on access
                                                  mode)
```

or

```
FILE *out_file ;
char test_results_file  [13] = "results.out" ;
out_file = fopen ( test_results_file , "w" ) ;   (double quotes on access
                                                  mode)
```

Include File

`#include <stdio.h>`   (contains function prototype for fopen())

See Also

fclose()	— close a file
fgetc()	— read a single character from a file
fgets()	— read a string of characters from a file
fprintf()	— format and write to a file
fread()	— read a record (structure) from a file
fwrite()	— write a record (structure) to a file
sscanf()	— extract numbers, characters, or strings from a string

Parameter Definitions

`FILE  *file_name;`

Equivalent to the COBOL FD *file-name*. You supply your own file name.

`char  dataset_name [n] = "ds_name";` -or- a string literal

The dataset name of the file. In C it is not uncommon to put the dataset name in the program.

`access_mode`

> Usually coded as a literal—"r," "w," or "a" (read, write, or append). It can be two letters and, since it is defined in the function prototype as a string, it must have double quotes, even if there is only one character.

Return Value

The address of the file buffer in memory that is assigned to `file_name`. If the `fopen()` call is not successful, `file_name` is set to `NULL`, which is hex zeroes. After you call `fopen()`, you check `file_name` to make sure it is not `NULL`. `NULL` means the program could not find or could not open the file.

After the `fopen()` call, you can forget about the address of the file buffer in memory and simply use `file_name`, as you do in COBOL.

When you open a file in COBOL, it assigns a memory address for a file buffer to *file-name*, which is defined in the `SELECT` and `FD` statements. But all you do in a program is open the file and then `READ` or `WRITE`. In C it's the same except you have to check whether the open function was successful.

Direction

Right to left.

Anatomy

```
file_name = fopen ( dataset_name , access_mode ) ;
```
                        |
                     Required

`file_name`

> The equivalent of *file-name* in the COBOL FD statement. In C you use `file_name` in the open, close, read, and write functions. `file_name` is declared with a pointer (address) declaration, `*`, which is not used again.
>
> `file_name` is also how you find out if `fopen()` was successful. If `fopen()` is not successful, `file_name` is set to `NULL`. You need to check that `file_name` is not set to `NULL` after `fopen()`. See the example program below.

`=`

> The assignment statement that moves the *address* of the file I/O area to `file_name`. The assignment statement moves `NULL` (hex zeroes) to `file_name` if `fopen()` is not successful.

`fopen`

The name of the function that opens a sequential file.

`dataset_name`

The name of the sequential file to be opened. This can be a hard-coded literal value, a string data element name, or a symbolic name. `dataset_name` has to obey the naming rules of the operating system you are using.

If you supply a literal value or a string that contains a literal value, the operating system assumes the file is in the same directory in which the program is being run. This is equivalent to having a piece of JCL in the program. This is acceptable in the C development environment, but in production environments datasets are not usually located in the same place as programs.

The solution for this is to use symbolic names. These are names defined in command files or scripts that execute programs. These command files are analogous to JCL, except that they are much simpler. Using symbolic names eliminates hard coding of production dataset names and locations. Symbolic names have different forms in different operating systems, so they will not be discussed in detail here. See your local operating system guru or the operating system documentation.

`access_mode`

Contains one of three values:

"r"	Read, or input
"w"	Write, or output
"a"	Write, and append to the end of the existing file

Six or eight other values are possible here, but typically they are not used in business systems. You can open a file to read, write, or append binary values. The values then would be "rb", "wb", or "ab". This is why double quotes are used: `access_mode` is defined as a string so the two-letter combinations can be used.

Discussion

C's file-handling ability is straightforward and simple: Open your file and then use it. If your requirements are more complex than nonindexed, nonkeyed sequential files can handle, you should access and update data through a database or file manager package.

The most common use for sequential files in business data processing is to write files that will then be printed. In COBOL you typically send the print output directly to a printer. In C you write a file and then use an operating system command or utility to print it.

The "w" (write) option replaces any existing file that has the same dataset name used in `fopen()`. This means previous data is lost. Also, if the user running the program does not have permission from the operating system to write the file, `fopen()` fails and returns `NULL`.

The "a" (append) option can be useful at times, but if you run a program multiple times with the append option, each new output file is appended to the set of previous output files. It grows and grows and grows. Use with care.

The file pointer declaration

```
FILE *in_file;
```

looks alien but in fact is exactly equivalent to the COBOL FD name. Both are pointers, which means that the memory they refer to is defined somewhere else. A pointer, in C and COBOL, is a single machine word of memory. The value in that word is the address of the beginning of the memory that is referred to.

In both languages the file buffer is defined outside the area where data elements are defined. The real difference here between C and COBOL is that C uses the asterisk to explicitly state that the memory being referred to is defined somewhere else. In the body of a C program, you always use file_name without the asterisk.

The following diagram shows a file definition in both C and COBOL. Assume the record is defined as 100 bytes. In both languages, only one machine word of memory is allocated where the file is declared. That word contains the address of (points to) the "real" memory of the file buffer. That other memory is where the record is stored in memory.

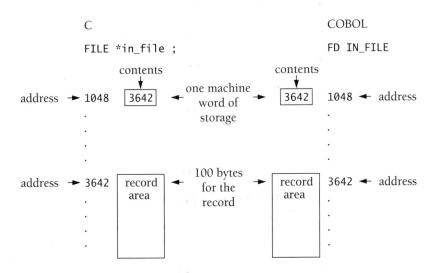

The fact is that in your program, in either language, you do not really care about this memory layout. You just define the file and then use it. Files are handled identically in each language from the programmer's point of view. In C you do what you do in COBOL: declare the file and then use it.

Common Error

Not checking the status of the call to fopen().

If fopen() fails and you do not check the status of the call, you get end-of-file indications from every read function you call. Always check the status of the fopen() call.

Example

```
/*                    fopen.c                      07/30/94              */
#include <stdio.h>                                 /* 1 for fopen() prototype    */
main()
{
  FILE *conv_file;
  FILE *in_file;

  char conv_dsn [9] = "conv.dat" ;

  in_file = fopen ( "testdata.dat", "r" );         /* 2 basic fopen()            */
  if (in_file == NULL)                             /* 3 check result             */
  {
    printf ("Could not open testdata.dat.\n" );
    return (1);
  }

  if ( (conv_file = fopen ( conv_dsn, "r" ) ) == NULL)    /* 4 common use        */
  {
    printf ("Could not open %s.\n", conv_dsn );
    return (1);
  }

  return (0);
}
```

Comments on the Example

Line 1 Brings in the include file `stdio.h`, which contains the function prototype for the `fopen()` function. A function prototype contains a template of the call parameters for the function. ANSI C uses this during compiling to check the call parameters.

Line 2 Shows the basic use of `fopen()`. `in_file` is the file name that will be used throughout the program for opening, reading, writing, and closing. "`testdata.dat`" is the dataset name of the input file. We know it's an input file because file access is "r", for read.

In COBOL the OPEN, READ, and CLOSE statements use *file-name*, and the WRITE statement uses `record-name`. C always uses `file_name`, and the `fread()` and `fwrite()` functions also use `record_name`.

Line 3 Checks to see that `fopen()` worked properly. If `fopen()` cannot open the file, it assigns a value of NULL (hex zeroes) to `in_file`.

NOTE: Notice the double equal sign for an equality check.

    If the program could not open the file, it prints a message giving the dataset name and returns to the operating system via the `return (1)` statement. The `return()` statement hands a value of 1 back to the operating system, which in the Unix world indicates failure. If you cannot open a file, there's no point in continuing.

Line 4   Gives a common, if hard to read, use of `fopen()`. This statement combines the `fopen()` call with checking its return value. It is exactly equivalent to lines 2 and 3. The statement is evaluated from the innermost set of parentheses to the outermost as follows:

```
if ( (conv_file = fopen ( conv_dsn, "r" )) == NULL)
```

becomes

```
if ( (conv_file = return_value          ) == NULL)
```

which becomes

```
if ( (conv_file                         ) == NULL)
```

`fopen()` is executed first because it has the innermost set of parentheses. The `fopen()` call is replaced by its return value. The return value is then assigned to `conv_file`. Then the `if` statement

```
if (conv_file == NULL )
```

is evaluated (notice the double equal sign for equality comparison). If the `fopen()` fails, `conv_file` is set to NULL. The statement is true, so the message is displayed on the terminal and the program returns control to the operating system with a value of 1, indicating a program error.

    For readability, lines 2 and 3 are preferable to line 4. Line 4 usage is common because it eliminates one line, but that is not a good reason to do it.

Close a sequential file.

C Keyword/Symbol/Function	`fclose()` (file close)

`fclose()` closes a sequential file that was opened using `fopen()`.

Syntax

```
close_status = fclose ( file_name );
```

Sample

```
file_status = fclose ( in_file );
```

Include File

`#include <stdio.h>`   (contains function prototype for `fclose()`)

See Also

`fgetc()`	— read a single character from a file
`fgets()`	— read a string from a file
`fopen()`	— open a file
`fprintf()`	— format and write to a file
`fread()`	— read a record (structure) from a file
`fwrite()`	— write a record (structure) to a file
`sscanf()`	— extract numbers, characters, or strings from a string

Parameter Definitions

`int  close_status;`

An integer that is assigned the return status of `fclose()`.

`FILE  *file_name;`

The same file definition you used in `fopen()`.

Return Value

The status of the file-closing operation. A zero (`NULL`) is returned if the file closes successfully. A –1 (negative 1) is returned if the close is not successful.

Direction

Right to left.

Anatomy

```
close_status = fclose ( file_name ) ;
```
Required

`close_status`

The data element that receives the return value from `fclose()`. It will contain `NULL` (hex zeroes) if the close is successful and –1 if the close is not successful.

```
fclose
```

The name of the sequential file close function.

```
file_name
```

The name of the file to close. `file_name` is the same as it was for `fopen()`. You only need to define `file_name` once.

```
;
```

A semicolon ends the statement.

Discussion

There's not much to say about closing a file. Close it when you are finished, and check the status of the close.

Common Error

Not checking the status of the call to `fclose()`.

This is a common omission. If you do not check the status of the close and there is a problem, it will not be evident until a subsequent program tries to use the file. Then the question is what happened and in what program. If you check the status of the close, you can identify any problem when it occurs.

Example

```
/*                      fclose.c                07/30/94                */
#include <stdio.h>                         /* 1 for fclose() prototype   */

main()
{
    int    file_status;
    FILE   *in_file;
    char   in_file_dsn [13] = "testdata.dat" ;

    in_file = fopen ( in_file_dsn, "r" );          /* 2 open the file     */

    if (in_file == NULL)                           /* 3 check result      */
    {
       printf ( "Could not open %s.\n", in_file_dsn );
       return (1);
    }
    ...
    file_status = fclose ( in_file );              /* 4  close the file   */
```

```
if (file_status != NULL)                        /* 5  check result              */
{
   printf (" Could not close %s.\n", in_file_dsn );
   return (1);
}

if ( fclose ( in_file ) != NULL)                /* 6  combine close             */
{                                               /*    and check                 */
   printf (" Could not close %s.\n", in_file_dsn );
   return (1);
}

return (0);
}
```

Comments on Example

Line 1 Brings in the include file stdio.h, which contains the function prototype for the fclose() function. A function prototype contains a template of the call parameters for the function. ANSI C uses this during compiling to check the call parameters.

Lines 2 and 3 The standard use of fopen() and a check of its return value.

Line 4 The call to fclose(). The file name, in_file, is passed as the parameter. The return value is assigned to file_status.

Line 5 Checks the return value from the fclose() call. If fclose() does not return NULL, a problem has occurred. If a problem occurs, the printf() statement displays a message on the terminal, and the return() statement hands a nonzero code back to the operating system.

Line 6 Shows a condensed version of lines 4 and 5. This statement is not as hard to read as its equivalent in fopen(). What happens here is that

```
if ( fclose ( in_file ) != NULL )
```

becomes

```
if ( return_value       != NULL )
```

The fclose() function executes and is replaced by its return value. If the close fails, return value is not set to NULL, the error message is displayed on the terminal, and the return() statement hands a nonzero code back to the operating system.

Line 6 is also the second close statement for the same file in this program. This is done to illustrate the technique. Line 6 actually fails, since the file has already been closed.

Reading Variable-Length Files

Usually sequential files in C are variable-length files, because C treats strings as variable length. In COBOL strings are always fixed length. When you are reading sequential files in

C, you generally need to parse the data. The two basic choices are to read one record at a time and extract the fields, or to read one character at a time and build up the fields. The latter choice is tedious, but sometimes it is the only choice.

The three functions commonly used in business for reading variable-length files are fgets(), fgetc(), and sscanf().

The fgets() function reads a specified number of characters or reads until it finds a line feed (\n or hex 0A), whichever happens first. The line feed is used as a record terminator. (It was inserted when the file was written by an fprintf() statement.) After using fgets() you need to extract the data with sscanf(). sscanf() is like printf() in reverse: It looks for the data in "*control string*" and puts it into the arguments.

If you need to examine records one character at a time, use fgetc(), which reads one character per call. You must then create a lot of logic to figure out what the data is. Do not use fgetc() routinely for business applications.

Read a string of characters from a file.

C Keyword/Symbol/Function	fgets() (get a string from a file)

fgets() reads a string of characters from a file. Typically, you read in a record that has a fixed number of fields but is variable in length due to the presence of strings.

Syntax

```
status = fgets ( destination_string, max_char_count, in_file_name ) ;
```

Sample

```
status = fgets ( input_rec, 81, in_file ) ;
```

Include File

#include <stdio.h>   (contains function prototype for fgets())

See Also

fclose()	— close a file
fgetc()	— read a single character from a file
fgets()	— read a string from a file
fopen()	— open a file
fprintf()	— format and write to a file
fread()	— read a record (structure) from a file
fwrite()	— write a record (structure) to a file
sscanf()	— extract numbers, characters, or strings from a string

Parameter Definitions

```
char  *status;
```

> Character pointer that receives the return status of `fgets()`. The function prototype for `fgets()` requires a character pointer (see the "Discussion" section below). The asterisk makes it a pointer, but you need not care about it being a pointer; just use the field to check for end-of-file.

```
char destination_string [n];
```

> String where the data read by `fgets()` is put.

```
int  max_char_count;
```

> Integer field or numeric literal with the maximum number of characters to be put in `destination_string`.

```
FILE  *in_file_name;
```

> Same file definition as used in the `fopen()` call.

Return Value

> NULL (zero) when the end-of-file is reached.

> **NOTE:** End-of-file indications are not consistent between `fgets()` and `fgetc()`.
>
> `fgets()` returns NULL (zero) when the end of the file is reached.
>
> `fgetc()` returns EOF (–1) when the end of the file is reached.

Direction

Right to left.

Anatomy

```
status = fgets ( destination_string, max_char_count, in_file_name ) ;
```
Required

status

> The field that receives the return value from the `fgets()` call. You ignore it except to check for an end-of-file. It equals NULL (zero) when the end of the file is reached.

`fgets`

The name of the function that reads a string of characters from the file identified by `input_file_name`.

`destination_string`

The data element that receives string of characters read from `input_file_name`. The size of `destination_string` must be *at least* the size of `max_char_count`, or memory is corrupted.

`max_char_count`

The maximum number of characters to be read into `destination_string`, unless a line feed (`\n` or hex 0A) is found first. `fgets()` reserves one character of `max_char_count` for a string terminator to be put in `destination_string` after the final character is copied.

If you are expecting a maximum of 80 characters, code 81 for `max_char_count`. If `fgets()` finds a line feed before 80 characters, say at 54, it stops there. `fgets()` puts the line feed character in position 54 and puts a null terminator in position 55 of `destination_string`. If `fgets()` does not find a line feed by character 80, it stops and puts a null terminator in position 81 of `destination_string`.

`fgets()` reads in any kind of character until it gets a line feed or end-of-file character (NULL), or until the character count reaches the value of "`max_char_count` – 1". Both spaces and string terminators are read in, which means that multiple strings can be read in with one `fgets()` call.

`input_file_name`

The name of the file you opened in the `fopen()` function with an access mode of "r".

`;`

A semicolon ends the statement.

Discussion

If you have to both read and write sequential files in a production system, you should set up the record definition as a structure and then use `fread()` and `fwrite()`, as discussed at the end of this chapter. The use of a structure creates a fixed-length record, and `fwrite()` and `fread()` write and read fixed-length records.

Since a line feed (record terminator) stops `fgets()`, the safe practice is to use a truly large number for `max_char_count`. If you code 10,000 and the records are 80 characters, `fgets()` stops at the line feed in column 81. If you code 81 and one or more records turn out to be larger than 80, your program fails. If you use 10,000 and there are some records that are 81 characters, `fgets()` reads the entire record. Of course, if you depend on a fixed format, the program will still have problems.

`fgets()` **does** read in the line feed if one is found before `max_char_count` characters are read. You may need to replace the line feed character (hex 0A) with a string terminator. See the following "Common Errors" section.

You should not use fgets() much in production programs, because in business applications you should have a database package or file manager taking care of directly reading and writing the application data. fgets() is usually used in programs that import data from some other system or in test data situations.

Common Errors

1. Memory corrupted.

   When max_char_count is larger than the size of destination_string, memory corruption occurs. fgets() performs the same way as every other string function in C: The source string size (defined by max_char_count) controls how many characters are copied. If the destination string is not large enough, memory is corrupted.

2. Line feed put in the destination string.

   fgets() does put the line feed character into the destination string if the line feed character is encountered before "max_char_count –1" is reached. Suppress it as follows:

   ```
   #define LINE_FEED 0xA      /* ASCII character for line feed */
                              /* hex 0A or decimal 10          */
   while ( fgets ( data_rec, 81, in_file ) != NULL)
   {
      if ( data_rec [ strlen (data_rec) – 1 ] == LINE_FEED )
      {
           data_rec [ strlen (data_rec) – 1 ] = '\0';
      }
      /* rest of processing */
   }
   ```

3. Program goes into an infinite loop.

   This can happen when you use the wrong value to check for an end-of-file. fgets() uses NULL to sense the end of the file, while fgetc() uses EOF. If you use EOF with fgets(), you'll get an infinite loop.

Example

```
/*                  fgets.c                         07/30/94            */
#include <stdio.h>                           /* 1 for fgets() prototype    */

main()
{
   char  data_rec     [81];
   char  in_file_dsn  [13] = "testdata.dat" ;
   FILE  *in_file;
   char  *status;

   in_file = fopen ( in_file_dsn, "r" );            /* 2 open the file        */
   if (in_file == NULL)                             /* 3 check result         */
```

```
{
    printf ( "Could not open %s.\n", in_file_dsn );
    return (1);
}
status = fgets ( data_rec, 81, in_file );          /* 4  single "read"      */
if ( status == NULL )                              /* 5  check status       */
{
    printf ( "End of file reached on 1st read.\n" );
    return (1);
}

while ( fgets ( data_rec, 81, in_file ) != NULL )   /* 6  basic read loop    */
{
    printf ( "Data record is: %s\n", data_rec );
    /* rest of loop processing goes here */
}

if ( fclose ( in_file ) != NULL)                    /* 7  close file         */
{
    printf ( "Could not close %s.\n", in_file_dsn );
    return (1);
}

    return (0);
}
```

Comments on Example

Line 1   Brings in the include file `stdio.h`, which contains the function prototype for the `fgets()` function. A function prototype contains a template of the call parameters for the function. ANSI C uses this during compiling to check the call parameters.

Lines 2 and 3   The standard use of `fopen()` and a check of its return value.

Lines 4 and 5   Represent a single read from `in_file`, which puts up to 80 characters of data into `data_rec` and assigns the return value of the `fgets()` call to `status`. Line 5 then checks `status` to see if end-of-file was reached.

These two lines are a syntactically correct way to use `fgets()` but one that you probably will not use. It does show the separate pieces, which makes it easier to understand, but it does not accommodate loop processing. See the comments about line 6.

Line 6   Shows how `fgets()` is typically used in a read loop controlled by a `while` statement. The `while` statement is discussed in detail in Chapter 10, "Flow of Control Statements." Here is a short summary:

```
while ( the_expression_between_the_parens_is_true )
{
    execute the C statements within the braces
}
```

The C `while` statement is equivalent to a COBOL PERFORM ... UNTIL, with a couple of minor differences. PERFORM executes *until* a condition is true, and `while` executes *while* a condition is true. The other difference is that the code executed by `while` follows it immediately, where in traditional COBOL PERFORM executes a paragraph somewhere else. COBOL II supports an in-line PERFORM.

Line 6 combines the `fgets()` call with the end-of-file check. The statement is evaluated from the innermost set of parentheses to the outermost, as follows:

```
while ( fgets ( data_rec, 81, in_file ) != NULL )
```

becomes

```
while ( return_value              ) != NULL )
```

The `fgets()` call is executed first. Up to 80 characters are put in `data_rec`, and a status is put in *return_value*. The `fgets()` call is replaced by its return value.

The resulting code executes the loop while the `fgets()` return value is not NULL; in other words, it calls `fgets()` as long as an end-of-file is not reached. The `while` condition happens to include a read, which is a trick you cannot do in COBOL.

The braces following the `while` contain the statements to be executed as long as an end-of-file is not reached. This is where your processing goes. The `printf()` statement is here to display what was read.

The `while` checks the `while` condition *before* it executes the statements following it. If the `while` condition is not true on the first evaluation, none of the conditional statements are executed, as in COBOL.

Line 7   Shows the combined file close and status check.

Format and extract field(s) from a string.

C Keyword/Symbol/Function   `sscanf()` (get and format fields from a string)

`sscanf()` extracts numbers, strings, or characters from a string using the format specifiers and puts these data items into the fields listed. It is used to extract data elements from strings that come in from the terminal or from a file.

Syntax

```
sscanf ( source_string, "control string", arg_1 [, arg_2,...] ) ;
```

Sample

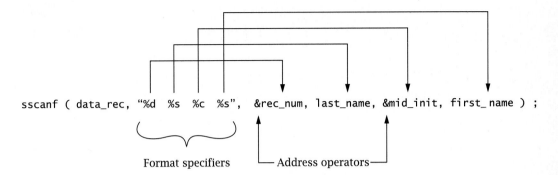

```
sscanf ( data_rec, "%d  %s  %c  %s",  &rec_num, last_name, &mid_init, first_name ) ;
```

Format specifiers   └─ Address operators─┘

Include File

```
#include <stdio.h>
```
   (contains function prototype for `sscanf()`)

See Also

`argc`	—the number of run-time parameters
`argv`	—the data in the run-time parameters
`fgets()`	—read a string of characters from a file
`gets()`	—get a string of characters from the terminal

Parameter Definitions

`source_string`

   A string data element you want to extract individual fields from.

"control string"

   A literal within the `sscanf()` call statement where the expected format of the string is described. It contains format specifiers that you expect will match the input.

`arg_1, arg_2, arg_3...`

   The *addresses* of the data elements that are to receive the values formatted according to the format specifiers in "*control string*". You put an ampersand (address operator) in front of the data name if it is a numeric or single character data type. If it is a string, the string's name also denotes its address.

Return Value

The number of input fields that were successfully moved. This is how you check that the input matches your expected format.

Direction

Left to right.

Anatomy

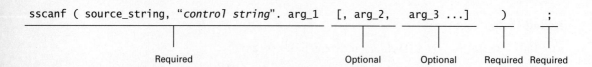

sscanf

> The name of the function that extracts numbers, characters, and strings from a string.

"*control string*"

> A literal within the sscanf() call statement. It is enclosed within double quotes. "control string" is a template that is compared to the string being parsed. It contains format specifiers for numerics and alphanumerics to be matched up. As sscanf() compares the input to the template, it formats and moves the data in the input into the data elements whose addresses are given in arg_1, arg_2, arg_3, and so on.

> Format specifiers are basically analogous to COBOL PICTURE clauses. A format specifier is identified by a percent sign (%) as the first character. Format specifiers are discussed in detail below.

arg_1 [, arg_2 , arg_3...]   (square brackets mean optional)

> The addresses of data items to be filled in based on matches between the contents of the string and the format specifiers in "*control string*". Substitutions occur from left to right. The data items can be any of the following:

Numeric data items	(int, long, double).
Single character data items	(char without []).
String data items	(char with [n] – n is number of characters).

Addresses of data items are coded as follows:

`int, long, double`	Data name preceded by an ampersand (&)
`char`	Data name preceded by an ampersand (&)
`char [n]`	Data name (no ampersand)

Format Specifiers

Format specifiers for `sscanf()` are a subset of those for `printf()`, plus one that `printf()` does not use.

Format specifiers are equivalent to the COBOL PICTURE clause. They specify the data types to be used when transferring data from the string to individual data elements. In C, format specifiers are identified by a percent sign (%) as the first character.

Format specifiers are coded as follows:

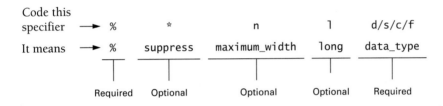

NOTE: The only required items are the % and the data type.

%

A single percent symbol tells `sscanf()` that this is the beginning of a format specifier.

*

An asterisk instructs `sscanf()` to skip the field. This can be handy if you have a lot of fields in a string (or file you've read into a string), but you're only interested in a few of the fields.

n

Tells `sscanf()` the *maximum* number of characters to extract for the data element, typically a string. If a string is wider than the maximum width, `sscanf()` stops when it has copied the number of characters specified by `maximum_width`, unless it finds a white-space character first.

Here are some sample entries:

%4   Tells `sscanf()` to take in a maximum of 4 characters
%20   Tells `sscanf()` to take in a maximum of 20 characters

This parameter is a potential troublemaker because it can stop in the middle of a string if the string is wider than the maximum number of characters specified.

l

The letter l tells `sscanf()` that the data is to be stored in either a `long` or a `double`. Many compilers now take care of this without explicit instruction.

d/s/c/f

Tells `sscanf()` the data type of this format specifier. The input data will be converted to this type, if possible. Common choices for business include the following:

Format Specifier	Data Type	Output
%d	long/int	Signed decimal integer
%c	char	A single character
%s	char [n]	The string of characters terminated by \0 or NULL
%f	double	Signed decimal number

Discussion

`sscanf()` can be a problem to use when the data is not uniform. For instance, if you are reading in `last_name`, `first_name`, and `middle_init`, there must always be a `middle_init` or `sscanf()` gets out of sync. The exact result is unpredictable, but it is certain to be bad. You can detect the problem as soon as it occurs by capturing the return value from the `sscanf()` call and comparing that to the number of fields that *should* be present. This allows you to handle the inevitable exceptions.

In production systems the only suitable method for dealing with sequential files is to use `fread()` and `fwrite()`. `sscanf()` is acceptable for quick and dirty solutions, but it does not belong in production systems.

Common Error

Data looks like garbage, or the program blows up.

This situation occurs when the data is not consistent. If you expect six fields and get five, the program is out of sync. If you capture the return value from `sscanf()` and compare it to the expected count of fields, you can trap this condition.

Example

```
/*                    sscanf.c                    07/30/94                    */
#include <stdio.h>                          /* 1 for sscanf() prototype        */
main()
{
    int     count;
    int     emp_no;
    char    first_name  [16];
    double  hourly_rate;
    char    last_name   [21];
    char    middle_init;
    long    pay_grade;

    char    ws_rec_in_1 [81] =
    "2629 Johnson       James       C 1280 12.50";   /* 2 six fields           */
                                                     /*   in string            */

    /*
    Assume that ws_rec_in_1 is an input record.
    File I/O is omitted for simplicity.
    */
    count = sscanf ( ws_rec_in_1, "%d",          /* 3 get one field out        */
                &emp_no );

    if (count != 1)                              /* 4 check count              */
    {
        printf ("Expected 1 field; got %d\n", count );

        return (1);

    }

    count = sscanf ( ws_rec_in_1,                /* 5 extract 6 fields         */
                "%d %s %s %c %ld %lf",           /*   from a string            */
                &emp_no,
                 last_name,
                 first_name,
                &middle_init,
                &pay_grade,
                &hourly_rate );
    if (count != 6)                              /* 6 check count              */
    {
        printf ("Expected 6 fields; got %d\n", count );
        return (1);
    }
    count = sscanf ( ws_rec_in_1,                /* 7 skip fields              */
                "%d * * * * * %lf",
                &emp_no,
                &hourly_rate );
```

```
    if (count != 2)                          /* 8 check count              */
    {
       printf ("Expected 2 fields: got %d\n", count );
       return (1);
    }

    return (0);
}
```

Comments on Example

Line 1   Brings in the include file `stdio.h`, which contains the function prototype for the `sscanf()` function. A function prototype contains a template of the call parameters for the function. ANSI C uses this during compiling to check the call parameters.

Line 2   Defines a string with six fields in it. This represents a record that is read and then parsed.

Line 3   Shows the simplest use of `sscanf()`, to pull one field out of a string. Notice that `emp_no` has the address operator, `&`, in front of it, which is required for numeric and single-character data types.

Line 4   Checks the count to see if the expected number of fields was extracted.

Line 5   A more typical use of `sscanf()`, extracting multiple fields from a string. The numeric data elements and the single-character data element have ampersands in front of them, indicating address. Also, the "long" editing symbol, `l`, is used for the `long` and `double` data elements. This is not necessary on all compilers.

Line 6   Checks the count after the `sscanf()` call to see if the expected number of fields was extracted.

Line 7   Skips four fields in the string. This call to `sscanf()` only picks up the first and sixth fields in the string, `emp_no` and `hourly_rate`. Asterisks are used to skip the second through fifth fields. Skipped fields do not have to be contiguous.

Line 8   Shows that the expected count is the number of format specifiers with percent signs. Fields represented by asterisks are skipped and not counted.

Read one character from a file.

C Keyword/Symbol/Function	`fgetc()` (get one character from a file)

`fgetc()` reads a single character from a file. You either get a usable character or the end-of-file character (`EOF`).

Syntax

```
character_from_file = fgetc ( input_file_name ) ;
```

Sample

```
input_char = fgetc ( in_file );
```

Include File

`#include <stdio.h>`   (contains function prototype for `fgetc()`)

See Also

`fclose()`   — close a file
`fgets()`   — read a string from a file
`fopen()`   — open a file
`fprintf()`   — format and write to a file
`fread()`   — read a record (structure) from a file
`fwrite()`   — write a record (structure) to a file
`sscanf()`   — extract numbers, characters, or strings from a string

Parameter Definitions

`char  character_from_file;`

The single-character field that receives the character read by `fgetc()`.

`FILE  *input_file_name`

The file definition of the file to be read.

Return Value

The single character retrieved by `fgetc()`. When the end of the file is reached, the value of the returned character is `EOF`. EOF is defined in the include file `stdio.h` as –1.

> **NOTE:** End-of-file indications are not consistent between `fgetc()` and `fgets()`.
>
> `fgetc()` returns EOF (-1) when end of file is reached.
>
> `fgets()` returns NULL (zero) when end of file is reached.

Direction

Right to left.

Anatomy

```
character_from_file = fgetc ( input_file_name ) ;
```

Required

`character_from_file`

The data element that receives the return value from `fgetc()`. It contains the next character in the file or the EOF character if the end of the file is reached.

`=`

The assignment statement that causes the character read by `fgetc()` to be put into `character_from_file`.

`fgetc`

The name of the function that reads a single character from the file defined by `input_file_name`.

`input_file_name`

The same file name you used in the `fopen()` call.

`;`

A semicolon ends the statement.

Discussion

`fgetc()` is the way to get one character at a time in from a file. This is sometimes necessary to parse variable format input. If you have to perform sequential file operations and you have a voice in the design, use `fwrite()` and `fread()` so you can deal with fixed-length records. It is much simpler than variable-length and variable-format sequential files.

If you have varying formats, use `fgetc()` so you can parse the input. `fgets()` is an alternative to get records into your program, but you then have to decide whether to use `sscanf()` (which works differently on different compilers) or to pick the data out of the string one character at a time. This latter method is the functional equivalent of using `fgetc()`.

Another available input file function, `fscanf()`, picks fields directly out of file input. It is regarded as unreliable on multiple compilers, which is why it is not discussed in this book.

Common Error

Program goes into an infinite loop.

This can be caused by using the wrong value to check for the end-of-file condition. `fgetc()` uses EOF to sense the end of the file, while `fgets()` uses NULL. If you use NULL with `fgetc()`, you'll get an infinite loop.

Example

```
/*                    fgetc.c                          07/30/94                */
#include <stdio.h>                                     /* 1 for fgetc() prototype    */

main()
{
   char  in_file_dsn  [30] = "testdata.dat" ;
   FILE  *in_file;
   char  input_char;

   in_file = fopen ( in_file_dsn, "r" );              /* 2 open the file        */
   if (in_file == NULL)                               /* 3 check result         */
   {
      printf ( "Could not open %s.\n", in_file_dsn );
      return (1);
   }

   input_char = fgetc ( in_file );                    /* 4 read one             */
                                                      /*    character           */
   if ( input_char == EOF )                           /* 5 check for EOF        */
   {
      printf ( "EOF reached on first read.\n" );
      return (1);
   }
   while ( (input_char = fgetc ( in_file ) ) != EOF ) /* 6 basic read           */
   {                                                  /*    loop; combines      */
      printf ( "%c", input_char );                    /*    read & EOF          */
                                                      /*    check               */
      /* rest of loop processing goes here */

      /* parse that input ! */
   }

   if ( fclose ( in_file ) != NULL)                   /* 7 close file           */
   {
      printf ( "Could not close %s.\n", in_file_dsn );
      return (1);
   }
   return (0);
}
```

Comments on Example

Line 1   Brings in the include file stdio.h, which contains the function prototype for the fgetc() function. A function prototype contains a template of the call parameters for the function. ANSI C uses this during compiling to check the call parameters.

Lines 2 and 3   The standard use of `fopen()`, and a check of its return value.

Line 4   Retrieves one character from `in_file` and puts it in the field `input_char`. Line 5 checks for the end-of-file condition.

Line 5   Checks `input_char` for EOF, which is defined in the include file `stdio.h` as –1. `input_char` does double duty: It receives a character read by `fgetc()`, or it receives the EOF character if the end-of-file has been reached.

Lines 4 and 5 are a syntactically correct way to use `fgetc()`, but you probably will not use this method. It does show the separate pieces, which makes it easier to understand, but it does not accommodate loop processing. See the comments on line 6.

Line 6   Shows how `fgetc()` is typically used, in a read loop controlled by a `while` statement. The `while` statement is discussed in detail in Chapter 10, "Flow of Control Statements." Here is a short summary:

```
while ( the_expression_between_the_parens_is_true )
{
    execute the C statements within the braces
}
```

The C `while` statement is equivalent to a COBOL PERFORM ... UNTIL, with a couple of minor differences. The PERFORM executes *until* a condition is true, and the `while` executes *while* a condition is true. The other difference is that the code executed by the `while` follows it immediately, where in traditional COBOL PERFORM executes a paragraph somewhere else. COBOL II allows an in-line PERFORM.

Line 6 combines the `fgetc()` call with the end-of-file check. The statement is evaluated from the innermost set of parentheses to the outermost. Each part is evaluated and then replaced by the result of the evaluation:

```
while ( (input_char = fgetc ( in_file ) ) != EOF )
```

becomes

```
while ( (input_char = return_value    ) != EOF )
```

which becomes

```
while ( input_char                    != EOF )
```

The `fgetc()` call is replaced by its return value. The return value is then assigned to `input_char`. The `while` statement compares `input_char` to EOF and continues to loop as long as `input_char` is not equal to EOF.

The braces following the `while` contain the statements to be executed as long as an end-of-file has not been reached. This is where your processing goes. The `printf()` statement is here just to display what was read.

The `while` checks the `while` condition before it executes the statements following it. If the while condition is not true on the first evaluation, none of the conditional statements are executed, just as in COBOL.

Line 7   Shows the combined file close and status check.

Printing and Writing Variable-Length Files

In C business systems you do not write directly to the printer. The technique is to write your print output to a file and then print the file using operating system commands. This technique preserves program or report output, so if you need to print again, you print the output file instead of running the program or report.

This is not the usual practice in the mainframe environment, but the fact is that disk space is extremely cheap in the workstation and PC environment. The amount of disk space taken by leaving reports on disk is a small fraction of the total disk space. It is cheaper to leave the reports on disk than to micro-manage the disk space. Of course, the disk will eventually fill up, and then space must be freed or added.

The way to print reports on a file is to use a C library function, fprintf() (formatted print to file). fprintf() works essentially the same way as printf(), except that it writes to a file instead of to stdout. There is one extra parameter in the fprintf() call—the file name—but otherwise it's the same as printf().

fprintf() is also commonly used to write sequential files that are not print files. These files typically are input for another system. fprintf() creates variable-length records by default, which is not a problem for printing. Variable-length files are harder to process correctly, as previous sections have noted.

You can use fprintf() to create fixed-length files by specifying a width for every data item you write. As long as all the data items fit within the specified widths, you'll get a fixed-length-field/fixed-length-record file. If a data item takes more space than you specify, fprintf() **will not** truncate. This generates variable-length records. For further discussion see the section called "How Long is a Record?" later in this chapter.

Format and write fields to a file.

C Keyword/Symbol/Function	fprintf() (format data and write (print) a record to a file)

fprintf() writes data values and/or literals to a file. It defines a record, moves data into it, and writes it. fprint() is very similar to printf().

Syntax

```
fprintf ( output_file_name, "control string" [, arg_1, arg_2,...] );
```

Sample

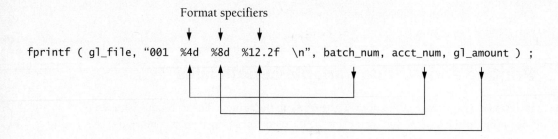

Include File

`#include <stdio.h>`   (contains function prototype for `fprintf()`)

See Also

`printf()`   — format and write to the terminal
`sprintf()` — format and write into a string

Parameter Definitions

`FILE  *output_file_name;`

  Defines a file buffer in the required C manner. The same file definition is used in `fopen()`, `fclose()`, and `fprintf()`.

`"control string"`

  A literal within the `fprintf()` call statement where the formatting is defined. It is usually a combination of literal characters and format specifiers for the data items that follow.

`arg_1, arg_2...`

  The data items to be moved into "`control string`". They can be data elements or literals.

Return Value

The number of characters written to the file. This is seldom used.

Direction

Arguments are substituted from left to right into the format specifiers in "`control string`".

Anatomy

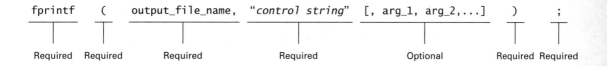

fprintf

    The function name for formatting data and writing it to a file.

output_file_name

    Names the file buffer that was defined at the top of the function. You use the same file name for the `fopen()`, `fprintf()`, and `fclose()` function calls. It's the equivalent of the COBOL FD name.

    In COBOL you read a file and write a record; in C you read a file and write a file.

"control string"

    A literal within the `fprintf()` call statement. It is enclosed by double quotes. It can contain literals and format specifiers for numerics and alphanumerics to be substituted into "*control string*". After `fprintf()` fills in all the values, it writes everything between the double quotes to the file named by `output_file_name`.

    Format specifiers are analogous to COBOL PICTURE clauses. A format specifier is identified by a percent sign as its first character. Format specifiers are discussed in detail later in this section.

    "*control string*" does not have to have any format specifiers in it. If there are no format specifiers, the literal within the quotes will be written to the output file as is.

[, arg_1, arg_2...]   [brackets mean optional]

    The optional data elements to be moved into "*control string*" where the format specifiers occur. If there are any data items to insert, a comma must follow "*control string*". After that comma the data names appear, separated by commas. Data elements are taken from left to right and inserted into the format specifiers from left to right. See the sample at the beginning of this section. The data items can be any of the following:

- Numeric data items
- Single character data items
- String data items
- Literals
- Expressions (computation results, return values of function calls)

;

A semicolon ends the statement.

Discussion

fprintf() combines COBOL's MOVE and WRITE statements. fprintf() works the same way as the printf() function, with the addition of a file name to write to.

Use fprintf() for both output files and for printer output. Using fprintf() does not print your data. It puts it into a file that you then print after the program runs. How you print files depends on your operating system.

If your program blows up before you close the file fprintf() is using, the output is usually lost.

fprintf() should be used in production systems so that a file is always produced. This makes it possible to reprint a job's output without having to rerun the job. Again, remember that disk space is very cheap in the workstation and PC environment.

Format Specifiers

Format specifiers are equivalent to the COBOL PICTURE clause. They give formatting directions to be applied to the data items in the argument list. Format specifiers are identified by a percent sign (%) as the first character. To have a percent sign in the control string, put two together (%%). This is similar to the technique for putting a single quote in a VALUE clause in COBOL.

Format specifiers for fprintf() are the same as the ones for printf().

Format specifiers are coded as follows:

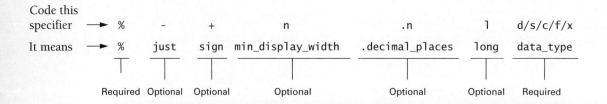

> **NOTE:**   The only required items are the % and the data type.

%

A single percent symbol tells fprintf() that this is the beginning of a format specifier.

– (dash)

Produces left justification of the data item. The default is right justification for everything, which is good for numbers and bad for strings. You must code the dash to left-justify strings.

+

Tells fprintf() to put a plus sign with the number if it is positive. The plus sign appears on the left. Minus signs are *always* inserted for negative numbers, whether or not you use +. A minus sign is displayed to the left of the number.

n

tells fprintf() the **minimum** width to format the data item. If, after formatting, the result string is wider than this value, fprintf() **will not** truncate, which is different from COBOL. Also, with double data elements the minimum width must account for integer digits, the decimal point, and the desired number of decimal places. Again, if the edited number comes out to be larger than specified minimum width, fprintf() writes all of the characters. This could lead to unexpected variable length strings and records. On the other hand, data is not lost.

If you want leading zeroes, code a zero in front of the number, as in %04d. This tells fprintf() to format an integer for at least four digits, with leading zeroes.

Here are some sample entries:

%4   Tells fprintf() to insert at least 4 characters
%-20   Tells fprintf() to insert left-justified for a minimum of 20 characters
%08   Tells fprintf() to insert at least 8 characters with leading zeroes

.n

Consists of a period and a number, which tells fprintf() how many decimal places to insert. For instance, %10.6 tells fprintf() to display a number in a minimum of ten characters, with a decimal point, and six decimal places. This leaves three characters for the integer value. If the integer value is larger than three characters, fprintf() displays as many characters as it takes to show it, leading to unexpected alignment. But again, you do not lose data.

fprintf() rounds to the number of decimal places you tell it to show. However, C compilers do not use the business rounding convention of rounding up .5. ANSI C compilers use the IEEE standard that rounds .5 down sometimes. This affects fprintf(), printf(), and sprintf(). For business applications you must use your own rounding routine. Appendix F contains a round() function that rounds according to business rules.

l

The letter l tells fprintf() that there is either a long or a double to be written. It is coded along with the data type, as in %ld or %lf. Most compilers now take care of this without explicit instruction.

d/s/c/f/x

Tells fprintf() the data type of the argument (parameter) for this format specifier. Common choices for business use include the following:

Format Specifier	Data Type	Output
%d	long/int	Signed decimal integer.
%c	char	A single character.
%s	char [n]	The string of characters until a \0 is found.
%s	string literal	The contents of the literal until the closing double quotes.
%f	double	Signed decimal number. If no precision is specified, the default format is to write all of the integer digits plus six decimal places.
%x	long/int	Unsigned hexadecimal.
%u	long/int	Unsigned decimal integer.
%o	long/int	Unsigned octal integer (seldom used in business).
%e	double	Exponential notation (seldom used in business).

Samples of Format Specifiers

These are a few samples of format specifiers for common data types. See the example program for more samples.

To Display	Use	Data	Result
A long or int in decimal form	%d	33	33
• With four digits	%4d	33	33
• With leading zeroes	%04d	33	0033
• Left-justified	%-4d	33	33
A single character (char)	%C	M	M
A string (char [n])	%s	Sirius	Sirius
• For 10 characters	%10s	Sirius	Sirius[1]
• 10 characters left-justified	%-10s	Sirius	Sirius
A double	%f	13.64	13.640000
• With 4 integers and 2 decimals	%7.2f	13.64	13.64
• With 1 integer and 6 decimals	%8.6f	.654321	0.654321
A long or int in hexadecimal form	%x	47	2f

[1]Right-justified is the default format for strings; this is the opposite of both COBOL and English.

How Long is a Record?

In COBOL this is an idle question because the records are generally fixed in length. In C a record is a set of characters, terminated by a line feed. You have to *explicitly* end a record with a \n, which becomes an ASCII 0A. This is the line feed character.

For files that will be printed, the records do not need to be fixed in length. This is different from COBOL. The columns should line up, of course, but if you have a short line you do not need to fill it out with spaces. Just send the line feed (\n).

If you need to write fixed-length records in C, you have two choices: format carefully with fprintf(), as shown in the following program fragment, or use fwrite() with a structure.

To get fixed-length records with fprintf(), put a number with each format specifier, so that each field comes out with the same length. This assumes that none of your data is wider than the minimum number of characters you specify in the format specification. Here is an example (a program fragment):

```
char last_name  [31] = "Jingleheimer" ;
char first_name [21] = "John" ;
char mid_init        = 'J' ;

main()
{
    fprintf (out_file, "%s %s %c \n",      last_name, first_name, mid_init );
    fprintf (out_file, "%30s %20s %c \n", last_name, first_name, mid_init );

    /*
    1st one writes "Jingleheimer John J "
    2nd one writes "Jingleheimer         John            J "

    (Quotes are for showing the effect of using %30s and %20s in fprintf().
    They are not written by the fprintf() shown above.)
    */
}
```

If you do not specify field sizes and you have string variables, you'll get variable-length records. If you do specify field sizes and some of your data is larger than your specification, you'll get variable-length records. If you do specify field sizes and they are as large as your largest data items, you'll get fixed-length records.

If you need to use fixed-length records, use fwrite() and fread().

Carriage Control

Since fprintf() is usually used to write print files as well as to write sequential files for other uses, carriage control is an issue.

To get line feeds/carriage returns, tabs, and page breaks to occur, put a backslash and a letter inside the format specification literal in the printf() call. Tabs are not recommended because they can be different widths on different printers. The tab on a terminal display can also be a different width than on a printer. Tabs cause more alignment problems than they solve.

To Get	Use	Example
Line feed/carriage return or a record terminator	\n	fprintf (rpt_file, "Total: %14.2f \n", amt); fprintf (gl_file, "001 HEADER \n");
Tab	\t	printf ("tab \t between \t words");
Form feed	\f	fprintf (rpt_file, "\f");

Printing Special Characters

Certain characters cannot be printed by themselves inside an fprintf() statement. To be displayed correctly, such characters require special character combinations such as the following:

To Get	Use	Example
Percent sign	%%	fprintf (outfile, "Weighted average is %d%% ", average);
Double quote	\"	fprintf (outfile, " \"Best Guess\" Totals ");
Backslash	\\	fprintf (outfile, "Run-time directory is C:\\run ");

FILLER

FILLER is a very handy thing in COBOL when creating print lines. There is nothing equivalent to it in the C language, but it's easy to get the same effect. You define a character string as

```
char filler [2] = " " ;
```

This creates a data element named filler, which has a single-space character and a string terminator. You can use filler as a data item to insert into a control string when you need 10, 20, 50 or any number of spaces in a print line or record. In the control string you specify a minimum width and then use filler as the data element to put there. fprintf() supplies spaces to create the minimum width:

```
fprintf( out_file, "GL100 %20s General Ledger Trial Run \n", filler );
```

becomes

```
GL100                    General Ledger Trial Run
123456789012345678901234567890123456789012345678901234567890
         1         2         3         4         5         6
```

The single spaces on each side of %20s in the control string are also inserted, which makes a total of 22 spaces. This is a much cleaner way to format print lines than holding your thumb on the space bar. This technique is also shown in the example program later in this section.

Final Comment on `fprintf()`

Again, you should not be writing a lot of reports in C; that's what report-writing packages are for. But even with a report writer package, you will write a certain number of reports in C, although it should be a small percentage of your reports.

Common Errors

1. Data that was written does not show up in the file, and there's a strange warning message from the compiler.

   If you omit the file name from the `fprintf()` statement, you will get an incomprehensible warning message, but the program will work, sort of. The data will not be written to the file.

   This happens because `fprintf()` and `printf()` are extremely similar in format and function. `fprintf()` does require the file name to work properly.

2. Bad value in the output, or the program blows up; more format specifiers than arguments.

   If you have three format specifiers in the format specification and two data elements, the value for the third format specifier is unpredictable. You would think the compiler could count the format specifiers and the arguments, but it does not. This compiles cleanly.

3. Missing value in the output, or the program blows up; more arguments than format specifiers.

   This is the converse of the previous error. If you have two format specifiers and three arguments, the third data item does not get inserted into the control string. This also compiles cleanly.

4. Strange value in the output, or the program blows up; a mismatch of format specifier and argument.

   If the data type of the argument cannot be reasonably converted to the data type of the format specifier, either you get a strange result or the program blows up. Some compilers generate a warning on this, and some do not. The common sources of a mismatch are as follows:

Format Specifier	Supplied Data Type
%s	int, long, double
%c	char [n], double
%d	char [n], double (decimal truncation)

As is often the case in C, you have to protect yourself because the compiler does not.

5. A number has rounded down.

fprintf() rounds a double to fit the number of decimal places you specify. Since the IEEE rounding method is used, in some cases .5 rounds down. Don't depend on fprintf(), sprintf(), or printf() to round your numbers. Use the round() function, which is discussed in Appendix F.

Example

```
/*                      fprintf.c                    07/30/94              */
#include <stdio.h>                              /* 1  for fprintf() prototype   */

main()
{
   FILE    *out_file;
   int     day              = 7 ;
   char    filler      [2]  = " " ;               /* 2  my friend FILLER        */
   char    first_name  [21] = "James" ;
   char    last_name   [31] = "Harkin" ;
   char    middle_init      = 'C' ;
   int     month            = 2 ;
   char    out_file_name [20] = "testfile.out" ;
   long    rec_count        = 12345 ;
   double  sales_tot        = 11234.65 ;
   long    table_size       = 255 ;
   int     year             = 1993 ;

   out_file = fopen ( out_file_name, "w" );       /* 3  basic fopen()           */
   if (out_file == NULL)                          /* 4  check result            */
   {
      printf ("Could not open %s.\n", out_file_name );
      return (1);
   }
                                                  /*    Result:                 */
   fprintf ( out_file, " '%s'   \n", "Totals: " );   /* 5  'Totals: '           */
   fprintf ( out_file, " '%-10s'\n", "Totals: " );   /* 6  'Totals:    '        */
```

```
    fprintf ( out_file, " '%10s' \n", "Totals: " );      /* 7  ' Totals: '               */
    fprintf ( out_file, " '%4s'  \n", "Totals: " );       /* 8  'Totals: '                */
                                                          /*     OVERFLOWS               */

    fprintf ( out_file, " '%s %c %s' \n",                 /* 9  'James C Harkin'         */
        first_name,
        middle_init,
        last_name );

    fprintf ( out_file, " 'GL100 %20s GL EOM RUN' \n",    /* 10 see below                */
        filler );
                            /* 'GL100              GL EOM RUN'                           */

    fprintf ( out_file, "\f" );                           /* 11 FORM FEED                */

    fprintf ( out_file, " '%d'   \n", rec_count );        /* 12 '12345'                  */
    fprintf ( out_file, " '%d'   \n", -23456   );         /* 13 '-23456'                 */
    fprintf ( out_file, " '%8d'  \n", rec_count );        /* 14 '   12345'               */
    fprintf ( out_file, " '%+8d' \n", rec_count );        /* 15 '  +12345'               */
    fprintf ( out_file, " '%08d' \n", rec_count );        /* 16 '00012345'               */
    fprintf ( out_file, " '%-8d' \n", rec_count );        /* 17 '12345   '               */
    fprintf ( out_file, " '%3d'  \n", rec_count );        /* 18 '12345'                  */
                                                          /*     OVERFLOWS               */

    fprintf ( out_file, " '%02d/%02d/%04d' \n",           /* 19 '02/07/1993'             */
        month,
        day,
        year );

    fprintf ( out_file, " '%f'     \n", sales_tot );      /* 20 '11234.650000'           */
    fprintf ( out_file, " '$%.2f'  \n", sales_tot );      /* 21 '$11234.65'              */
    fprintf ( out_file, " '%.0f'   \n", sales_tot );      /* 22 '11235'                  */
    fprintf ( out_file, " '%11.2f' \n", sales_tot );      /* 23 '   11234.65'            */
    fprintf ( out_file, " '%011.2f' \n", sales_tot );     /* 24 '00011234.65'            */
    fprintf ( out_file, " '%6.2f'  \n", sales_tot );      /* 25 '11234.65'               */
                                                          /*         OVERFLOWS           */

    fprintf ( out_file, " '%x'   \n", table_size );       /* 26 'ff'                     */
    fprintf ( out_file, " '%4x'  \n", table_size );       /* 27 '  ff'                   */
    fprintf ( out_file, " '%04x' \n", table_size );       /* 28 '00ff'                   */
    fprintf ( out_file, " '%x'   \n", middle_init );      /* 29 '43'                     */
                                                          /*     (ASCII value)           */

    if ( fclose ( out_file ) != NULL)                     /* 30 close file               */
    {
       printf (" Could not close %s.\n", out_file_name );
       return (1);
    }

    return (0);
}
```

Comments on Example

Line 1 Brings in the include file stdio.h, which contains the function prototype for the fprintf() function. A function prototype contains a template of the call parameters for the function. ANSI C uses this during compiling to check the call parameters, except when the function has a variable-length parameter list, which fprintf() has. With fprintf() you are on your own.

Line 2 The first part of how to get the effect of FILLER into a C program. Define filler as a two-character string with a value of a space. The other character is the string terminator. filler is used in line 10 to provide spaces in the output.

Lines 3 and 4 The standard use of fopen(), and a check of its return value.

Lines 5–8 Show the effects of various format specifiers on a string literal. The results would be the same if a string variable were named.

Line 5 is the minimal specification. The width will be the length of the string contents.

Line 6 shows how to get left-justified alphanumerics with a specified width.

Line 7 shows default justification for alphanumerics, which is right justification. This is obviously the opposite at what COBOL does.

Line 8 shows how fprintf() does not truncate if you specify a width smaller than the data element turns out to be. Four characters are specified, and eight characters are formatted. **Programmer beware!**

Line 9 Combines first name, middle initial, and last name in one field. Note that middle_init is a single-character field, char, and thus uses the %c substitution symbol.

Line 10 Shows how to use filler to get spaces between fields. filler is especially useful when you have a wide report with 40 or 50 spaces between some of the fields in the header. If you don't use this technique, you have fprintf() statements with a lot of spaces in the control string. If you use filler, you can make changes more easily.

Line 11 Causes a form feed. It is easier to find form feeds in a program if each one is put on a line by itself.

Lines 12–18 Examples of various format specifiers for integer data types int and long.

Line 12 is the basic int/long specification. All the digits in the number will be formatted.

Line 13 shows the same thing, with a negative number. fprintf() automatically puts the negative sign on the left.

Line 14 directs fprintf() to use eight characters to format the number. The defaults in effect are right justification and no leading zeroes.

Line 15 shows how to get a plus sign to show up with a number. If the number is positive, the plus sign always appears on the left side.

Line 16 uses a zero in front of the minimum width number to get leading zeroes to appear.

Line 17 uses the minus sign in the editing symbol, which means left-justify. Since there are five digits and a minimum width of eight, there will be three spaces on the right.

Line 18 shows an overflow condition. `fprintf()` does not truncate numbers or any other data type if the data is wider than the specified minimum width. `fprintf()` just puts out the data. **Programmer beware!**

Line 19 Shows a common use of `fprintf()` to format dates into a readable form. The control string is hard to read. It says put in 2 integer digits with leading zeroes, a slash, two more integer digits with leading zeroes, another slash, and four integer digits. The arguments then supply `month`, `day`, and `year` to be inserted. The result is a date in a normal format for printing.

Lines 20–25 Show various format specifiers to handle a floating point number, a `double` in this case.

Line 20 uses the default formatting for a `double`, which will format to whatever width the `double` is, and show six decimal places. Note that there are only two nonzero digits to the right of the decimal point, and C shows six anyway.

Line 21 puts a dollar sign in front of the number and limits it to two decimal places. The only problem here is that C **never** puts commas in numbers. Also, C will not float a dollar sign over to the first nonzero digit. If you want commas in your numbers, use the `dollar_comma()` function, which is discussed in Appendix F.

Line 22 rounds the number and shows no decimal places. A potential problem here is that the IEEE rounding method sometimes rounds .5 down.

Line 23 right-justifies, suppresses leading zeroes, and shows two decimal places.

Line 24 right-justifies, shows leading zeroes, and shows two decimal places.

Line 25 specifies a minimum width (six), which is smaller than the data (eight). `fprintf()` does *not* truncate, and formats all the data. If you are expecting columns of data to line up, they won't if any of the numbers, after formatting, are larger than the minimum width specification. **Programmer beware!**

Lines 26–29 Show various effects of displaying numbers in hexadecimal form.

Line 26 is the basic hex format, with no minimum width specified.

Line 27 specifies a minimum width of four characters. Defaults of right justification and suppression of leading zeroes are in effect.

Line 28 specifies leading zeroes and a minimum width of four characters.

Line 29 shows how to get the hexadecimal value of a single character.

Line 30 Shows the combined file closing and status check.

Fixed-Length Record Processing

As mentioned repeatedly in this book, in the C business environment you should not be performing a lot of sequential file processing. In some cases, however, such as interfaces with other systems, sequential files may be required. Often these files must be fixed-length records, which you are familiar with from COBOL. The simplest method to produce such files in C is to create structures for the records and to use `fread()` and `fwrite()` to read and write the files.

In this section `fwrite()` is discussed first because you have to write using this technique before you can read using it.

Write a fixed-length record to a file.

C Keyword/Symbol/Function	`fwrite()` (write a fixed-length record to a file)

`fwrite()` writes a fixed-length record to a file. It takes a structure and writes it to a sequential file, the same way COBOL writes a fixed-length record to a sequential file.

Syntax

```
fwrite ( address_of_structure, bytes_to_write, recs_to_write, output_file_name );
```

Sample

```
fwrite ( &gl_rec, sizeof (gl_rec), 1, gl_file );
```

Include File

```
#include <stdio.h>
```
(contains function prototype for `fwrite()`)

See Also

`fclose()`	— close a file
`fopen()`	— open a file
`fprintf()`	— format and write data to a file
`fread()`	— read a record (structure) from a file

Parameter Definitions

`address_of_structure`

The name of the structure you want to write, with the address operator **&** in front of the name.

bytes_to_write

Integer value. Can be a hard-coded literal or a call to `sizeof()`.

recs_to_write

Integer value, usually hard coded as **1**.

FILE *output_file_name;

File name that you use in `fopen()` and `fclose()`.

Return Value

The number of records written to the file. It usually is the same number that you specified to write. However, if `fwrite()` fails, the return value will contain zero (`NULL`).

Direction

Left to right.

Anatomy

```
fwrite (address_of_structure, bytes_to_write, recs_to_write, output_file_name);
```

Required

fwrite

The name of the function that writes a fixed-length record.

address_of_structure

The name of the structure with the address operator **&** in front of it. `fwrite()` uses the address to know where to begin writing.

bytes_to_write

Can be hard coded as a number, but the usual practice is to let the compiler figure it out by using `sizeof (struct_name)`, where `struct_name` is the name of the structure you want to write.

recs_to_write

Usually coded as a literal **1**. The parameter exists to allow multiple occurrences of an array to be written in one call to `fwrite()`. The ordinary business requirement is to write one record at a time.

`output_file_name`

> The name of the file you opened for output with `fopen()`. The file access option is "w" (write) for output.

`;`

> A semicolon ends the statement.

Discussion

`fwrite()` writes records to a sequential file exactly as COBOL does, creating a fixed-length-field/fixed-length-record file with no line feeds at the end of records. If you look at a hexadecimal display of a file written by `fwrite()`, you will see that there is neither a space nor a line feed between records. The first byte of the second record immediately follows the last byte of the first record. However, the compiler may pad a structure to get it to end on a machine-word boundary. This can cause the structure to have one to three extra bytes on the end of it, depending on whether the compiler has a two-byte word or a four-byte word.

`fwrite()` is used to accomplish fixed-length record processing. There is not a lot of that in C. To repeat the sermon briefly, if you are developing business DP systems using C, you should also be using a database/file manager package, a screen generator package, and a report writer package.

Common Error

Records don't line up when you use `fread()` on a file written by `fwrite()`.

> Some C compilers cannot write an odd-length record. This can appear as records having a longer length than the structure. Another possible effect is `fwrite()` writing one or two even-length records followed by odd-length records. When you later use `fread()` to read the file, the read process gets out of sync. With the bad data, the program may blow up.

> In both cases you need to look at compiler options to see what the compiler does with odd-length structures. You may need to tell the compiler to pad structures to get them to end on word boundaries.

Input Data for the Example

The example program creates a fixed-length-field/fixed-length-record file from a file that does not have fixed-length fields or fixed-length records. The input data is a typical C sequential file: a set of fields strung together, where the strings are variable in length and the records are terminated with the line feed character.

The goal of this `fwrite()` example is to transform this file into fixed-length-field/fixed-length-record file. It uses `fgets()` to bring in the data and `sscanf()` to extract the fields. Remember that `sscanf()` needs the data to be "well behaved"; that is, every specified field will have a nonspace value. That is why `sscanf()` checks the count of fields extracted.

The contents of the file convdata.dat are

```
173882331 William C McNeil 14 13.90
164398875 Earl O Harwood 15 14.50
224612793 Gloria A Davis 20 18.85
262907432 Anne L Jones 21 22.25
104836592 James R Martin 10 11.00
291483556 Carolyn C King 12 11.50
384835584 Desmond A Morris 15 15.25
192740034 Colleen P Ferris 09 10.00
261027694 Joseph H Winfield 13 12.80
112834565 Helen H Dixon 14 13.50
```

Example

```
/*                    fwrite.c               08/01/94           */
#include <stdio.h>                           /*1  for fwrite() prototype  */

main()
{
    int    count;
    char   data_rec      [81];
    char   in_file_dsn   [13] = "convdata.dat";
    char   out_file_dsn  [13] = "pay_mstr.out";

    FILE  *in_file;
    FILE  *out_file;

    struct                                   /* 2  create structure       */
    {
        long    soc_sec_no;
        char    last_name   [31];
        char    middle_init;
        char    first_name  [21];
        int     pay_grade;
        double  hourly_rate;

    } pay_rec;

    in file = fopen ( in_file_dsn, "r" );    /* 3  open input file         */

    if (in_file == NULL)                     /* 4  check result            */
    {
        printf ( "Could not open %s.\n", in_file_dsn );
        return (1);
    }

    out_file = fopen ( out_file_dsn, "w" );  /* 5  open output file        */

    if (out_file == NULL)                    /* 6  check result            */
    {
        printf ( "Could not open %s.\n", out_file_dsn );
        return (1);
    }
```

```
while ( fgets ( data_rec, 81, in_file ) != NULL )     /* 7  basic read loop     */
{
   count = sscanf ( data_rec, "%ld %s %c %s %d %lf",  /* 8  extract six         */
      &pay_rec.soc_sec_no,                            /*      fields & put       */
       pay_rec.first_name,                            /*      in structure       */
      &pay_rec.middle_init,
       pay_rec.last_name,
      &pay_rec.pay_grade,
      &pay_rec.hourly_rate );
   if ( count != 6 )                                  /* 9  check sscanf()       */
   {
      printf ("Six fields expected. %d found\n",
                 count );
      return (1);
   }
   /* any other loop processing goes here */          /* 10 real work here       */

   fwrite ( &pay_rec, sizeof (pay_rec), 1, out_file );    /* 11 write one        */
                                                          /* fixed length        */
                                                          /* record              */
}

if ( fclose ( in_file ) != NULL)                      /* 12 close input file     */
{
   printf ( "Could not close %s.\n", in_file_dsn );
   return (1);
}
if ( fclose ( out_file ) != NULL)                     /* 13 close output file    */
{
   printf ( "Could not close %s.\n", out_file_dsn );
   return (1);
}
return (0);
}
```

Comments on Example

Line 1   Brings in the include file stdio.h, which contains the function prototype for the fwrite() function. A function prototype contains a template of the call parameters for the function. ANSI C uses this during compiling to check the call parameters.

Line 2   Creates a structure to be used for writing fixed-length records. If you were doing this for a production program, you would create this structure as a template and put it in an include file. Then each program that uses this record layout would include that include file and use the template to allocate an area for the record. Using the template and putting it into an include file ensures that all programs use the same record layout.

Lines 3 and 4   Open the input file and check the status of the call to open it.

Lines 5 and 6   Open the ouput file and check the status of the call to open it.

Line 7 The basic fgets() read loop, using the while keyword. It reads the input file one record at a time and assumes that no record is larger than 80 characters (line feed makes 81). If you want to make sure that you get a whole record every time, make the max_char_count field large, say 10,000. fgets() does not go past a line feed and so does not read in more than one record at a time (assuming your record size is less than 10,000 bytes).

Line 8 Uses sscanf() to pick the data out of the string just read in. The data elements are assigned to members of the structure. Note that the address operator & is used on numbers and single characters. String names are inherently addresses, so they don't require the address operator.

Line 9 Checks the number of fields retrieved by sscanf(). If you use sscanf(), you should check the field count to know if the input matched what you expected.

Line 10 Where you put statements to operate on the data being read.

Line 11 Writes a fixed-length-field/fixed-length-record file. fwrite() is straightforward: You simply hand it the address the structure to write, &pay_rec; the number of bytes to write, sizeof (pay_rec); the number of records to write, 1; and the file name to write them to, out_file.

The return value contains the number of records written. The expected value is 1, because the statement is writing one record. However, if fwrite() fails, it returns a zero in the return value. This happens so infrequently that people don't write code to capture the return value. If fwrite() does fail, it's a safe bet that the fclose() will fail too.

Line 12 Closes the input file and checks the status of the close.

Line 13 Closes the output file and checks the status of the close.

Read a fixed-length record from a file.

C Keyword/Symbol/Function   fread() (read a fixed-length record from a file)

fread() is the mirror of fwrite(). It reads a fixed-length record (structure) from a file. fread() actually reads a number of bytes rather than a record. How many bytes is determined by the product of bytes_to_read and recs_to_read. It reads that number of bytes and puts them into the structure whose address has been supplied. recs_to_read typically has a value of 1, so one record at a time is read.

Syntax
```
fread ( address_of_structure, bytes_to_read, recs_to_read, input_file_name );
```

Sample
```
fread ( &gl_rec, sizeof (gl_rec), 1, gl_file_in );
```

Include File

`#include <stdio.h>`   (contains function prototype for `fread()`)

See Also

`fclose()`   — close a file
`fopen()`   — open a file
`fwrite()`   — write a record (structure) to a file

Parameter Definitions

`address_of_structure`

>   The name of the structure you want to read into, with the address operator & in front of the name.

`bytes_to_read`

>   Integer value. Can be a hard-coded literal or a call to `sizeof()`.

`recs_to_read`

>   Integer value, usually hard coded as 1.

`FILE *input_file_name;`

>   File name that you use in `fopen()` and `fclose()`.

Return Value

The number of records read from the file. When an end-of-file is reached, the value is zero (NULL). This is how processing is terminated.

Direction

Left to right.

Anatomy

```
fread (address_of_structure, bytes_to_read, recs_to_read input_file_name);
```
_____

                                    |
                                Required

`fread`

>   The name of the function that reads a fixed-length record.

`address_of_structure`

The name of the structure with the address operator & in front of it. `fread()` uses the address to know where to put the data.

`bytes_to_read`

Can be hard coded as a number, but the usual practice is to let C figure it out by using `sizeof (struct_name)`, where `struct_name` is the name of the structure you want to read into.

`recs_to_read`

Usually coded as a literal 1. As in COBOL, most of the time you only want to see one record at a time.

`input_file_name`

The name of the file you opened for input with `fopen()`. The file access option is "r" (read) for input.

`;`

A semicolon ends the statement.

Discussion

`fread()` reads records from a sequential file written by calls to `fwrite()`. These records are fixed-length-field/fixed-length records with no line feeds at the end of records. They are exactly like sequential records written in COBOL, except that in structures in C the strings are null terminated, so there may be garbage at the end of the strings. This doesn't matter, because when you print or use strings you get the contents up to the null terminator, but not beyond.

Since `fread()` is reading a specified number of bytes, it does not care about special characters. Every character in the file, including line feeds, nulls, escape characters, and so on, can be read without a problem.

Common Errors

1. Records don't line up or seem to "walk."

    When you use `fread()` you will see any alignment problem that `fwrite()` generates. For instance, records may be shifted one byte per record. This causes programs to behave badly.

    As mentioned in the `fwrite()` section, you may have to set an option in the compiler regarding odd-length structures. See your compiler documentation.

2. Infinite loop from `fread()`.

    If you check for EOF instead of NULL in `fread()`, the program goes into an infinite loop. This is different from COBOL, where, graciously or not, the program does stop if you attempt to read past an end-of-file. C doesn't care. `fread()` returns NULL every time it is called at or after an end-of-file. Use NULL to terminate `fread()`.

Example

```
/*                      fread.c                    08/04/94                */
#include <stdio.h>                                 /* 1  for fread() prototype   */

main()
{
   char  in_file_dsn   [30] = "pay_mstr.in";
   char  out_file_dsn  [30] = "pay_mstr.out";
   FILE  *in_file;
   FILE  *out_file;

   struct                                          /* 2  create structure        */
   {
      long    soc_sec_no;
      char    last_name   [31];
      char    middle_init;
      char    first_name  [21];
      int     pay_grade;
      double  hourly_rate;
   } pay_rec;

   in_file = fopen ( in_file_dsn, "r" );           /* 3 open input file           */
   if (in_file == NULL)                            /* 4 check result              */
   {
      printf ( "Could not open %s.\n", in_file_dsn );
      return (1);
   }

   out_file = fopen ( out_file_dsn, "w" );         /* 5  open output file         */
   if (out_file == NULL)                           /* 6  check result             */
   {
      printf ( "Could not open %s.\n", out_file_dsn );
      return (1);
   }
                                                   /* 7  basic read loop          */
   while ( (fread ( &pay_rec, sizeof (pay_rec), 1, in_file ) ) != NULL )
   {
      /* any loop processing goes here */          /* 8  do work here             */
      pay_rec.hourly_rate += 1.0;                  /*     change output           */
      fwrite ( &pay_rec, sizeof (pay_rec), 1, out_file );  /* 9  write fixed      */
                                                   /*     length record           */
   }
```

```
   if ( fclose ( in_file ) != NULL)                   /* 10 close input file          */
   {
      printf ( "Could not close %s.\n", in_file_dsn );
      return (1);
   }
   if ( fclose ( out_file ) != NULL)                  /* 11 close output file         */
   {
      printf ( "Could not close %s.\n", out_file_dsn );
      return (1);
   }

   return (0);
}
```

Comments on Example

Line 1 Brings in the include file `stdio.h`, which contains the function prototype for the `fread()` function. A function prototype contains a template of the call parameters for the function. ANSI C uses this during compiling to check your call parameters.

Line 2 Creates a structure to be used for writing fixed-length records. If you were doing this for a production program, you would create this structure as a template using `typedef` and put it in an include file. Then each program that uses the record layout would include that include file and use the template for record definition. Using the template and putting it into an include file ensures that all programs use the same record layout.

Lines 3 and 4 Open the input file and check the status of the call to open it.

Lines 5 and 6 Open the ouput file and check the status of the call to open it.

Line 7 The basic `fread()` read loop, using the `while` keyword. This `while` statement boils down to "while not end-of-file, perform `fread()`." The `while` is evaluated from the innermost set of parentheses to the outermost set as follows:

```
      while ( (fread ( &pay_rec, sizeof (pay_rec) , 1, in_file )) != NULL )
```

becomes

```
      while ( (fread ( &pay_rec, 68              , 1, in_file )) != NULL )
```

which becomes

```
      while ( return_value                       ) != NULL )
```

`sizeof()` has the innermost set of parentheses. The compiler evaluates the `sizeof()` call and replaces it with its return value, **68**. (Assume there is a two-byte `int` and that the compiler pads the structure to be an even number of bytes.)

`fread()` is executed next. This `fread()` reads 68 bytes times 1 record from `in_file` into `pay_rec`. The `fread()` statement is replaced by its return value, which contains the number of records it read. This is 1 until it reaches the end-of-file, when it is zero (`NULL`). The program executes this call, puts the record in `pay_rec`, and replaces the `fread()` call with the return value of the call.

If the return value is 1, the loop continues. When the end-of-file is reached, the return value is zero (`NULL`) and the `while` loop stops.

Line 8 Where you put statements that operate on the data being read.

Line 9 Writes a fixed-length-field/fixed-length-record file. `fwrite()` is straightforward: You simply hand it the address of the structure to write, the number of bytes in the structure, the number of records to write, and the file name to write to.

The return value contains the number of records written. The expected value is 1, since the statement is writing one record. However, if `fwrite()` fails, it returns a zero in the return value. This happens so infrequently that people don't write code to capture the return value. This is lazy but common. If `fwrite()` does fail, it's a safe bet that the `fclose()` will fail too.

Line 10 Closes the input file and checks the status of the close.

Line 11 Closes the output file and checks the status of the close.

A Final Comment

You really should not be doing a lot of sequential file processing in a C business data processing environment. If you are using C, that should imply you are also using a software package to handle screens, a database/file manager package to manage the data, and a report writer package to handle most reports. C should be used for the internal processing. If you are performing master and transaction file processing in C, you're better off in COBOL.

Summary

In this chapter we examined the kinds of sequential file processing commonly used in business systems in C. The most common use of sequential files is as print image files which are then printed. The other common use is for files to transfer data to another system. Sequential master and transaction file processing should not be done in C.

File operations in C are conducted by calling functions. This is different from COBOL, where reserved words do the work. Files are opened and closed using the `fopen()` and `fclose()` functions.

Sequential files in C tend to consist of variable-length records, due to the inherently variable length of strings in C. Variable-length record files are usually read by calling `fgets()` and `sscanf()`, or by calling `fgetc()`. Using either of these techniques requires extracting fields, one by one, from the file.

Writing variable-length records is handled by `fprintf()`, which works the same way as `printf()`, with the addition of a file name parameter. Variable-length records in a print file are not a problem in C. You can write a fixed-length record with `fprintf()` if you specify the size of every string and no string exceeds the specified size.

For true fixed-length record processing, use `fread()` and `fwrite()`. These two functions read and write structures, which by definition are fixed-length.

It is a fundamental assumption of this book that business systems in C should use a database or a file manager package, and therefore a minimum of sequential files. If you are writing a lot of programs which use sequential files, you should be using COBOL.

CHAPTER 7

Moving Data

Introduction

In COBOL you use the keyword MOVE, which really means copy, when you want to copy a value to somewhere else. In C when you want to copy a number, a single character field, or a structure, you *assign* it. The assignment operator is the **single** equal sign. When you want to copy a *string* (an alphanumeric of two or more characters), you use one of the string copy library functions. You cannot use the assignment operator on strings.

The following table is a summary of the operators and functions used for moving data and determining the size of data items. A short overview of numeric/single-character moves follows. The section on the assignment operator is followed by an overview of moving string data and descriptions of the functions used in moving string data.

Desired Action	C Keyword/Symbol/Function	
Move a number	=	(assign)
Move a single character	=	(assign)
Move a structure (group item)	=	(assign)
Move a string	strcpy()	(string copy)
Move the first *n* characters of a string	strncpy()	(string copy *n* characters)
Find the length of a string	strlen()	(find length of a string)
Find the defined size of any data item	sizeof()	(find size of)

| Move and format strings and/or numbers into a string | sprintf() (copy and format data into a string) |
| Append one string to another one | strcat() (string concatenate) |

Moving Numeric and Single-Character Data

As mentioned in Chapter 3, "Defining Data in C," both numeric and single-character data items can usually be manipulated by symbol operators or keywords. The assignment operator = is used to move numeric data items, numeric literals, single-character data items, and single-character literals.

In C the single equal sign works the same way that a single equal sign works in a COBOL COMPUTE statement: It takes the item or expression on the right side of the equal sign and copies the item or the result of the expression into the data item on the left side of the equal sign.

```
tax_amount   = 0.0;                    COMPUTE TAX-AMOUNT   = 0.
tax_amount   = gross_pay * tax_rate;   COMPUTE TAX-AMOUNT   = GROSS-PAY * TAX-RATE.
prev_cust_no = cust_no;                COMPUTE PREV-CUST-NO = CUST-NO.
```

This shows a novel way to use COMPUTE, but for numeric data items it is equivalent to the C assignment statement. C goes a step further by using the assignment operator for single-character data elements as well. The point here is to read C assignment statements the way you read COMPUTE statements, which is from right to left.

> **CAUTION:** A single equal sign, =, **always** means move or copy in C. When you write if statements, you must use a double equal sign, ==, for comparisons. If you use a single equal sign, C assigns the right data item to the left data item and then evaluates the left data item. The intended comparison does not occur. See further discussion in Chapter 9, "If, Case (EVALUATE), and Class Test."

Desired Action	C Keyword/Symbol/Function
Move a number	= (assign)
Move a single character	= (assign)
Move a structure	= (assign)

The C assignment operator, a single equal sign, acts like the COBOL MOVE statement but with reversed syntax.

Syntax

```
to_data_item = from_data_item;
```

COBOL Equivalent

```
MOVE FROM-DATA-ITEM TO TO-DATA-ITEM.
```

Samples

Assignment Statements in C

```
sub_1 = 1;
mid_init = 'I';
hours_worked = timecard_hours;
```

MOVE Statements in COBOL

```
MOVE 1 TO SUB-1.
MOVE 'I' TO MID-INIT.
MOVE TIMECARD_HOURS TO HOURS-WORKED.
```

See Also

`strcpy()`   (copy a literal or string to another string)

Scope

Works on all numeric data types, the *single* character data type, and structures. Does not work on strings (alphanumerics of two or more characters). Use `strcpy()` for strings.

Direction

Works from right to left.

Anatomy

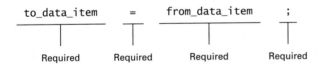

`to_data_item`

The name of the target data item.

`—`

The assignment operator. It means "take the value of the data item or expression on the right of the assignment operator and assign (move or copy) it to the data item on the left side."

`from_data_item`

The source data item to copy (move). `from_data_item` can be a data_name, a numeric constant, a character constant, a structure, or an expression. An expression can be a C statement fragment (`gross_pay * tax_rate`) or a function call that returns a value. See the following example program.

`;`

A semicolon ends the statement.

Discussion

The assignment operator takes the data element or literal on the right side of the equal sign and puts it into the data element on the left side. C uses this method both for copying data and for assigning results in computations. The syntax is actually like the COMPUTE statement, without the COMPUTE keyword:

COBOL	C
COMPUTE TAX-RATE = .028.	tax_rate = .028;

The assignment operator will seem more familiar if you think of it in terms of the COMPUTE statement syntax. The only thing odd is that it doesn't work on strings. It is a quirk of C that you must use library functions to manipulate strings. But for single-character fields, numeric fields, and structures, the assignment operator is the way to copy data.

The assignment operator can also be used to copy the contents of one structure into another structure. This is equivalent to moving a group item in COBOL. There is a significant difference in C, however. Both structures must be defined using the same template defined by using typedef. This is one of the few places where C is more restrictive than COBOL.

Common Errors

1. Decimal truncation after assignment.

   If you assign a double to an int or to a long, any decimal places in the double will be lost. Both int and long are integers, which by definition have no decimal places.

2. Strange numbers or negative numbers as a result of assignment.

   This occurs when there is overflow. If you assign a large number to a data element with a smaller capacity, an overflow condition can occur. This can happen when moving a double to a long or to an int. It can also happen when moving a long to an int. Make sure the receiving field is defined with a data type as large as or larger than the sending field, or be prepared for the consequences.

3. Nothing happens in the assignment statement.

   The reverse of the common error of using a single equal sign in an if statement is to use double equal signs in an assignment statement. If you accidentally code

   ```
   line_count == 0;
   ```

   the compiler evaluates it, rather than moving zero to line_count. It generates a true or false condition, but no action. It is a "no-op" statement.

4. Using a single equal sign in an if statement.

    This is the classic mistake that everyone makes. The single equal sign is the equality comparator in FORTRAN, Pascal, BASIC, and COBOL. In C the single equal sign is the assignment operator. When you use it in an if statement, the data element or literal on the right is moved into the data element on the left, and *then* the if statement is evaluated. If the assignment results in a nonzero value, the if statement is true. If the assignment results in a zero value, the if statement is false.

    Here's an incorrectly coded if statement:

    ```
    if (line_count = 66 )
    ```

    The first thing that happens is that 66 is assigned to the data element line_count. Then the if statement evaluates

    ```
    if (line_count)
    ```

    which reads as

    ```
    if (66)
    ```

    66 is not zero, so the if statement evaluates as true. The intended comparison does not occur.

Example

```
/*        assign.c              07/16/94                        */

#include <stdio.h>              /* 1  for I/O function prototypes    */
#include <string.h>             /* 2  for strcpy() prototype         */
#include <stdlib.h>             /* 3  for atoi() prototype           */
#define HEADER_LENGTH  7        /* 4  define program constants       */
#define NO             'N'      /* 5  single quote for single character */

main()
{
   int    acct_num;
   long   dept_num;
   char   disc_ind;
   double emp_gross_amt;
   char   input_num    [4] = "346";   /* 6  double quotes for string   */
   int    line_count;
   long   prev_dept_num      = 0;
   char   prev_disc_ind;
   long   record_count;
   double tax_amt;
   double tax_rate;

   typedef struct                      /* 7  typedef means template     */
   {
      long    cust_no;
```

```
    char    cust_name [31];
    double  current_bal;
} CUST_REC;

CUST_REC tran;                              /* 8  use the template                     */
CUST_REC prev_tran;

disc_ind = 'Y';                             /* 9  assign literal to character field    */
                                            /*     (single quote for single character) */

prev_disc_ind = disc_ind;                   /* 10 assign char field to char field      */
disc_ind = NO;                              /* 11 assign #define value to char field   */

dept_num   = 17;                            /* 12 assign literal to a numeric          */
line_count = HEADER_LENGTH;                 /* 13 assign #define value to a numeric    */
prev_dept_num    = dept_num;                /* 14 assign one numeric to another        */
record_count     = 453;                     /* 15 assign literal to long int           */
tax_rate         = .045;                    /* 16 assign literal to double             */
emp_gross_amt    = 25642.31;                /* 17 assign literal to double             */
tran.cust_no     = 6642;                    /* 18 assign literal into a structure      */
tran.current_bal = 994.32;                  /* 19 assign literal into a structure      */
strcpy (tran.cust_name, "AA Auto" );        /* 20 copy string into structure           */
                                            /*     (double quotes for string)          */

prev_tran = tran;                           /* 21 assign one structure to another      */
acct_num = atoi (input_num);                /* 22 assign return value of a function    */
                                            /*     to a numeric                        */

tax_amt = emp_gross_amt * tax_rate;         /* 23 assign result of expression          */
return (0);                                 /* 24 return to O/S                        */
}
```

Comments on the Example

Line 1   Brings in the perennial favorite `stdio.h`. This include file contains function prototypes for the basic I/O functions that almost all C programs use. A function prototype contains a template of the call parameters and the return value for the function. ANSI C uses this during compiling to check the call parameters.

Line 2   Includes the file `string.h`, which contains the function prototype for `strcpy()` (string copy). `strcpy()` is used later in the program.

Line 3   Contains the function prototype for `atoi()` (alphanumeric to int), which is used later in the program.

Line 4   Begins two lines of program constant definitions using the `#define` preprocessor directive. The preprocessor substitutes the values where the names occur in the program. When the compiler gets the program, only the values are present.

Line 5   Defines a single-character literal to be used by name in the program. Single quotes are used for single-character literals, and double quotes are used for strings.

Line 6   Defines a character array (string) field. An initial value is supplied, which must be placed inside double quotes.

Line 7   Begins the definition of a structure template. We know this because the `typedef` keyword precedes the `struct` keyword. The template name, CUST_REC, is given at the end of the template definition.

Line 8   Shows two invocations of the template. This is the last appearance of the CUST_REC name. `tran` and `prev_tran` define *instances* of CUST_REC, and those are the names used later in the program.

Line 9   Assigns a single-character literal to a single-character field. Note that single quotes are used. Use single quotes on single-character fields and double quotes on strings (character fields of two or more characters).

Line 10   Assigns a single-character field to another single-character field.

Line 11   Assigns a program constant value to a single-character field. The constant was defined on line 5. Its value is substituted here by the preprocessor. When the compiler gets the program, this line will look like

```
disc_ind = 'N';
```

Note that on line 5 `#define` uses single quotes for this single-character literal.

Line 12   Assigns a numeric literal to a numeric field.

Line 13   Assigns a `#define` value to a numeric field. In this case `#define` defines a numeric value. When the compiler gets the program, this line will look like

```
line_count = 7;
```

Line 14   Assigns one numeric field to another. Both are `long` integer types.

Line 15   Assigns a numeric literal to a `long` (long integer). Don't assign decimal values to an integer type (`int` or `long`), because the decimal part will be truncated.

Line 16   Assigns a numeric literal that has only a decimal value to a `double` (floating point number with decimal places). If `tax_rate` were defined as an `int` or `long`, the result would be zero, because C forces a conversion to the receiving field type. Integers don't have decimal places, so any decimal places in the sending field are truncated.

Line 17   Assigns a number with a decimal portion to a `double`. The only difference from line 16 is that there is also an integer portion. It works the same way as line 16.

Line 18   Assigns an integer literal to a `long` in a structure. You must qualify the member name with the structure name.

Line 19   Assigns a literal with decimal places to a `double` in a structure. Qualify the name of the structure member.

Line 20   Assigns (copies) a string value into a structure using the string copy function strcpy(). This function call copies "AA Auto" into cust_name in the tran structure. Qualify the name of the structure member.

Line 21 Assigns (copies) one whole structure to another structure. This is equivalent in COBOL to copying a record or group item to another record or group item. However, it only works in ANSI C if both structures are defined using the same typedef.

Line 22 Assigns the return value of the function atoi() to a field. This is how to capture the return value of a function. The return value is the "invisible parameter" in a function call. atoi() performs an alphanumeric-to-int conversion. It returns the int (integer) value of input_num.

There is no exact COBOL equivalent, but if there were, it would look like this:

```
ACCT-NUM = CALL 'ATOI' USING (INPUT-NUM).
```

where the equal sign assigns the result of the alpha to integer conversion.

Line 23 Assigns the result of an expression. This is easily recognizable as the COMPUTE statement without the COMPUTE reserved word. In COBOL it would read

```
COMPUTE TAX-AMT = EMP-GROSS-AMT * TAX-RATE.
```

Line 24 Uses the return keyword, which returns control to either the calling function on the operating system. Since this is the main() function, control is returned to the operating system. A value of zero is returned. Zero is often used to indicate successful completion.

Moving String Data

Strings—alphanumerics of two or more characters—are not a fundamental data type in C. C treats a string as an array (table) of single characters. Because a string is not a fundamental data type, it cannot be manipulated with language operators. In C you use library functions to work with strings.

Since a string is an array, this section briefly discusses array notation. Most of the library functions that work on strings can use several forms of array notation. Definition and use of arrays is covered in depth in Chapter 12, "Table Handling."

Array notation topics covered in this chapter include array definition, array and subscript notation, and referencing an array by the whole array and by individual occurrences.

Array Definition

Recall from Chapter 3 that a string definition uses the form of

```
char data_name [n];
```

This syntax declares a data element that is an array of single characters. The square brackets identify it as an array, and the number inside the brackets defines the size of the array (string). You need to define a character array one character larger than the maximum expected size to leave a byte for the null terminator. The following string definition will be used for the rest of this discussion:

```
char  date_time  [21] = "Jul 16 1994 03:25 PM";
```

This declares a character array or string with the data name of date_time and a size of 21 characters. No value for date_time is expected to be larger than 20 characters so the last byte will be available for the null terminator.

Array and Subscript Notation

Having defined date_time as a character array, you have several choices in the way you can refer to it. You can pick up the whole string by using the name by itself: date_time. You can also reference individual characters by using C subscript notation, as in date_time [1].

If you could define this string in COBOL the same as in C, you would code

```
01 DATE-TIME     PIC X(20).
01 DATE-TIME     REDEFINES DATE-TIME
                 PIC X
                 OCCURS 20.
```

This obviously would not compile in COBOL, but it does show the concept of using the same name for a whole array and for individual characters within it.

C subscript notation is like COBOL's except it uses square brackets rather than parentheses. As in COBOL, you can use either a numeric literal for the subscript or a data name of an integer field. One other difference is that C subscripts begin at zero, because they use the offset rather than the count. For example,

```
date_time [0]
```

refers to the first character in date_time.

Referencing Arrays

As previously mentioned, you use the array name by itself to refer to the whole array and use the name with a subscript to refer to an individual element of the array.

For most uses of string library functions, you use the name of the string without a subscript and without the address operator. The strcpy() function copies strings. The typical use is as follows:

```
char  date_time     [21] = "Jul 16 1994 03:25 PM";
char  pr_date_time [21];
...
strcpy ( pr_date_time, date_time );
```

This tells strcpy() to copy the string in date_time into pr_date_time.

However, sometimes you want to copy *from* the middle of a string or copy *into* the middle of a string. In these cases you use both the subscript and the address operator. If you have two fields defined as

```
char  time       [9];
char  date_time [21] = "Jul 16 1994 03:25 PM";
```

and you want to pick the time out of `date_time`, you need the string that starts in offset 12 (character 13) of `date_time`. You specify this in a call to `strcpy()` as follows:

```
strcpy ( time, &date_time [12] );
```

This function call tells `strcpy()` to copy the string beginning in offset 12 in the field `date_time` into the field `time`.

Conversely, if you have a value in `time` that you want to copy into `date_time`, you code

```
strcpy ( &date_time [12], time );
```

This tells `strcpy()` to copy the string in the `time` field into the `date_time` field beginning at offset 12 (character 13). The first 12 characters of `date_time` are not affected.

While you won't use these techniques every day, they are fairly common in string manipulation in C. They are also shown in the program examples for string functions in this chapter.

Move a string.

C Keyword/Symbol/Function	`strcpy()` (string copy)

`strcpy()` copies the contents of one string or literal into another string. It then puts a null terminator (`'\0'` or hex `00`) after the last character copied. It is *somewhat* like the COBOL `MOVE` statement for alphanumeric data, except that in C the *sending* field controls how many characters are moved, not the receiving field.

`strcpy()` can easily corrupt memory. This is a big difference from COBOL.

Syntax   COBOL Equivalent

`strcpy ( to_string, from_string ) ;`   `MOVE FROM-STRING TO TO-STRING.`

Samples

`strcpy()` Statements in C	MOVE Statements in COBOL
`strcpy (prev_dept_name, dept_name );`	`MOVE DEPT-NAME   TO PREV-DEPT-NAME.`
`strcpy (last_name,      "Bosworth" );`	`MOVE 'BOSWORTH' TO LAST-NAME.`
`strcpy (first_name,     "Barry    " );`	`MOVE 'BARRY'     TO FIRST-NAME.`

Include File

`#include <string.h>` (contains function prototype for `strcpy()`)

See Also

`sprintf()` — move and format alphanumerics and/or numerics into a string
`strcat()` — append one string to the end of another
`strlen()` — find the length of a string
`strncpy()` — copy the first *n* characters of one string to another

Parameter Definitions

`char  to_string [n];`

Character string. n represents its size. Add 1 for the null terminator.

`char  from_string [n];` or `"Some literal in double quotes"`

Character string or string literal for the source data item. n represents the size of the character string. Add 1 for the null terminator.

Return Value

`strcpy()` returns the address of the destination string. This is usually not used.

Scope

Used for strings only.

Direction

Works from right to left.

Anatomy

`strcpy`

The name of the string copy function.

`to_string`

    The name of the string you want to copy *to*.

`from_string`

    The name of the string you want to copy *from*. This can be a string literal or a data element.

> **NOTE:** All string literals in C must use double quotes. The ANSI compiler will tell you if you don't.

`;`

    A semicolon ends the statement.

Discussion

`strcpy()` has one *huge* difference from the COBOL `MOVE` statement: The *source* data item controls how many characters will be moved, *not* the destination item. If you copy a longer string or literal into a shorter string, C happily keeps copying until it finds the end of the source string or literal. This causes memory to be corrupted, which COBOL cannot do with a `MOVE` statement involving alphanumeric elementary items.

> **It is the programmer's responsibility to ensure that the to string is long enough to receive the from string.**

Common Error

Memory corrupted

    As mentioned, if you copy a longer string or string literal into a shorter string, memory is corrupted. This is about the only error there is with `strcpy()`, but it's very popular. The effect shows up in two main ways, neither of which points directly at `strcpy()`. Basically, either some other data element gets corrupted or the program blows up because you copied data over instructions.

    C allocates program memory differently than COBOL does. C does not necessarily allocate memory for fields in the order you declare them. So while an incorrect `strcpy()` call corrupts memory, the field immediately following the destination string is not necessarily the one clobbered.

    Happy hunting.

Example

```
/*                     strcpy.c                  07/16/94                    */
#include <stdio.h>
#include <string.h>                              /* 1 for strcpy() prototype  */

main()
{
    char  date_time       [25] = "Mar 11 1993 09:53 AM" ;
    char  dept_name       [9];
    char  prev_dept_name  [9];
    char  report_title    [61];
    char  time            [9];

    strcpy ( dept_name, "ABCDEFGH" );            /* 2 copy same-sized         */
                                                 /*   literal                 */

    strcpy ( dept_name, "Sales" );               /* 3 copy shorter literal    */

    strcpy ( prev_dept_name, dept_name );        /* 4 copy string to          */
                                                 /*   string                  */

    strcpy ( time, &date_time [12] );            /* 5 copy FROM inside a      */
                                                 /*   string @ offset 12      */

    strcpy ( &date_time [12], "04:27:00 PM" );   /* 6 copy TO inside a        */
                                                 /*   string @ offset 12      */

    strcpy ( report_title, "GL100 General "      /* 7 continue a literal      */
                           "Ledger EOM Trial" ); /*   to next line            */

    return (0);
}
```

Comments on Example

C considers a string to be an array (table) of single characters. Recall that all arrays in C are referenced by their *offsets* rather than by their occurrence count. In COBOL you can't have a subscript or index with a value of zero, while in C you *must* have a subscript with a value of zero to reference the first element (or character) in an array. See Chapter 12, "Table Handling," for further discussion of tables/arrays.

Line 1 The include file `string.h` contains the function prototype for `strcpy()`, which is used in the program. A function prototype contains a template of the call parameters for the function. ANSI C uses this during compiling to check the call parameters.

Line 2 Copies a string literal to a string of the same size. This literal "ABCDEFGH" has eight characters. The null terminator, which `strcpy()` puts into the receiving field, makes nine. `strcpy()` puts a null terminator, `\0` (hex zeroes), after the last character copied.

For many compilers, memory in a C program starts out with every unassigned character having a value of hex zero, also known as `null`, `\0`, `NULL`, `NUL`, or `LOW-VALUE`. However, automatic initialization of all memory to hex zeroes is not guaranteed for all compilers.

Memory before `strcpy ( dept_name, "ABCDEFGH" );` is as follows:

Field	dept_name								
Offset	0	1	2	3	4	5	6	7	8
Character	\0	\0	\0	\0	\0	\0	\0	\0	\0

Memory after the statement is

Field	dept_name								
Offset	0	1	2	3	4	5	6	7	8
Character	A	B	C	D	E	F	G	H	\0

Line 3   Copies a string literal to a string. The literal is shorter than the defined size of the destination string. `strcpy()` puts a null terminator, 0 (hex zeroes), after the last character copied.

Memory before `strcpy ( dept_name, "Sales" );` is as follows:

Field	dept_name								
Offset	0	1	2	3	4	5	6	7	8
Character	A	B	C	D	E	F	G	H	\0

Memory after the statement is

Field	dept_name								
Offset	0	1	2	3	4	5	6	7	8
Character	S	a	l	e	s	\0	G	H	\0

This shows a significant difference between C and COBOL. C does not space-fill the receiving field. It just overlays the characters you copy and puts a null terminator on the end. The first null terminator ends the string, not the length of the receiving field.

Any string function that uses `dept_name` only picks up "`Sales`" because the null terminator follows "`Sales`" in position 6, which is offset 5.

Short strings are not a problem.

Line 4   Copies one string data field to another. `strcpy()` handles string literals and string data items the same way.

Note again that `strcpy()` stops when it finds the first `\0` in the source string, `dept_name`. The characters "GH" are not copied.

Memory before `strcpy ( prev_dept_name, dept_name );` is as follows:

Field	dept_name								
Offset	0	1	2	3	4	5	6	7	8
Character	S	a	l	e	s	\0	G	H	\0

Field	prev_dept_name								
Offset	0	1	2	3	4	5	6	7	8
Character	\0	\0	\0	\0	\0	\0	\0	\0	\0

Memory after the statement is

Field	dept_name (no change in source field)
Offset	0 1 2 3 4 5 6 7 8
Character	S a l e s \0 G H \0

Field	prev_dept_name
Offset	0 1 2 3 4 5 6 7 8
Character	S a l e s \0 \0 \0 \0

Line 5 Shows how to copy from inside a source string to its end. This example picks up the time part of a date/time field and puts it in a separate field. Instead of using the string name, you use the address of the character position you want to start copying from. Put the address operator **&** in front of the source string name, and put the *offset* in square brackets after the string name. Remember, the offset is one number lower than the count of characters, because the offset starts at zero. In this case, time begins at character 13, offset 12.

Memory before `strcpy ( time, &date_time [12] );` is as follows:

Field	date_time
Offset	0 1 2 3 4 5 6 7 8 9 10 11 12 13 14 15 16 17 18 19 20 21 22 23 24
Character	M a r 1 1 1 9 9 3 0 9 : 5 3 A M \0 \0 \0 \0 \0

Field	time
Offset	0 1 2 3 4 5 6 7 8
Character	\0 \0 \0 \0 \0 \0 \0 \0 \0

Memory after the statement is

Field	time
Offset	0 1 2 3 4 5 6 7 8
Character	0 9 : 5 3 A M \0

Line 6 Shows how to copy a string or a string literal to inside a destination string. This example copies a new time into the date/time field.

Instead of using the destination string name, you use the address of the character position you want to start copying into. Put the address operator **&** in front of the destination string name and put the *offset* in square brackets after the string name. Again, the offset is one number lower than the count of characters, because the offset starts at zero.

Memory before `strcpy ( &date_time [12], "04:27:00 PM" );` is as follows:

Field	date_time
Offset	0 1 2 3 4 5 6 7 8 9 10 11 12 13 14 15 16 17 18 19 20 21 22 23 24
Character	M a r 1 1 1 9 9 3 0 9 : 5 3 A M \0 \0 \0 \0 \0

Memory after the statement is

Field	date_time
Offset	0 1 2 3 4 5 6 7 8 9 10 11 12 13 14 15 16 17 18 19 20 21 22 23 24
Character	M a r 1 1 1 9 9 3 0 4 : 2 7 : 0 0 P M \0 \0

The same rules apply here regarding copying string data shorter or longer than the receiving field. If you copy in something shorter, the destination field is treated as shortened, because `strcpy()` puts a null terminator in the destination field immediately after the shorter data.

If you copy in a literal or a field that is longer than the rest of the receiving field, strcpy() just keeps copying. **Let the copier beware!**

Line 7 Shows how to continue a string literal onto the next line. Put double quotes at the end of the first line and resume the literal with double quotes on the next line. This allows you to align the literal any way you want. The compiler throws away white-space characters (space, tab, line-feed) between one ending double quote and the next beginning double quote and continues the literal. This is a nice feature.

Move the first *n* characters of a string.

C Keyword/Symbol/Function	`strncpy()` (string copy *n* characters)

`strncpy()` copies the first *n* characters of `from_string` to `to_string`. *n* is supplied as either an integer literal or a data element. The copy is terminated when the specified number of bytes is copied or a null terminator is copied from the source string. `strncpy()` **does not put** a null terminator in the destination string if it does not find one within the first *n* bytes of the source string. You have to do it.

Syntax

```
strncpy (to_string, from_string, bytes_to_copy );
```

Sample

```
strncpy (month_abbrev, month_name, 3 );
```

Include File

`#include <string.h>` (contains function prototype for `strncpy()`)

See Also

`strcat()` — append one string to the end of another
`strcpy()` — copy a literal or string to another string
`strlen()` — find the length of a string
`sprintf()` — move and format alphanumerics and/or numerics into a string

Parameter Definitions

`char to_string [n];`
  Character string for the destination string.

```
char from_string [n];
```
    Character string for the source string.

```
int bytes_to_copy;
```
or a numeric literal

    Integer literal or data element for how many characters you want to copy.

Return Value

`strncpy()` returns the address of `to_string`. This is seldom used.

Scope

Used for strings only.

Direction

Works from right to left.

Anatomy

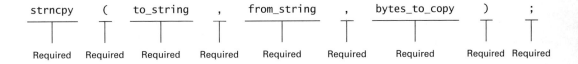

strncpy

    The name of the function to string copy *n* characters.

to_string

    The name of the string you want to copy *to*.

from_string

    The name of the string you want to copy *from*.

bytes_to_copy

    The number of bytes in `from_string` that you want to copy, starting from the first character. If you want to copy six bytes, put 6 in the statement. No offsets are used here.

;

    A semicolon ends the statement.

Discussion

`strncpy()`, like `strcpy()`, is different from the COBOL `MOVE` statement in that the *source* data item, combined with `bytes_to_copy`, controls how many characters will be moved, not the *destination* item. If you copy a longer string into a shorter string, strncpy() will happily keep copying until it copies the specified number of characters or finds the end of the source string. This can cause memory to be corrupted, which cannot happen with a COBOL MOVE statement involving elementary alphanumeric items. It is the C programmer's responsibility to ensure that the destination string is long enough to receive what is copied from the source string.

Common Error

Memory corrupted.

> strncpy() can corrupt memory the same way that strcpy() does. If both the number of bytes to be copied and the source string are larger than the destination string, memory is corrupted.

Example

```
/*              strncpy.c                      7/15/94                    */
#include <stdio.h>
#include <string.h>                            /* 1    for strncpy() prototype    */

main()
{
   char  date       [21] = "07/03/95 13:27:14.38";
   char  date_time  [21] = "Mar 11 1993 09:53 AM";
   char  hh_mm      [9]  = "03:20 PM";
   char  new_time   [6]  = "11:45";

   strncpy ( date, date_time, 11 );            /* 2.1 copy first 11 characters    */
                                               /*        of date_time             */
   date [11] = '\0';                           /* 2.2 terminate destination       */
                                               /*        string                   */
   strncpy ( hh_mm, &date_time [12], 5 );      /* 3.1 copy 5 characters FROM       */
                                               /*        inside string @offset 12 */
   hh_mm [5] = '\0';                           /* 3.2 terminate destination       */
                                               /*        string                   */
   strncpy ( &date_time [12], new_time, 5 );   /* 4    copy 5 characters TO        */
                                               /*        inside string @ offset 12*/
   return (0);                                 /* 5    return to O/S               */
}
```

Comments on Example

Line 1   The include file string.h contains the function prototype for strncpy(). A function prototype contains a template of the call parameters for the function. ANSI C uses this during compiling to check the call parameters.

Line 2.1 Shows the basic use of `strncpy()`, which is to copy out the first *n* characters of a string. In this case `strncpy()` copies "Mar 11 1993" into `date`. However, `strncpy()` does not terminate the string. See the comments about line 2.2.

Line 2.2 Finishes the work of line 2.1 by assigning the null terminator '\0' to `date`, in offset 11, which is character 12. `strncpy()` does not put the null terminator in the destination field. You have to do it. (`strcpy()` does put in the null terminator.)

  `date` is a string, or a character array. When you use `date`, you get the whole string. When you want to do something to one character in a string, use the string name and put the character offset in brackets, as in `date [11]` on this line. Offset 11 is character 12.

Line 3.1 Demonstrates the technique of using `strncpy()` to copy out a number of bytes from within a string. The two keys here are the address operator `&` and the offset `[12]`. What this statement does is copy five characters out of `date_time` from offset 12 (position 13).

  The result is to copy "09:53" into `hh_mm`.

  `strncpy()` expects the address of a string. In C the name of a string, or character array, is also the address of that string. Thus, in line 1 the name `date_time` is implicitly also the address of `date_time`. You only have to get explicit about the address if you're not starting from the beginning.

Line 3.2 Shows the same thing as line 2.2: you must terminate the destination string yourself.

Line 4 The inverse of line 3.1. Instead of copying *from* inside a string, this line copies *into* the middle of a string. The same rule applies, however. If you're going to write into the middle of a string, you need to use the address operator `&` and an offset in brackets, `[12]` in this case.

  The result of this statement is to write the five characters "11:45" in `new_time` *into* `date_time` at offset 12.

  After the function call, `date_time` looks like

    Mar 11 1993 11:45 AM

This time it's advantageous that `strncpy()` didn't terminate the string it copied into: It left "AM" in `date_time`.

Line 5 The `return(0)` statement ends the program and returns control to the operating system with a return value of zero.

Find the length of a string.

C Keyword/Symbol/Function	`strlen()` (string length)

`strlen()` counts the number of characters in `string_to_check` before it finds a null terminator. It does not count the null terminator. `strlen()` then returns the count in the return value. This is not something you need to do in COBOL, but you do it fairly often in C.

Syntax

```
string_length = strlen ( string_to_check ) ;
```

Sample

```
length = strlen (date_time );
```

Include File

`#include <string.h>`   (contains function prototype for `strlen()`)

See Also

`strcat()`   — append one string to the end of another
`strcpy()`   — copy a literal or string to another string
`strncpy()`   — copy the first *n* characters of one string to another

Parameter Definitions

`int  string_length;`

Integer field to receive the return value of `strlen()`.

`char  string_to_check  [n];`

Character string you want to get the length of.

Return Value

`strlen()` returns the number of bytes in `string_to_check` as an `int`. Since the return value is important in this function, you must assign (move) it to another field or examine it on the fly. See the following example program.

Scope

Used for strings only.

Direction

Works from right to left.

Anatomy

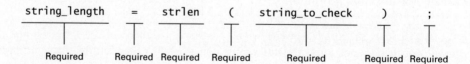

`string_length`

The name of the integer data item that receives the return value of `strlen()`.

`=`

The assignment operator that moves the return value of `strlen()` into `string_length`.

`strlen`

The name of the function to count the number of characters in a string.

`string_to_check`

The name of the string data item to be counted.

`;`

A semicolon ends the statement.

Discussion

Dealing with alphanumerics in COBOL is much simpler than it is in C. In COBOL the receiving field truncates a longer field being moved to it. In C the longer field overwrites memory. That is one reason you may need to find out how long a string is.

In C you also tend to perform more operations character by character on strings. This means you use a `for` or `while` loop to copy or examine a string one character at a time. `strlen()` typically is used in these cases to get the length in order to terminate the loop. See the following example program.

Common Error

Calling `strlen()` but not assigning the result.

The length that `strlen()` obtains is passed back in the return value. If you don't assign or use the return value, the `strlen()` call has no effect in the program. The following statement does nothing useful:

```
strlen (date_time);
```

and it will not be flagged by many compilers.

Example

This program uses a `for` statement in line 5. `for` is like an in-line `PERFORM VARYING` statement in COBOL. The full discussion of the `for` loop statement is in Chapter 10, "Flow of Control Statements."

```
/*                strlen.c                    7/15/94                      */
#include <stdio.h>
#include <string.h>                    /* 1 for strlen() prototype        */

main()
{
   char  date      [16];
   char  date_time [31] = "Mar 11 1993 09:53 AM" ;
   int   i;
   int   length;
   int   space_count;

   length = strlen (date_time );         /* 2 assign return value         */

   if ( strlen (date_time) < 16 )        /* 3 use return value in IF      */
   {
      strcpy (date, date_time );         /* 4 copy date_time to date      */
   }

   for ( i = 0; i < strlen (date_time); i++ )  /* 5 control loop w/ strlen. */
   {                                     /*    loop counts spaces         */
      if (date_time [i] == ' ' )         /* 6 test for space              */
      {
         space_count += 1;               /* 7 add 1 to space_count        */
      }
   }

   printf ("Length = %d\n", strlen (date_time) );  /* 8 use return value   */
                                         /*    in printf()                */

   return (0);                           /* 9 return to 0/S               */
}
```

Comments on Example

Line 1   The include file string.h contains the function prototype for strlen(). A function prototype contains a template of the call parameters for the function. ANSI C uses this during compiling to check the call parameters.

Line 2   Shows the basic use of strlen(). strlen() uses the return value to hand back the result, which is the number of bytes in the string that was passed. Return values must be captured to be useful. The basic method for capturing the return value is to use a single equal sign to assign it to a variable.

strlen() tells you how many bytes are currently in the string. This is not necessarily the same as the declared size of the string.

The value of length after the call to strlen() is 20.

Line 3   An example of capturing the return value on the fly. This statement is evaluated from the innermost set of parentheses outward. What happens first is that strlen (date_time) is executed. Since its return value is not assigned (no equal sign is used), strlen (date_time) is replaced by its return value, which is 20.

```
    if ( strlen (date_time)   < 16 )
```

becomes

```
    if ( 20                   < 16 )
```

Now the if statement tests if 20 is less than 16, which evaluates as false. Since the length of the contents of date_time is larger than the size of date, date_time is not copied into date. Memory is not corrupted.

In a production system you would not hard code a size as this statement does. You would use the sizeof keyword, which is discussed in the next section.

Note that the strlen() call does not have a semicolon when it is inside another statement.

Line 4 Would perform a string copy of date_time into date, if the contents of date_time would fit. Since the if statement is false, this statement is not executed.

Line 5 Shows a for loop controlled by the use of a strlen() call. This for loop counts spaces in date_time. A for loop is much like a COBOL PERFORM ... VARYING ... FROM ... BY ... UNTIL.

The for loop says to perform the following code (delimited by braces) varying i from 0, by 1, while i is less than the length of date_time.

The main difference between for and PERFORM is that for continues *while* something is true and PERFORM continues *until* something is true. Also, the for's loop code is immediately after the for, which cannot be done in traditional COBOL. COBOL II allows an in-line PERFORM statement.

As in line 3, the return value of the strlen() call replaces strlen (date_time):

```
    for ( i = 0; i < strlen (date_time);    i++ )
```

becomes

```
    for ( i = 0; i < 20               ;     i++ )
```

The value of i is incremented from 1 by 1 each time the loop iterates. When the value of i reaches 20, the for statement stops.

Line 6 An if statement that tests the current subscripted character of date_time to see if it is a space. Single quotes are used for a single character. Subscript notation in C is essentially the same as in COBOL, except that C uses square brackets for the subscript while COBOL uses parentheses.

Note that the equality comparison uses the double equal (==). Remember that a single equal sign in an if statement does not generate the desired comparison.

Line 7 Adds 1 to space_count when the if statement is true. The += operator is equivalent to the COBOL ADD ... TO ..., except that in C the order is reversed.

Line 8 Uses the return value of a `strlen()` call to get an integer value to substitute into a `printf()` call. `strlen (date_time)` is replaced by 20, and then 20 is inserted into the `printf()` statement where the %d is. The result will be displayed on the terminal as

```
Length = 20
```

Terminal I/O is discussed in Chapter 5, "Terminal Input/Output."

Line 9 The `return(0)` statement ends the program and returns control to the operating system with a return value of zero.

Find the defined length of any data item.

C Keyword/Symbol/Function   `sizeof()` (find size of some data item)

`sizeof()` counts the number of characters in `item_to_check` based on the defined size of `item_to_check`. `item_to_check` can be a structure, an elementary data type, an array, or any other legally defined data item in C. `sizeof()` returns the count in bytes in *return value*. You can either assign the return value to a data element or use the return value on the fly.

Syntax

```
item_size = sizeof ( item_to_check ) ;
```

Samples

```
date_length = sizeof ( date_time ) ;
int_size    = sizeof ( int );
name_size   = sizeof ( last_name ) ;
```

Include File

None. Although `sizeof` looks like a function, it is a keyword. There are no prototypes for keywords.

See Also

```
calloc()   — allocate memory to your program while it is running
fread()    — read a record (structure) from a file
fwrite()   — write a record (structure) to a file
strlen()   — find the length of a string
```

Parameter Definitions

`int item_size;`

> Integer field to receive the return value of `sizeof()`.

`item_to_check`

> This can be any data type, from C a data type, such as `int`, to a programmer data type, such as a structure or array.

Return Value

`sizeof()` returns the number of bytes in the definition of `item_to_check`. Since the return value is important in this function, you must assign (move) it to another field or examine it on the fly. See the example program on page 211.

Scope

Used for any data type you can think of.

Direction

Works from right to left.

Anatomy

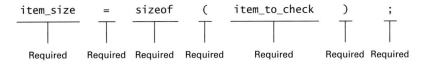

`item_size`

> The name of the integer data item that receives the return value of `sizeof()`.

`=`

> The assignment operator that moves the return value of `sizeof()` into `item_size`.

`sizeof`

> The name of the keyword that counts the number of bytes in a data item.

`item_to_check`

> The name of the data item you want to know the size of.

`;`

> A semicolon ends the statement.

Discussion

Although sizeof looks and acts like a function, it is a keyword. The statement sizeof (some_thing) is replaced by the compiler with the defined size of some_thing. The sizeof keyword is evaluated at compile time and replaced by the size of the data element checked. If it compiles cleanly, it will work at run time.

The primary uses of sizeof() in business systems are to read and write fixed-length records and to allocate memory dynamically to the program. The rest of the time you usually don't care how big a data item is.

The difference between sizeof() and strlen() is that sizeof() tells you how large the string was originally defined to be, and strlen() tells you how many characters are currently in it.

fread() and fwrite() read and write a number of characters based on a parameter you send. This typically is the size of the structure (record) you are reading or writing. Rather than hard coding the size of the structure, you should use the sizeof() function. This eliminates a maintenance problem when the structure is inevitably changed. Using sizeof() always gets the current size. fread() and fwrite() are discussed in Chapter 6, "File Input/Output."

The other main use of sizeof() is for allocating memory to the program at run time. This is something you basically cannot do in COBOL. If you have a table in a program in C and you don't know how large to make it, you can size it at run time and then allocate memory. You would get a count at run time of how many occurrences you need and then use sizeof() on the table structure and multiply the return value times the number of occurrences. This is discussed further in Chapter 12, "Table Handling." Most of the time it should be acceptable to figure out the size of a table in advance and let the compiler allocate the memory.

Common Errors

1. Calling sizeof() but not assigning the result.

   The length that sizeof() obtains is passed back in the return value. If you don't assign or use the return value, the sizeof() call has no effect in the program. The following statement does nothing useful:

   ```
   sizeof (date_time);
   ```

   and it will not be flagged by many compilers.

2. Using sizeof on a structure tag name.

   If you create a structure template by using a tag name instead of using typedef, you can't use sizeof() on the tag name. You have to use sizeof() on a structure that uses the tag name as a template.

   You can use sizeof() on the typedef name or the instance name of a structure.

Example

```
/*                    sizeof.c              2/13/94                    */
#include <stdio.h>
#include <string.h>                    /* 1  for strlen() prototype    */

main()
{
    char  date_time      [31] = "Mar 11 1993 09:53" ;
    int   date_time_size;
    int   double_size;
    int   fed_size;
    int   int_size;
    int   long_size;
    int   member_size;
    int   pay_rec_size;
    long  state_vote_cnt [50];          /* 2  50 occurrences of long   */
    int   string_length;
    int   table_size;
    int   tag_name_size;

    typedef struct                      /* 3  typedef = template       */
    {                                   /*     definition. No memory   */
        double  tax_rate;               /*     is allocated.           */
        double  tax_amt;
    } TAX_DATA;

    struct                              /* 4  NO typedef; struct       */
    {                                   /*     will allocate memory    */
        long     soc_sec_no;
        char     last_name [31];
        char     middle_init;
        char     first_name      [21];
        double   hourly_rate;
        TAX_DATA fed;                   /* 5  use template             */
        TAX_DATA state;                 /*     use template            */
        TAX_DATA local;                 /*     use template            */
    } pay_rec;

    int_size = sizeof (int );           /* 6  get size of int          */

    long_size = sizeof (long );         /* 7  get size of long         */

    double_size = sizeof (double );     /* 8  get size of double       */

    date_time_size = sizeof (date_time );   /* 9  get size of a string */
                                        /*     DEFINITION              */

    string_length = strlen (date_time );    /* 10 get LENGTH of a      */
                                        /*     string's CONTENTS.      */
                                        /*     Not same as sizeof()    */

    printf ("Int size = %d\n", sizeof (int) );  /* 11 use return value */
                                        /*     in printf()             */
```

```
pay_rec_size = sizeof (pay_rec );          /* 12 get size of a        */
                                           /*    structure            */
fed_size = sizeof (pay_rec.fed );          /* 13 get size of included */
                                           /*    structure            */
member_size = sizeof (state_vote_cnt [0] );/* 14 get size of 1st member*/
                                           /*    in array (table)     */
table_size = sizeof (state_vote_cnt );     /* 15 get size of array    */
return (0);
}
```

Comments on Example

Line 1 The include file `string.h` contains the function prototype for `strlen()` (get string length), which is used later in the program. A function prototype contains a template of the call parameters for the function. ANSI C uses this during compiling to check the call parameters.

There is no include file for `sizeof()` because it is a keyword masquerading as a function.

Line 2 Defines `state_vote_cnt` as an array (table) of 50 occurrences. C's array declaration is simpler than COBOL's. To do this in COBOL, you would have to do something like

```
01  STATE-VOTE-CNT-TABLE.
    05 STATE-VOTE-CNT      OCCURS 50 TIMES
                           PIC 9(8) COMP.
```

The C declaration is obviously more compact. Also, in C you treat all arrays as subscripted. There is no separate concept of indexing as in COBOL.

Line 3 Creates a structure template definition via `typedef`. No memory is allocated. TAX_DATA will be used below as a data type.

Line 4 Declares a structure. Since there is no tag name, memory is allocated.

Line 5 These three lines use the structure template TAX-DATA to create three sets of tax data: `fed`, `state`, and `local`. Memory is allocated when the template is invoked. Note that the data type is TAX-DATA and the data name (`fed`, `state`, `local`) will refer to a structure of the type TAX-DATA.

Line 6 Gets the size, in bytes, of a data type, `int`. This is one of the few places, other than data declarations, where you can use a data type keyword such as `int`. `sizeof()` figures out the size of `int` and hands back the number in the return value. The return value is captured by assigning it to the variable `int_size`.

On a PC `int_size` is usually two bytes. On many workstation computers it is four bytes. Run it on your compiler and see what you get.

Line 7 The same as line 6, except the data type is `long`. `long` is usually four bytes on both PCs and workstations.

Line 8   Checks the size of a `double`. It is generally eight bytes.

Line 9   Gets the *defined size* of `date_time`. The `sizeof()` operator tells you the original defined size of the data item. It ignores the length of any string that may be in `date_time`. All that is checked is the defined size.

   The *size* of `date_time` is 31.

Line 10   Finds out the length of the *contents* of `date_time`. `strlen()` tells you how many bytes are in a string before it finds the null terminator. It does not count the null terminator. The number could be lower or higher than the defined size of the string. It could be larger because, if you copy a longer string to a shorter one, C will not truncate. So `strlen()` can return a value that is greater than the defined size of the string.

   The *length* of (the string in) `date_time` is 17.

Line 11   Uses the return value of `sizeof()` on the fly. The fragment `sizeof (int)` is evaluated and replaced with 2 on a two-byte `int` compiler. The statement

```
printf ("Int size = %d\n", sizeof (int) );
```

becomes

```
printf ("Int size = %d\n", 2            );
```

and the result is

```
Int size = 2
```

Line 12   Shows `sizeof()` getting the size of a structure. This is one of the handy uses of `sizeof()` when using `fread()`, `fwrite()`, and `calloc()`. These functions all need a count of bytes to read, write, or allocate memory.

   The size of `pay_rec` is 113.

Line 13   Gets the size of an included structure. There's nothing special here except that the notation uses the structure member operator, or period, to qualify `fed`. Even though `fed` is itself a structure, it is a member of another structure, `pay_rec`, and so it must be qualified when referred to.

   The size of `fed` is 16.

Line 14   Finds the size of an element in an array. Subscript notation in C is basically the same as in COBOL, except that square brackets are used instead of parentheses and C starts counting from zero. The first element is represented by `[0]` (offset zero).

   The size of the first occurrence (offset zero) of `state_vote_cnt` is four bytes, because it is a `long`. On most C compilers a `long` is four bytes.

Line 15   Gets the size of the whole array, which is more useful than a single element's size. The notation here uses the name of element that occurs, without any subscript. This technique is also handy for finding the size of an array for which you want to dynamically allocate memory with `calloc()`. This should not be very common in business systems.

   The size of the whole array (50 occurrences) of `state_vote_cnt` is 200.

Move and format strings and/or numbers into a string.

C Keyword/Symbol/Function   sprintf() (copy and format data into a string)

sprintf() copies literals and/or data values into a string. sprintf() is the equivalent in COBOL of defining a print line format in WORKING-STORAGE and moving data into it. It is a formatting move function. sprintf() is very similar to both printf() and fprintf().

Syntax

```
sprintf (to_string, "control string" [, arg_1, arg_2...] ) ;
```

Format specifier
↓

```
sprintf (print_line, "GL100  End Of Month Run   Page: %3d", page_num ) ;
```

↑   ↓

Result: GL100   End Of Month Run   Page: 14

Sample

Include File

#include <stdio.h>   (contains function prototype for sprintf())

See Also

fprintf()   — format and write data to a file
printf()   — format and display data on the terminal

Parameter Definitions

char to_string [n];

   Character string where the result of formatting goes.

"control string"

   This is a literal within the sprintf() call statement where the formatting is defined. It is usually a combination of literal characters and format specifiers for the data items that follow.

arg_1, arg_2...

   These are the data items to be moved into "control string". They can be data elements or literals.

Return Value

`sprintf()` returns the number of characters copied into `to_string`. This is seldom used.

Scope

Used for strings only.

Direction

Arguments are substituted from left to right into the format specifiers in "`control string`".

Anatomy

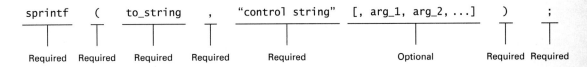

sprintf

The name of the function to copy and format data into a string.

to_string

The name of the string you want the result of all the formatting to go into.

"control string"

A literal within the `sprintf()` call statement. It is enclosed by double quotes. It can contain literals and format specifiers for numerics and alphanumerics to be substituted in the "`control string`". `sprintf()` fills in all the values and copies the result into `to_string`.

Format specifiers are analogous to COBOL PIC clauses. A format specifier is identified by a percent sign (%) as the first character. Format specifiers are discussed in detail below.

Format specifiers are not required to appear in "`control string`". If there are no format specifiers, the literal within the quotes will be moved as is into `to_string`.

Here are a few examples of control strings with some parameters and their results:

Control String	Result
"Tax rate is %f", tax_rate	Tax rate is .28
"GL100 Final Run Page: %d", page_num	GL100 Final Run Page: 13
"Cust No Tran Date Order No"	Cust No Tran Date Order No

[, arg_1, arg_2...] [brackets mean optional]

These are the optional data elements to be moved into "`control string`" where the format specifiers occur. If there are any data items to insert, a comma must follow "control string". After that comma, the data names appear, separated by commas. Data elements are taken from left to right and inserted into the format specifiers from left to right. The data items can be any of the following:

- Numeric data items
- Single character data items
- String data items
- Literals
- Expressions (computation results, return values of function calls)

;

A semicolon ends the statement.

Format Specifiers

Format specifiers are equivalent to the COBOL PIC clause. They give formatting directions to be applied to the data items in the argument list. Format specifiers are identified by a percent sign (%) as the first character. To move a percent sign into a string, put two together (%%). This is similar to the technique for putting a single quote in a VALUE clause.

Format specifiers for sprintf() are the same as for printf().

Format specifiers are coded as follows:

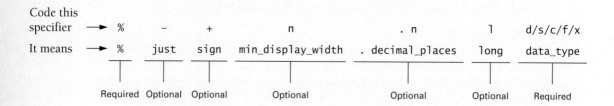

NOTE: The only required items are the % and the data type.

%

A single percent symbol tells sprintf() that this is the beginning of a format specifier.

– (dash)

Produces **left** justification of the data item. The default is right justification for everything, which is good for numbers and bad for strings. You must code the dash to left-justify strings.

+

Tells `sprintf()` to put a plus sign with the number if it is positive. The plus appears on the left. Minus signs are *always* inserted for negative numbers whether or not you use +. A minus sign also appears to the left of the number.

n

Tells `sprintf()` the **minimum** width to format the data item. If, after formatting, the result string is wider than this value, `sprintf()` **will not** truncate, which is different from COBOL. Also, with `double` data elements this is the total display width, including integers, the decimal point, and the desired number of decimal places. Again, if the edited number comes out to be larger than specified minimum width, `sprintf()` moves all of the characters. This could lead to unexpected variable-length strings. On the other hand, data is not lost.

If you want leading zeroes, code a zero in front of the number, as in `%04d`. This tells `sprintf()` to format an integer for at least four digits, with leading zeroes.

Here are some sample entries:

`%4`	tells `sprintf()` to insert at least 4 characters.
`%-20`	tells `sprintf()` to insert left justified for a minimum of 20 characters.
`%08`	tells `sprintf()` to insert at least 8 characters with leading zeroes.

.n

Consists of a period and a number, which tells `sprintf()` how many decimal places to insert. For instance, `%10.6` tells `sprintf()` to insert a number in a minimum of ten characters, with a decimal point, and six decimal places. This leaves three characters for the integer value. If the integer value is larger than three characters, `sprintf()` inserts as many characters as it takes to show it, leading to unexpected variable-length records or column misalignment for a print file. But, again, you don't lose data.

`sprintf()` rounds to the number of decimal places you tell it to show. However, C compilers **do not** use the business rounding convention of rounding up .5. ANSI C compilers use the IEEE standard that rounds .5 to the nearest round number. This affects `sprintf()`, `printf()`, and `fprintf()`. What it means is that for business applications you must use your own rounding routine. Appendix F contains a `round()` function written by the author, which rounds according to business rules.

l

The letter l tells `sprintf()` that there is either a `long` or a `double` to be written. It is coded along with the data type, as in `%ld` or `%lf`. Most compilers now take care of this without explicit instruction.

d/s/c/f/x

tells `sprintf()` the data type of the argument (parameter) for this format specifier. Common choices for business use include the following:

Format Specifier	Data Type	Output
%d	long/int	Signed decimal integer.
%c	char	A single character.
%s	char [n]	The string of characters until a \0 is found.
%s	string literal	The contents of the literal until the closing double quotes.
%f	double	Signed decimal number. If no precision is specified, the default format is to write all of the integer digits plus six decimal places.
%x	long/int	Unsigned hexadecimal.
%u	long/int	Unsigned decimal integer.
%o	long/int	Unsigned octal integer (seldom used in business).
%e	double	Exponential notation (seldom used in business).

Samples of Format Specifiers

These are a few samples of format specifiers for common data types. See more in the example program.

To Display	Use	Data	Result
A long or int in decimal form	%d	33	33
• With four digits	%4d	33	33
• With leading zeroes	%04d	33	0033
• Left-justified	%-4d	33	33
A single character (char)	%c	M	M
A string (char [n])	%s	Sirius	Sirius
• For 10 characters	%10s	Sirius	Sirius[1]
• 10 characters left-justified	%-10s	Sirius	Sirius
A double	%f	13.64	13.640000
• With 4 integers and 2 decimals	%7.2f	13.64	13.64
• With 1 integer and 6 decimals	%8.6f	.654321	0.654321
A long or int in hexadecimal form	%x	47	2f

[1]Right-justified is the default format for strings; this is the opposite of both COBOL and English.

Discussion

As previously mentioned, sprintf() both defines a format for a string and moves data to it. It is really a "super move" statement.

sprintf() has the same potential to corrupt memory that strcpy() does. In the case of sprintf(), if the result of all substitutions into "control string" is longer than the receiving field, sprintf() just keeps writing. There is no truncation.

There are two other functions, printf() and fprintf(), that are similar to sprintf(). All three use the same rules for format specifiers and substitution. Here is a short comparison of the three.

sprintf()

Used for formatting strings, but not for printing them. The most typical use of sprintf() is to format dates as MM/DD/YYYY.

Here is a sample:

```
sprintf ( pr_date, "Run Date: %02d/%02d/%4d", month, day, year) ;
```

After the call to sprintf(), the contents of pr_date are "Run Date: 02/17/1994".

printf() (print formatted)

Formats a string and displays it on stdout (standard output device). printf() works like the COBOL DISPLAY statement showing a formatted line. Its syntax is similar to that of sprintf().

fprintf() (file print formatted)

Used to format a string and write the formatted string (a print line or a record) to a file. This is the equivalent of the COBOL WRITE command. Its syntax is also similar to that of sprintf().

sprintf() also works like strcpy() in that the *source* string length controls how many characters are moved, *not* the destination string length. After sprintf() formats the data values, it writes the result into to_string. If the formatted string is longer than to_string, sprintf() will just keep writing over memory. It's the programmer's responsibility to make sure that to_string is long enough to receive everything in "control string" after substitution for format specifiers.

Common Errors

1. Bad value in the string, or the program blows up; more format specifiers than arguments.

   If you have three format specifiers in "control string" and two data elements, the value for the third format specifier is unpredictable. You would think the compiler could count the format specifiers and the arguments, but it doesn't. This compiles cleanly.

2. Missing value in the string, or the program blows up; more arguments than format specifiers.

   This is the converse of the previous error. If you have two format specifiers and three arguments, the third data item does not get inserted into the string. This also compiles cleanly.

3. Strange value in the string, or the program blows up; a mismatch of format specifier and argument.

   If the data type of the argument cannot be reasonably converted to the data type in the format specifier, you either get a strange result or the program blows up. Some compilers generate a warning on this, and some don't. The common sources of mismatch are as follows:

Format Specifier	Supplied Data Type
%s	int, long, double
%c	char [n], double
%d	char [n], double (decimal truncation)

   As is often the case in C, you have to protect yourself because the compiler doesn't.

4. A number has rounded down.

   sprintf() rounds a double to fit the number of decimal places you specify. Since the IEEE rounding method is used, in some cases .5 rounds down. Don't depend on sprintf(), printf(), or fprintf() to round your numbers. Use the round() function, as discussed in Appendix F.

Example

```
/*                      sprintf.c                    07/16/94                    */
#include <stdio.h>                              /* 1  for sprintf() prototype    */

main()
{
  int     day            = 7 ;
  char    first_name [21] = "James" ;
  char    last_name  [31] = "Harkin" ;
  char    middle_init    = 'C' ;
  int     month          = 2 ;
  char    work_str   [50];
  long    rec_count      = 12345 ;
  double  sales_tot      = 11234.65 ;
  long    table_size     = 255 ;
  int     year           = 1993 ;


                                                /*      Result:                  */
  sprintf ( work_str, " '%s %c %s' ",           /* 2  'James C Harkin'           */
    first_name,
    middle_init,
    last_name );

  sprintf ( work_str, "%s Sales %f.",           /* 3  self-concatenation         */
    work_str,
    sales_tot );
                                   /* result: 'James C Harkin' Sales 11234.650000. */

  sprintf ( work_str, " '%02d/%02d/%4d'",       /* 4  '02/07/1993'               */
    month,                                      /*    date formatting            */
    day,
    year );

  sprintf ( work_str, " '%s'     ", "Totals: " ); /* 5  'Totals: '               */
  sprintf ( work_str, " '%-10s' ", "Totals: " ); /* 6  'Totals:    '             */
  sprintf ( work_str, " '%10s'  ", "Totals: " ); /* 7  '  Totals: '              */
  sprintf ( work_str, " '%4s'    ", "Totals: " ); /* 8  'Totals: '               */
                                                /*    OVERFLOWS WIDTH            */

  sprintf ( work_str, " '%d'    ", rec_count ); /* 9  '12345'                    */
  sprintf ( work_str, " '%d'    ",  23456    ); /* 10 '-23456'                   */
  sprintf ( work_str, " '%8d'  ", rec_count ); /* 11 '   12345'                  */
  sprintf ( work_str, " '%+8d' ", rec_count ); /* 12 '  +12345'                  */
  sprintf ( work_str, " '%08d' ", rec_count ); /* 13 '00012345'                  */
  sprintf ( work_str, " '%-8d' ", rec_count ); /* 14 '12345   '                  */
  sprintf ( work_str, " '%3d'   ", rec_count ); /* 15 '12345'                    */
                                                /*     OVERFLOWS WIDTH           */
```

```
sprintf ( work_str, " '%f'      ", sales_tot );    /* 16 '11234.650000'        */
sprintf ( work_str, " '$%.2f'   ", sales_tot );    /* 17 '$11234.65'           */
sprintf ( work_str, " '%.0f'    ", sales_tot );    /* 18 '11235'               */
sprintf ( work_str, " '%11.2f'  ", sales_tot );    /* 19 '   11234.65'         */
sprintf ( work_str, " '%011.2f' ", sales_tot );    /* 20 '00011234.65'         */
sprintf ( work_str, " '%6.2f'   ", sales_tot );    /* 21 '11234.65'            */
                                                   /*    OVERFLOWS WIDTH       */

sprintf ( work_str, " '%x'   ", table_size );      /* 22 'ff'                  */
sprintf ( work_str, " '%4x'  ", table_size );      /* 23 '  ff'                */
sprintf ( work_str, " '%04x' ", table_size );      /* 24 '00ff'                */
sprintf ( work_str, " '%x'   ", middle_init );     /* 25 '43'                  */
                                                   /*    (ASCII value)         */

return (0);
}
```

Comments on Example

Line 1   The include file `stdio.h` contains the function prototype for `sprintf()`. A function prototype contains a template of the call parameters for the function. ANSI C uses this during compiling to check the call parameters. Since `sprintf()` has a variable number of parameters, the compiler does not bother to perform parameter checking. This means the compiler does not catch a short or a long parameter list.

Line 2   Combines first name, middle initial, and last name in one field. Note that `middle_init` is a single character field, `char`, and thus uses the `%c` substitution symbol.

Line 3   Shows how to use `sprintf()` successively to self-concatenate strings. You could use `strcat()` to do some of this, but `sprintf()` also allows substitution of data elements, which `strcat()` does not.

> **CAUTION:** Not all compilers interpret this as self-concatenation. Some compilers just drop the current contents of `work_str` and create a result of "`Sales 11234.65000`". If you are concerned about portability, avoid this technique.

Line 4   Shows a common use of `sprintf()` to format dates into a common form. "`control string`" is hard to read. It says put in two integer digits with leading zeroes, a slash, two more integer digits with leading zeroes, another slash, and four integer digits. The arguments then supply `month`, `day`, and `year` to be inserted. The result is a date in a normal format for printing.

Lines 5–8   Show the effects of various editing symbols on a string literal. The results would be the same if a string variable were named.

Line 5 is the minimal specification. The width will be the length of the string contents.

Line 6 shows how to get left-justified alphanumerics with a specified width.

Line 7 shows default justification for alphanumerics, which is right justication. This is obviously the opposite of what COBOL does.

Line 8 shows how `sprintf()` does not truncate if you specify a width smaller than the data element turns out to be. Four characters are specified, and eight characters are formatted. **Programmer beware!**

Lines 9–15   Examples of various editing symbols for integer data types `int` and `long`.

Line 9 is the basic `int/long` specification. However many digits are in the number will be formatted.

Line 10 shows the same thing, with a negative number. `sprintf()` automatically puts the negative sign on the left.

Line 11 directs `sprintf()` to use eight characters to format the number. The defaults in effect are right justification and no leading zeroes.

Line 12 shows how to get a plus sign to show up with a number. If the number is positive, the plus sign always appears on the left side.

Line 13 uses a zero in front of the minimum width number to get leading zeroes to appear.

Line 14 uses the minus sign in the editing symbol, which means left-justify. Since there are five digits and a minimum width of 8, there will be three spaces on the right.

Line 15 shows an overflow condition. `sprintf()` does not truncate numbers, or any other data type, if the data is wider than the specified minimum width. `sprintf()` just puts out the data. **Programmer beware!**

Lines 16–21   Show various editing symbols to handle a floating point number, a `double` in this case.

Line 16 uses the default formatting for a `double`, which will format to whatever width the `double` is, and show six decimal places. Note that there are only two nonzero digits to the right of the decimal point and C shows 6 anyway.

Line 17 puts a dollar sign in front of the number and limits it to two decimal places. The only problem here is that C never puts commas in numbers. Also, C will not float a dollar sign over to the first nonzero digit. If you want commas in your numbers, use the `dollar_comma()` function, as discussed in Appendix F.

Line 18 rounds the number and shows no decimal places. A potential problem here is that the IEEE rounding method sometimes rounds .5 down.

Line 19 right justifies, suppresses leading zeroes, and shows two decimal places.

Line 20 right justifies, shows leading zeroes, and shows two decimal places.

Line 21 specifies a minimum width (six), which is smaller than the data (eight). `sprintf()` does not truncate, and formats all the data. If you are expecting columns of data to line up, they won't if any of the numbers, after formatting, are larger than the minimum width specification.

Lines 22–25 Show various effects when displaying numbers in hexadecimal form.

Line 22 is the basic hex format, with no minimum width specified.

Line 23 specifies a minimum width of four characters. Defaults of right justification and suppressing leading zeroes are in effect.

Line 24 specifies leading zeroes and a minimum width of four characters.

Line 25 shows how to get the hexadecimal value of a single character.

Append one string to another one.

C Keyword/Symbol/Function	strcat() (string concatenate)

strcat() appends one string of characters onto another string of characters. append_string can be either a string data item or a string literal.

Syntax

```
strcat ( to_string, append_string ) ;
```

Sample

```
strcat ( print_line, date);
```

Include File

`#include <string.h>`   (contains function prototype for `strcat()`)

See Also

`sprintf()`   — format and move alphanumerics and/or numerics into a string
`strcpy()`   — copy a literal or string to another string
`strncpy()`   — copy the first *n* characters of one string to another

Parameter Definitions

`char to_string [n];`
   Character string data item that will be added to.

`char append_string [n];`
   Character string data item or literal that will be appended to `to_string`.

Return Value

`strcat()` returns the address of `to_string`. This is seldom used.

Scope

Used for strings only.

Direction

Works from right to left.

Anatomy

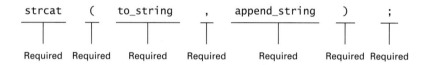

strcat (to_string , append_string) ;

Required Required Required Required Required Required Required

`strcat`

> The name of the function to append one string to another string.

`to_string`

> The name of the string you want to append characters to.

`append_string`

> The source of characters to append. This can be a string data item or a string literal.

`;`

> A semicolon ends the statement.

Discussion

`strcat()` keeps appending characters until it finds a string terminator, no matter what size `to_string` is defined as. In COBOL the destination data item controls how many characters are moved. In C it's the source that controls how many characters are moved. `strcat()` can and will corrupt memory.

Common Error

Memory corrupted.

> As previously mentioned, `strcat()` works the same way that `strcpy()` and `strncpy()` do: The source data item controls how many characters are copied. It is up to you to avoid corrupting memory.

Example

```
/*                    strcat.c                   07/16/94                    */
#include <stdio.h>
#include <string.h>                         /* 1 for strcat() prototype      */

main()
{
    char  date          [13] = "Nov 26 1992 ";
    char  date_time      [25] = "Mar 11 1993 09:53 AM" ;
    char  print_line    [133];

    strcat ( print_line, "GL100 Run: " );     /* 2 concatenate a literal     */

    strcat ( print_line, date );              /* 3 concatenate a string to   */
                                              /*   a string                  */

    strcat ( print_line, &date_time [12] );   /* 4 concatenate FROM inside   */
                                              /*   a string                  */

    strcat ( print_line, "     General "      /* 5 concatenate a literal     */
                "Ledger EOM Trial" );         /*   which continues to the    */
                                              /*   next line                 */
    return (0);
}
```

Comments on Example

Line 1 The include file `string.h` contains the function prototype for `strcat()`. A function prototype contains a template of the call parameters for the function. ANSI C uses this during compiling to check the call parameters.

Line 2 Shows building a string by concatenation, using a string literal. The effect is the same if you use a string variable. `print_line` was uninitialized when it was declared in the program. Its length, by definition, is zero. If you use `strcat()` to append a string to an empty string, it will put it at the beginning.

After this statement `print_line` looks like

```
GL100 Run:
```

with a space after the colon.

Line 3 Appends the field `date` to `print_line`. The effect would be the same if a string literal were used.

After this statement `print_line` looks like

```
GL100 Run: Nov 26 1992
```

Line 4 Picks up a substring to append to another string. If you want to use a part of another string, use the address operator & and the offset of the character you want to start with. In this case the offset is 12 for the beginning of the time part of `date_time`. `strcat()` starts at offset 12 and stops when it finds the end of `date_time`.

After this statement `print_line` looks like

```
GL100 Run: Nov 26 1992 09:53 AM
```

Line 5   Concatenates a string literal that is continued on the next line. Put double quotes at the end of the first line and resume the literal with double quotes on the next line. This allows you to align the literal any way you want. The compiler throws away white-space characters (space, tab, line-feed) between one ending double quote and the next beginning double quote and continues the literal.

After this statement `print_line` looks like

```
GL100 Run: Nov 26 1992 09:53 AM   General Ledger EOM Trial
```

Summary

How you move (copy) data in C depends on what kind of data it is. This is different from COBOL, where the MOVE reserved word takes care of all cases. The assignment operator (=) is used to copy numeric data types, single characters, and structures. An assignment statement reads like a COMPUTE statement without the COMPUTE reserved word. Strings are copied using function calls.

The `strcpy()` function copies one string or string literal to another string. In `strcpy()`, as in all functions involving strings in C, the *source* string controls how many characters are copied, not the destination string. This makes it easy to corrupt memory. It is also the reverse of COBOL.

`strncpy()` copies a specified number of characters from one string to another. `strcat()` appends one string or string literal to another string. The `strlen()` function tells you how many characters are in a string.

When you want to know the defined size in bytes of any data item, including strings, use `sizeof`. The difference between `sizeof` and `strlen()` is that `sizeof` gives the originally defined size of a string data element and `strlen()` gives the length of the current contents of the string. The typical use of `sizeof` is to get the size of a structure.

Use `sprintf()` to format and move data into a string. It uses the same format specifiers and substitution rules as `printf()` and `fprintf()`. It has a parameter which is the data name of the string where the result of formatting goes, but otherwise it works the same way as `printf()`.

Moving data in C is not as straightforward as it is in COBOL, but it is not complicated. The primary caution is to be careful with string functions, since they can easily corrupt memory.

CHAPTER 8

Arithmetic

Introduction

This chapter covers basic arithmetic operations in C, including the following topics:

- Types of business arithmetic usually performed in C
- Common mistakes in arithmetic in C, including rounding numbers, which does not operate in C the way it does in COBOL
- A detailed examination of arithmetic operations

Types of Business Arithmetic in C

Arithmetic statements fall into four categories in C:

Basic arithmetic—"compute" style—works like the COBOL COMPUTE statement but without the COMPUTE reserved word. The syntax is the same as the COMPUTE statement. This is the most common form of arithmetic in C.

Basic arithmetic—"add to" style—works like COBOL ADD TO, SUBTRACT FROM, MULTIPLY BY, DIVIDE INTO, and DIVIDE INTO ... REMAINDER statements but without the GIVING clause. As in COBOL, this type of operation is used less frequently than the preceding form, but it still has many uses.

Increment/decrement are C language statements which increase or decrease a data item by 1. The increment and decrement operators are similar to the COBOL ADD 1 TO and SUBTRACT 1 FROM statements but are more compact. They are used to count records, control loop iterations, move through tables, and more.

Absolute value functions return the absolute value of an integer or a floating point number. When you need the positive value of a number, you can call one of C's absolute value functions instead of writing two to four lines of code.

The following table lists arithmetic operations, the C arithmetic operators and functions used for them, and the corresponding COBOL statements.

C and COBOL Arithmetic Operators/Keywords		
Operation	**C**	**COBOL**
Basic Arithmetic—"Compute" Style		
Addition	+	+
Subtraction	–	–
Multiplication	*	*
Division	/	/
Remainder (modulus)	%	/ GIVING ... REMAINDER
Basic Arithmetic—"Add To" Style<		
Add to	+=	ADD ... TO ...
Subtract from	–=	SUBTRACT ... FROM ...
Multiply by	*=	MULTIPLY ... BY ...
Divide into	/=	DIVIDE ... INTO ...
Remainder into	%=	DIVIDE ... INTO ... REMAINDER ...
Increment / Decrement		
Add 1 to a data element	++	ADD 1 TO ...
Subtract 1 from a data element	––	SUBTRACT 1 FROM ...
Absolute Value		
Get absolute value of an integer	abs()	IF AMT < 0
Get absolute value of a long integer	labs()	MULTIPLY AMT BY –1.
Get absolute value of a double	fabs()	

Common Arithmetic Mistakes in C

The most common mistakes in arithmetic in C involve intermediate results and overflowing integers.

Intermediate Results

C handles intermediate results of calculations differently than COBOL does. This will cause problems for you, primarily in division. The difference is due to the handling of the decimal portions of intermediate results.

COBOL looks at the whole arithmetic expression to determine how many decimal places to maintain for the expression. For intermediate results COBOL maintains a number of decimal places equal to the smallest number of places for any internal decimal number in the whole expression. Integers gain this number of decimal places so they can be divided without losing the decimal portion of the result.

C does not look at the whole expression to determine the size of intermediate results. C looks at each pair of numbers being added, subtracted, multiplied, or divided and decides whether the result (intermediate or final) will be an integer or a floating point number.

If both numbers are integers, the result of the arithmetic operation will be an integer. If at least one number is floating point, the result will be a floating point number, which has a large number of decimal places. In C you cannot specify the number of decimal places for a number; it either has them (`double` and `float`) or it does not have them (`int` and `long`).

This example illustrates the difference:

COBOL:

```
01  BATTING-AVERAGE       PIC V999  VALUE 0.
01  AT-BATS               PIC 9(3)  VALUE 300.
01  HITS                  PIC 9(3)  VALUE 100.
       COMPUTE BATTING-AVERAGE = HITS / AT-BATS.
```

This yields the expected result of .333. COBOL maintains three decimal places for the result because BATTING-AVERAGE has three decimal places in its definition.

C:

```
double  batting_average = 0.0;
int     at_bats         = 300;
int     hits            = 100;

batting_average = hits / at_bats ;
```

This yields the unexpected result of `0.0`. For each arithmetic operation, C looks at the two number types involved and creates an intermediate result based on whether the two numbers are both integer types. If they are, then the result (intermediate or final) is an integer and has no decimal places. If at least one of the numbers (which could be a previous intermediate result) is floating point, then the result will be floating point and the decimal places will be preserved. Therefore, when you divide integers in a C program, you must be careful to preserve the decimal portion of the results. One simple way to do this is multiply any integer numbers by 1.0 before dividing.

```
batting_average = ( hits * 1.0 ) / ( at_bats * 1.0 ) ;
```

This creates two intermediate results, both of which are floating point. Then the two floating point results are divided, and `batting_average` becomes a respectable `.333`.

The example program for "compute" style arithmetic in this chapter has more examples of preserving and losing decimal portions of intermediate results.

Casting

Another way to preserve decimal values in integer computations is to use a technique called *casting*. Casting tells C to convert a data element to some data type before using it. Cast syntax consists of a data type in parentheses preceding the data element to be cast, or converted to another type. Using casting in the previous example gives

```
batting_average = ( (double) hits ) / ( (double) at_bats ) ;
```

Casting occurs before any other operation in an arithmetic statement. The example above casts `hits` and `at_bats` to be `doubles`, which means that decimal places are preserved. In fact, casting one of them is sufficient, because C preserves decimal values for any arithmetic operation that has at least one floating point number in it.

Casting a data element causes a temporary variable to be created. The original data element's data type is not changed.

Arithmetic results are the same whether you cast numbers or multiply them by `1.0`.

Overflow

Overflow refers to adding a value to an integer that yields a value greater than it can hold. In COBOL you can trap this with `ON SIZE ERROR`. In C there is no way to trap it.

Signed integer types, such as `int` and `long`, generally go negative when addition causes them to exceed their maximums. This is due to the fact that `int` and `long` variables use the high-order bit of the number both as a value and as a sign. When the high-order bit is turned on, it signifies a negative number.

If your compiler has a two-byte `int` and you have an `int` with a value of 32,767, the hexadecimal value is `7fff`. When you add 1 to that, the hexadecimal value becomes `8000`. The high-order bit is now turned on, so the number is interpreted as negative. Hex `8000` is translated to −32,768 decimal for a two-byte `int`.

With `unsigned int` and `unsigned long` data types, the numbers *roll over* (go to zero and start up again). Because they are unsigned, the high-order bit does not act as a sign bit. If you have a two-byte `unsigned int` with a value of 32,767 and you add 1 to it, the result will be +32,768. The number will roll over to zero if you add 1 to a value of 65,535.

The `unsigned` qualifier for `int` and `long` is not used much in business because usually you want to handle negative numbers.

The following table shows the results of adding and subtracting at the ends of the range of values for integer types. Assume the compiler has a two-byte `int` and a four-byte `long`.

Results of Adding or Subtracting 1 to/from Maximum Values of Integer Data Types					
Data Type	——— Maximum Value ——— Decimal	Hex	Arithmetic Operation	——— Resulting Value ——— Hex	Decimal
int	+32,767	7fff	Add 1	8000	–32,768
	–32,768	8000	Subtract 1	7fff	+32,767
long	+2,147,483,647	7fffffff	Add 1	80000000	–2,147,483,648
	–2,147,483,648	80000000	Subtract 1	7fffffff	+2,147,483,647
unsigned int	+65,535	ffff	Add 1	0	0
unsigned long	+4,294,967,295	ffffffff	Add 1	0	0

You have to be careful to choose number types that will be large enough to maintain your results correctly. It is safer to use long instead of int for counters likely to stay under 2 billion. If your counts can get larger than this, use double.

For all numbers with decimal places, use double. There is no reason to use float anymore: The memory saved is insignificant and the error potential is very large. Memory is cheap and programming errors are expensive.

Rounding

C compilers do not round the way you would expect them to in a business environment. Rounding in C occurs when displaying, converting or writing floating point numbers using the functions printf(), sprintf(), and fprintf(). These functions typically use the default compiler rounding method. It is the wrong method for business programming.

Business rounding always rounds .5 *up* to the next number.

Most C compilers use the IEEE (Institute of Electrical and Electronics Engineers) rounding method, which rounds .5 "to the nearest round number." The nearest round number is based on the binary representation within a floating point number. You cannot determine from the decimal representation whether the number will round up or down. In scientific programming this rounding method is considered a useful feature because it distributes .5 values both up and down. In business programming it will get you in trouble.

Here are two examples that show the problem. Assume the numbers are stored as doubles.

Value	Number of Places to Round	Format Specifier	Result
2.5	0	%.0f	2
1.335	2	%.2f	1.33

You can definitely lose pennies by relying on the compiler. While some compilers allow you to choose the rounding method to use, the safest course is to use a rounding routine. This makes the code independent of a particular compiler's default or chosen rounding routine.

Decimal truncation in C is a problem, but for a different reason. The only way to truncate in the standard library is to use `fprintf()`, `printf()`, and `sprintf()` and specify the number of decimal places you want. Since all these functions round, there is no decimal truncation.

Appendix F discusses and provides listings for a rounding routine, `round.c`, and a truncation routine, `truncate.c`. These routines were written by the author for business use. They round and truncate according to normal business rules.

Use them and don't lose pennies!

Basic Arithmetic—"Compute" Style

Desired Action	C Keyword/Symbol/Function
Addition	+
Subtraction	–
Multiplication	*
Division	/
Remainder (modulus)	%

Syntax

Addition	`sum`	`= num_1 + num_2 ;`
Subtraction	`diff`	`= num_1 – num_2 ;`
Multiplication	`product`	`= num_1 * num_2 ;`
Division	`quotient`	`= num_1 / num_2 ;`
Remainder (modulus)	`remainder`	`= num_1 % num_2 ;`

Samples

Addition	`total_hours`	`= reg_hours + ot_hours ;`
Subtraction	`net_pay`	`= gross_pay – total_deductions ;`
Multiplication	`fed_tax_amt`	`= gross_pay * fed_tax_rate ;`
Division	`take_home_pct`	`= net_pay / gross_pay ;`
Remainder (modulus)	`remainder_days`	`= est_days % 7 ;`

Basic arithmetic in C has the structure of the COBOL COMPUTE statement without the word COMPUTE:

```
COBOL:    COMPUTE A = B + C.
C:             a = b + c;
```

This type of arithmetic statement is a three-operand statement: One operand is the result, and the other two operands are used by the operator.

Basic arithmetic in C also works the same as the COBOL COMPUTE in that the data items on the right side of the equal sign (assignment operator) are not changed by the arithmetic operation. A computation is performed, and the resulting number is assigned (moved) to the data item on the left side of the equal sign.

Here is a summary of "compute"-style arithmetic in C:

Addition

```
COBOL:    COMPUTE TOTAL-HOURS = REGULAR-HOURS + OVERTIME-HOURS.
C:        total_hours        = regular_hours + overtime_hours;
```

Subtraction

```
COBOL:    COMPUTE NET-PAY = GROSS-PAY - TOTAL-REDUCTIONS.
C:        net_pay         = gross_pay - total_deductions;
```

Multiplication

```
COBOL:    COMPUTE GROSS-PAY = HOURS-WORKED * HOURLY-RATE.
C:        gross_pay        = hours_worked * hourly_rate;
```

Division

```
COBOL:    COMPUTE AVERAGE-SALARY = TOTAL-SALARY / EMPL-COUNT.
C:        average_salary        = total_salary / empl-count;
```

Remainder (modulus)

```
COBOL:    DIVIDE TOTAL-DAYS BY 7 GIVING   TOTAL-WEEKS
                                  REMAINDER EXTRA-DAYS.
C:        extra_days = total_days % 7;
```

The term *modulus* is commonly used in C to mean remainder. It has a precise definition in mathematics that does not quite mean remainder. This text uses the term *remainder* because it is more obvious. The percent sign, %, is the remainder operator in C. C's remainder operator is much more elegant than COBOL's. Just use the percent sign instead of the divide sign. COBOL has an advantage in that if you want both the result and the remainder, you can get it in one statement. In C it takes two statements: one for the division and one for the remainder:

```
total_weeks = total_days / 7;
extra_days  = total_days % 7;
```

C is more concise when you want only the remainder. COBOL is more concise when you want both the result and the remainder.

Common Error

Losing the decimal value on division.

If you divide one integer by another and assign the result to a `double`, you will not get any decimal places. This is a tricky difference from COBOL, because the equivalent statement in COBOL preserves the decimal value.

In C the result of each arithmetic operation depends on the data types of the two operands involved. If both are integer data types, the result will be an integer, which has no decimal places. This is consequential primarily on division.

When there are two integers being divided, the solution is to make sure at least one integer gets treated as a floating point number. This is accomplished either by multiplying one of the integers by 1.0 or by casting one of the integers as a `double`. See lines 8 and 9 in the example program.

Example

```
/*              compute.c                    9/05/94                */
#include <stdio.h>
main()
{
   long    estimated_days   = 74;
   long    estimated_weeks;
   long    ot_hours         = 15;
   long    reg_hours        = 40;
   long    remainder_days;
   long    total_hours;

   double  gross_pay        = 32517.53;
   double  hourly_wage      = 17.50;
   double  fed_tax_amt;
   double  fed_tax_rate      = .28;
   double  net_pay;
   double  ot_ratio_1;
   double  ot_ratio_2;
```

```
double  take_home_pct;
double  total_deductions = 7450.45;
double  weekly_pay;

total_hours = reg_hours + ot_hours;             /* 1 addition               */
net_pay = gross_pay - total_deductions;         /* 2 subtraction            */
fed_tax_amt = gross_pay * fed_tax_rate;         /* 3 multiplication         */
take_home_pct = net_pay / gross_pay;            /* 4 division               */
remainder_days = estimated_days % 7;            /* 5 remainder              */

weekly_pay = total_hours  * hourly_wage;        /* 6 mixing integer and     */
                                                /*   floating point         */

estimated_weeks = estimated_days / 7;           /* 7 integer division       */
                                                /*   ignoring fraction      */

ot_ratio_1 = (ot_hours    * 1.0) /              /* 8 integer division       */
             (total_hours * 1.0) ;              /*   preserving fraction    */

ot_ratio_2 = (double) ot_hours /                /* 9 integer division       */
             total_hours;                       /*   preserving fraction    */

return (0);
}
```

Comments on the Example

Line 1 Basic addition.

All numbers on line 1 are `long` (long integer). When all the numeric types are the same in addition, no decimal values are lost. If you mix floating point numbers and integers, make sure the number on the left of the equal sign is a floating point number, or you'll lose the decimal portion of the result.

The value of `total_hours` is 55 after this statement.

Line 2 Basic subtraction.

All numbers on line 2 are `double` (double-precision floating point). When all the numeric types are the same in subtraction, no decimal values are lost. If you mix floating point numbers and integers, make sure the number on the left of the equal sign is a floating point number, or you'll lose the decimal portion of the result.

The value of `net_pay` is 25,067.08 after this statement.

Line 3 Basic multiplication.

All numbers on line 3 are `double` (double-precision floating point). When all the numeric types are the same in multiplication, no decimal values are lost. If you mix floating point numbers and integers, make sure the number on the left of the equal sign is a floating point number, or you'll lose the decimal portion of the result.

The value of `fed_tax_amt` is 9,104.9084 after this statement. In a production environment this result would need to be rounded.

Line 4 Basic division.

All numbers on line 4 are `double` (double-precision floating point). When all the numbers in a division are defined as `double`, no decimal values are lost.

If you have all integer numbers in a division, you will lose any fractional result. See the comments about lines 7 through 9 and the "Common Error" section for considerations when dividing integers.

If you mix floating point numbers and integers, make sure the number on the left of the equal sign is a floating point number, or you'll lose the decimal portion of the result.

The value of `take_home_pct` is .770879 after this statement.

Line 5   The remainder operation.

All numbers on line 5 are `long` (long integer). The remainder operator does not work for floating point numbers: It is an integer (`long` or `int`) operation. It always gives the remainder of the division of two integers as an integer.

The value of `remainder_days` is 4 after this statement.

Line 6   Multiplication using floating point and integer numbers.

As long as you assign the result to a floating point number, you will get correct results when multiplying a floating point and an integer number.

The value of `weekly_pay` is 962.50 after this statement.

The decimal part of the result is preserved because the compiler converts integers to floating point numbers if it finds a floating point number in a single arithmetic operation (add, subtract, divide, or multiply two numbers).

After multiplicaton the interim result, a floating point number, is assigned to the final result field according to its numeric type. If the final result field is a floating point number, the decimal part of the result is preserved. If the final result field is an integer (`long` or `int`), the decimal part of the interim result is truncated. This is seldom the desired result.

If you were to assign the result to an integer field, the value would be 962. This works the same way as in COBOL. Where C works differently is with division involving two integers. See also the "Common Error" section.

Line 7   Integer division which *loses* the decimal portion of the result.

This example works the same way it would in COBOL. If you divide one integer by another and assign the result to an integer, the decimal portion of the result is truncated.

The value of `estimated_weeks` is 10 after this statement.

Line 8   Integer division that *preserves* the decimal portion of the result.

To preserve the decimal portion when dividing two integers, you must convert at least one of them to a floating point number. This line multiplies each number by 1.0 to turn them into floating point numbers, which are then divided. Line 9 gets the same effect by type casting.

In COBOL you don't have to do this because defining the receiving field as having decimal places causes decimal places to be preserved in intermediate results.

In C each intermediate result can be an integer or a floating point number. It does not depend on the receiving field. It depends on each pair of numbers in an arithmetic operation. If they are both integers, the intermediate result will be an integer. If at least one number is a floating point number, then the result will be a floating point number.

The value of `ot_ratio_1` is `0.272727` after this statement.

Line 9   Integer division that *preserves* the decimal portion of the result.

This line is equivalent to line 8. It converts `ot_hours` temporarily to a `double` by casting. This will cause the result of the division to be a `double`, which is then assigned to `ot_ratio_2`. Decimal places are preserved.

The value of `ot_ratio_2` is `0.272727` after this statement.

Basic Arithmetic—"Add To" Style

Desired Action	C Keyword/Symbol/Function
Add to	+=
Subtract from	−=
Multiply by	*=
Divide into	/=
Remainder into	%=

Syntax

Add to	`sum`	`+= num_1 ;`
Subtract from	`diff`	`-= num_2 ;`
Multiply by	`product`	`*= num_3 ;`
Divide into	`quotient`	`/= num_4 ;`
Remainder into	`remainder`	`%= num_5 ;`

Sample

Add to	`line_count`	`+= 2 ;`
Subtract from	`leave_balance`	`-= hours_taken ;`
Multiply by	`take_home_pct`	`*= 100.0 ;`
Divide into	`total sales amt`	`/= 1000.0 ;`
Remainder into	`estimated_days`	`%= 7 ;`

These arithmetic operators work like the COBOL ADD TO and SUBTRACT FROM statements. The result of the arithmetic operation is placed in one of the two data items in the statement. They are two-operand statements.

In COBOL it is the *right* operand that receives the new value. In C it is the *left* operand that receives the new value.

In C this kind of operator is called a *combined assignment* operator. It performs an arithmetic operation and assigns the result with a single operator.

> **CAUTION:** Combined assignment operators alter the data item on the left. If you need to preserve the value of that data item, don't use these operators. Use the "compute"-style statements as discussed in the previous section.

Here is a summary of "add to"-style arithmetic in C:

Add To

C: `ytd_gross += weekly_gross;`

which is the same as

```
ytd_gross = ytd_gross + weekly_gross;
```

COBOL: `ADD WEEKLY-GROSS TO YTD-GROSS.`

To keep running totals in C, you can either use the addition assignment operator or repeat the total field.

Subtract From

C: `leave_balance -= leave_hours_taken;`

which is the same as

```
leave_balance  = leave_balance - leave_hours_taken;
```

COBOL: `SUBTRACT LEAVE-HOURS-TAKEN FROM LEAVE-BALANCE.`

If you have totals that are subtracted from, you can either use the subtraction assignment operator or repeat the total field.

Multiply By

C: `gross_pay *= .9235;`

which is the same as

```
gross_pay = gross_pay * .9235;
```

COBOL: `MULTIPLY .9235 BY GROSS-PAY.`

This operator is less common than the previous two, since a running result of multiplication is seldom useful. If you need to do it, however, the multiplication assignment operator keeps you from having to repeat the name of the field being multiplied.

Divide Into

C: `annual_salary /= 26.1;`

which is the same as

`annual_salary = annual_salary / 26.1;`

COBOL: `DIVIDE 26.1 INTO ANNUAL-SALARY.`

The same comments apply to division as to multiplication. You overwrite the data item being divided. This may not be the desired result.

Remainder Into

C: `days %= 7;`

which is the same as

`days = days % 7;`

COBOL: `DIVIDE DAYS BY 7 GIVING WEEKS REMAINDER DAYS.`

COBOL does not have a remainder into operation.

The same virtue/problem occurs here as in multiplication and division—the original data item gets replaced with the result of the operation.

Common Error

Incorrect result.

The common error when using the combined assignment operators is that the left operand is changed when it should not be. If you use a combined assignment operator, the original value of the left operand is lost.

The problem usually is choosing the combined operator syntax instead of the "compute"-style syntax. "Compute"-style syntax assigns the result of the arithmetic operation to a result field and does not affect the fields used to create the result.

Example

```
/*              add_to.c                    9/05/94                    */
#include <stdio.h>
main()
{
    long    estimated_days  = 74;
    long    estimated_weeks;
    double  hours_taken     = 13.5;
    long    line_count      = 0;
    double  leave_balance   = 118.5;
    double  take_home_pct   = .784706;
    double  total_sales_amt = 1222333.44;

    line_count += 2 ;                  /* 1 add to running count        */

    leave_balance -= hours_taken;      /* 2 subtract from running       */
                                       /*   balance                     */

    take_home_pct *= 100.0;            /* 3 make percent be between     */
                                       /*   1 and 100                   */

    total_sales_amt /= 1000.0;         /* 4 express total_sales_amt     */
                                       /*   as thousands                */

    estimated_weeks = estimated_days / 7;  /* 5.1 find number of weeks  */

    estimated_days %= 7;               /* 5.2 make estimated_days       */
                                       /*     have the remainder        */

    return (0);
}
```

Comments on Example

Line 1 Add to operation. This is the common way to keep running totals for processing or reports.

   The value of line_count is 2 after this statement.

Line 2 Subtract from operation. This is not used as commonly as the += operator, but it works the same way.

   The value of leave_balance is 105.0 after this statement.

Line 3 Multiply by operation. This is how to raise percents to whole numbers.

   The value of take_home_pct is 78.4706 after this statement.

CAUTION: This statement will work the same way using 100 and 100.0, but it is always better when working with floating point numbers to use the decimal point. When you mix integers and floating point numbers there are cases where you lose the fraction part of the floating point number. See the section on intermediate results at the beginning of this chapter.

Line 4 Divide into operation. When you need to state numbers as thousands or millions, use the /= operator to move the decimal place.

The value of `total_sales_amt` is `1,222.333440` after this statement.

See the **Caution** on page 242.

Lines 5.1 and 5.2 Show the use of the remainder assignment (remainder into) operator. Usually when you want a remainder, you also want the quotient. Since the modulus assignment operator replaces the original number with the remainder, you must be careful to preserve the quotient.

Line 5.1 saves the quotient and truncates the decimal value at the same time. Decimal truncation occurs because both `estimated_days` and 7 are integers. Integer division is desirable in this case, since we want a count of weeks. The value of `estimated_weeks` is `10` after this statement.

Line 5.2 replaces the original value of `estimated_days` with the remainder of dividing `estimated_days` by 7. The value of `estimated_days` is 4 after this statement. Note that the original value of `estimated_days` is now lost.

Incrementing/Decrementing a Data Item

Desired Action	C Keyword/Symbol/Function
Add 1 to a data element	++
Subtract 1 from a data element	--

Syntax

Add 1	`counter++ ;` or `++counter ;`
Subtract 1	`counter-- ;` or `--counter ;`

Sample

Add 1	`record_count++ ;` or `++record_count ;`
Subtract 1	`records_remaining-- ;` or `--records_remaining ;`

C has two very compact features for adding or subtracting 1 from a numeric data element or a pointer: the increment and decrement operators. They are like COBOL `ADD 1 TO` ... and `SUBTRACT 1 FROM` ... statements. Looking at the following comparisons, you can see that the COBOL and C statements are equivalent, but the C statement is more compact.

```
C:      record_count++;
COBOL:  ADD 1 TO RECORD-COUNT
```

The increment operator is useful in counting records and controlling the number of times a loop is executed.

```
C:        records_remaining--;
COBOL:  SUBTRACT 1 FROM RECORDS-REMAINING.
```

The decrement operator is useful when you need to count down.

The compiler allows you to use the increment or decrement operator as a prefix or postfix (suffix) on a data element. The effect of a prefix operator can be different than that of a postfix operator if you mix it with other operators or function calls in the same statement. If you use the increment or decrement operator by itself on a line, as in the examples above, the effect is always the same.

When you use an increment or decrement operator as a prefix, it increments or decrements the value of the data element before the rest of the expression is evaluated. When you use it as a postfix operator, the expression is evaluated first, and then the increment or decrement operation occurs.

Here is a code fragment that shows this effect:

```
int    rec_count = 8;
printf ("rec_count = %d\n", rec_count   );   /* 1 no change       */
printf ("rec_count = %d\n", --rec_count );   /* 2 decrement before */
printf ("rec_count = %d\n", rec_count   );   /* 3 no change       */
printf ("rec_count = %d\n", rec_count++ );   /* 4 increment after */
printf ("rec_count = %d\n", rec_count   );   /* 5 no change       */
```

Here are the results:

```
rec_count = 8
rec_count = 7
rec_count = 7
rec_count = 7
rec_count = 8
```

In line 2 the decrement operation occurs *before* `rec_count` is used by `printf()`, so its value appears as 7. In line 4 the increment operation occurs *after* `rec_count` is used by `printf()`, so the value of `rec_count` is the value before the increment operation, 7. The last `printf()` displays 8, which is the value of `rec_count` after the increment operation.

This can get confusing in more complex statements. The safe and simple thing to do is to increment or decrement the data item in one statement and then use the value in a following statement, as shown here:

```
rec_count++;
printf ("rec_count = %d\n", rec_count );
```

If you use these operators in statements by themselves, it does not matter whether you use them as prefix operators or postfix operators. Just be consistent.

Common Error

The data item is being incremented or decremented before or after it should be.

This occurs when you lose control of an increment or decrement operator in a complex statement. The order of evaluation is not always obvious when you look at the code. The best solution is to avoid using the increment and decrement operators in complex statements. Put them on lines by themselves.

Example

```
/*                      inc_dec.c       9/09/94                          */
#include <stdio.h>
#define MAX 30                          /* 1 declare program constant    */

main()
{
    int    i;                           /* 2 declare subscript           */
    int    line_count       = 0;
    int    records_remaining = 61;
    double sales_amt [MAX]   = { 0 };   /* 3 define array of totals      */
                                        /*   and init to zeroes          */

    line_count++ ;                      /* 4 increment by 1              */

    records_remaining-- ;               /* 5 decrement by 1              */

    for ( i = 0;  i < MAX; i++ )        /* 6 use ++ to control loop      */
    {
       printf ("sales_amt = %f \n", sales_amt [i] );
    }

    return (0);
}
```

Comments on Example

Line 1 Uses the #define preprocessor directive to declare a program constant. MAX is used to define the size of an array and to control processing the array.

Line 2 Shows the nearly universal C declaration of a subscript. By widespread convention, an int with the data name of i is used for subscripts. j and k are also commonly used for second and third subscripts.

Line 3 Declares an array of MAX occurrences (30) of a double. This is a simple one-dimensional array. The assignment = { 0 } initializes the array to zeroes.

Line 4 Incrementing an integer counter by 1 is the commonest use of the ++ operator. This is how most loop counts, record counts, line counts, and page counts are kept.

The value of line_count is 1 after this statement.

Line 5 When you want to subtract 1 from an integer, the -- operator is the most convenient way to do it.

The value of records_remaining is 60 after this statement.

Line 6 The ++ and -- operators are also commonly used to control loop sections of code. The for statement in C is equivalent to the PERFORM ... VARYING ... BY ... UNTIL ... statement in COBOL. In this particular loop i is used both as the loop counter and as a subscript. This is a common use of i.

This for statement says "perform the following statements, varying i from 0, by 1, *while* i is less than MAX." "The following statements" are delimited by the braces { and }. The only statement in this loop is a printf() statement, which prints the value of sales_amt in the array.

for statements usually vary i from zero, because subscripting in C starts at zero, not at 1. Subscripts in C are based on the offset from zero. Zero offset is the first occurrence.

The main difference between looping in COBOL and C is that COBOL performs *until* some condition is true, and C performs *while* some condition is true. This is explored more fully in Chapter 10, "Flow of Control Statements."

Absolute Value of a Number

Introduction

In business data processing there are times when you must have a positive number, as when sending data to an accounting system. If your source system allows negative numbers, you have to convert any negative numbers to positive numbers.

C has several functions for getting the absolute value of a number. There are separate functions for int, long, and double. There is no function for float. This is yet another reason for not using the float data type.

The absolute value functions are

abs()	for int (integers)
labs()	for long (long integers)
fabs()	for double (double precision floating point numbers)

The reason for multiple functions is that these number types have different sizes and internal bit layouts. int and long are binary integers of two and four bytes when the compiler has a two-byte int.[1] A double is usually eight bytes and has three portions: integer, fraction, and exponent. In the beginning C only had int, and there was only abs(). Later

---

[1] If a compiler has a four-byte int and a four-byte long (common on workstation compilers), there is no difference between abs() and labs(). You still need to use fabs() when a number is defined as a double.

`long` and `double` were added to the language, and since their internal formats are different, separate absolute value functions were also added.

The purpose of these three functions is to strip a negative sign from a number, if one exists. If the number is positive, it is not changed. You can use these functions, or you can write your own `if` statement in the following form:

```
if ( gl_amount < 0)
{
    gl_amount = gl_amount * -1.0 ;
}
```

which is equivalent to

```
gl_amount = fabs ( gl_amount ) ;
```

The function calls are shorter and more elegant. However, you must choose the correct function for the data type of the number for which you want the absolute value. If you do not match the function to the data type of your number, "results are unpredictable," to use the famous phrase.

For example, if you call `abs()` with a `double`, it will not generate a warning message on most compilers. You will get the absolute integer value of the double number and lose the fractional amount. This may be useful occasionally, but most often it is an error.

Get the absolute value of an integer (`int`).

C Keyword/Symbol/Function	`abs()`

`abs()` returns the absolute (positive) value of an `int` (integer) as an `int`. If the number is already positive, it is returned unchanged.

Syntax

```
positive_integer = abs ( some_integer ) ;
```

Sample

```
edited_hour_count = abs ( input_hour_count ) ;
```

Include File

```
#include <stdlib.h>
```
(contains function prototype for `abs()`)

See Also

`labs()`   — get the absolute value of a `long` (long integer)
`fabs()`   — get the absolute value of a `double` (double-precision floating point)

Parameter Definitions

`int positive_integer;`

Integer field that receives the return value of `abs()`.

`int some_integer;`

Integer that you want the positive value of.

Return Value

`abs()` returns the absolute (positive) value of `some_integer`. Since the return value is important in this function, you have to assign (move) it to another field or capture it on the fly. See the following example program.

Scope

Used for `int` (integer) only.

Direction

Works from right to left.

Anatomy

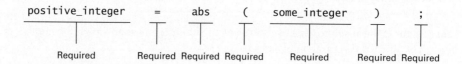

`positive_integer`

The name of the integer data item that receives the return value of `abs()`.

`=`

The assignment statement that moves the return value of `abs()` into `positive_integer`.

`abs`

The name of the function that returns the absolute value of an integer field.

`some_integer`

The name of the integer that you want to get the absolute (positive) value of.

`;`

A semicolon ends the statement.

Discussion

This function is useful when you have an integer that may have a negative value, but you require a positive value. Remember that abs() only works on int (integer). For long (long integer) numbers, you must use labs(), and for double (double-precision floating point) numbers, you must use fabs().

Common Errors

1. Decimal values are truncated.

   If you pass a double to abs() and assign the return value to a double, you will lose any decimal values. abs() returns the absolute integer value of a number. Use fabs() for numbers defined as double.

2. Number returned by abs() is different than the one passed.

   This is usually the result of an overflow condition. If you pass a number that is larger than your compiler's capacity for the int data type, the number is be corrupted. Use atol() for numbers defined as long.

Example

```
/*                    abs.c                        9/09/94              */
#include <stdio.h>
#include <stdlib.h>                            /* 1 for abs() prototype    */

main()
{

    int  edited_hr_count;
    int  input_hr_count    = -74;

    edited_hr_count = abs ( input_hr_count ) ;   /* 2 basic use of abs()     */

    if ( abs ( input_hr_count ) > 24 )           /* 3 use return value in    */
    {                                            /*    if statement          */
        printf ("More than one day needed. \n" );
    }

    return (0);
}
```

Comments on Example

Line 1 The function prototype for abs() is contained in the file stdlib.h. Including the prototype allows ANSI C to compare the parameter list you send to the function with the parameter list in the prototype. This reduces errors.

Line 2   This is the basic use of abs(). The absolute (positive) value of input_hr_count is obtained and assigned to edited_hr_count.

   The value of edited_hr_count is 74 after this statement.

Line 3   This statement evaluates the return value of the abs() function, rather than assigning the return value and then evaluating it. This is a common shortcut, although it is hard to read at first.

   The if statement is evaluated from the innermost set of parentheses outward. The call to abs() contains the innermost set of parentheses. The statement is evaluated as follows:

```
if ( abs ( input_hr_count )  > 24  )
```

becomes

```
if ( abs ( -74            )  > 24  )
```

which becomes

```
if ( 74                   )  >  24  )
```

The call to abs() is replaced by its return value, which is then evaluated by the if statement. Since 74 is greater than 24, the statement within the braces that appears after the if is executed.

   The result of that printf() statement is

```
More than one day needed.
```

Get the absolute value of a long integer (long).

C Keyword/Symbol/Function	labs()

labs() returns the absolute (positive) value of a long (long integer) as a long. If the number is already positive, it is returned unchanged.

Syntax

```
positive_long = labs ( some_long_int ) ;
```

Sample

```
edited_rec_count = labs ( input_rec_count ) ;
```

Include File

```
#include <stdlib.h>
```
   (contains function prototype for labs())

See Also

abs()   — get the absolute value of an int (integer)

`fabs()` — get the absolute value of a `double` (double-precision floating point)

Parameter Definitions

`long positive_long;`
  Long integer field that receives the return value of `labs()`.

`long some_long_int;`
  Long integer that you want the positive value of.

Return Value

`labs()` returns the absolute (positive) value of the parameter `some_long_int`. Since the return value is important in this function, you have to assign (move) it to another field.

Scope

Used for `long` (long integer) only.

Direction

Works from right to left.

Anatomy

positive_long   =   labs   (some_long_int   )   ;

Required   Required Required Required   Required   Required Required

`positive_long`
  The name of the long integer data item that receives the return value of `labs()`.

`=`
  The assignment statement that moves the return value of `labs()` into `positive_long`.

`labs`
  The name of the function that returns the absolute value of a long integer field.

`some_long_int`
  The name of the long integer that you want to get the absolute (positive) value of.

`;`
  A semicolon ends the statement.

Discussion

labs() is useful when you have a long (long integer) that may have a negative value, but you require a positive value. Remember that labs() only works on long. For int (integer) numbers you must use abs(), and for double (double-precision floating point) numbers you must use fabs().

Common Errors

1. Decimal values are truncated.

    As with abs(), if you pass a double to labs() and assign the return value to a double, you lose any decimal values. labs() returns the absolute long integer value of a number. Use fabs() for numbers defined as double.

2. Number returned by labs() is different than the one passed.

    This is usually the result of an overflow condition. It can be caused by assigning the result of labs() to an int instead of a long or by passing a double that has a value larger than a long can hold. Make sure that you're using data elements defined as long for both the passed value and the return value of labs().

Example

```
/*                      labs.c                        9/09/94              */
#include <stdio.h>
#include <stdlib.h>                              /* 1 for labs() prototype  */

main()
{

    long  edited_rec_count;
    long  input_rec_count    = -675332;
    long  second_count       = -93500;

    edited_rec_count = labs ( input_rec_count ) ;   /* 2 basic use of labs()  */

    if ( labs ( second_count ) > 86400 )            /* 3 use return value in   */
    {                                               /*   if statement          */
       printf ("More than one day needed. \n" ) ;
    }

    return (0);

}
```

Comments on Example

Line 1   The function prototype for labs() is contained in the file stdlib.h. Including the prototype allows ANSI C to compare the parameter list you send to the function with the parameter list in the prototype. This reduces errors.

Line 2 This is the basic use of `labs()`. The absolute (positive) value of `input_rec_count` is obtained and assigned to `edited_rec_count`.

The value of `edited_rec_count` is 675,332 after this statement.

Line 3 This statement evaluates the return value of the `labs()` function, rather than assigning the return value and then evaluating it.

The `if` statement is evaluated from the innermost set of parentheses outward. The call to `labs()` contains the innermost set of parentheses. The statement is evaluated as follows:

```
if ( labs ( second_count )  > 86400 )
```

becomes

```
if ( labs ( -93500       )  > 86400 )
```

which becomes

```
if ( 93500               )  > 86400 )
```

The call to `labs()` is replaced by its return value, which is then evaluated by the `if` statement. Since 93,500 is greater than 86,400, the statement within the braces that appears after the `if` is executed.

The result of that `printf()` statement is

```
More than one day needed.
```

Get the absolute value of a double **(double)**.

C Keyword/Symbol/Function	`fabs()`

`fabs()` returns the absolute value of a `double` (double-precision floating point number) as a `double`. If the number is already positive, it is returned unchanged.

Syntax

```
positive_double = fabs ( some_double ) ;
```

Sample

```
gl_amount = fabs ( fed_tax_amount ) ;
```

Include File

`#include <math.h>`   (contains function prototype for `fabs()`)

NOTE: This is not the same file as for `abs()` and `labs()`.

See Also

`abs()` — get the absolute value of an `int` (integer)
`labs()` — get the absolute value of a `long` (long integer)

Parameter Definitions

`double positive_double;`

Double-precision floating point field that receives the return value of `fabs()`.

`double some_double;`

Double-precision floating point number that you want the positive value of.

Return Value

`fabs()` returns the absolute (positive) value of `some_double`. Since the return value is important in this function, you have to assign (move) it to another field or capture it on the fly. See the following example program.

Scope

Used for `double` (double-precision floating point numbers) only.

Direction

Works from right to left.

Anatomy

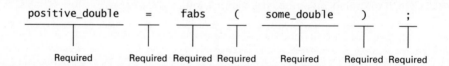

`positive_double`

The name of the `double` data item that receives the return value of `fabs()`.

`=`

The assignment statement that moves the return value of `fabs()` into `positive_double`.

`fabs`

The name of the function that returns the absolute value of a `double` field.

some_double

> The name of the `double` field that you want to get the absolute (positive) value of.

;

> A semicolon ends the statement.

Discussion

This function is useful when you have a money field defined as a `double` that may have a negative value, but you require a positive value. Accounting systems typically don't like negative numbers, but you may be storing some dollar fields in the database as negative numbers. You'll need to convert the negatives before going to the accounting system.

Remember that `fabs()` only works on data type `double`. There is no function that returns the absolute value of a `float` data type, which is another reason not to use `float`.

Common Error

Decimal values are truncated.

> If you pass a `double` to `fabs()` and assign the return value to a `long` or an `int`, you lose any decimal values. The assignment operator causes a data conversion to whatever data type is to the left of the equal sign. This means decimal places are truncated if the target field is an `int` or a `long`.

Example

```
/*              fabs.c                        9/08/94              */
#include <stdio.h>
#include <math.h>                             /* 1  for fabs() prototype   */
                                              /*    NOT SAME AS OTHERS!    */


main()
{
   double  fed_tax_amt       = -63278.14;
   double  gl_amount;
   double  total_expense_amt = -13476.50;

   gl_amount = fabs ( fed_tax_amt );          /* 2 basic use of fabs()     */

   if ( fabs ( total_expense_amt ) > 0.0 )    /* 3 use return value in     */
   {                                          /*    if statement           */
      printf ("Send this to the G/L.\n" );
   }

   return (0);
}
```

Comments on Example

Line 1   The function prototype for `fabs()` is contained in the file `math.h`. Note that this is not the same include file as for `abs()` and `labs()`. When you include the prototype, ANSI C can compare the parameter list you send to the function with the parameter list in the prototype. This reduces errors.

Line 2   This is the basic use of `fabs()`. The absolute (positive) value of `fed_tax_amt` is obtained and assigned to `gl_amount`.

   The value of `gl_amount` is `3,278.14` after this statement.

Line 3   This statement evaluates the return value of the `fabs()` function, rather than assigning the return value and then evaluating it.

   The if statement is evaluated from the innermost set of parentheses outward. The call to `fabs()` contains the innermost set of parentheses. The statement is evaluated as follows:

```
if ( fabs ( total_expense_amt )  > 0.0 )
```

becomes

```
if ( fabs ( -13,476.50          ) > 0.0 )
```

which becomes

```
if ( 13,476.50                  ) > 0.0 )
```

The call to `fabs()` is replaced by its return value, which is then evaluated by the `if` statement. Since `13,476.50` is greater than `0.0`, the statement within the braces that appears after the `if` is executed.

   The result of that `printf()` statement is

```
Send this to the G/L.
```

Summary

Basic arithmetic in C follows the same two forms COBOL does: "add to" style and "compute" style. The main difference is that C arithmetic statements are coded with symbol operators instead of keywords. C also has symbol operators for incrementing and decrementing a variable by 1. Absolute values of numbers are obtained by function calls.

   The most common arithmetic mistake in C is losing decimal values during division involving integers. This occurs because C handles intermediate results differently than COBOL. It is avoided by multiplying integers by 1.0 before dividing or by casting them as `doubles` before dividing. Another common mistake is "overflowing" integers when adding. A two-byte `int` has a positive maximum of 32,765, which makes it unsuitable for most totals. Declare total fields as `long` or `double`.

   Rounding (and truncation) in C does not conform to business rules, so a rounding function is required to get acceptable results for business. There is a rounding routine and a truncation routine in Appendix F which operate according to business rules.

"Compute" style arithmetic follows the form of a = b + c, the same form as the COBOL COMPUTE statement. C uses the symbol operators +, −, *, /, and %. The percent sign is the remainder operator.

"Add to" style arithmetic works the same way as the COBOL ADD TO construct, but you read the C statement from right to left. ADD 2 TO COUNT becomes count += 2 in C. The symbol operators are +=, −=, *=, /=, and %=. The last one is the "remainder into" operator.

Incrementing and decrementing a variable by 1 are handled by the ++ and −− symbol operators. These operators can be coded before or after the variable they modify. They are best used as single statements on lines by themselves.

Absolute values are obtained by calling one of three functions: abs(), labs(), and fabs(). To get correct results you must match the function with the data type of the variable: abs() for int, labs() for long, and fabs() for double.

CHAPTER 9

If, Case (EVALUATE), and Class Tests

Introduction

if statements in C correspond closely to IF statements in COBOL. The differences are that C uses only symbols for comparison and C's punctuation is different from COBOL's.

In both C and COBOL, the generic form of the if statement is:

IF *condition*
>   *statements-to-execute-if-true*

ELSE
>   *statements-to-execute-if-false*

Comparing strings in C requires calling the function strcmp(). Typically you code a call to strcmp() within an if statement and you also typically check only equality or inequality. strcmp() is covered in its own section following the section on the if statement.

C and COBOL II each have a case statement. A case statement tests a variable and has a block of code for each permissible value. COBOL II has the EVALUATE reserved word to accomplish this. Traditional COBOL does not have a case statement, but the effect is obtained through a nested IF statement that repeatedly tests a variable.

The class test in COBOL determines whether a data element is alphabetic or numeric. C has a dozen class test functions that determine whether a single-character is alphabetic, alphanumeric, decimal digit, printable, and so on.

Test one or more conditions.

C Keyword/Symbol/Function	if

The C if statement is basically the same as the COBOL IF statement. In C there is:

- An if keyword
- A test condition
- Action if the test condition is true
- An else, which is optional
- Other action if the test condition is false

Syntax

```
if ( one-or-more-conditional-statements )    Notice there's no semicolon
{
   one-or-more-C-statements;
}
else
{
   one-or-more-C-statements;
}                                            Notice there's no semicolon
```

Sample

```
if ( hours_worked > 40 )
{
   overtime_hours = hours_worked - 40;
}
else
{
   overtime_hours = 0;
}
```

Include File

None: if is a keyword and does not require an include file.

See Also

strcmp() — compare one literal or string to another string
switch   — case statement; evaluate multiple values for one variable

Parameter Definitions

Since if is a C keyword and not a function, the statement has no parameters.

Return Value

Since if is not a function, the statement has no return value.

Direction

Left to right, top to bottom.

Anatomy

```
if ( one-or-more-conditional-statements )    ← No semicolon
```

The first line of an if statement has the if, one or more test conditions inside a pair of parentheses, *and no semicolon at the end.* You are probably ready by now to end every line in a program with a semicolon. Don't do it on an if statement. It will cause the compiler to always execute the statements after the if.

To be complete, an if statement needs at least one statement to be executed for the true condition:

```
if ( one-or-more-conditional-statements )
{
    one-or-more-C-statements-if-true;
}
```

The first statement or statements after the conditional statements are what is executed if the conditional statements evaluate true (in this book such statements are called true-condition statements). If you have only one statement to execute when the conditions are true, the compiler does not require the curly braces shown above. If you have more than one statement to execute on true, you must use curly braces to get the desired result.

The C statements which execute when the test conditions are true can be any valid C statements. Each of these C statements *does* end with a semicolon.

As in COBOL, there is an else clause for the false condition:

```
else
{
    one-or-more-C-statements;
}
```

The else part of the if statement is optional, as it is in COBOL.

The else code executes when the if evaluates false. The statement(s) that follow the else work the same way as those that follow the if.

The C statements that execute when the test conditions are false (referred to here as false-condition statements) can be any valid C statements. Each of these C statements *does* end with a semicolon.

Discussion

As stated before, C and COBOL if statements are structurally very similar but with different symbols. While COBOL allows reserved words for relational operators in the test condition, C uses only symbol operators.

The following table compares features of if statements in both languages. The major groupings are String Comparisons, Numeric and Single Character Comparisons, Test Condition Delimiters, and Other Features.

COBOL and C If Statements Compared	
COBOL IF Statements	**C if statements**
String (alphanumeric) Comparisons	
EQUAL or =	strcmp()
NOT EQUAL or NOT =	strcmp()
Numeric and Single-Character Comparisons	
EQUAL and =	== (double equal sign)
NOT EQUAL and NOT =	!=
GREATER THAN and >	>
LESS THAN and <	<
NOT GREATER THAN	<= (less than or equal)
NOT LESS THAN	>= (greater than or equal)
GREATER OR EQUAL and >=[1]	>=
LESS OR EQUAL and <=[1]	<=
Test Condition Delimiters	
IF	if
ELSE	else
AND	&&
OR	||
IF ... THEN	n/a
Parentheses	Parentheses
Nested IF	Nested if
Terminating Nested IF with END-IF	Terminating Nested if with { }
Other Features	
NEXT SENTENCE (Do Nothing)	; (Do Nothing)
Implied Subjects	n/a
Condition-names	n/a

[1]COBOL II supports both reserved words and symbols for the "greater than or equal" and the "less than or equal" comparisons.

String Comparisons

Strings cannot be directly compared using relational operators. You must use the function `strcmp()`, which is discussed beginning on page 273.

Numeric and Single-Character Comparisons

To compare numeric and single-character data items, C uses the symbol operators on page 262, which are equivalent to reserved words in COBOL.

Comparisons of numeric and single-character data elements are done solely with symbol operators in C. These comparison operators work for

Numeric data types	`int, long, float, double`
Numeric literals	`17, 14933, 1.39943`
Single-character data type	`char` (with no square brackets)
Single-character literals	'a', '6', 'L', '@', '2' (always have single quotes)

Numeric and single comparison symbol operators are discussed individually below. If statements in both COBOL and C are shown for each.

Equal ==

Equality comparison is the same in COBOL and C, but the symbols are different. C does not have a keyword for equal; there is only the symbol operator `==` (double equal). This is the source of many problems in C programs.

The equal comparisons read

```
IF A = B
if ( a == b)
```

The single equal sign is used in C as the assign (move) operator. If you code a single equal sign in your test condition, the value of the data item on the right is assigned (moved) to the data item on the left. The resulting value will then be tested: if the value is not zero, the statement is true; if the value is zero, the statement is false. The intended comparison does not occur.

```
if ( hours_worked = 40  )
```

becomes

```
if ( 40                )
```

Since 40 is not zero, the if statement is intrepreted as true no matter what value is in hours_worked. If you wrote

```
if ( overtime_hours = 0 )
```

it would always be false, because the assignment results in a zero value, which is evaluated as false.

C's use of the double equal sign for equality causes more errors than anything else in C.

Not equal   !=

There is no keyword in C for equal and there also is no keyword for not. C uses != (called bang equal or not equal). It functions the same way as NOT = in COBOL. There is no ambiguity here as there is with the ==.

The not-equal comparisons read

```
IF A NOT = B
if ( a != b)
```

Greater than   >

COBOL allows both the > symbol and the words GREATER THAN. C allows only the symbol operator. It works the same in both languages.

The greater-than comparisons read

```
IF A > B
if ( a > b)
```

Greater Than or Equal   >=

COBOL II has the exact equivalent of this with >=. COBOL II also allows GREATER OR EQUAL. Traditional COBOL requires you to code NOT LESS THAN in order to get this comparison. The symbol operator >= is concise and uses positive logic.

The greater-than-equal comparisons read

```
IF A >= B
if ( a >= b)
```

Less Than   <

COBOL allows both the words LESS THAN and the symbol <. C allows only the symbol operator. It works the same way in both languages.

The less-than comparisons read

```
IF A < B
if ( a < b)
```

Less Than or Equal   <=

COBOL II has the exact equivalent in <=. COBOL II also allows LESS OR EQUAL. Traditional COBOL requires NOT GREATER THAN.

The less-than-equal comparisons read

```
IF A <= B
if ( a <= b)
```

Test Condition Delimiters

The if and else keywords in C work the same way as their equivalents in COBOL. They are discussed in the "Anatomy" section on page 261.

And and Or

COBOL uses AND for and and uses OR for or.

C   uses && for and and uses || for or.

```
IF A = B AND C = D
if ( a == b && c == d )

IF A = B OR C = D
if ( a == b || c == d)
```

No big sticking points here. The C statements are just not very readable.

IF . . . THEN

COBOL allows the IF...THEN construct.

C   Has no keyword for then.

```
IF A > B THEN
if ( a > b )
```

THEN is an optional part of COBOL's IF statement which is rarely used. C looks for the last matching right parenthesis after the if to terminate the test condition.

Parentheses

COBOL allows the use of parentheses to group test conditions.

C   also allows the use of parentheses.

```
IF (    A = B )   AND ( C = D   OR E = F)
if ( ( a == b ) &&   ( c == d || e == f) )
```

You use parentheses in C the same way you do in COBOL: to ensure that the ANDs (&&) and ORs (||) are grouped exactly the way you want them. It is a good rule never to allow the compiler of any language to choose which conditions to bind to the ands and ors. Notice that in the C if statement always has an outermost set of parentheses to contain all the test conditions.

C, like every other computer language, has a hierarchy of precedence of operators and symbols, as shown in Appendix E. When using C, as with every other language, you should use parentheses and not rely on the precedence hierarchy. Parentheses force the compiler to evaluate the expression based on your grouping.

Nested if Statements

COBOL allows nested IF statements.

C   also allows nested ifs.

```
IF A = B
      IF C = D
            MOVE 1 TO E
      ELSE
            MOVE 1 TO F.

if ( a == b )
{
   if ( c == d )
   {
      e = 1;
   }
   else
   {
      f = 1;
   }
}
```

The structure of the nested if is basically the same in C as in COBOL. The C construct has more symbols—the curly braces.

Terminating Nested If Statements

COBOL II uses END-IF for explicit termination of nested IF statements.

C   uses curly braces.

```
IF A = B
     IF C = D
             MOVE 1 TO E
     ELSE
             MOVE 1 TO F
     END-IF
     PERFORM 2400-GET-NEXT-RECORD.

if ( a == b )
{
  if ( c == d )
  {
    e = 1;
  }
  else
  {
    f = 1;
  }
  a2400_get_next_record();
}
```

COBOL II has added END-IF as an explicit terminator for the IF. This allows multiple true-condition statements within a nested IF, which you can't do in traditional COBOL. The END-IF construct is equivalent to the curly braces in a C if statement.

Curly Braces { } and Why You Should Use Them

Although C does not require the curly braces after an if statement, your quality of life will be much better if you *always* use curly braces in *all* if statements.

If you do not use curly braces, the C compiler *assumes* that there is only one statement to execute after the if or the else. Any statements after that are *always* executed, whether the if is true or not.

OK, you say, but I have only one statement to execute when the if is true. That may be true today, and today the if statement works properly.

But if you need to go back and add another statement to execute when true, you must *always* remember to add the curly braces or you won't get the desired results. Life is just a lot easier if you always put the curly braces after both the if and the else. This is especially helpful when you are working on a program after the unwelcome phone call in the middle of the night. Would you always remember to add braces to an if statement at two in the morning?

The following code fragments show the different outcomes with and without curly braces.

1. ```c
   if ( hours_worked > 40 )
       overtime = hours_worked - 40;
   ```

   A "bare" if statement. There's only one statement after the if, so the compiler executes it if hours_worked > 40 is true.

2. ```c
   if ( hours_worked > 40 )
       overtime = hours_worked - 40;
       overtime_flag = 'y';
   ```

   Because of the indentation, this looks like there are two statements to execute if hours_worked > 40 is true. However, the compiler doesn't see it that way. There are no curly braces, so only one statement is attached to the if. In this example, overtime_flag is *always* set to 'y'.

3. ```c
   if ( hours_worked > 40 )
   {
       overtime = hours_worked - 40;
       overtime_flag = 'y';
   }
   ```

   This if executes both statements when, and only when, hours_worked exceeds 40. The curly braces ensure that all the intended statements are attached to the if. Do it this way.

Other Features

There are several other features of if statements which do not fit neatly into the above categories. These are discussed below.

NEXT SENTENCE (Do Nothing)

COBOL uses an explicit statement for doing nothing in an IF statement.
C   uses a semicolon by itself.

```cobol
IF CUST-NO = PREV-CUST-NO AND
   BILL-NO = PREV-BILL-NO
      NEXT SENTENCE
ELSE
      PERFORM 3600-BILL-SUMMARY.
```
```

```
if        (cust_no == prev_cust_no &&
   bill_no == prev_bill_no      )
{
   ;   /* null statement – nothing happens */
}
else
{
   a3600_bill_summary();
}
```

This construct is useful when you are dealing with sorted data with multiple sort keys. It is often easier to use positive logic to determine that a break has *not* occurred and use the false case to handle a break. Otherwise you can find yourself writing multiple "and not" statements. So if key values are the same, do nothing; otherwise perform the break logic. In COBOL you use NEXT SENTENCE, and in C you place a single semicolon on a line by itself.

Implied Subjects

COBOL allows implied subjects.

C   does *not* allow implied subjects.

```
IF A = B AND NOT = C
if ( a == b && a != c)
```

If you don't repeat the first subject in COBOL, the compiler assumes it's the same subject for the second condition. If you don't repeat the first subject in C, you get a compile error.

Condition-names

COBOL allows the use of 88 level names that can be used directly in IF statements.

C   has nothing like COBOL's condition-names.

COBOL has a clear advantage here. In C you must compare a data element to another data element or a program constant.

Common Errors

1. The if statement is always true (or always false).

    This is the result of a single equal sign being used. A single equal sign causes the right operand to be assigned to the left operand. The left operand is then evaluated. If it is not zero, the if statement is true. If it is zero, the if statement is false. The intended comparison does not occur.

2. All the true-condition statements except the first one execute every time.

This is usually due to a lack of braces. If you do not put braces after an if statement, only the first statement after the if is executed when the condition is true. Always use braces.

3. All the true-condition statements execute every time.

This is typically caused by having a semicolon at the end of the conditional statement, as shown here:

```
if ( hours_worked > 40 );
{
    overtime = hours_worked - 40;
    overtime_flag = 'y';
}
```

Compilers should flag this, but most do not. The compiler interprets this as "do nothing if true." The fact that there are braces after the if does not matter to the compiler. overtime is always calculated and could be negative. overtime_flag is always set to 'y'. The compiler does not consider these statements to be part of the if.

Example

```
/*                        ifthen.c                      9/13/94                    */
#include <stdio.h>
#define PAGE_LENGTH 60

main()
{
    char    break_ind      = 'N';
    int     exempt_count   = 0;
    double  hours_worked   = 48.0;
    int     line_count     = 48;
    long    mast_cust_no   = 3124;
    long    mast_bill_no   = 17;
    char    match_ind      = 'N';
    long    mismatch_count = 0;
    double  overtime_hours = 0.0;
    long    rec_count      = 0;
    char    run_option     = 'f';
    long    tran_bill_no   = 17;
    long    tran_cust_no   = 3124;
    char    type      [31] = "exempt";
```

```
if ( rec_count == 0 )                        /* 1 compare equality        */
{                                            /*    use double equal ==    */
   printf ( "Beginning processing\n" );
   rec_count++;
}

if ( match_ind != 'Y' )                      /* 2 compare NOT equal       */
{
   mismatch_count++;
}

if ( hours_worked > 40 )                     /* 3 compare greater than    */
{
   overtime_hours = hours_worked - 40.0;
}

if ( line_count >= PAGE_LENGTH )             /* 4 compare GT or equal     */
{
   fprintf (rpt_file, "\f" );
   line_count = 0;
}

if ( mast_cust_no == tran_cust_no  &&        /* 5 "and" comparison        */
     mast_bill_no == tran_bill_no        )
{
   match_ind = 'Y';
}

if ( run_option == 'f' ||                    /* 6 "or" comparison         */
     run_option == 'F'    )                  /*    with else              */
{
   printf ("This is a Final Run \n" );
}
else
{
   printf ("This is a Trial Run \n" );
}

if ( mast_cust_no == tran_cust_no  &&        /* 7 NEXT SENTENCE           */
     mast_bill_no == tran_bill_no        )
{
   ;      /* next sentence */
}
else
{
   break_ind = 'Y';
   /* do break processing  */
}

if ( type [0] == 'e' )                       /* 8 character in a string   */
{
   exempt_count++;
}

return (0);
}
```

Comments on Example

Line 1 Is the basic equality comparison *with two (2) equal signs*. If `rec_count` is equal to zero, a message is printed and `rec_count` is incremented.

After this statement the value of `rec_count` is 1.

Line 2 Shows the not-equal comparison. This line is a single-character comparison, but the `!=` symbol operator is also used for numeric comparisons. If this statement is true, then `mis_match_count` is incremented by 1.

After this statement the value of `mis_match_count` is 1.

Line 3 Uses the greater-than symbol operator. If `hours_worked` is greater than 40, then `overtime_hours` is computed.

The value of `overtime_hours` after this statement is 8.0.

Line 4 Performs a comparison that traditional COBOL cannot: compare greater than or equal to. This is more straightforward than NOT LESS THAN. COBOL II has this same `>=` symbol, as well as GREATER OR EQUAL.

Since `line_count` is less than `PAGE_LENGTH`, the true-condition statements are not executed.

After this statement the value of `line_count` is still 48.

Line 5 Shows the use of `&&` for "and" comparison (there is no keyword in C for and). Both parts of the comparison must be true for the true-condition statement(s) to execute. In this case they do match.

After this statement the value of `match_ind` is 'Y'.

Line 6 Uses the `||` symbol operator to perform an or comparison (there is no keyword in C for or). If either condition is true, the true-condition statement(s) execute.

Since `run_option` does contain one of the compared values,

```
This is a Final Run
```

is displayed on the screen.

Line 7 Shows how to get the NEXT SENTENCE construct in C: put a single semicolon within the curly braces after the conditional part of the `if` statement.

Sometimes in programs it is much simpler to describe a condition using positive logic and then execute statements only when that condition is false. An example is the one shown here: key breaks in a sort sequence. Coding the logic to catch the sort break can involve a lot of "and not" logic, which is hard to read. It is simpler and easier to understand that if the keys are still the same, do nothing, else perform the break processing.

Line 8 Is an example of using subscript/index notation to examine a single character in a string. Offset 0 refers to the first character in the string.

Since the first character is an 'e', the value of `exempt_count` after this statement is 1.

String Comparisons

Desired Action	C Keyword/Symbol/Function

Compare two strings:
   Equal
   Not equal
	strcmp()
	strcmp()

Compares two strings and sends the result back in the return value. Format 1 tests two strings for equality and format 2 tests two strings for inequality.

Format 1

```
if ( strcmp ( left_string, right_string ) == 0 )
```

Format 2

```
if ( strcmp ( left_string, right_string ) != 0 )
```

Samples

```
Format 1   if ( strcmp ( prev_dept_code, dept_code ) == 0 )
Format 2   if ( strcmp ( prev_dept_code, dept_code ) != 0 )
```

Include File

`#include <string.h>`   (contains function prototype for `strcmp()`)

See Also

`if`   — compare numerics or single characters
`switch`   — case statement; evaluate multiple values for one variable

Parameter Definitions

`char  left_string [ n ] ;`
   A string data item or a string literal you want to compare.

`char  right_string [ n ] ;`
   The other string data item or a string literal you want to compare.

Return Value

The result of the comparison in integer form. It can be interrogated within an if statement, as shown in the samples, or it can be assigned to an integer data item. The return value is usually evaluated "on the fly" within an if statement.

If the two strings are exactly equal, strcmp() returns zero. If the left string is greater than the right string, the return value is positive. If the left string is less than the right string, the return value is negative.

Direction

Left to right.

Anatomy

```
strcmp      (     left_string,   right_string      )        ;
  |         |          |              |             |        |
Required  Required  Required       Required     Required  Required
```

strcmp
    The name of the function that compares two strings.

left_string
    A string literal or the name of a string data item to be compared.

right_string
    A string literal or the name of the other string data item to be compared.

;
    A semicolon ends the statement.

Discussion

strcmp() is almost always used inside if statements, as shown in the formats and samples above and in the example program below. The return value of strcmp() is what reveals the relationship between the two strings/string literals. When they are identical, zero is placed in return value. For the following example, assume prev_dept_code has a value of "C40" and dept_code has a value of "A16". The statement

```
if ( strcmp ( prev_dept_code, dept_code ) == 0 )
```

becomes

```
if ( strcmp ( "A16"        , "C40"   ) == 0 )
```

which becomes

```
    if ( 2                      ) == 0 )
```

The `strcmp()` call is replaced by its return value. The return value is compared to zero. It does not equal zero, so this `if` statement is false.

`strcmp()` returns three kinds of values: negative numbers, zero, and positive numbers. Which value you get depends on whether `left_string` is less than `right_string`, identical to `right_string`, or greater than `right_string`. Determining less than and greater than involve both the contents and the lengths of the strings.

Typically in business data processing, you do not have to worry about the greater-than or less-than cases. Generally you are concerned with equality or inequality. Does `pay_rcpt_code` equal "PAY"? Does `dept_id` equal `prev_dept_id`? Either it matches or it doesn't. You don't care whether it's less than or greater than. The sort sequence takes care of that.

Common Error

A compile error occurs, with a message like "`Lvalue required in function main.`"

This is the result of coding a single equal sign in an `if` statement that uses `strcmp()`. If you have a statement such as

```
    if (strcmp (pay_rcpt_code, "PAY" ) = 0 )
```

the compiler interprets this as trying to assign 0 to the return value of `strcmp()`. This is not allowed. The virtue of this error is that it is uncovered at compile time, before it can blow up your program.

Example

```
/*                      strcmp.c              09/13/94              */
#include <stdio.h>
#include <string.h>                           /* 1 for strcmp() prototype    */

main()
{
  char  dept_name      [20] = "Sales";
  long  dept_rec_count      = 0;
  long  pay_count           = 0;
  char  pay_rcpt_code  [4]  = "PAY";
  char  prev_dept_name [20] = "Sales";

  if (strcmp (prev_dept_name, dept_name ) == 0 )    /* 2 compare equality      */
  {                                                 /*   double equal ==       */
    dept_rec_count++;
  }

  strcpy ( dept_name, "Support" );                  /* 3 set up next compare    */
```

```
if (strcmp (prev_dept_name, dept_name ) != 0 )        /* 4 compare NOT equal         */
{
  strcpy ( prev_dept_name, dept_name );
  dept_rec_count = 0;
}

if (strcmp (pay_rcpt_code, "PAY" ) == 0 )             /* 5 compare string and       */
{                                                     /*    literal                 */
  pay_count++;
}

return (0);
}
```

Comments on Example

Line 1 The include file `string.h` contains the function prototypes for `strcmp()` (string compare) and `strcpy()` (string copy). A function prototype contains a template of the call parameters for the function. ANSI C uses this during compiling to check the call parameters.

Line 2 The basic string compare for equality. It uses the double equal sign. If the two strings are identical, do something(s).

After this statement the value of `dept_rec_count` is 1.

Line 3 Sets up line 4. For this example it's equivalent to reading a new record.

Line 4 Performs a test for two strings *not* being equal. If they are not equal, the return value from `strcmp()` is not zero. We don't care if one string is less than or greater than the other string, only whether they match.

Since they do not match, the return value is not zero, so the `if` statement evaluates as true. The value of `dept_name` is copied to `prev_dept_name`, and the counter is reset.

After this statement the value of `prev_dept_name` is "Support", and the value of `dept_rec_count` is 0.

Line 5 Shows the comparison of a string data element and a string literal. This is quite common. The same rules of comparison apply. This statement evaluates as true because `pay_rcpt_code` contains "PAY".

After this statement the value of `pay_count` is 1.

Case (EVALUATE) Statements

Evaluate a variable for multiple values.

C Keyword/Symbol/Function	
	switch and case

The `switch` statement in C is a form of `if` statement where multiple values for the same variable can be acted on. It is similar to, but less powerful than the EVALUATE command in COBOL II. An expression is evaluated by the `switch` keyword and then the statements following the matching `case` value are executed.

Syntax

```
switch ( expression )              Notice there's no semicolon
{
   case value_1 :                  Notice case ends with a colon
      one-or-more-C-statements ;
      break ;
   case value_2 :
      one-or-more-C-statements ;
      break ;
   default :
      one-or-more-C-statements ;

}
```

Sample

C:
```
switch ( pay_code )
{
   case 10:
      a8100_hourly_wage();
      break;
   case 20:
      a8200_weekly_wage();
      break;
   case 30:
      a8300_biweekly_wage();
      break;
   default:
      a9900_pay_code_error;
}
```

COBOL II:
```
EVALUATE PAY-CODE
   WHEN 10  PERFORM 8100-HOURLY-WAGE
   WHEN 20  PERFORM 8200-WEEKLY-WAGE
   WHEN 30  PERFORM 8300-BIWEEKLY-WAGE
   WHEN OTHER PERFORM 9900-PAY-CODE-ERROR
END-EVALUATE.
```

See Also

`if`   — compare numerics or single characters
`strcmp()`   — compare one literal or string to another string

Include File

There is no include file for `switch` because it is a keyword.

Scope

`switch` works on all integer data types and on the single-character data type. It also works on the return value of a function call when the function returns an integer data type or a single character. It does not work on strings or floating point numbers.

Direction

Works from top to bottom and left to right.

Anatomy

```
switch ( expression )  ◄──────────  Notice there's no semicolon
{
    case value_1 :  ◄──────────  Notice case ends with a colon
        one-or-more-C-statements;
        break ;
    case value_2 :
        one-or-more-C-statements;
        break ;
    default :
        one-or-more-C-statements;
}
```

`switch`

The keyword that begins a `switch` statement.

expression

An integer data element, a single-character data element, or a function call that returns one of those types. The return value of the function call is substituted for *expression*.

`case`

The keyword that begins a block of instructions based on one value for *expression*.

value_1/value_2, etc.

An integer literal or a single-character literal that is compared to the value of *expression*. It can also be a `#define` that defines an integer literal or a single-character literal. The integer value can be negative.

one-or-more-C-statements

Executed if the value of *expression* is the same as *value_1*, *value_2*, and so on.

`break`

The keyword that tells `switch` to go to the next statement after `switch`. If you don't have `break` within a `case`, the program continues within the `switch` statement and executes the logic for each subsequent `case`, without testing the `case`, until `break`, `default`, or the end of the `switch` is encountered. If there is a `default`, that logic is also executed.

`default`

> The keyword that tells `switch` to execute a set of C statements when none of the `case` conditions has been met. `default` is not required, but if you don't code it you will not know if a condition slipped through your `switch` statement.

Discussion

Two key facts about `switch` are (1) it only deals with integer or single-character data types, and (2) the compiler does not require `break` statements, but most business data processing does.

The EVALUATE statement in COBOL II is a broader implementation of the case construct than C's `switch` statement. EVALUATE is not restricted to certain data types and can evaluate multiple conditions in one statement. The case construct in COBOL II is more powerful than the one in C. Traditional COBOL does not have a case construct. To get the effect of a case statement, you must code a nested IF statement.

In the C `switch` statement the data element or return value to be evaluated must be either an integer value or a single-character value (no strings). The values don't have to start with 1. Integer values can be negative. They also don't have to be in numerical or character sequence, though readability requires such a sequence.

You can stack `case` statements in a `switch` statement:

```
switch ( rate_variance )
{
   case -1:
   case 2:
   case 4:
      rate_code = 1;
      break;

   case 8:
      rate_code = 2;
      break;

   default
      rate_code = 4;
}
```

This fragment shows `rate_code` set to 1 when `rate_variance` has a value of –1, 2, or 4. Use this technique when you have multiple values that require the same action.

Also note that the C statements within a `case` can include function calls, as is shown in the example program below. Any valid C statement can be used inside a `case`.

Final Words of Wisdom

1. Always code `break`.

    This prevents the program from "falling through."

2. Always code `default`.

You always want to catch unrecognized values, if only to generate a warning message.

3. Always use `default` to identify unrecognized values.

Don't use `default` for common processing; use it for error processing.

Common Errors

1. The default always executes.

Common sources of this error are as follows:

a. No `break` statement or missing `break` statements.
Not having any break statements causes all the `case` statements to execute, as well as the `default`. Any `case` statement that does not have a `break` causes the program to continue through subsequent cases. It executes the logic for all subsequent cases and the `default` if there is no `break` statement.

b. Variable being used for `switch` is a `double` or a string.
This usually causes the `switch` variable to be evaluated as zero. If you have a case for zero, that case executes. Otherwise, only the `default` executes.

c. Negative value in integer variable used by `switch`, and no negative `case` statements.
`switch` does not convert integers to positive values. If there are possible negative values in the data, you need to code `case` statements with negative numbers.

2. Multiple `case` statements are executing.

This is usually due to one or more missing `break` statements. Every `case` statement needs a `break` statement.

3. There is a compiler warning about nonportable or suspicious pointer conversion.

If you use a string variable as the `switch` variable, you may get one or more warning messages. If you execute the program, the `switch` statement will probably fall through to the `default`.

Example

```
/*              switch.c                09/13/94                */

#include <stdio.h>
#include <string.h>                /* 1 for strcpy() prototype   */
#include <ctype.h>                 /* 2 for toupper() prototype  */

#define ERR_READ   53              /* 3 error message constants  */
#define ERR_UPDATE 59
#define ERR_DELETE 71
```

```
main()
{
    char  err_code          = 'f';
    char  err_desc    [31];
    long  err_no            = 8;
    long  rate_code;
    long  remaining_years = 2;
    long  severity_code;
    char  step_name  [5];
    long  step_number       = 3;

    switch ( step_number )                          /* 4 basic switch/case          */
    {
        case 1:
            strcpy (step_name, "PAY" );
            break;

        case 2:
            strcpy (step_name, "REC" );
            break;

        case 3:
            strcpy (step_name, "SUM" );
            break;

        default:
            strcpy (step_name, "???" );
    }

    switch ( remaining_years )                      /* 5 same action for            */
    {                                               /*   multiple values            */
        case 1:
        case 2:
        case 3:
            rate_code = 1;
            break;

        case 4:
            rate_code = 2;
            break;

        case 5:
            rate_code = 3;
            break;

        default:
            rate_code = 4;
    }

    switch ( err_no )                               /*  6 use #defines in switch    */
    {
        case ERR_READ:
            printf ( "ERROR reading \n" );
            severity_code = 3;
            break;
```

```
      case ERR_UPDATE:
        printf ( "ERROR updating \n" );
        severity_code = 4;
        break;

      case ERR_DELETE:
        printf ( "ERROR deleting \n" );
        severity_code = 5;
        break;

      default:
        printf ( "ERROR UNKNOWN ERROR \n" );
        severity_code = 9;
  }

  switch ( toupper (err_code) )            /* 7  use return value of      */
  {                                        /*     function call; switch on */
    case 'E':                              /*     a single character       */
      strcpy (err_desc, "Error" );
      break;

    case 'F':
      strcpy (err_desc, "Fatal" );
      break;

    case 'W':
      strcpy (err_desc, "Warning" );
      break;

    default:
      strcpy (err_desc, "???" );

  }
  return (0);

}
```

Comments on Example

Line 1   The include file `string.h` contains the function prototype for `strcpy()` (string copy), which is used later in the program. A function prototype contains a template of the call parameters for the function. ANSI C uses this during compiling to check the call parameters.

Line 2   `ctype.h` contains the function prototype for `toupper()`, which is used later in the program.

Line 3   A sample set of integer constants, defined by #define statements. These are used in line 6 to provide values for the `case` statements in a `switch`.

Line 4   Represents the basic `switch/case` example. An integer variable (a `long` in this example) is tested for the values 1, 2, and 3 to determine what step a process is in. Note that there is a **break** after each **case**. This causes control to be transferred to the statement after **switch** when one of the conditions is satisfied. Note also that there is a **default** to catch any value of **step_number** not caught by one of the **case** statements above it.

A **switch** statement only needs one set of curly braces to contain the whole statement. After this statement the value of **step_name** is "SUM".

Line 5   Shows one of the real virtues of **switch**: Multiple values can be used for one set of action statements. If **remaining_years** is equal to 1, 2, or 3, then **rate_code** is set to 1. This statement shows the **case** values in continuous numerical sequence, but that is not required. The values could be 10, 17, and 21 and they could still be stacked over the same set of action statements.

After this statement the value of **rate_code** is 1.

Line 6   Demonstrates that **case** values do not have to be hard coded. This is highly desirable in production systems. In this example the **case** statements use **#define** names that represent integer values. In a production system these error codes would be put in a separate include file. Both the processing programs and the error-handling program would include that file, and all the programs would use error names rather than error numbers. It is especially important in **switch** statements in error handler functions to have a **default**; not using it defeats the purpose of the error handler if you don't catch all the errors.

After this statement the value of **severity_code** is 9. An error number was used which was not in the list of case values and therefore the **default** was executed.

Line 7   Runs a **switch** using the return value of a function call. In this example the function **toupper()** returns a single character. After executing **toupper()** the compiler evaluates the single character in return value and passes control to the appropriate **case** statement.

You can also use a function call that returns an integer value. It does not matter to the compiler whether it is a library function or one you have written. The return value is the only thing that's important.

The compiler, as always, evaluates the statement from the innermost set of parentheses to the outermost. It evaluates the statement as follows:

```
switch ( toupper (err_code ) )
```

becomes

```
switch ( toupper ( 'f'     ) )
```

which becomes

```
switch ( 'F'               )
```

The **toupper()** function call is replaced by its return value. **switch** then switches based on the return value. The second **case** will match.

After this statement the value of **err_desc** is "Fatal".

Class Test

Desired Action	C Keyword/Symbol/Function
Test a single character:	Call this function:
Alphabetic	isalpha (single_character_field)
Alphanumeric	isalnum (single_character_field)
ASCII character range	isascii (single_character_field)
ASCII control character	iscntrl (single_character_field)
C language white space	isspace (single_character_field)
Decimal digit	isdigit (single_character_field)
Hexadecimal digit	isxdigit (single_character_field)
Lowercase letter	islower (single_character_field)
Printable character	isprint (single_character_field)
Printable character but not a space	isgraph (single_character_field)
Punctuation character	ispunct (single_character_field)
Uppercase letter	isupper (single_character_field)

is___() is a set of single-character test routines. The is___() functions test a single character against a class of characters. Each one tests the character against a particular list. If single_character_field is in that list, the is___() returns a nonzero value (true). Otherwise, it returns zero (false).

NOTE: For discussion purposes the above functions are referred to generically as is___().

Syntax

```
test_result = is___ ( single_character_field ) ;
```

Samples

```
test_result = isalpha ( middle_init ) ;
test_result = isdigit ( formatted_digit ) ;
```

Include File

#include <ctype.h> (contains function prototype or macro code for is___() routines)

See Also

The is___() functions are primarily used for character string processing, which this book does not emphasize.

Parameter Definitions

```
int    test_result;
```
Integer field to receive the return value of is____().

```
char    single_character_field;
```
A single-character field you want to test. It can be a single character from a string referenced by subscripting. See the example program on page 287.

Return Value

The is____() functions return either zero or a nonzero value, based on the content of the character that is passed. is____() returns a nonzero value (1 on most compilers) if the character tested is in the list for that test. A nonzero value evaluates as true; otherwise, is____() returns a zero, which evaluates as false.

Table of Values for is____() Functions		
Function	**Test**	**Valid Values**
isalnum()	Alphanumeric	0-9, a-z, A-Z
isalpha()	Alphabetic	a-z, A-Z
isascii()	ASCII character	hex 00 – hex 7f
iscntrl()	Control character	hex 00 – hex 1f and hex 7f
isdigit()	Decimal digit	0-9
isgraph()	Printable & not space	hex 21 – hex 7e
islower()	Lowercase	a-z
isprint()	Printable	hex 20 – hex 7e
ispunct()	Punctuation	! " # $ % ' ( ) * + , - . / : ; < = > ? [\ ] ^ _ { | } ~ space
isspace()	C white space	space, tab, line-feed hex 20, hex 09, hex 0a
isupper()	Uppercase	A-Z
isxdigit()	Hexadecimal digit	0-9, a-f, A-F

Scope

Used for single characters only.

Direction

Works from right to left.

Anatomy

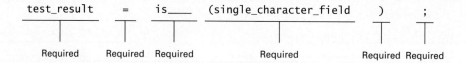

test_result
: The name of the integer data item that receives the return value of the is____() function.

=
: The assignment operator that moves the return value of is____() into **test_result**.

is____
: The name of the function to test a single character. is____() is a generic description for isalpha(), isdigit(), ispunct(), and so on.

single_character_field
: The name of the single-character data item to be tested.

;
: A semicolon ends the statement.

Discussion

The is____() routines can be implemented by a compiler as functions or macros or both. A macro is one or more lines of code that are substituted into the program at compile time. Macros are, in effect, copy members with parameters. From the programmer's point of view, there is no difference between function and macro implementation of the is____() routines. For simplicity they are referred to as functions in this discussion.

The is____() functions were originally written to handle text processing on a character-by-character basis. This is not usually a requirement in business data processing.

You should not have to use these functions very often in a business environment. The assumption is that for C to be productive in a business DP environment you should use a screen-handling package, a database package, and a report-writing package. The screen handling package should take care of editing input and thus cover input character processing.

However, sometimes you will need one or more of these. One example is in the dollar_comma() routine in the Appendix F. isdigit() is useful in that function to count the numeric digits being formatted.

The syntax and sample sections above show a return value being assigned to a variable. In practice the is____() calls are coded inside if statements, and the return value is evaluated within the if. The return value is seldom, if ever, assigned to a variable. See the example program below.

Common Error

Nothing changes after the call to is_____().

> If you do not assign the return value of a call to an is_____() function, nothing is affected. The is_____() functions are tests only. You have to use the return value to make something happen. If you code
>
> ```
> isspace (middle_init);
> ```
>
> a return value is produced but not assigned or used. Nothing happens.

Example

```
/*                        is_____.c              9/13/94                    */

#include <stdio.h>
#include <ctype.h>                       /* 1 for is_____() prototypes       */
#include <string.h>                      /* 2 for strlen()  prototype        */

main()
{
   char  edit_string [31] = "  111222333.99" ;
   int   i               = 0;
   int   length          = 0;
   int   space_count     = 0;
   int   digit_count     = 0;

   length = strlen (edit_string);        /* 3 length of edit_string          */

   for ( i = 0; i < length; i++ )        /* 4 loop through edit_string       */
   {
      if ( isspace (edit_string [i]) != 0 )   /* 5 explicit compare in 'if'   */
      {                                       /*    test for space            */
         space_count++;
      }
      if ( isdigit (edit_string [i]) )   /* 6 common use of is_____()        */
      {                                  /*    in an if statement            */
         digit_count++;
      }
   }

   return (0);
}
```

Comments on Example

Line 1 The include file `ctype.h` contains the function prototypes and the macro code for the `is____()` routines. We don't have to worry about whether the compiler implements these as macros or functions, because they operate the same way in either case.

Line 2 The include file `string.h` contains the function prototype for the `strlen()` function, which is used later in the program. A function prototype contains a template of the call parameters for the function. ANSI C uses this during compiling to check the call parameters.

Line 3 Gets the length of `edit_string` so it can be used to control the loop processing in line 4. After this statement the value of `length` is 16.

Line 4 This `for` statement says "perform the following statements," varying `i` from 0 by 1, while `i` is less than `length`. "The following statements" are delimited by the braces `{` and `}`. There are two `if` statements in this loop. `for` statements are discussed in detail in Chapter 10, "Flow of Control Statements."

This `for` statement goes through `edit_string` character-by-character while `i` is less than `length`. The value of `length` is 16. It starts with a value of zero for `i` because strings (and other arrays) are referenced by offset not occurrence number. The first character in a string is at offset zero. The `for` statement goes from offset 0 through offset 15, which corresponds to the 1st through 16th occurrences of characters in `edit_string`. When `i` is incremented to 16, the loop stops.

The code following the `for` statement performs actions on the character in the string that `i` subscripts.

Line 5 Tests whether the current character is a space. The `if` statement is evaluated from the innermost set of parentheses outward. Assume the value of `i` is 2:

```
if ( isspace ( edit_string [i] ) != 0 )
```

becomes

```
if ( isspace ( edit_string [2] ) != 0 )
```

which becomes

```
if ( isspace ( ' '          ) != 0 )
```

which becomes

```
if ( 1                      ) != 0 )
```

The `isspace()` function call is replaced by its return value. Since `edit_string [2]` does contain a space, `isspace()` returns 1 (nonzero value = true). Since 1 does not equal 0, the following line increments `space_count`.

This `if` statement uses negative logic to ask a positive question. It is explicit but awkward. See the next line for positive logic.

Line 6 Provides the more common and more readable version of the `is____()` test. The statement

```
if ( isdigit ( edit_string [i] ) )
```

can be read as "if it's a digit." This if statement is unusual because it does not have a comparison operator in it. It only tests a condition for true or false. The condition is the return value of the isdigit() call. Assume the value of i is 7. This if statement is evaluated from the innermost set of parentheses outward as follows:

```
if ( isdigit ( edit_string [i] ) )
```

becomes

```
if ( isdigit ( edit_string [7] ) )
```

which becomes

```
if ( isdigit ( 2              ) )
```

which becomes

```
if ( 1                        )
```

The call to isdigit() is replaced by its return value, which is 1 because edit_string [7] contains the digit 2. A return value of 1 is not zero and therefore true. The following statement is executed and increments digit_count.

Summary

This chapter covered if statements, case statements, and class tests.

The structure of if statements in C is basically the same as in COBOL. Both languages have if, else, and, or, and comparison operators. C uses symbol operators exclusively for its comparison operators, where COBOL can use either symbols or reserved words. You can write nested if statements in both languages. Parentheses have the same effect in C and in COBOL. While C does not have keywords equivalent to NEXT SENTENCE, you can get the same effect with a semicolon on a line by itself.

The biggest difference is that C uses a double equal sign for equality comparison. This is complicated by the fact that if you incorrectly use a single equal sign in an if statement, it will compile cleanly but it will not generate the intended comparison. This is the source of many errors in C programs.

Another difference is that the comparison operators are used with numeric data types and the single character data type, but not with strings. To compare strings you call the strcmp() function inside an if statement.

C has a case statement, in which blocks of statements are executed when a condition is matched. The switch, case, break, and default keywords are used for a switch statement in C. The switch statement is equivalent to EVALUATE in COBOL II, but switch is not as powerful.

There is a richer set of class tests in C than in COBOL, but they all operate on a single character at a time. There are a dozen tests which cover every reasonable classification of a character. They are not used frequently in business systems, but are valuable when needed.

CHAPTER **10**

Flow of Control Statements

Introduction

PERFORM, CALL, GO TO, GOBACK and STOP RUN are the reserved words in COBOL for controlling the flow of logic in a program. C has the same functionality and a few extras to boot.

Two common variants of PERFORM have very similar counterparts in C. PERFORM ... VARYING ... UNTIL has a close cousin in the C for statement. PERFORM ... UNTIL is much like the C while statement.

COBOL's basic PERFORM format is the same as calling a function in C. Functions in C are hybrids that can act like COBOL paragraphs or COBOL subprograms.

COBOL's CALL reserved word also relates to calling a function in C. Calling functions is discussed in Chapter 11, "Calling Functions (Subprograms)."

Getting to the bottom of a loop without terminating the loop is handled by the continue keyword. It is equivalent to coding a GO TO EXIT in COBOL. continue has the additional virtue of not being able to go anywhere else.

C also allows a loop to be terminated completely from inside the loop with the break keyword. Traditional COBOL can't do this. If it could, it would mean coding a statement inside the PERFORM loop that directly transferred control to the statement *after* the PERFORM statement. You can do this in COBOL II with a NEXT SENTENCE in an in-line PERFORM.

GOBACK and STOP RUN equivalents exist in C, with more features than their COBOL counterparts. return can function the same as either GOBACK or STOP RUN and can pass back a value in almost any data format. exit() returns control directly to the operating system, as STOP RUN does. exit() can also pass a value to the operating system.

The C `goto` is completely unnecessary. It is included in this book to acknowledge that it exists and so I can tell you not to use it. It is unnecessary because C structured programs can do everything they need to do without using `goto`.

The following table shows the common COBOL flow of control statements and their equivalents in C.

Desired Action	C Keyword/Symbol/Function COBOL Equivalent
Execute a loop while a condition is true, while varying the condition	`for` `PERFORM ... VARYING ... UNTIL`
Execute a loop while a condition is true	`while` `PERFORM ... UNTIL`
Call a function which has no parameters	*call a function* `PERFORM`
Call a function with parameters	*call a function* (see Chapter 11) `CALL`
Go to the bottom of a loop	`continue` `GO TO` exit of `PERFORM`
Terminate a loop and go to the following statement	`break` Terminate a `PERFORM`[1]
Go to	`goto` `GO TO`
Return control to calling function or to operating system	`return()` `GOBACK`
Return control to operating system	`exit()` `STOP RUN`

[1]In a COBOL II in-line PERFORM, NEXT SENTENCE has the same effect as `break` in C if the in-line PERFORM has no periods. In traditional COBOL you cannot terminate a loop from within the loop. It is the equivalent of terminating a performed paragraph in the middle and transferring control to the statement following the PERFORM.

This chapter covers all the topics above except for calling a function which has parameters. That is the subject of Chapter 11, "Calling Functions (Subprograms)."

Execute a loop, while a condition is true, while varying the condition (PERFORM ... VARYING ... UNTIL).

C Keyword/Symbol/Function	for

for is a loop statement similar to the COBOL PERFORM ... VARYING ... UNTIL. It sets an initial value, executes a loop, varies a value, than checks a condition to see if it should terminate.

SEMICOLONS !!　　　*NO SEMICOLONS !!*

Syntax　　　↓　　　↓　　　↓↓

```
for ( initialization_expr ; while_true_expr ; varying_expr  )
{
   one_or_more_c_statements_to_execute;
}
```

Sample   **COBOL II Equivalent**

```
for ( i = 0; i < 10; i++ )    PERFORM VARYING I FROM 0 BY 1
{                                     UNTIL I = 10
   dept_tot = 0;                   MOVE 0 TO DEPT-TOT
}                             END-PERFORM.
```

Include File

None. for is a keyword and therefore does not require an include file.

See Also

break	— terminate a for or while loop
continue	— transfer control to the bottom of a for or while loop without terminating the loop
while	— PERFORM ... UNTIL equivalent
call a function	— PERFORM paragraph equivalent

Parameter Definitions

for is a keyword, not a function, and therefore has no parameters.

Return Value

for is not a function and therefore has no return value.

Direction

Left to right.

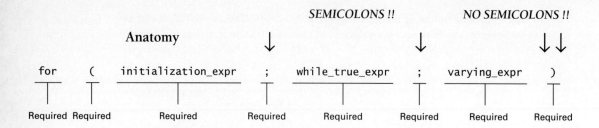

for

> The keyword that is analogous to PERFORM . . . VARYING . . . UNTIL. It executes a set of instructions in a loop. Notice that it does *not* end with a semicolon.

initialization_expression

> Equivalent to VARYING . . . FROM in PERFORM. initialization_expression is a C expression that initializes one or more data elements. It typically sets a counter to zero. (C counts from zero most of the time.)

;

> A semicolon follows initialization_expression.

while_true_expression

> Evaluated and resolved in the same way as an if statement. It results in either a nonzero value (true) or zero (false). It operates under the same rules as the C if statement.
>   In the statement
>
>   for (i = 0; i < 10; i++)
>
> i < 10 is the while_true_expression. In effect it becomes "if i < 10, proceed with the following statements."
>
> while_true_expression is basically analogous to UNTIL *condition-1* in PERFORM. The difference is that in COBOL you say execute *until:*
>
>   SUBSCRIPT > TABLE_SIZE.
>
> while in C you say execute *while:*
>
>   subscript < table_size
>
> *While* means execute while true and *until* means execute until true. See the "Discussion" section on page 295 for additional discussion of *while* versus *until.*

;

> A semicolon follows while_true_expression.

varying_expression

> Equivalent to VARYING . . . BY in PERFORM. for statements, typically use the increment operator (++) or decrement operator (--) to move a subscript or counter up or down

by 1. However, as in COBOL, you can vary the subscript or counter by any value you want to use.

`varying_expression` is executed after the last statement within the loop, just as `VARYING` is in COBOL. If you use `continue` in a `for` loop to get to the bottom of the loop, `varying_expression` still executes. `continue` is equivalent to a `GO TO EXIT` in a COBOL PERFORMed paragraph.

No semicolon after `varying_expression`

This seems inconsistent, but the compiler will generate an error if you code a semicolon after `varying_expression`.

No semicolon after the right parenthesis

`for`, `if`, `while`, and `switch` *do not* have semicolons after the parentheses that follow them. Each one is a block statement command: They are followed by one or more C statements contained by curly braces.

```
{
    one_or_more_c_statements_to_execute;
}
```

The loop code immediately follows the `for` statement. It consists of one or more C statements enclosed in curly braces. In a COBOL II in-line `PERFORM`, these statements would immediately follow the `PERFORM` and be terminated by an `END-PERFORM`. In traditional COBOL the statements in the loop would be in the paragraph being performed. In C they immediately follow the `for` statement. Whatever you want to do in the loop is put in here. The curly braces are necessary the same way they are in an `if` statement: If there are no curly braces, the compiler assumes the `for` has only one statement in the loop.

Discussion

The structure of `for` is much like the in-line `PERFORM ... VARYING` in COBOL II and different from performing a paragraph in traditional COBOL. But, aside from the fact that you don't have to turn pages to find out what's being done in the loop, `for` operates nearly identically to `PERFORM ... VARYING`.

Here is how the parts of a `for` statement compare to COBOL:

Parts of **for** Statement	COBOL Equivalents
for	PERFORM
initialization_expression	VARYING *identifier-1* FROM *value-1*
while_true_expression	UNTIL *condition-1*
varying_expr	BY *value-2*

The big difference is the sense of *while* compared to the sense of *until*. "While true" is equivalent to "until false." The only problem with this is that the COBOL expression is "until true." Translating the thought process from `PERFORM ... VARYING` to `for` requires using the inverse of the `PERFORM` condition.

Another consideration is that subscripts in C begin from zero rather than 1. This is because C subscripts count offsets from zero rather than occurrence number. The first occurrence in an array in C has a subscript of zero. Here is an example of array definition and subscript values to illustrate:

COBOL Table Definition	C Array Declaration
| ```
01  TABLE.
    05  DEPT-TOT  OCCURS 10
                  PIC S9(6)V99.
``` | `double dept_tot [10];` |

Attributes	COBOL	C
Occurrences	10	10
Subscript range	1–10	0–9
Subscript of first occurrence	1	0
Subscript of tenth occurrence	10	9

The value of a subscript in C is always 1 less than the occurrence number. Because of this, and the fact that we are using *while* instead of *until*, the *while* test is usually expressed as "while sub < max," as shown here:

COBOL	C
`UNTIL PAY-SUB > TABLE-SIZE`	(while) `pay_sub < table_size`
`UNTIL SUB-1 > 10`	(while) `sub_1 < 10`

`for` evaluates its while-true condition before executing the first time, just as `PERFORM ... VARYING ... UNTIL` checks the until condition before it executes. `for` will not execute the loop at all if `while_true_expression` is false.

Array Initialization

One of the primary uses of `PERFORM ... VARYING ... UNTIL` in COBOL is the initialization of arrays (tables) in `WORKING-STORAGE`. (This requirement is essentially eliminated if you
```

use INITIALIZE in COBOL II.) Typically an array has packed fields that must be initialized to zero. This type of initialization is not necessary in C for two reasons.

First, every C numeric data type has the same byte configuration for a value of zero: hex zeroes (LOW-VALUES). COBOL, on the other hand, has a different byte configuration for zeroes for each numeric type: numeric display, binary, packed, short-precision floating point, and long-precision floating point.

Second, C allows array initialization at compile time. If you use = { 0 } as an initial assignment, all members of the array are set to zero. This works for single-dimensional arrays, multidimensional arrays, and arrays of structures, as shown here:

```
double  div_sales_tot  [10]              = { 0 };

double  dept_sales_tot [MAX_DEPTS] [50] = { 0 };

struct
{
    long     sales_count;
    double   tax_total;
    double   net_sales_total;
    double   labor_total;
}
report_total [5] [12] [8] = { 0 };
```

CAUTION: Some, but not all, ANSI C compilers initialize program memory to zeroes when the program starts. If this were part of the ANSI C standard, I would recommend letting the compiler do it. This is not the case, however. It is simple to initialize arrays when you declare them. Do it.

Common Errors

1. Only one statement seems to be in the loop.

   This is typically due to a lack of curly braces after a for statement that has more than one statement *intended* to be in the loop:

   ```
   for ( i = 0; i < 10; i++ )
       sales_amt    += 100.0;
       dept_tot [i] = sales_amt;
   ```

   This statement has been indented to show two statements in the loop, but the compiler doesn't see it that way. Since there are no curly braces, the compiler includes in the loop only the first statement after the for. Use curly braces.

2. The program goes beyond the end of the array.

   This problem often has the same cause as the first one. The last time the subscript is incremented it gets a value beyond the end of the array. If a subsequent statement uses the subscript, it is using a value beyond the end of the array. Results are unpredictable.

3. The loop does not execute.

This is usually due to a hard-to-find error: a semicolon on the end of the `for` statement. Compilers should always issue a warning on this, but few do. In the beginning, it is fairly easy to write a statement like this:

```
for ( i = 0; i < 10; i++ );
{
    printf ("Dept total = %f \n", dept_tot [i] );
}
```

The semicolon on the end of the `for` line tells the compiler that the only thing to do in this `for` statement is to increment i from 0 by 1 while i is less than 10. The only result of the `for` statement is to change the value of i from 0 to 10 (incrementing to 10 stops the loop). The `for` finishes and proceeds to the next statement, which uses i with a value out of range of the array.

The next statement is a `printf()`, which will only execute once, with an incorrect value for i. Results are unpredictable.

4. You receive a compile error message something like

```
For statement missing ; in function xxxx
```

If you code a for statement with commas instead of semicolons, as in

```
for ( i = 0, i < 10, i++ )
```

you get an error message from the compiler. Use semicolons (two only) inside the `for` statement.

5. You receive a compile error message something like

```
Expression syntax in function xxxx.
```

If you code three semicolons in a for statement, as in

```
for ( i = 0; i < 10; i++; )
```

you get a compile error message. There is no semicolon after the varying expression in a `for` statement.

Example

```
/*                      forloop.c              9/16/94                    */
#include <stdio.h>
#include <ctype.h>                             /* 1 for isdigit() prototype    */
#define PERIOD '.'                             /* 2 replace punctuation        */

main()
```

```
{
   double  dept_tot     [10] = { 0 };        /* 3 array of doubles          */
   long    digit_count      = 0;
   char    edited_amt   [12] = " 111222.34";
   int     i;
   int     j;
   double  net_amt [5] [10] = { 0 };         /* 4 two dimensional array     */
   double  sales_amt        = 0;

   for ( i = 0; i < 10; i++ )                /* 5 load array                */
   {
      sales_amt += 100.0;

      dept_tot [i] = sales_amt;
   }
   for ( i = 0; i < 10; i++ )                /* 6 display array             */
   {
      printf ("Dept total = %f \n", dept_tot [i] );
   }

   for ( i = 0; edited_amt [i] != PERIOD; i++ )   /* 7 use for on a string  */
   {
      if ( isdigit (edited_amt [i] ) )
      {
         digit_count++;
      }
   }

   for ( i = 0; i < 5; i++ )                 /* 8 display 2-D array         */
   {
      for ( j = 0; j < 10; j++ )            /* 9 nested for                */
      {
         printf ("net_amt = %f \n", net_amt [i] [j] );
      }
   }

   return (0);
}
```

Comments on the Example

Line 1   The file ctype.h contains the function prototype or macro definition for isdigit(), which is used later in the program.

Line 2   Uses a #define to create a name for the period character used in line 6. C has too much punctuation for human comprehension as it is. Use #define to make code more readable.

Line 3   Creates an array (table) of 10 occurrences for dept_tot and initializes it to zeroes. The numbers are of type double because you want to preserve decimal portions of numbers. C's array declaration is more compact than COBOL's. If COBOL could do it directly, the equivalent line would look like

```
01 DEPT-TOT       PIC S9(7)V99   OCCURS 10.
```

Line 4   Defines a two-dimensional array and initializes it to zeroes. This array will be used to show how nested `for` statements work. Arrays (tables) are discussed in Chapter 12.

Line 5   Shows the use of a `for` statement to add to values in an array. `i` is the usual data name for an `int` or `long` that is used as a subscript in a C program. This statement also shows the common C method of processing arrays by starting at zero. Again, this is because C subscripting starts from zero rather than 1. C loops generally read as "from zero while subscript < max." The first occurrence is the "zeroth" offset and the last occurrence is the "max − 1" offset.

`i = 0` is the initialization expression, and it assigns a value of zero to `i`. This is exactly the same as the `VARYING ... FROM` phrase in COBOL.

`i < 10` is the while-true expression. Before `for` executes the first time and after every iteration, `i` is tested to see if it is less than `10`. If it is, the loop continues. If not, the loop terminates and control is transferred to the next statement after the `for`. This is equivalent to the COBOL `UNTIL` phrase, with the difference between *until* and *while*, as explained in the "Discussion" section above.

`i++` (with no semicolon) is the varying expression. It is the same as a `VARYING I BY 1` phrase in COBOL.

The two statements inside the braces are executed every time the `for` iterates. The first statement adds `100.0` to `sales_amt`. The second statement

```
dept_tot [i] = sales_amt;
```

assigns the value of `sales_amt` to the current subscripted occurrence of `dept_tot`.

This loop will stop after 10 iterations—offset 0 through offset 9.

Line 6   Uses the same `for` statement conditions. This time the loop is displaying the data. Note that the `printf()` parameter, `dept_tot [i]`, picks the occurrence of `dept_tot` based on the value of the subscript `i`.

Line 7   Demonstrates another common use of `for`: string processing. In C a string is really an array of characters. A string can be referenced as a whole by using the name with no qualifier, which makes it seem like it's not really an array. A string can also be referenced character by character by specifying a subscript. That's what this `for` statement does.

This `for` statement wants to know how many digits are to the left of the decimal point in a number that has been moved to a string. A formatting routine would want to know this.

The initialization and varying expressions are the same as previously discussed. The while-true expression

```
edited_amt [i] != PERIOD;
```

says to continue the loop as long as the current character in `edited_amt` is not a period. Use of the `#define` makes this more readable than

```
edited_amt [i] != '.' ;
```

The `if` statement in the loop checks a character for being a decimal digit and adds 1 to `digit_count` if it is.

Lines 8 and 9   Show a use of a nested `for` statement to go through a two-dimensional array.

Line 8 uses the i subscript to control iteration through the first level of the array defined on line 4. The first level occurs five times, so the while expression reads i < 5. For each value of i between 0 and 4, the second `for` statement executes.

Line 9 contains the only statement in the `for` loop of line 8. This statement is also a loop. It goes through the second level of the array, which occurs 10 times. This for statement uses j as a subscript. It varies j from 0 by 1 while j < 10. It displays 10 lines for each value of i.

Execute a loop while a condition is true (`PERFORM ... UNTIL`).

C Keyword/Symbol/Function	`while`

while executes one or more C statements in a loop as long as a condition is true. If the condition is false at the beginning, `while` does not execute any of the C statements in the loop.

NO SEMICOLON !!

Syntax   ↓

```
while ( while_true_expression )
{
   one_or_more_c_statements_to_execute;
}
```

Sample   **COBOL II Equivalent**

```
while ( acct_pd <= end_pd )         PERFORM 2400-CHECK-BAL
{                                         UNTIL ACCT-PD > END-PD
  ...                                     ...
  increment_period (acct_pd);         CALL 'INCRPER' USING ACCT-PD.
}                                   END-PERFORM.
```

Include File

None. `while` is a keyword and therefore does not require an include file.

See Also

`break`   — terminate a `for` or `while` loop

`continue`	— transfer control to the bottom of a `for` or `while` loop without terminating the loop
`for`	— PERFORM ... VARYING ... UNTIL equivalent
call a function	— PERFORM paragraph equivalent

Parameter Definitions

`while` is a keyword, not a function, and therefore has no parameters.

Return Value

`while` is not a function and therefore has no return value.

Direction

Left to right.

NO SEMICOLON !!

Anatomy

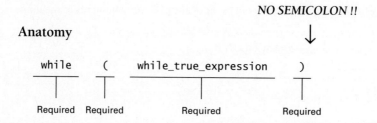

`while`

The keyword that is analogous to PERFORM ... UNTIL. `while` directs the compiler to execute the set of instructions that immediately follow it.

`while_true_expression`

The `while_true_expression` is evaluated and resolved in the same way as an `if` statement. Its result is either a nonzero value (true) or zero (false). It operates under the same rules as the C `if` statement. It also allows and/or logic via **&&** and **||**. However, it is better for comprehension if a single condition is written.
In the statement

```
while ( i < 10 )
```

`i < 10` is the `while_true_expression`. It becomes in effect "if `i < 10`, proceed with the following statements."

`while_true_expression` is basically analogous to UNTIL *condition-1* in PERFORM. The difference is in COBOL you say execute *until*:

```
SUBSCRIPT > TABLE_SIZE.
```

while in C you say execute *while*:

```
subscript < table_size
```

While means execute while true and *until* means execute until true. For additional discussion of *while* versus *until,* see the "Discussion" section below.

No semicolon after the right parenthesis

`while`, `for`, `if`, and `switch` *do not* have semicolons after the parentheses that follow them. Each one is a block statement command: They are followed by one or more C statements, which are contained in curly braces.

```
{
    one_or_more_c_statements_to_execute;
}
```

Following the `while` statement is the loop code—one or more C statements enclosed in curly braces. In a COBOL II in-line `PERFORM`, these statements would immediately follow the `PERFORM` and be terminated by an `END-PERFORM`. In traditional COBOL the statements in the loop would be in the paragraph being performed. In C they immediately follow the `while` statement. Whatever you want to do in the loop you put here. The curly braces are necessary the same way they are in an `if` statement: If there are no curly braces, the compiler assumes the `while` only has one statement in the loop.

Discussion

Before the first iteration and each time `while` finishes the C statement(s) in the loop, it checks `while_true_expression`. As long as `while_true_expression` is true, `while` continues the loop. You must initialize the test condition before the loop. Also, you must increment or decrement counters or subscripts inside the loop, just as with `PERFORM ... UNTIL`.

`while` has two primary uses: processing a set of data from the middle of the set and sequential file processing. The `for` statement is more commonly used for array processing, and the `while` statement is more commonly used for sequential file processing.

`while` is generally used to process a set of data from some point to the end when the initial subscript value is provided by the data. An example is having an array of totals by month, where each record needs to be added to every total from the month in the record to the end of the array. You can use the value of the month in the data as a subscript and go to the end.

If you are going to process a whole array, `for` is the statement to use: It declares an initial value, gives a while-true expression, and takes care of the increment/decrement logic. By contrast, `while` assumes there is an initial value (which you must provide), and you have to handle the increment/decrement logic within the loop.

The sequential file processing functions in this book (`fgets()`, `fgetc()`, and `fread()`) are commonly coded in `while` statements that read "while not end of file, get a string/character/record from this file." Those functions are discussed in Chapter 6, "File Input/Output," which covers how to use `while` with each read function, so they will not be discussed further here.

The structure of while is much like the COBOL II in-line PERFORM . . . UNTIL. It is different from performing a paragraph in traditional COBOL because the loop code immediately follows the while. But, aside from the fact that you don't have to turn pages to find out what's being done in the loop, while operates nearly identically to PERFORM . . . UNTIL.

Parts of **while** Statement	COBOL Equivalents
while	PERFORM
while_true_expression	UNTIL *condition-1*

The big difference is the sense of *while* compared to the sense of *until*. This situation is exactly the same as discussed in the section on the for statement earlier in this chapter. All the comments about *while* versus *until* and how C uses subscripts also apply to the while statement.

while evaluates its while-true condition before executing the first time, just as PERFORM . . . UNTIL checks the until condition before it executes. while will not execute the loop if while_true_expression is false.

Infinite Loops (Intentional)

In the development process there are times when you want a test program to run over and over again while you submit different data to it from the screen. The simple solution is to use a while (1) statement in a main() function and call the test program or function from inside the loop. Here's an example:

```
main()
{
    ...
    while ( 1 )
    {
        printf ("Enter a number: \n" );
        gets (input_data);
        /* call the test function and display results */
    }
    return (0);
}
```

You can also do this with the for statement by coding

```
for ( ; ; )
{
    /* statements */
}
```

It does not matter which one you use.

Common Error

The only common error with the `while` statement is inadvertently creating an infinite loop. The most popular ways to do this are

1. Coding a `while` loop without curly braces.

   The following seemingly innocuous `while` statement

   ```
   while ( i < 13 )
       ytd_totals [i] += month_amt;
       i++;
   ```

   looks like it has two statements in the loop, but it does not. As with both the `if` and `for` statements, a `while` statement without curly braces is intrepreted by the compiler as having only one statement in the loop. If the first statement is not the increment/decrement statement, the while-true expression is never altered from its initial state. If the while-true expression is true on the first iteration, it is true forever. Always use braces.

2. Coding a `while` statement with a semicolon on the end.

   If you slip up and put a semicolon on the end of a `while` statement, as in

   ```
   while ( i < 13 );
   {
       ytd_totals [i] += month_amt;

       i++;
   }
   ```

   the increment/decrement logic is never reached, so the while-true expression is always true (if it is true at the beginning).

3. Forgetting to increment/decrement the subscript.

   Another seemingly innocent `while` statement

   ```
   while ( i < 13 )
   {
       ytd_totals [i] += month_amt;
   }
   ```

   does not change the value of `i` within the loop. If `i` is less than 13 when the loop starts, the loop runs forever. If you use `while`, you must change the value of the data element in the while-true expression.

4. Using `continue` to get to the bottom of the loop but not incrementing/decrementing the subscript before the `continue;`.

You use `continue` when you want to skip over remaining code in the current iteration of the loop. The following code neglects to change the value of `i` if `month_amt` is less than zero:

```
while ( i < 13 )
{
    if (month_amt < 0 )
    {
        continue;
    }
    ytd_totals [i] += month_amt;
    i++;
}
```

This code causes an infinite loop if `month_amt` is ever less than zero. Any `continue` statement in a `while` loop must be preceded by maintenance of the data element in the while-true expression.

Example

```
/*              whilee.c              9/17/94              */
#include <stdio.h>

main()
{
    double  dept_tot    [10] = { 0 };          /* 1 array of doubles          */
    int     i;
    int     month        = 7;
    double  month_amt    = 150.20;
    double  sales_amt    = 0;
    double  ytd_totals [13] = { 0 };           /* 2 13 totals for months      */
                                               /*   use month for subscript   */

    i = 0;                                     /* 3 i needs value before while */
    while ( i < 10 )                           /* 4 load array                 */
    {
        sales_amt += 100.0;

        dept_tot [i] = sales_amt;

        i++;                                   /* 5 increment subscript        */
    }

    while ( month < 13 )                       /* 6 add until end of array     */
    {
        ytd_totals [month] += month_amt;

        month++;                               /* 7 increment month            */
    }
```

```
    while ( 1 )                                      /* 8 infinite loop on purpose        */
    {
       printf ("Enter some data: \n" );
       /* test code here      */
    }

    return (0);
}
```

Comments on Example

Line 1   The same array (table) of numbers as in the for example. `dept_tot` is a `double` and occurs `10` times.

Line 2   Shows how to set up an array when the buckets represent months. Since C handles arrays by offsets, and offsets start from zero, create 13 occurrences when you want to deal with 12 months. Then you can use the month number as a subscript. The first occurrence, at offset zero, is never used.

If you are doing this with `for` statements, the initialization expression is coded as `i = 1`.

Lines 3–5   Show a `while` that is really a `for`. If you are going to initialize the subscript and use an increment or decrement operator to maintain the subscript, you may as well use `for`.

Line 3 assigns a value to the subscript `i`. A more realistic case would be a value for the subscript that is supplied at run time via a read or a database retrieval.

Line 4 is the `while` statement. It is in effect the middle part of a `for` statement. As long as `i` is less than `10`, the loop continues.

Line 5 shows that you must increment/decrement the subscript yourself in a `while` statement.

Lines 6–7   Represent a more typical `while` statement. A value for `month` comes (you can assume) from input data, and you want to apply a number from that month through the end of the year. This statement loops from months 7 through 12 (7 is supplied in lieu of an I/O function call).

Line 7 increments `month`. Incrementing/decrementing is the programmer's responsibility in a `while` loop. When month has a value of `13`, the loop stops.

Line 8   Uses `while` to create an intentional infinite loop. This is a useful technique for test situations, when you want to test some function repeatedly.

The while-true expression here is `1`, which is not zero and therefore true. No data element appears inside the parentheses, so you cannot change it and it is *always* true.

This statement loops until you terminate the program. That is typically done with the Ctrl-C key combination but may vary depending on your operating system. Inside this infinite loop you typically ask for one or more data values, call some function, display results, and then start over.

Call a function which has no parameters (PERFORM).

C Keyword/Symbol/Function	*call a function*

A function that is written like a COBOL paragraph has no parameters and uses file global data elements or program global data elements. To call such a function, code the function name followed by empty parentheses, as `a4000_add_totals()`. In ANSI C you also need to create a function prototype, which is a template of call parameters.

Syntax

`void function_name (void);`	Function prototype
`function_name ();`	Function call
`void function_name (void)`	Function header

Sample

```
void a4000_add_totals (void);
main()
{
   a4000_add_totals();
   return (0);
}
void a4000_add_totals (void)
{
   dept_tot_amt  += sales_amt;
   grand_tot_amt += sales_amt;
   return;
}
```

COBOL Equivalent

```
PROCEDURE DIVISION.

    PERFORM 4000-ADD-TOTALS.
    GOBACK.

4000-ADD-TOTALS.

    ADD SALES-AMT TO DEPT-TOT-AMT.
    ADD SALES-AMT TO GRAND-TOT-AMT.


5000-WRAP-UP.
    ...
```

Include File

None. Calling a function does not require an include file.

See Also

call a function	— Chapter 11, "Calling Functions (Subprograms)"
for	— PERFORM . . . VARYING . . . UNTIL equivalent
while	— PERFORM . . . UNTIL equivalent

Parameter Definitions

Since you are writing functions to behave like paragraphs, there are no parameters.

Return Value

May or may not be used in this technique. Not using a return value is indicated by void at the beginning of both the function prototype and the function header. You can use a return value to indicate success or failure of the function, for instance. It is determined by you when you write the function. If you choose to return a value, you code the data type of the return value as the first item in both the function prototype and the function header. You also code return (expression) in the function to return that value. A return value is not required.

Direction

Read function calls from left to right.

Anatomy (Function Prototype)

```
void function_name (void);
```
Required

void

The keyword used as the return value of a function prototype when the function does not generate a return value. You can choose to have the function return a value to indicate success or failure. If you want to return a value, replace void with the data type of the value you are going to return (int, long, double, and so on).

function_name

The name you assign to the function. It is the equivalent of a paragraph name.

void

The keyword that tells the compiler that there will be no parameters for this function. When you write functions to act like paragraphs, you do not include parameters.

;

A semicolon ends the function prototype.

Anatomy (Function Call)

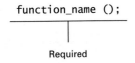

```
function_name ();
```
Required

When you call the function, you code its name, a pair of empty parentheses, and the semicolon.

NO SEMICOLON !!

Anatomy (Function Header)

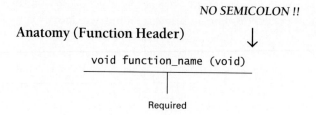

```
void function_name (void)
```

Required

The function header must match the function prototype on each of three things: return value data type, function name, and parameter list. It also must *not* have a semicolon at the end.

The only other requirement for a function is an opening curly brace and a closing curly brace. A function will compile cleanly without instructions. This is a valid function:

```
void a4000_add_totals (void)
{
}
```

The three lines above constitute a function that has no instructions. You may want to do this during the early part of developing a program to provide a stub. It compiles cleanly.

Discussion

The COBOL PERFORM reserved word performs a paragraph/section that is in the same program (and source dataset) as the PERFORM statement. The performed paragraph name is known within the program, but the paragraph name is not known to the link editor. This means that no program can perform paragraphs in any other program.

COBOL does not allow passing of parameters to paragraphs; all the data defined in the program is available to all paragraphs. COBOL's data is global *within* the program. This is called *file global data.*

C has a different arrangement. Instead of paragraphs there are functions, which can act like paragraphs, subprograms, or "super paragraphs." Also, there is no perform keyword. Coding the function name tells the compiler to perform/call it. In C you can also make a data element available to functions in files other than the one it is defined in. This is *program global data.*

C functions can be written to behave like

- COBOL paragraphs (with access to file global data)
- COBOL subprograms (with parameters passing data)

- COBOL "super paragraphs" or "super subprograms" (with access to all globally defined data in a linked program)

This section discusses only the first type of function. The other two types are covered in Chapter 11, "Calling Functions (Subprograms)."

In COBOL, all data defined in the Data Division is available to all paragraphs in the file. A file is generally the same as a program in COBOL.

You can write C programs to define in a global manner at the top of the file. The data is then available to all functions within the file/program without passing parameters in the call to the function. Do this by declaring your data elements above `main()`. Use the `static` storage class if you want the elements to be used only in that file. This kind of C program operates like a COBOL program with paragraphs.

Common Error

A compile error occurs on the function header line or the line following it.

This is commonly due to having a semicolon at the end of the function header. It typically happens during copying and pasting the function prototype to use as the function header. A function prototype *does* have a semicolon at the end, and a function header *does not* have a semicolon at the end:

Prototype: `void a2000_add_to_totals (void) ;` ←— semicolon

Header: `void a2000_add_to_totals (void)` ←— no semicolon

The message from the compiler may be incomprehensible such as `Need an identifier to declare`

Example

```
/*              callfunc.c                  09/16/94                 */
#include <stdio.h>

void a2000_add_to_totals (void);      /* 1  function prototype for a2000  */
void a4000_print_totals  (void);      /* 2  function prototype for a4000  */

double  grand_tot_amt;                /* 3  program global variables      */
double  region_tot_amt;
double  sales_amt       = 10570.49;

main()                                /* 4  beginning of main()           */
{
   a2000_add_to_totals();             /* 5  call a2000_add_to_totals      */

   return (0);                        /* 6  return to operating system    */
                                      /*    (GOBACK.)                     */

}
```

```
void a2000_add_to_totals (void)            /* 7  function header            */
{
  /* read loop could go here */
  region_tot_amt += sales_amt;
  grand_tot_amt  += sales_amt;
  a4000_print_totals();                    /* 8  call a4000_print_totals    */
  return;                                  /* 9  return to main()           */
}

void a4000_print_totals (void)             /* 10 function header            */
{
  printf ("region_tot_amt = %f \n",
    region_tot_amt );
  printf ("grand_tot_amt = %f \n",
    grand_tot_amt );
  return;                                  /* 11 return to a2000            */
}
```

Comments on Example

Lines 1–2   Contain the function prototypes for the two functions called in this program. No prototype is required for `main()`. Function prototypes have the form

    return_value_data_type function_name (parameter_list) ;

Since this program is designed to have functions that work like COBOL paragraphs, these functions will not have return values and will not have parameters, thus the use of

    void function_name (void);

The compiler checks function headers and function calls to see if they match the prototype. The number of parameters must match. Data types for the return value and the parameters must match or be able to be converted or coerced by the compiler to the data type of the prototype. If they do not match, a compile error is generated. This is good, because it's a lot easier to find these errors when the compiler points them out, rather than to find them by combing through a program that blew up because of such a mismatch. This is the voice of experience speaking.

Notice that the function names begin with aXXXX, where XXXX is a four-digit number. This is as close as you can get to COBOL paragraph numbering. C does not allow a data name or function name to begin with a number. Numbering functions makes sense for the same reason that numbering paragraphs does: Eventually someone is going to have to print the program and read it. Functions are easier to find if they are numbered and in order. Also remember to give the function a descriptive name as well. You have 31 characters to use.

Line 3   Shows typical C program data declarations. Whether consciously chosen or not, these data elements are program global. They are available to every function in any file that is link edited with this one. They are global to the program because they are defined above `main()` and they are not qualifed by having the `static` keyword precede them. For example,

```
static double grand_tot_amt;
```

would be a file global variable, and

```
double grand_tot_amt;
```

would be a program global variable. In programs with all the functions in one file, such as this one, this is not a big concern. This is the way memory works in COBOL programs. As C programs grow larger and multiple files are involved, however, program global memory becomes a significant consideration with regard to data integrity. If every function can change a data element, which one did it last?

For further discussion see Chapter 11, "Calling Functions (Subprograms)."

Line 4   The beginning of the `main()` function. Data elements defined above this line are either program global or file global.

This is where mainline logic goes. The `main()` function should be short, just as the mainline of a COBOL program should be short. Call an initialization function, call a primary processing loop, call a wrap-up function, and stop the run.

Line 5   Calls (performs) the function `a2000_add_to_totals()`. The parentheses tell the compiler that this is a function call. The emptiness between the parentheses tells the compiler that no parameters are being passed. This is equivalent to performing a paragraph in COBOL.

Line 6   Uses `return` to stop the run. Zero is being returned to the operating system, which means success, by convention in the C world. This is opposite of how `if`, `for`, and `while` statements work. Zero means false in `if`, `for`, and `while`, while a nonzero value means true. Using zero on the return to the operating system is done to allow multiple values for failure. If a program succeeds, you need only one code: success. If a program fails, you often want to have a variety of codes that can be translated to different failure messages.

For further discussion see `return` and `exit()` later in this chapter.

Line 7   The function header for the `a2000_add_to_totals()` function. It is equivalent to the paragraph name at the beginning of a paragraph, with the additions of specifying a return value data type and a parameter list.

Recall that function header syntax is the same as function prototype syntax, except that the function header does *not* have a semicolon at the end.

The function boundaries are the first left curly brace after the function header and the right curly brace that matches it. Any legal C statements are acceptable within a function. This function has a comment that suggests a read loop would be appropriate, two addition statements, a call to another function, and a `return` statement.

Line 8 Calls (performs) the a4000_print_totals() function. This function is also written in the manner of a COBOL paragraph, so no parameters are passed.

Line 9 Returns control to the calling function, main() in this case. Since the function prototype declares that there is no return value for a2000_add_to_totals(), the keyword return is used without an expression. It is equivalent to a COBOL exit paragraph.

Line 10 The function header for a4000_print_totals(). The comments for line 7 apply here also.

Line 11 Returns control to the calling function, a2000_add_to_totals(). This line operates exactly like line 9.

Go to the bottom of a loop (GO TO EXIT of PERFORM)

C Keyword/Symbol/Function	continue

Transfer control to the bottom of a for or while loop without terminating the loop. That is the only place continue can go. It is as though GO-TO-EXIT were a reserved word in COBOL.

Syntax

```
continue ;
```

Sample   ### COBOL Equivalent:

```
  while ( acct_pd <= end_pd )              PERFORM 2400-CHECK-BAL
  {                                            UNTIL ACCT-PD > END-PD.
    if (acct_bal == 0 )
    {                                      2400-CHECK-BAL.
      continue;                              IF ACCT-BAL = 0
    }                                            GO TO 2400-EXIT.
    ...                                      ...
  }                                        2400-EXIT.
                                             EXIT.
```

Include File

None. continue is a keyword and therefore does not require an include file.

See Also

break   — terminate a for or while loop

```
for        — PERFORM ... VARYING ... UNTIL equivalent
while      — PERFORM ... UNTIL equivalent
```

Parameter Definitions

Since `continue` is a keyword, not a function, it needs no parameters.

Return Value

Since `continue` is not a function, it has no return value.

Scope

`continue` is used only inside `for` and `while` loops.

Direction

To the bottom of the `for` or `while` loop.

Anatomy

```
continue      ;
```
Required   Required

`continue`

    The keyword that transfers control to the bottom of the current `for` or `while` loop. There really isn't anything else to say about it.

`;`

    A semicolon ends the statement.

Discussion

When you're inside a COBOL paragraph that is being performed, it is common to GO TO the paragraph exit when some condition is met. This is typically the only allowed use of GO TO in COBOL shops (these days). When you're inside a PERFORM and go to the paragraph exit, the flow of control returns to the PERFORM statement.

    In the body of the C `for` and `while` statements, there is an exact equivalent of GO TO EXIT, only it's better. You code the `continue` statement inside the `for` or `while` loop when you want to go to the bottom of the loop without terminating the loop. The *only place* a `continue` can go is to the bottom of the current `for` or `while` loop. You can't go to the wrong exit. You can't go to the top of the loop. Use it the same way you use a GO TO EXIT—whenever you need to skip the rest of the statements in the loop.

The CONTINUE reserved word in COBOL II *is not equivalent* to the continue keyword in C. CONTINUE is a *no op* statement: It does nothing. Its primary use is in the EVALUATE statement to deal with a data value that requires no action.

COBOL II has an in-line PERFORM that you can use like either the for or while in C, but with an important exception. There is no way to transfer control to the bottom of the current iteration of an in-line PERFORM. This was probably omitted by design, to encourage relatively simple logic for in-line PERFORMs. You can write an in-line PERFORM with enough nested IF statements to get around the lack of a transfer control statement. But, if the logic is complicated, it makes more sense to create separate paragraphs and use PERFORM THRU. Then you can use GO TO EXIT to get to the bottom of the current iteration.

Common Error

Using continue to get to the bottom of a while loop but not incrementing/ decrementing the subscript.

You use continue when you want to skip remaining code in the current iteration of a while loop. The following code neglects to change the value of i if month_amt is less than zero:

```
while ( i < 13 )
{
    if (month_amt < 0 )
    {
        continue;
    }
    ytd_totals [i] += month_amt;
    i++;
}
```

It will cause an infinite loop if month_amt is ever less than zero. Any continue statement in a while loop must be preceded by maintenance of the data element in the while-true expression.

Example

```
/*                continu.c                9/17/94                        */
#include <stdio.h>

main()
{
    int     month        = 7;
    double  ytd_total [13] = { 0 };          /* 1  13 totals for months;    */
                                             /*     use month as subscript  */
```

```
for (month = 1; month < 13; month++ )      /* 2  process whole array         */
{
  if ( ytd_total [month] == 0.0 )          /* 3  check if zero balance       */
  {
    continue;                              /* 4  go to bottom of loop        */
  }
  ...
}                                          /* 5   continue goes here, then   */
                                           /*     for goes back to line 2    */

month = 3;
while ( month < 13 )                       /* 6  process til end of array    */
{
  if ( ytd_total [month] == 0.0 )          /* 7  check if zero balance       */
  {
    month++;                               /* 8  maintain subscript          */
    continue;                              /* 9  go to bottom of loop        */
  }
  ...
  month++;                                 /* 10 maintain subscript          */
}                                          /* 11 continue goes here, then    */
                                           /*    while goes back to line 6   */

return (0);
}
```

Comments on Example

Line 1   An array (table) of 13 occurrences of `ytd_total`, which is defined as a `double` (decimal places desired). It is initialized to zeroes. This shows how to set up an array when the buckets represent months. Since C handles arrays by offsets, and offsets start from zero, you must create 13 occurrences when you want to deal with 12 months. Then you can use the month number as a subscript. The first occurrence at offset zero is never used.

   If you are performing "month processing" with `for` statements, the initialization expression is coded as $i = 1$, rather than the usual $i = 0$, so the subscript will start with January.

Line 2   Demonstrates how to code a `for` statement that deals with 12 months. Set `month` to 1 and remain in the loop while `month` is less than 13.

Line 3   A test for whether the logic in the rest of the loop should be executed or skipped. Your business case will determine what such an `if` statement looks like.

Line 4   Transfers control to the bottom of the loop when the `if` statement on line 3 is true. This `continue` statement transfers control to the ending curly brace of the `for` statement, which is on line 5. `continue` is equivalent to a GO TO EXIT in a COBOL paragraph that is being performed in a loop.

Line 5   The ending curly brace of the `for` statement on line 2. From here the logic returns to the `for` statement and tests the while-true condition.

Line 6   Shows a `while` statement that is executing from a point within the array to the end of the array. The line before this, which sets month to 3, is arbitrary; in real life the starting value comes from a read, a function call, or a database access.

Line 7   The same as line 3—a test that indicates the need to skip the rest of the logic in the loop.

Line 8   Maintains the subscript before the continue is executed. This is a necessary piece of housekeeping because a while statement assumes the programmer will take care of incrementing/decrementing the subscript. A while statement also assumes the programmer will take care of setting the initial value of the subscript.

Line 9   Transfers control to the bottom of the while loop when the if statement on line 7 is true. The loop is not terminated. Control is transferred to the closing curly brace on line 11. continue operates exactly the same way in for statements and in while statements.

Line 10   Maintains the subscript when the rest of the loop is executed.

Line 11   The closing curly brace of the while statement that begins on line 6. The logic goes from here back to the while statement, where the while-true condition is checked.

Terminate a loop and go to the following statement (No COBOL equivalent)

C Keyword/Symbol/Function	break

break causes an immediate exit from the current for, while, and switch statements. Control passes to the next statement after the for, while, or switch. Use break when you have a reason to quit the loop altogether.

Syntax

```
break ;
```

Sample

```
while (acct_pd <= end_pd )
{
    ...

    if (error_code == 'F' )
    {
        break;
    }
}
C_statement_after_while_or_for;
```

COBOL II Equivalent:

```
PERFORM UNTIL ACCT-PD > END-PD

    ...

    IF ERROR-CODE = 'F'
        NEXT SENTENCE
    END-IF

END-PERFORM.

COBOL-STATEMENT-AFTER-PERFORM.
```

(You can't do this in traditional COBOL.)

Include File

None. `break` is a keyword and therefore does not require an include file.

See Also

`continue`	— transfer control to the bottom of a for or while loop without terminating the loop
`for`	— `PERFORM ... VARYING ... UNTIL` equivalent
`switch`	— case statement used to evaluate multiple values for one variable
`while`	— `PERFORM ... UNTIL` equivalent

Parameter Definitions

Since `break` is a keyword and not a function, it has no parameters.

Return Value

Since `break` is not a function, it has no return value.

Scope

`break` is used inside `for` and `while` loops and within the `switch` statement.

Direction

Down to the next statement after the bottom of the `for` or `while` loop or to the statement following the `switch` statement.

Anatomy

break ;

Required

`break`

The keyword that terminates the current `for` or `while` loop or terminates a `switch` statement. The difference between `break` and `continue` is that `continue` stays within the loop, although it transfers control to the bottom of the loop. When `break` is executed, control passes out of the `for`, `while`, or `switch` statement. (`continue` is not used with the `switch` statement.)

`;`

A semicolon ends the statement.

Discussion

In COBOL II you can terminate an in-line PERFORM by using NEXT SENTENCE if there are no periods in the loop until the END-PERFORM. This works the same way as the break statement in C: The current loop is terminated. You can't do this in traditional COBOL.

If you need to terminate a PERFORM in traditional COBOL, you do it by setting the value of *condition-1* named in the UNTIL clause and then going to the paragraph exit. Control is then returned to the PERFORM, the UNTIL is checked and found true, and control is transferred to the statement following the PERFORM.

C has a simple method: Just code break and you're out of the for, while, or switch statement. If there are nested loops, control returns to the next outermost loop. This is shown in the example program below.

The varying expression is not executed when break is used to terminate a for statement. This means any subscript still has the last value used in the loop. This is different from continue, which *will* cause the varying expression to be executed.

break is also used to exit a switch statement. This is discussed with switch in Chapter 9, "If, Case (EVALUATE), and Class Tests."

Common Errors

1. A switch statement executes many or all cases plus default.

   This is usually due to forgetting to use the break statement in each case.

2. Losing control of nested for or while statements.

   Nested for and while statements can be problematic, especially when they exceed two or three levels. If each loop has one or more break statements it can be difficult to figure out a problem. The only real advice is to try to keep nested for and while statements to a few levels.

Example

```
/*              breakk.c                    9/17/94                      */
#include <stdio.h>

main()
{
    int     i;
    int     j;
    int     month        = 7;
    double  net_amt  [5] [10] = { 0 };      /* 1  two dimensional array    */
    double  ytd_total [13]    = { 0 };      /* 2  13 totals for months;    */
                                            /*    use month as subscript   */
```

```
for (month = 1; month < 13; month++ )        /* 3  process whole array       */
{
  if ( ytd_total [month] < 0.0 )             /* 4  check negative balance    */
  {
    break;                                   /* 5  exit loop completely      */
  }
  ...
}

month = 3;                                   /* 6  break comes to this line  */
while ( month < 13 )                         /* 7  process til end of array  */
{
  if ( ytd_total [month] < 0.0 )             /* 8  check negative balance    */
  {
    break;                                   /* 9  exit loop completely      */
  }
  ...
  month++;                                   /* 10 maintain subscript        */
}

printf ("Resume. \n" );                      /* 11 break comes to this line  */

for ( i = 0; i < 5; i++ )                    /* 12 display 2-D array         */
{
  for ( j = 0; j < 10; j++ )                 /* 13 nested for                */
  {
    if (net_amt [i] [j] < 0 )
    {
      break;                                 /* 14 terminate inner loop      */
    }
    printf ("net_amt = %f \n",
      net_[i] [j] );
  }                                          /* 15 end of nested for loop    */
  printf ("End of set %d\n", i );            /* 16 break comes here          */
}                                            /* 17 end of "outer" for loop   */

return (0);
}
```

Comments on Example

Line 1 Defines a two-dimensional array and initializes it to zeroes. This array will be used to show how break is used in a nested for statement.

Line 2 An array (table) of 13 occurrences of ytd_total, which is also initialized to zeroes. This shows how to set up an array when the buckets represent months. Since C handles arrays by offsets, and offsets start from zero, you must create 13 occurrences when you want to deal with 12 months and use the month number as a subscript. The first occurrence, at offset zero, is never used.

   If you are doing month processing with for statements, the initialization expression is coded as i = 1, rather than the usual i = 0, so the subscript will start with January.

Line 3 Demonstrates how to code a `for` statement that deals with 12 months. Set `month` to 1 and remain in the loop while `month` is less than 13.

Line 4 A test for whether the loop logic should be terminated. In some cases a condition tells you that you don't have to go through the rest of the iterations. Your business case will determine what such an `if` statement looks like.

Line 5 Transfers control to the next statement after the bottom of the loop. This `break` statement transfers control to line 6, which is the next line after the closing curly brace of the `for` statement on line 3. The value of `month` is not incremented because `break` breaks out of the loop.

Line 6 Sets up the `while` statement on line 7. This is where the `break` statement on line 5 transfers control.

Line 7 Shows a `while` statement that is executing from a point within the array to the end of the array. The line before this, which sets `month` to 3, is arbitrary; in real life the starting value comes from a read, a call, or a database access.

Line 8 The same as line 4—a test that indicates the need to stop loop processing altogether.

Line 9 Transfers control to the next statement after the bottom of the `while` loop. `break` operates exactly the same way in both `for` and `while`.

Line 10 Maintains the subscript in the `while` statement as long as it continues to loop.

Line 11 The next statement after the `while` loop that starts on line 7. If the `break` statement is executed, this is where control is transferred.

Line 12 Begins a `for` statement that contains another `for` statement. The entire statement displays all the values in the `net_amt` array. This `for` loop controls the first subscript and prints a line at the end of each iteration of the second subscript.

Line 13 The nested `for` statement. It contains the `printf()` statement for `net_amt [i] [j]` and also a check for an out-of-range condition.

Line 14 If `net_amt` is less than zero, this `for` loop will be terminated by this `break` statement. Control is transferred to the next statement after this `for` statement, line 16. Line 16 is a `printf()` statement in the outer `for` loop.

Line 15 The closing curly brace of the nested `for` statement. It is skipped by the `break` statement if `break` executes. If `break` does not execute, control is transferred from here back to line 13, the beginning of the nested `for` statement.

Line 16 The second statement in the outer `for` statement that begins on line 12. The `printf()` is the next statement executed if the `break` statement on line 14 executes.

Line 17 Terminates the outer `for` statement that begins on line 12. This `for` statement is unaffected by the `break` statement in the nested `for` statement. The value of `i` is incremented, and the inner `for` statement is executed again if `i` is still less than 5. The inner `for` sets `j` to 0 and goes through the next set of occurrences of the array.

GO TO (GO TO).

C Keyword/Symbol/Function	goto

DON'T USE goto.

COBOL has one valid use for GO TO, and that is to get to the exit paragraph for the current paragraph. C solves this problem by providing the `continue` and `break` statements. Therefore, there are no valid uses for `goto` in C.

    `continue` transfers control to the bottom of the current `for` or `while` loop without terminating the loop. `break` terminates the loop and transfers control to the next statement after the bottom of the current `for` or `while` loop. `break` is also used to transfer control to the statement following a `switch` statement.

    You don't need `goto`.

See Instead:

`break`   — terminate a `for` or `while` loop
`continue`   — transfer control to the bottom of a `for` or `while` loop
                   without terminating the loop

Return control to calling function or to operating system (GOBACK).

C Keyword/Symbol/Function	return

`return` terminates the execution of a C function and returns control to the calling function (or to the operating system if used in `main()`). If a literal, a data element, or an expression is coded after the `return` keyword, its value is given back to the calling program or operating system. The `return` keyword and that value are the source of the return value that is talked about so much in this book.

Format 1:

```
return ( return_value ) ;
```

Format 2:

```
return;
```

Sample	COBOL Equivalent:
`return ( 4 );`	`MOVE 4 TO RETURN-CODE.` `GOBACK.`

`return ( status_code ) ;`
`return ( SUCCEED ) ;`
`return ( FAIL ) ;`	

`return;`	`GOBACK.`

Include File

None: `return` is a keyword and therefore does not require an include file.

See Also

call a function	— PERFORM paragraph equivalent
call a subprogram	— CALL ... USING equivalent
`exit()`	— return control to the operating system

Parameter Definitions

`return_value`

Can be just about anything: `char`, `char [x]`, `int`, `long`, `double`, a structure, or an expression that evaluates to any of these. Typically it's a number.

Return Value

`return` is the keyword that causes a return value to be passed back to the calling program or operating system. Any value that follows the `return` keyword is the return value for the function.

Direction

Left to right.

Anatomy

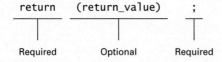

return	(return_value)	;
Required	Optional	Required

`return`

The keyword that terminates a function and optionally provides a return value.

`return_value`

An optional value to be returned to the calling function.

`;`

A semicolon ends the statement.

Discussion

A return value operates basically the same way `RETURN-CODE` does in IBM COBOL, except that a return value can be just about any data type. `RETURN-CODE` is not commonly used in IBM COBOL subprograms, but it can be used to pass a status back to the calling program. In IBM COBOL you have to move a number to `RETURN-CODE`, while in C you can use a number, a single character, a string literal, a data name, or a value declared by a `#define` statement for the return value.

How a return value is used depends on how the function is defined. If the function does not have a return value, its prototype reads

```
void function_name ( parameter_list ) ;
```

In such a function `return` must be used alone; it cannot return a value. `void` as the return value data type means no return value. Code it as

```
return;
```

On the other hand, if a function prototype reads

```
double function_name     ( parameter_list ) ;
```

that function must return a value that is a `double` or can be converted to a `double`. It can return a data element (the result of the function), a numeric literal, or a `#define` value. If the value is not a `double`, the compiler forces a conversion. If the compiler cannot convert the data type, a compile error is generated. Code this kind of return as

```
return (data-name);
```

Return Value Convention When Returning to a Calling Function

When returning to a calling function, C really has no convention. Whatever type value needs to be returned is returned. The result can be a number, a character string, or a status (or anything else). This is dictated either by the design of a new function or by the function prototype for an existing function. When using `return()` to indicate the success or failure of a function other than `main()`, the general practice is to follow the `if` statement evaluation rule:

nonzero value = true = success

zero   = false = failure

The easy way to set this up is to create two `#define` values in an include file used by the project. These two lines

```
#define SUCCEED   1
#define FAIL      0
```

allow you to use `return (SUCCEED)` or `return (FAIL)` without ever having to try to remember whether success is zero or a nonzero value. Program constants are much more obvious than zero and one.

Return Value Convention When Returning to the Operating System

There is a general C convention for a return value when you are returning control to the operating system. It is the opposite of the `if` statement evaluation rule. When returning to the operating system, zero generally indicates success and a nonzero value indicates failure. The reason for the inversion is that if a program succeeds, you don't really need to know anything else. If a program fails, many application systems and operating systems have lists of return values that indicate the kind of failure that occurred.

Most ANSI C compilers generate a warning message if you use `exit()` in `main()` instead of `return()`. If this occurs, use `return()` and get rid of the message.

Common Error

`return()` is not easy to use incorrectly, but if you use no function prototypes, or default function prototypes, you can have a serious mismatch on the return value data type, and the compiler will not catch it. Always create full function prototypes, and the compiler will tell you if you are attempting an illegal type conversion with `return()`.

Example

```
/*                returnn.c              09/18/94                    */
#include <stdio.h>

#define FAIL      0             /* 1  #defines for return values   */
#define SUCCEED 1

int  a2000_add_totals   (void);  /* 2  function prototypes          */
void a4000_print_totals (void);

double  grand_tot_amt;           /* 3  declare global data elements */
double  sales_amt    = 10570.49;
int     read_status = SUCCEED;   /* 4  initialize to #define value  */
double  region_tot_amt;

main()
{
   if ( a2000_add_totals() != SUCCEED )   /* 5  exec a2000 and check ret val */
   {
      return (-1);               /* 6  return to O/S with error     */
   }
   return (0);                   /* 7  return to O/S with success   */
}
```

```
int a2000_add_totals (void)
{
   /* assume some I/O call */
   if ( read_status != SUCCEED )              /* 8  check status of I/O call   */
   {
      return (FAIL);                          /* 9  return to main() w/ FAIL   */
   }
   region_tot_amt += sales_amt;
   grand_tot_amt += sales_amt;
   a4000_print_totals();
   return (SUCCEED);                          /* 10 return to main() w/ SUCCEED */
}
void a4000_print_totals (void)
{
   printf ("region_tot_amt = %f \n",
      region_tot_amt );
   printf ("grand_tot_amt = %f \n",
      grand_tot_amt );
   return;                                    /* 11 return to a2000 – no ret val */
}
```

Comments on Example

Line 1   Uses #define to set up two program constants that are referred to later in the program. These follow the if statement evaluation rule:

nonzero value == true == SUCCEED
zero   == false == FAIL.

Line 2   The function prototypes are declared here. a2000_add_totals() returns an integer value. a4000_print_totals() does not return a value. Neither function has parameters. The lack of parameters also tells us these functions use global data.

Line 3   Begins global data element declaration. Since you want to use these data elements without passing them as parameters, you define them above main(). Use the static storage class if you want their use restricted to the file where they are declared.

   For further discussion of global data, see Chapter 11, "Calling Functions (Subprograms)."

Line 4   Uses a #define value to initialize a variable. A 1 is substituted for SUCCEED by the preprocessor. When the program goes into the compilation step, this line will read

```
   int   read_status  = 1;
```

Line 5   Calls a2000_add_totals() and checks the status inside an if statement. After the preprocessor substitutes a value for SUCCEED, the statement is evaluated from the innermost set of parentheses outward as follows:

```
        if ( a2000_add_totals() != SUCCEED )
```

becomes

```
        if ( a2000_add_totals() != 1       )
```

which becomes (assuming success)

```
        if ( 1                   != 1      )
```

a2000_add_totals() is replaced by its return value. It returns a value of type int (see function prototype and function header). Assume success, so return value will be 1. What's left is a simple if statement. If it is true (return value is not equal to SUCCEED), line 6 is executed.

Line 6   Executes if the if statement on line 5 is true, which indicates a failure in a2000_add_totals(). Line 6 returns a –1 to the operating system. It returns to the operating system because it is located in the main() function.

Line 7   The normal return to the operating system at the end of the main() function. Zero generally indicates success.

Line 8   Tests the status from an assumed I/O call just above it. In a real program there would be a database or file I/O operation before this.

Line 9   Transfers control back to the calling function, main(), if read_status did not equal SUCCEED. The preprocessor substitutes 0 for FAIL during the compile. The return statement is passing back an integer value, 0, which the if statement on line 5 will evaluate.

Line 10   Transfers control back to the calling function, main(), when there is a normal end in this function. The preprocessor substitutes 1 for SUCCEED during the compile, and so 1 is the integer value returned by this statement.

Line 11   The a4000_print_totals() function has no return value defined, so all it can do is use the return keyword without anything else. This statement returns control to a2000_add_totals(), which called it.

Return control to operating system (STOP RUN)

C Keyword/Symbol/Function	exit()

exit() terminates the execution of a C program. The integer value of status_code is returned to the operating system.

Syntax

```
        exit ( status_code ) ;
```

Samples

```
exit ( 4 );                    MOVE 4 TO RETURN-CODE.
                               STOP RUN.
exit ( 0 ) ;
exit ( -1 ) ;
exit ( EXIT_SUCCESS ) ;
exit ( EXIT_FAILURE ) ;
```

Include File

```
#include <stdlib.h>
```
(contains function prototype for `exit()`)

See Also

`return` — return control to calling program or operating system

Parameter Definitions

```
int    status_code;
```

This can be an integer data item, an integer literal, or a `#define` name for an integer literal.

Return Value

The value of `status_code` that you call `exit()` with. Whatever value you put between the parentheses is returned to the operating system. In the call to `exit()`, the programmer controls the return value. You typically use a zero value for success and a nonzero value for failure. This is the reverse of the sense of `if` statements. See the "Discussion" section below.

Direction

Left to right.

Anatomy

```
exit (status) ;
```

Required

`exit`

The name of the C function that terminates a program and returns control directly to the operating system.

`status_code`

A required integer value to be returned to the operating system.

`;`

A semicolon ends the statement.

Discussion

You can use either `exit()` or `return()` to end a C program. However, ANSI C compilers usually complain when `return()` is not used at the end of a `main()` function. If your compiler generates a warning on this, use `return()` with a status value.

As with COBOL's STOP RUN, it is possible to use `exit()` in the middle of a subprogram. You should *not* use `exit()` this way, however, for the same reason you should not use STOP RUN this way: It is too easy for such a termination to bypass clean-up functions needed on program termination. In C, as in COBOL, it is best to pass your error status up the call chain so the `main()` function can perform any clean-up functions before termination.

`status_code` operates basically the same way RETURN-CODE does in IBM COBOL. In C you can either hard code a number inside the parentheses, use a numeric data item, or use a program constant value.

The operating system can interrogate `status_code` and decide whether to continue with other jobs. This is the same way that OS JCL handles RETURN-CODE.

When returning to the operating system from a C program, zero generally means success, and a nonzero value means failure.

Common Errors

1. A warning message comes from the compiler.

    Using `exit()` at the end of `main()` generates a warning message from an ANSI compiler. Replace `exit()` with `return()`.

2. The program comes to an abrupt halt before it should.

    If you use `exit()` instead of `return()` in any function, the program ends when the `exit()` statement is executed. This is equivalent to coding STOP RUN in a COBOL subprogram. Use `return()` to pass control up the calling structure.

Example

```
/*              exitt.c                      03/23/94                */
#include <stdio.h>
#include <stdlib.h>                  /* 1 for exit() prototype        */

#define FAIL    0
#define SUCCEED 1

int  a2000_main_loop (void);         /* 2 a2000 function prototype    */
```

```
main()
{
    if ( a2000_main_loop() != SUCCEED )       /* 3 call a2000 and check ret val    */
    {
        exit (-1);                            /* 4 exit to O/S if not success      */
    }

    /* close files/database etc. */

    exit (0);                                 /* 5 exit to O/S with success        */
}
int a2000_main_loop (void)
{

    ...

    return (SUCCEED);                         /* 6 function uses return            */
}
```

Comments on Example

Line 1   The include file `stdlib.h` contains the function prototype for the `exit()` function. A function prototype contains a template of the call parameters for the function. ANSI C uses this during compiling to check the call parameters.

Line 2   Contains the function prototype for `a2000_main_loop()`, which returns an integer value. It has no parameters.

Line 3   Calls `a2000_main_loop` and checks its return value, which is defined to be a status for success or failure. For a detailed explanation of how the function call, return value, and `if` statement work together, see the example program for the `return()` function in the section immediately before this one.

Line 4   Calls `exit()` and returns control to the operating system with a return value of –1. Since the value is not zero, this is interpreted as a failure in the program.

Line 5   Calls `exit()` and returns control to the operating system with a return value of zero. This is interpreted as a normal termination of the program.
    In a real program, this line is preceded by calls to close files, the database, and so on.

Line 6   Shows that called functions use `return()`, not `exit()`, to return control to the calling function.

Summary

Flow of control statements in C are generally equivalent to those in COBOL. C also offers several features that COBOL does not have.

The `for` statement in C has an initialization clause, executes a loop while a condition is true, and has a "varying" clause. It has the same features as COBOL's PERFORM ... VARYING ... UNTIL, with two differences. The `for` statement executes *while* a condition is true where COBOL executes *until* a condition is true. This requires an adjustment in thinking about controlling loops. The other difference is that array subscripts in C begin with zero, rather than with 1. The result of this is that `for` loops generally use "from 0 while less than max" logic. The equivalent COBOL logic is "from 1 until greater than max."

The equivalent of the COBOL PERFORM ... UNTIL statement is found in the C `while` statement, with the same differences as noted above. It is fairly easy to create infinite loops (both unintentional and intentional) with the `while` statement.

The basic PERFORM statement in COBOL is found in C in a call to a function which has no parameters. This method depends on either "file global" or "program global" data. Figuring out which function updated global data can be difficult. Because of this problem, this method is recommended primarily for programs of under 1,000 lines with all code in a single file.

Calling a C function which has parameters is equivalent to calling a subprogram in COBOL. It is the subject of Chapter 11, "Calling Functions (Subprograms)."

Jumping to the bottom of a loop is done by use of the `continue` statement. It is similar to the GO TO exit technique in COBOL, except that `continue` cannot go anywhere else. The `break` statement exits the current loop and transfers control to the next statement after the bottom of the current loop. NEXT SENTENCE can be equivalent to `break` in certain situations in COBOL in-line PERFORM statements.

Using `break` and `continue` eliminates any need for a Go To statement in C, but one exists anyway. It is properly banned in almost all standards documents.

Returning control to either the calling function or to the operating system is handled by the `return()` statement. It is identical to GOBACK in how it transfers control. It is more powerful than GOBACK because `return()` can pass a value of any data type. This value is called the return value.

C's `exit()` statement returns control to the operating system the same way that STOP RUN does. `exit()` can also pass a value. Most ANSI compilers now issue a warning message if they find an `exit()` statement in the `main()` function. In order to get compiles with no warning messages, use `return()`.

11

Calling Functions (Subprograms)

Introduction

This chapter examines calling functions in C. Program design in C involves creating functions that are called by other functions. You need to be able to write functions and to call functions that you and other people have written.

The chapter begins with a brief discussion on the relationship of functions and files. That discussion is brief because it can quickly become a discussion of program design, which is not the subject of this book. Next the chapter discusses the scope, or visibility, of data in a C program and then shows three different ways functions can behave. The primary focus of this chapter, however, is how C handles *parameters*—data passed to or returned from functions. Calling functions and general rules for parameter passing are examined. Pointers are explained (most of the time they behave like COBOL parameters), and the concept of the return value is revisited in greater depth. The second half of the chapter shows in detail how to code and call functions with parameters that can be changed and parameters that cannot be changed. Parameter passing for elementary data elements, arrays, structures, and members of structures is also covered.

Files and Functions

So far in the book, we have been calling library functions to do useful work in the example programs. These programs have almost all consisted of a single function, `main()`, which does some work with operators and some work by calls to library functions. Business programs are coded this way too, with the addition of calls to functions written by the programmer or others.

In the real world, business programs are too large and complex for all the code to fit in the `main()` function. Functions are designed to break up a problem into smaller, more manageable pieces. Business programs typically have many functions, ranging in size from several dozen to several hundred lines.

As you design functions, you make choices about what the function does and what the parameters will be. In C, as in COBOL II, data passed as parameters can be either changed or protected from change.

Programs in the real world are often too large or have too many different functions to reasonably place in a single file. The functions get *packaged*, or put together, in multiple files. The only compiler rule about packaging is that you can have no more than one `main()` function in any set of files submitted for compiling and linking.

The following is a simple example of a general ledger (`gl`) program. The diagram below shows that this program consists of four functions packaged into two files.

File name: `gl_main.c`   File name: `gl_output.c`

```
#include stdio.h              #include stdio.h

main()                        write_gl_detail()

{                             {

    ...                           ...

    ...

    ...                       }

}
                              create_gl_rollup()
get_gl_data()
                              {
{
                                  ...
    ...
                              }
}
```

Each file would be compiled separately into an object module. The object modules would typically be named `gl_main.obj` and `gl_output.obj` (the suffix varies depending on the compiler). The link edit process would combine these two object modules with any necessary C library object modules to make an executable, with a name chosen by the programmer. One and *only* one `main()` function must be in the set of files used to create an executable.

Scope of Data

Scope, or visibility, of data refers to how much of the program can access a given data element. In C, data has the following three levels of scope, listed in order of increasing broadness:

1. Local function data.

   Available *only* within the function where it is defined. Local function data is not available to other functions in the same source file or in other source files in the linked program, except through parameter passing. `main()` is no different from any other function in this regard. Local variables are the best kind to use, because they are the most protected. In COBOL, local function data would be like having data definition within paragraphs, with the data available only inside the paragraph.

2. File global data.

   Available to every function contained in the source file where it's defined. Except through parameter passing, file global data is not available to functions *in other files* in the linked program. This is the same as `DATA DIVISION` data in a COBOL program that does not use `GLOBAL` names.

   File global data is defined above the first function declaration in a file, and it uses the reserved keyword `static` in front of the data type.

   Use of this kind of global data is reasonable in programs that are no larger than 1000 lines and are composed of several functions contained in one file. It is fairly easy to get up to 1,000 lines in a batch program that uses a database. You should avoid creating a huge file for a program in order to use file global data. Break it up and pass parameters.

3. Program global data.

   Available to every function in the linked program, across files. Data defined above `main()` is global to the program. Functions in other files can access global data directly by using the same data name as in `main()`, preceded by the keyword `extern`, as in:

   ```
   extern int page_count;
   ```

   This instructs the compiler to use the memory associated with the original definition of `page_count`, located above `main()`.

The linked program can contain object modules from one or more source files. Traditional COBOL has no program global data definition, but COBOL II does allow data elements to be declared GLOBAL. You should minimize your use of global data in both C and COBOL, because data can easily be corrupted and it is difficult to find the cause.

The following sample program includes the three types of data.

```
#include <stdio.h>

int         page_count;            /* program global       */
char        run_date      [12];    /* program global       */

static int  record_count;          /* file global          */
static char dept_name     [21];    /* file global          */

main()
{
   int      cust_no;               /* local to this function */
   char     cust_name    [31];     /* local to this function */

   ...
   return (0);
}
```

Three Types of Functions

Functions in C can be designed to work in three different ways with respect to parameters and shared memory. Listed here in order from the most desirable to the least desirable C functions can be made to work like

1. COBOL subprograms (with parameters passing data).

2. COBOL paragraphs (with access to file global data).

3. COBOL "super paragraphs" or "super subprograms" with access to all data defined in a linked program (program global data).

Each type of function is discussed below. The examples in this chapter are for first type, subprogram-style functions. Examples for paragraph-style functions are in Chapter 10, "Flow of Control Statements." This book does not include examples of "super paragraphs or subprograms" because they can lead to difficulties in problem determination and in maintenance and enhancement.

C Functions That Work Like COBOL Subprograms

COBOL subprograms are programs that are called by another program and have a par-ameter list. The parameters are named in the PROCEDURE DIVISION USING statement, and they are defined in the LINKAGE SECTION. The called subprogram can have its own DATA DIVISION (file global data), but the only data in the calling program that it knows about is what is passed to it. This assumes you do not use global data in COBOL II.

One of the tenets of good design is that you should design functions on a "need to know" basis. In other words, a function should *not* have access to any more data elements than it needs to do its own well-defined job. This strategy pays off during the life cycle of the program when enhancements and maintenance occur. If a function uses only the data passed to it and the data defined locally to that function, it is much less likely to affect other functions when it is changed. It is also much less likely to be affected when other functions change.

Generally, you should design C functions with parameters, named and defined in the function prototype and the function header. The *called* function should not have access to any of the data defined in the *calling* function, except through parameters. All the C library routines discussed in this book, such as strcpy(), printf(), fopen(), are designed this way.

C Functions That Work Like COBOL Paragraphs

In COBOL, all data defined in the DATA DIVISION is available to all paragraphs in the file. A file is generally the same as a program in COBOL.

C programs can be written so that data is defined in a file global manner at the top of the file. The data is then available to all functions within the file without passing parameters in the call to the function. This kind of C program operates like a COBOL program with paragraphs.

This method has a role in business systems, in particular in small and medium-sized batch programs. For a batch program that consists of several functions in one file, file global data is generally not a problem, because all the functions that use the data are in one file.

C Functions That Work Like COBOL "Super Paragraphs" or "Super Subprograms" with Program Global Data

Traditional COBOL has nothing like this, but COBOL II allows global data declaration, this means a paragraph or subprogram can access data defined in another subprogram in the same link edit list. This is what program global data means.

C also allows program global data definition. This is both a blessing and a curse, but mostly a curse. It's a blessing because it can be very handy to avoid passing parameters five or ten levels deep in a subprogram structure. It's a curse because program global data is subject to corruption, which is usually hard to track down. If a global data element is available to 10 or 15 functions, figuring out which function clobbered the data can be very difficult. Program global data can also mask poor design. An example of this would be having a function use 10 or 20 global data elements. If these were being passed as parameters, it would be obvious that the parameter list is excessive and further design is needed. Use of global data can hide this.

Function Calls

Functions in C can be written in several different ways, depending on the scope of data they are using, but they are called in the same way no matter what design. C function calls are very similar to COBOL subprogram calls.

C Function Call	Equivalent Call in COBOL

compute_fica (emp_ssno,
               hourly_wage,
               hours_worked);
	CALL 'COMPFICA' USING EMP-SSNO,
	                    HOURLY-WAGE,
	                    HOURS-WORKED.

To translate a COBOL call to C, drop CALL, USING, and the quotes. Put the parameters inside parentheses. At first it looks funny to call a function without using CALL and USING, but you get used to it after a while.

The COBOL CALL statement invokes another program, usually called a subprogram. The CALL statement can optionally pass parameters to the subprogram. The subprogram does some work and hands control back with the GOBACK statement. The subprogram does not have access to any of the data in the calling program except for the data items passed in the LINKAGE SECTION.

Functions in C typically operate like the COBOL subprogram. C functions are called from another function; they are passed a list of parameters. They do some work and return control with the return statement. Properly designed functions don't know about any data in the calling function other than passed parameters. The C library routines that come with your compiler, such as printf(), gets(), fclose(), and so on, are designed this way.

Memory Between Function Calls

When you call a subprogram in COBOL using the CALL 'PROGNAME' syntax and use the NODYNAM compile option, the program named by PROGNAME is statically called. This means all WORKING-STORAGE values are maintained from one call to the next, and memory is not released.

In C the default is the opposite of this. If you declare variables in a function without using a storage class, it defaults to auto. Memory for automatic variables is allocated when a function is called and released when the function returns.

When an auto variable has no initial assignment, memory contents can be garbage when the function begins. When an auto variable has an initial assignment, that value is put in the variable. All memory associated with an automatic variable is released when the function returns. No values are maintained from one call to the next for an auto variable. This means the function cannot depend on its internal values from a previous call.

However, as always in C, there is a way. Use of the static storage class causes a variable to be maintained in memory from one call to the next. If you need a variable to maintain its value from one call to the next, precede the data type with the static keyword, as shown below:

```
void print_error_messages ( int err_no,
                            char err_message [] )

{

        int message_length;  /* value reset on every call  */
    static int page_count;      /* value maintained across calls */
    ...
    return;
}
```

Parameter Passing

In C, parameters are passed by reference (which means a subprogram can change the parameter) or by value (which means a subprogram *cannot* change the parameter). When you pass parameters by reference, you are passing the data the way you normally do in COBOL. In COBOL you use the data name in the parameter list; in C you put an ampersand (&) in front of the data name. The ampersand is the *address operator* and indicates that the address of this data element should be used. In both C and COBOL, what you are passing is the address of that data item in the calling program. This means that the subprogram uses the data item in the calling program and can change it.

C offers another option for numbers, single-character fields, and structures: passing by value. When you pass any number, a single-character field, or a structure by value, you simply use the data name. This tells the compiler to pass a *copy* of the contents of the field or structure to the called function. The called function can do anything it wants to that data item, but the original value in the calling function is not affected. Thus the data in calling programs is protected. The COBOL II equivalent to passing by value is using the CALL BY CONTENT construct.

Unfortunately, you cannot pass arrays or strings as by-value parameters. Recall that a string is the char data type with square brackets and two or more characters declared. It is an array of characters. For arrays and strings, the data name, without square brackets, *is* by definition the address of the beginning of the array or string. You do not put an ampersand in front of the name of the array or string to say "address of." An array or string is always passed by reference and can be changed by the called function.

The following table summarizes the rules for passing by reference and passing by value:

Type of Data	Data Declaration		Pass by Reference	Pass by Value
Number	int	reg_hrs;	&reg_hrs	reg_hrs
	long	rec_count	&rec_count	rec_count
	double	tax_amt;	&tax_amt	tax_amt
Single character	char	ot_ind;	&ot_ind	ot_ind
Structure	CUST_REC	master;	&master	master
String	char	last_name [31];	last_name	N/A
Array	double	div_total [5];	div_total	N/A
An occurrence of				
a string	char	last_name [31];	&last_name [4]	last_name [4]
an array	double	div_total [5];	&div_total [3]	div_total [3]

Example

The following example shows what by-value and by-reference parameters look like in code. The program includes a main() function and a call to another function.

```
/*                        call_by.c        10/04/94            */

#include <stdio.h>

main()
{

    double  gross_pay;                       /* a number           */
    double  tax_amount          = 0.0;       /* another number     */
    char    run_option;                      /* a single character */
    char    excess_ind          = 'N';       /* another one        */
    char    state_code      [3];             /* a string           */
    double  state_tax_total [50] = { 0 };    /* array of numbers   */

    ...
```

```
        compute_tax_amt ( gross_pay,           /* pass by value     */
                          &tax_amount,         /* pass by reference */
                           run_option,         /* pass by value     */
                          &excess_ind,         /* pass by reference */
                           state_code,         /* pass by reference */
                           state_tax_total );  /* pass by reference */

        return (0);

    }
```

Comments on the Example

In this example some lines have been omitted in order to focus on parameter passing. `tax_amount` and `excess_ind` are passed by reference, which means the address is passed. `compute_tax_amt()` can change their values. This is the way COBOL works by default.

gross_pay and run_option are passed by value, which means that `compute_tax_amt()` will receive a *copy* of each parameter and cannot change the data element in `main()`. COBOL II gets this effect by using `CALL BY CONTENT`.

`state_code` is a string, which can only be passed by reference in C. This means `compute_tax_amt()` can change `state_code`, even if that is inappropriate. The same thing is true for `state_tax_total`, which is an array. Arrays, whether of numbers or characters, cannot be passed by value in C.

To pass parameters two different ways, two kinds of syntax are required in the *calling* function. There are two kinds of syntax in the *called* function as well. In the called function, parameters that are passed by reference are known as *pointers* and have an asterisk in front of their names. This is explained in the next section and the following example.

Pointers Explained in English

The primary use of pointers in C business systems relates *exactly* to one thing in COBOL: a parameter that can be changed by a subprogram. That is the truth, the whole truth, and nothing but the truth.

In order to focus on parameters that can be changed, we will leave aside for the moment the COBOL II `CALL BY CONTENT` construct. We are only interested in the default attributes of parameter passing in COBOL, where the subprogram can change the value of the data in the calling program.

`LINKAGE SECTION` parameters do *not* get memory allocated for the size of the parameter according to the `PIC` clause. What is allocated is one word of memory for an address. A `LINKAGE SECTION` parameter links a parameter name to a data element in the calling program. `LINKAGE SECTION` parameters are actually addresses of data elements in the calling program.

Here is a sample `LINKAGE SECTION`, along with how the COBOL compiler sees it.

What You Code	What the Compiler Generates
LINKAGE SECTION.	LINKAGE SECTION.
01 SOC-SEC-NO PIC 9(9) COMP-3.	01 SOC-SEC-NO PIC 9(8) COMP.
01 LAST-NAME PIC X(30).	01 LAST-NAME PIC 9(8) COMP.
01 MIDDLE-INIT PIC X.	01 MIDDLE-INIT PIC 9(8) COMP.
01 LINE-COUNT PIC 99.	01 LINE-COUNT PIC 9(8) COMP.

The COBOL compiler allocates four bytes for each parameter no matter what you code in the LINKAGE SECTION. The four bytes contain the address of the parameter in the *calling* program. But you don't care about addresses in COBOL. You just pass parameters that the subprogram can change. In fact we are passing pointers.

In C, pointers operate in the same way as COBOL parameters: They allocate one word of memory for an address. They link (point) the parameter name to a data element in the calling function. They are addresses of data elements in the calling function.

Since C allows parameters that can be changed and parameters that can't be changed, there must be a way to distinguish between the two types. The calling function puts the address operator in front of the parameter name when it allows a function to change the contents of the parameter. If there is no address operator preceding the parameter, a copy of the data is passed.

In the *called* function, the distinction must also be made between a by-value parameter and a by-reference parameter. The default is by-value: The name is used without any modifier. You use the pointer operator, *, in front of the parameter name for a by-reference parameter.

When you see *data_name in a C program, think "This is a COBOL-type parameter. The memory for it is allocated somewhere else. When I change *data_name, I am changing the data where it is defined."

The vast majority of pointers in C business systems are parameters for data elements that the *called* function can change. The presence of the asterisk tells you that the memory for this data item is defined somewhere else and you can change the contents of the data item. That's all you need to know.

Example

Now you are ready to see what pointers look like in a program. In the previous example compute_tax_amt() is called using by-reference and by-value parameters. The following example shows the compute_tax_amt() function itself so you can see how the parameters are handled in the *called* function.

```
void compute_tax_amt ( double   gross_pay,              /* copy of gross_pay        */
                       double  *tax_amount,            /* tax_amount in main()     */
                       char     run_option,            /* copy of run_option       */
                       char    *excess_ind,            /* excess_ind in main()     */
                       char     state_code [],         /* string in main()         */
                       double   state_tax_total [] )   /* array in main()          */
{
   *tax_amount = gross_pay * tax_rate;                 /* change it in main()      */

   ytd_gross_amt += gross_pay;

   if (ytd_gross_amt > FICA_MAX_AMT)
   {
      *excess_ind = 'Y';                               /* change it in main()      */
   }

   strcpy (state_code, "XX" );                         /* change it in main()      */

   state_tax_total [3] += *tax_amount;                 /* change it in main()      */

   gross_pay = 0.0;                                    /* NO EFFECT in main()      */

   run_option = 'X';                                   /* NO EFFECT in main()      */

   return;
}
```

Comments on Example

This example is a continuation of the previous example. Like the previous example, this program also has some lines omitted in order to focus on parameter handling.

Note that pointer syntax is used in the function header for compute_tax_amt(). Pointer syntax continues inside the function. When you use a parameter that has been declared as a pointer, you use the asterisk prefix. If you leave off the asterisk, you are dealing with the address of the data rather than the data. This is not right when you are manipulating the parameter as data.

*tax_amount and *excess_ind are passed as pointers: They refer to data elements in the calling function, and this function can change their contents. gross_pay and run_option are being passed by value; there is a local copy created of the value of the data element in main(). The assignment statements for these two elements only affect the local copies; the corresponding fields in main() are unchanged.

Since state_code is a string (an array of characters), it is by definition being passed as a pointer; no special syntax is required. The change to state_code affects the original in main(). The same things are true for state_tax_total, which is an array of numbers. The key fact is that these data elements are arrays. Their syntax and the limitation on the way they can be passed is a quirk of C.

Data names in the called function are the same as in the calling function. This is not required, but it is highly desirable for comprehensibility. Utility functions that are called by multiple functions are an exception to this principle, since the names cannot be made to match multiple calling functions.

Using a Pointer as a Parameter in Another Call

So far we have looked at a `main()` function that calls another function. In the real world, calls are likely to go down three, four, or more levels. Unfortunately, the syntax changes for by-reference parameters from the first to the second level of use. It is consistent from the second call down.

When you pass a data element by reference (so the called function can change the value), use the address operator, &, in front of the item name when it is a number, a single character field, or a structure:

```
main()
{
   double tax_amount;

   . . .

   figure_tax ( &tax_amount );
}
```

Both the function prototype and the function header for `figure_tax()` show `tax_amount` as a pointer (a parameter that the *called* function can change in the *calling* function):

```
void figure_tax ( double *tax_amount);    /* function prototype */

void figure_tax ( double *tax_amount)     /* function header    */
{
   . . .
}
```

However, if `figure_tax()` wants to pass `tax_amount` by reference to another function, it does not use the address operator & or the pointer symbol *, because *`tax_amount` refers to the *contents* of `tax_amount` in `main()`. To continue to pass the *address* of `tax_amount` in `main()`, from the second level down, you use `tax_amount` in the call list, with no & and no *. The function prototypes and function headers continue to use *`tax_amount`, as do the functions, except when passing it again:

```
main()
{
double tax_amount;

   . . .

   figure_tax ( &tax_amount );              /* pass by reference        */
}
void figure_tax ( double *tax_amount)       /* it's a pointer           */
{
   . . .

   *tax_amount = 0.0;                        /* pointer syntax: contents */
                                             /* of tax_amount in main()  */
```

```
      get_fica_tax ( tax_amount );          /* address of tax_amount  */
                                            /* in main()              */
}
void get_fica_tax ( double *tax_amount)    /* still a pointer         */
{
    ...
    *tax_amount = .143 * gross_pay_amt;    /* pointer syntax: contents */
                                           /* of tax_amount in main()  */

}
```

Once `tax_amount` has been passed by reference, it has two identities: `*tax_amount` and `tax_amount`. The first, `*tax_amount`, refers to the *contents* of the passed field in the calling program. This is what you use when you want to change the value. `tax_amount`, without the asterisk, is the *address* of the passed field in the calling program. The primary use in business systems of a pointer without the asterisk is to pass the field or structure again, by reference, to another function.

If this seems somewhat confusing, it is. One thing to note again is that from the second level down, the handling is consistent. Three example programs later in this chapter show parameter passing by reference and by value through several levels of calls; `parm_1.c` on pages 351–353 shows passing numbers, strings, and arrays, `parm_2.c` on pages 357–359 shows passing structures, and `parm_3.c` on pages 362–363 shows passing members of structures. The comments after the programs discuss these issues in detail. I do not try to remember all this syntax, I just refer to the example programs.

Return Value of a Function, Part 2

As mentioned in Chapter 4, C functions have a very useful feature that has only a limited correspondence in COBOL. Every C function can return an invisible parameter, called the return value. The return value is assigned by the `return` statement in the *called* function. This is similar to a combination of setting RETURN-CODE and coding GOBACK/STOP RUN in COBOL. However, C's return value can be in the form of any data type: `int`, `double`, user-defined structure, and so on. In addition, a return value can be returned to any calling function, while RETURN-CODE can only be passed back to the operating system.

A common use of return value in C is to return the data result of a function. This works fine when there is only one data result in a function, such as the absolute value of a number. However, in business data processing it is common to use database packages to retrieve data. A correctly designed program must always check the status from a database call. This means that at least two pieces of data always come back from a function that calls a database package: status and one or more data elements. As a result, such functions typically use the return value to indicate status, as in

```
                        return (SUCCEED);
```

SUCCEED and FAIL are usually defined in an include file that is used throughout a project. Typical values are

```
    #define SUCCEED  1
    #define FAIL     0
```

These two definitions are common but not universal. These values correspond to the way an if statement evaluates a condition. If a condition evaluates to a nonzero value, it is true. If it evaluates to zero, it is false. The return value tells you if the function finished successfully. The data is then passed back through parameters, as either an element, a list of elements, or a structure.

A return value can contain the following:

- A status of how the function performed, such as SUCCEED/FAIL or TRUE/FALSE. For example:

  ```
   return (SUCCEED);
  ```

- A useful single result from the called function, such as a numeric result. For example:

  ```
   return (tax_amount);
  ```

- A result from the called function that usually is not used. Some functions may have a return code that is only interesting for certain coding techniques and not for normal usage. This is common in C library string functions. They often return the number of characters affected, which is seldom interesting. For example:

  ```
   return (num_characters_moved);
  ```

- Nothing, which is called void. This is equivalent to not using RETURN-CODE in COBOL. For example:

  ```
   return;
  ```

The following example program shows four called functions that return a variety of data types.

Example

```
/*                      ret_val.c            10/04/94                    */
#include <stdio.h>
#define  SUCCEED 1                           /* 1 define constant SUCCEED    */
#define  FAIL    0                           /* 2 define constant FAIL       */
double  get_abs_val  (double  amount );      /* 3  function prototypes       */
int     check_range  (double  gl_amt);
long    print_error  (int     status,
                      (char    err_message [] );
```

```
void    print_end_msg (char    end_message [] );

main()
{
   int    status     = SUCCEED;              /* 4  initialize status      */
   double  gl_amt;
   double  expense_amt = -65.37;
   char    err_message [133];
   char    end_message [133]
                    = "JOB IS OVER";

   gl_amt - get_abs_val (expense_amt );      /* 5  function returns       */
                                             /*    result as a double     */

   status = check_range (gl_amt );           /* 6  function returns       */
                                             /*    status as integer      */

   print_error (status,                      /* 7  function returns       */
              err_message);                  /*    error_count. We're     */
                                             /*    not interested in it.  */

   print_end_msg (end_message);              /* 8  function returns       */
                                             /*    nothing                */


   return (0);
}
/*************************** end of main() *****************************************/
double get_abs_val (double amount )           /* 9  function header        */
{
   double positive_amt;
   if (amount < 0.0 )
   {
     positive_amt = amount * -1;
   }
   else
   {
     positive_amt = amount;
   }
   return (positive_amt);                     /* 10 return a double        */
}
/*************************** end of get_abs_val() *****************************/
int check_range (double gl_amt)               /* 11 function header        */
{
   if (gl_amt > 10000.00)
   {
     return (FAIL);
   }
   if (gl_amt < 0.00)
   {
     return (FAIL);
   }
```

```
    return (SUCCEED);                                /* 12 return an int          */
}
/*************************** end of check_range() *********************************/
long print_error (int  status,                       /* 13 function header         */
              char err_message [] )
{
    static long error_count;                         /* 14 keep error_count in memory */
    if (status == FAIL)
    {
        fprintf (stderr, "ERROR\n" );
        error_count += 1;
    }
    else
    {
        fprintf (stderr, "WARNING\n" );
    }
    fprintf (stderr, "%s\n", err_message );

    return (error_count );                           /* 15 return a long           */
}
/*************************** end of print_error() *********************************/
void print_end_msg (char end_message [] )            /* 16 function header         */
{
    fprintf (stderr, "%s\n", end_message);
    return;                                          /* 17 return nothing          */
}
/*************************** end of print_error() *********************************/
```

Comments on Example

Lines 1 and 2   Define two constant values used later in the program. Constants allow the use of meaningful names instead of numbers. Again, in a production system these would be defined in a common include file.

Line 3   Begins a set of function prototypes for functions in this program. get_abs_val() will return a value as a double. check_range() will return an int. print_error() will return a long, and print_end_msg() will return nothing.

Line 4   Uses a constant to assign an initial value to a data element.

Line 5   Calls get_abs_val(), passes it a copy of expense_amt, and assigns the return value to gl_amt, which is a double.

Line 6   Calls check_range(), passes it a copy of gl_amt, and puts the result in status.

Line 7   Calls print_error(), passes it a copy of status, and passes err_message. Since err_message is a string, it is being passed by reference, by definition. print_error()

returns a value as a `long`, but this program is not interested in it, so it doesn't assign the return value.

Line 8   Calls `print_end_msg()` with the string `end_message`. Since strings by definition are passed by reference, `print_end_msg()` could change its contents. The prototype for `print_end_msg()` shows that return value is defined as `void`. This means that there is no return value. The `return` statement in `print_end_msg()` cannot send a value.

Line 9   The function header for `get_abs_value()`. It must match the function prototype for the data type of its return value, number of parameters, and data types of parameters.

Line 10   The return statement that returns a `double` data value to the calling function. `positive_amt` is defined as a `double` inside `get_abs_val()`. It is used to hold the absolute value during the function and then returned.

Line 11   The function header for `check_range()`. It must also match its function prototype.

Line 12   Returns an `int` as `SUCCEED` if the value of `gl_amt` passes the two `if` statements. Notice there are three `return` statements in this function. The `if` statements will return control with a return value of `FAIL` if `gl_amt` fails either test.

This is like the use of `GOBACK` in COBOL, except that people usually only have one `GOBACK` in a subprogram. In C it is common to have more than one `return` in a function. It is preferable to nested `if` statements that go on for pages to avoid a `return` statement. It is also preferable to putting every statement inside an `if` statement that reads `if (NO_ERROR_SO_FAR)`. It is simpler to use `return` when conditions are satisfied. Its use is similar to the `GO TO EXIT` construct in COBOL.

Line 13   The function header for `print_error()`. It must also match its function prototype.

Line 14   Shows how to keep a value in memory after a function returns. Recall that if you do not specify a storage class for a variable, it defaults to `auto`. Automatic variables are allocated memory when a function begins, and that memory is released when the function returns. This means that when you call a function a second time, no automatic variable retains its previous value.

Most of the time this is preferable. As a rule, functions should not "remember" values from a previous call. However, sometimes you want to maintain the value in a variable from one call to the next. You do this by using the `static` storage class when you declare the variable, as shown on this line.

Line 15   Shows `print_error()` returning a running `error_count`. In this program the code calling `print_error()` does not capture the return value. The return value just disappears without any effect.

Line 16   The function header for `print_end_msg()`. It must conform to its function prototype.

Line 17   Returns with no value. Control is transferred back to the calling function, but no data comes in the return value. This is how `return` is used when the function prototype shows `void` as the return value data type.

Calling Functions Using Elementary Data Items

The following example uses integers, single-character fields, a string (an array of characters), and an array of long integers to show how to pass parameters by value and by reference through three levels of calls. Note that everything done in this set of functions using
int is done in the exact same manner for long, double, and any other numeric data type.
As previously noted, the handling of pointer parameters changes in the first called function. It is consistent from that level down.

The example consists of a main() function and three lower functions. The calling hierarchy is as follows:

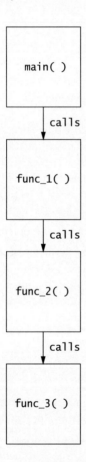

Example

```
/*                    parm_1.c            10/04/94                              */
#include <stdio.h>
#include <string.h>                 /* 1  for strcpy() prototype                */
void func_1 ( int   integer_1,      /* 2  func_1() prototype                    */
              int  *integer_2,
              char  char_1,
              char *char_2,
              char  string_1 [],
              int   rec_cnt [] );

void func_2 ( int   integer_1,      /* 3  func_2() prototype                    */
              int  *integer_2,
              char  char_1,
              char *char_2,
              char  string_1 [],
              int   rec_cnt [] );

void func_3 ( int   integer_1,      /* 4  func_3() prototype                    */
              int  *integer_2,
              char  char_1,
              char *char_2,
              char  string_1 [],
              int   rec_cnt [] );
main()
{
   int   integer_1    = 55;         /* 5  define int & initialize               */
   int   integer_2    = 11;         /* 6  ditto                                 */

   char  char_1       = 'N';        /* 7  define character & initialize         */
   char  char_2       = 'A';        /* 8  ditto                                 */

   char  string_1 [30] = "change me";   /* 9  define string & initialize       */

   int   rec_cnt  [10] = { 0 };     /* 10 define array & initialize             */

   func_1 ( integer_1,              /* 11 pass a copy of integer_1              */
              &integer_2,           /* 12 pass the address of integer_2         */
                char_1,             /* 13 pass a copy of char_1                 */
              &char_2,              /* 14 pass the address of char_2            */
                string_1,           /* 15 pass the address of string_1;         */
                rec_cnt );          /* 16 pass address of rec_cnt array         */

   return(0);                       /* 17 end of function main()                */

}
/***************************** end of main() *********************************/
void func_1 ( int  integer_1,       /* 18 copy of a number                      */
              int *integer_2,       /* 19 pointer to a number                   */
              char  char_1,         /* 20 copy of a single character            */
              char *char_2,         /* 21 pointer to a single character         */
              char  string_1 [],    /* 22 string name is always pointer         */
              int   rec_cnt  [] )   /* 23 array name is always pointer          */
```

```
{
    integer_1  = 99;                /* 24 put 99 in local copy of integer_1      */
    *integer_2 = 44;                /* 25 put 44 in integer_2 in main()          */

    char_1     = 'X';               /* 26 put 'X' in local copy of char_1        */
    *char_2    = 'R';               /* 27 put 'R' in char_1 in main()            */

    strcpy (string_1, "Bert" );     /* 28 put "Bert" in string_1 in main()       */

    rec_cnt [7]    += 50;           /* 29 add 50 to rec_cnt [7] in main()        */

    func_2 ( integer_1,             /* 30 pass a copy of the copy of integer_1   */
             integer_2,             /* 31 pass address of integer_2 in main()    */
             char_1,                /* 32 pass a copy of the copy of char_1      */
             char_2,                /* 33 pass address of char_2 in main()       */
             string_1,              /* 34 pass address of string_1 in main()     */
             rec_cnt );             /* 35 pass address of rec_cnt array in main() */

    return;                         /* 36 return to main()                       */
}
/****************************** end of func_1() ******************************/
void func_2 ( int    integer_1,     /* 37 parm list same as in func_1            */
              int    *integer_2,
              char   char_1,
              char   *char_2,
              char   string_1 [],
              int    rec_cnt [] )
{
    integer_1  = 77;                /* 38 put 77 in local copy of integer_1      */
    *integer_2 = 22;                /* 39 put 22 in integer_2 in main()          */

    char_1     = 'm';               /* 40 put 'm' in local copy of char_1        */
    *char_2    = 'u';               /* 41 put 'u' in char_1 in main()            */

    strcpy (string_1, "Ernie" );    /* 42 put "Ernie" in string_1 in main()      */

    rec_cnt [7] += 25;              /* 43 add 25 to rec_cnt [7] in main()        */

    func_3 ( integer_1,             /* 44 pass a copy of the copy of ...         */
             integer_2,             /* 45 still the address in main()            */
             char_1,                /* 46 pass a copy of the copy of ...         */
             char_2,                /* 47 still the address in main()            */
             string_1,              /* 48 still the address in main()            */
             rec_cnt );             /* 49 still the address in main()            */

     return;                        /* 50 return to func_1()                     */
}
/****************************** end of func_2() ******************************/
void func_3 ( int    f3_integer_1,  /* 51 no changes in method after             */
              int    *f3_integer_2, /*     first level down                      */
              char   f3_char_1,
              char   *f3_char_2,    /*     data name changes OK                  */
              char   f3_string_1 [],
              int    f3_rec_cnt [] )
```

```
{
 return;
}
/******************************* end of func_3() *******************************/
```

Comments on Example

Line 1   The file `string.h` contains the function prototype for `strcpy()`, which is used later in the progam. Including the prototype allows ANSI C to compare the parameter list you send to the function with the parameter list in the prototype. This reduces errors.

Line 2   Defines the function prototype for `func_1()`, which will be called by `main()`. For simplicity, the called functions in this example do not return values. This is indicated by `void` in front of the function name.

   Parameter definitions and names are inside the parentheses. `*integer_2` and `*char_2` are pointers. A pointer, which is identified by an asterisk in front of the name, refers to a parameter that can have its data changed by the called function. It is a by-reference parameter. COBOL parameters are normally by-reference parameters: The called program can change the value of the parameter in the calling program.

   `integer_1` and `char_1` are not preceded by the pointer symbol (an asterisk), so their contents in the calling program *cannot* be changed by the called function. These are by-value parameters. A copy of the value of `integer_1` and `char_1` will be passed.

   `string_1` is a special case, as strings usually are in C. By definition a string always can be changed in the called function, and it doesn't require the asterisk in front of the name. All strings are passed by reference, so they can be changed by the called function.

Lines 3 and 4   The other two function prototypes for this program. They are set up with exactly the same parameters as `func_1()`.

Lines 5 and 6   Two `int` data elements that will be used as parameter examples. They are defined inside `main()` and given initial values. Since they are defined inside `main()`, they are not directly accessible to any other function. `integer_1` will be passed by value, and `integer_2` will be passed by reference.

Lines 7 and 8   Two single-character fields (`char`) that will be used as parameter examples. They also are defined inside `main()` and given initial values. Notice that a *single quote* is used for single-character field value assignments. `char_1` will be passed by value, and `char_2` will be passed by reference.

Line 9   A string field that will be used as a parameter example. Strings can be passed only by reference. Notice that *double quotes* are used for string value assignments.

Line 10   Declares a one-dimensional array of 10 integers and initializes the array to zeroes. Numeric arrays are treated the same as character arrays when passing them to functions.

Lines 11–16   A function call to `func_1()`, with six parameters. It is equivalent to CALL ... USING ... in COBOL.

Lines 11 and 13 are the parameters being passed by value (the name of the field is used, *without* the address operator). A copy of the value in `integer_1` and `char_1` is being passed to `func_1()`. No matter what `func_1()` does, it cannot change the contents of these two data items in the `main()` function. `func_1()` has a separate, local copy of each of these parameter's contents.

Lines 12 and 14 are the parameters being passed by reference. They are being used the same way as COBOL parameters, but the syntax is different—the address operator, `&`, is used. `func_1()` is being passed the addresses of these elements. Thus, when `func_1()` changes the contents of these parameters, the result occurs in the data item in the `main()` function. This is exactly the way COBOL parameters work.

Line 15, a string, is a parameter being passed by reference. Notice that `string_1` does *not* have the address operator, because in C a string's name means the address of the string. String parameters can be passed only by reference.

Line 16 is the parameter passing the entire array of 10 occurrences of `rec_cnt`. An array of numbers is passed the same way as an array of characters. Arrays can only be passed by reference. They are passed without the address operator, and the parameter uses the name of the array without brackets.

Line 17 Returns control to the operating system with a status of zero, which means success.

Lines 18–23 Function header for the function `func_1()`. Both the parameter type and the parameter name are shown for each parameter. The function header must match the function prototype or the compiler will generate an error.

Lines 18 and 20 are the parameters that are *copies* of the contents of the fields in the calling function, `main()`. They are being passed by value. This is denoted by the *lack of* a pointer declaration (`*`) in front of the parameter definition.

Lines 19 and 21 are the numeric and single character parameters that are being passed by reference. This is the way COBOL parameters are normally passed. Remember that a pointer represents a parameter that has its memory defined in the calling function.

Line 22 is the odd case, passing an array (string). In C a string's name is its address. However, there is no pointer declaration (`*`) for a string. `string_1` is being passed by reference because that's the only way strings can be passed in C. The square brackets indicate a string. Do not put a number inside the brackets; size is indicated only in the original declaration.

Line 23 Shows the same case for an array of numbers. An array is always passed by reference and therefore does not get a pointer declaration put in front of the parameter name.

Line 24 Assigns a value of 99 to `func_1()`'s *copy* of `integer_1`. `integer_1` in `main()` still has a value of 55. COBOL II allows this kind of parameter passing in the CALL BY CONTENT construct.

Line 25   Assigns a value of 44 to `integer_2` in `main()`. This is the same way parameters normally work in COBOL. When you change it in the *called* program, it is changed in the *calling* program. Notice that the pointer declaration symbol, the asterisk, is used in the assignment statement.

Line 26   Assigns a value of 'X' to `func_1()`'s *copy* of `char_1`, a single-character field. `char_1 in main()` still has a value of 'N'. Again, `CALL BY CONTENT` works this way.

Line 27   Assigns a value of 'R' to `char_2` in `main()`. This is the same way parameters normally work in COBOL. When you change it in the called program, it is changed in the calling program. Notice that the pointer declaration symbol, the asterisk, is used in the assignment statement.

Line 28   Assigns a value of "Bert" to `string_1` in `main()`. This is the same way parameters normally work in COBOL. When you change it in the *called* function, it is changed in the *calling* function. Notice that no pointer declaration symbol (*) is used in this assignment statement. The name of a string can always be used as the address of the string.

Line 29   Adds 50 to the seventh offset of the `rec_cnt` array in `main()`. Since arrays in C start counting from zero, this is added to the eighth occurrence. The important point is that the array in `main()` is updated. Array notation is no different for a passed array than for a locally defined one. You can use `for`, `while`, `printf()`, or any other operators or functions on a passed array without using pointer syntax.

Lines 30–35   A function call to `func_2()`, with six parameters.

Line 30 passes a copy of `integer_1` in `func_1()`, which itself is a copy of `integer_1` in `main()`. You know it's a copy because it was defined as a by-value parameter in the function header.

Line 31 passes along the address of `integer_2` in `main()`. It was passed as an address (with the &) in the call to `func_1()`. A pointer without the asterisk is the address of the data element referred to by the pointer, rather than the contents of that data element.

Line 32 passes yet another copy of `char_1`. You know it's a copy because it was defined as a by-value parameter in the function header on line 20.

Line 33 passes along the address of `char_2` in `main()`. It was passed as an address (with the &) in the call to `func_1()`. You know it is an address because it is a pointer without an asterisk, as in line 31.

Line 34 is a string's name, which also is its address. No pointer/address symbols are used.

Line 35 is an array name, which also represents its address. There is no pass by value option for arrays.

Line 36   Returns control to `main()`. Since the function prototype says there is no return value (`void`), `return` is used alone.

Line 37   Begins the function header for `func_2()`. After the first level of called functions, there are no more changes in the parameters. Notice that the parameter list, types, and the parameter declarations are all the same as in `func_1()`.

Line 38 Assigns a value of 77 to its own local copy of `integer_1`. `integer_1` in `func_1()` is not affected, and `integer_1` in `main()` is not affected.

Line 39 Places a value of 22 in `integer_2` in `main()`. This is the same as if a COBOL subprogram called another subprogram using one of the parameters it was called with.

Line 40 Assigns a value of 'm' to its own local copy of `char_1`. `char_1` in `func_1()` is not affected, and `char_1` in `main()` is not affected.

Line 41 Places a value of 'u' in `char_2` in `main()`. This is the same as if a COBOL subprogram called another subprogram using one of the parameters it was called with.

Line 42 Places a value of "Ernie" in `string_1` in `main()`. Strings can always be changed by a called function.

Line 43 Adds 25 to the seventh offset of the `rec_cnt` array in `main()`. Arrays can only be passed by reference. Therefore, any change to an array passed as a parameter updates the original. The value of `rec_cnt [7]` in `main()` is now 75. Array notation is no different for a passed array. There is no pointer syntax.

Lines 44–49 Calls another function, `func_3()`, with six parameters. Again note that there are no differences in the handling of parameters after the first called function, `func_1()` in this example. This call list is the same as the one used for calling `func_2()`.

Line 50 Returns control to `func_1()`. Since the function prototype says there is no return value (`void`), `return` is used alone.

Line 51 After the first level down, there are no further changes in the handling of parameters. Notice that the data names in the function header are different from the data names used to call the function. This will compile cleanly. As a general rule, you should use the same names to avoid confusion.

Calling Functions Using Structures

The program in this section follows the same pattern as the previous program, except that the data items used are structures. There is a syntax difference between by-reference parameters that are elementary items and by-reference parameters that are members of structures.

When you are dealing with a structure in a function where it has been declared, you use the structure member operator, the period, to qualify the member name by the structure name:

```
fed_tax.tax_amt
```

C always requires structure members to be qualified. If you pass a structure by value, a copy of the structure will be passed to the called function. The called function then uses the structure member operator to access members of that structure. This is the same as if the structure had been defined in the called function. In effect it has been, because the called function has a copy of the structure.

When a structure is passed by reference, the *called* function is actually operating on the structure in the *calling* function. As with elementary data items, pointers (parameters that represent data that is defined in the calling function) are used, but the syntax is different. Applying pointer syntax, the code would be

```
*fed_tax.tax_amt
```

The only problem with this is that it generates a compile error. What the compiler allows and what is correct is

```
(*fed_tax).tax_amt
```

This is awkward, even by C standards. An alternative syntax, called the *structure pointer operator*, is less awkward. The symbol for it is ->, which is a minus sign followed by a greater-than sign. The structure pointer operator is used in place of the period when a structure has been passed by reference. For a locally defined structure or for a structure passed by value,

```
fed_tax.tax_amt
```

is used. For a structure passed by reference,

```
fed_tax->tax_amt
```

is used. This example shows the same four levels of functions as the previous example. It also shows the use of the structure pointer operator and the transition in using address for reference parameters.

Example

```
/*                    parm_2.c              10/05/94                      */
#include <stdio.h>
#include <string.h>                  /* 1  for strcpy() prototype         */

typedef struct                       /* 2  create structure template      */
{
  long  cust_no;
  char  status;
  char  cust_name  [31];
} CUST_REC;                          /* 3  template/typedef name           */

void func_1 ( CUST_REC master,       /* 4  func_1 prototype                */
              CUST_REC *tran );

void func_2 ( CUST_REC master,       /* 5  func_2 prototype                */
              CUST_REC *tran );

void func_3 ( CUST_REC master,       /* 6  func_3 prototype                */
              CUST_REC *tran );
```

```
main()
{
   CUST_REC master;                                  /* 7  declare master & tran as      */
   CUST_REC tran;                                     /* 8  structs of type CUST_REC      */

   master.cust_no= 2244;                              /* 9  assign initial values         */
   master.status = 'C';
   strcpy (master.cust_name, "AAA Auto" );

   tran.cust_no = 3355;                               /* 10 assign initial values         */
   tran.status  = 'D';
   strcpy (tran.cust_name, "ZZZ Eats" );

   func_1 ( master,                                   /* 11 pass a copy of master         */
            &tran );                                  /* 12 pass the address of tran      */

   return (0);                                        /* 13 end of function main()        */
}
/******************************** end of main() ********************************/
void func_1 ( CUST_REC master,                        /* 14 copy of master                */
              CUST_REC *tran )                         /* 15 pointer to tran               */

{
   master.cust_no= 9988;                              /* 16 put values in copy of master  */
   master.status = 'F';
   strcpy (master.cust_name, "CCC Bank" );

   tran->cust_no= 1199;                               /* 17 put values in tran in main()  */
   tran->status = 'S';
   strcpy (tran->cust_name, "HHH Hats" );

   func_2 ( master,                                   /* 18 pass a copy of the copy of master */
            tran );                                   /* 19 pass the address of tran in main() */

   return;                                            /* 20 return to main()              */
}
/******************************** end of func_1() ********************************/
void func_2 ( CUST_REC master,                        /* 21 parm list same as func_1()    */
              CUST_REC *tran )
{
   master.cust_no= 7766;                              /* 22 put values in local copy of   */
   master.status = 'M';                               /*    master from func_1()          */
   strcpy (master.cust_name, "LLL News" );

   tran->cust_no= 6633;                               /* 23 put values in tran in main()  */
   tran->status = 'Q';
   strcpy (tran->cust_name, "MMM Bike" );

   func_3 ( master,                                   /* 24 pass a copy of the copy of ... */
            tran );                                   /* 25 pass the address of tran in main() */
   return;                                            /* 26 return to func_1()            */
}
```

```
/****************************** end of func_2() ******************************/
void func_3 ( CUST_REC master,           /* 27 no change in parm list        */
              CUST_REC *tran )           /*     after first level down       */
{
   return;
}
/******************************* end of func_3() ******************************/
```

Comments on Example

Line 1   The file `string.h` contains the function prototype for `strcpy()`, which is used later in the progam. Including the prototype allows ANSI C to compare the parameter list you send to the function with the parameter list in the prototype. This reduces errors.

Line 2   Creates a template, or record definition, for a structure used later in the program. This structure template contains a long integer field, a single-character field, and a string. They will all behave in their usual manner.

Line 3   Gives the template, or `typedef`, its name. This structure is invoked whenever the name `CUST_REC` is used as the data type in a data declaration.

Lines 4–6   The function prototypes for the three functions called by `main()`. Each function has two parameters. One parameter is a by-value parameter and is a `CUST_REC` structure with the name `master`. The other parameter is a `CUST_REC` structure with the name `*tran`. It is a by-reference parameter, denoted by the asterisk in front of `tran`. `*tran` is a pointer, which means that the data is defined in the calling function and can be changed there by the called function.

While `master` and `tran` have not yet been defined in the program, the `CUST_REC` data type has been. In function prototypes the parameter *data types* must be defined prior to their use in a prototype, but the *data names* are strictly documentation as far as the compiler is concerned. Parameter data names help people understand what data is being passed to a function and should therefore be supplied.

Line 7 and 8   Two instances of the `CUST_REC` structure type. `master` and `tran` will have the same layout, since they share the same `typedef` type.

Line 9   Assigns initial values to the `master` structure. The structure member operator, a period, is used to qualify the data names in the structure.

Line 10   Shows similar assignment statements to the `tran` structure.

Lines 11 and 12   The call to `func_1()`. The calling convention for structures is the same as it is for data elements: structure name alone to pass by value and the address operator in front of the structure name to pass by reference.

A copy of the `master` structure is being passed to `func_1()`. This is denoted by the use of `master` structure name *without* an address operator. This is the default. Nothing in `func_1()` will be able to change the data in the `master` structure in `main()`. COBOL II allows this with the `CALL BY CONTENT` construct.

For the `tran` structure, however, the address is being passed. This is denoted by the address operator, `&`. This is the way COBOL normally passes parameters. There is no separate copy of the `tran` structure. Anything done by `func_1()` to the `tran` structure will affect the `tran` structure defined in `main()`. Again, this is what normally happens in COBOL.

Line 13 Is the end of the `main()` function. Control is returned to the operating system with a value of zero, or success.

Lines 14 and 15 Comprise the function header for `func_1()`. Two parameters are defined. `master` will be a copy (by value), since there is no pointer symbol. `*tran` will be the address of the `tran` structure (passed by reference) in the calling function. `*tran` will refer to the contents of the `tran` structure, but the structure pointer operator manipulates the member data elements.

Line 16 Shows three lines assigning values to the copy of the `master` structure in `func_1()`. Notice that the structure member operator, the period, is used because master is local to `func_1()`. None of these statements will affect the contents of the master structure in `main()`.

After these statements the values in `master` in `main()` are unchanged:

```
master.cust_no   = 2244
master.status    = C
master.cust_name = AAA Auto
```

The values in the local copy of `master` in `func_1()` are

```
master.cust_no   = 9988
master.status    = F
master.cust_name = CCC Bank
```

Line 17 Shows three lines assigning values to the `tran` structure in `main()`. Although the function prototype and the function header show `*tran`, when you access *members* of a structure passed by reference, you use `tran->`. The structure pointer operator, `->`, replaces the structure member operator (period) when referring to members of a structure that has been passed by reference. It is not consistent, but it is the way you have to do it.

After these statements the values in `tran` in `main()` are

```
tran.cust_no   = 1199
tran.status    = S
tran.cust_name = HHH Hats
```

There is no local copy of `tran` in `func_1()`.

Lines 18 and 19 The call to `func_2()`. A copy of `func_1()`'s copy of the `master` structure is passed to `func_2()`. Also, the address of `tran` in `main()` is passed to `func_2()`. The same rule applies here as in the previous example. The pointer `*tran` represents the data in the `tran` structure in `main()`. The pointer without the asterisk, `tran`, represents the *address* of the `tran` structure in `main()`. We want to continue to pass the address of the `tran` structure in `main()`.

Line 20 Returns control to `main()`. The function prototype and the function header declare that there is no return value by using `void` as the return value data type. Therefore, `return` is used alone.

Line 21 The function header for `func_2()`. It is expecting a copy of `master` and the address of `tran`. It is set up the same way as both `func_1()` and `func_3()`.

Line 22 Shows three lines assigning values to the *copy* of the `master` structure in `func_2()`. Notice that the structure member operator, the period, is used because master is local to `func_1()`. None of these statements will affect the contents of the `master` structure in `main()`.

After these statements the values in `master` in `main()` are unchanged:

```
master.cust_no   = 2244
master.status    = C
master.cust_name = AAA Auto
```

The values in the local copy of master in `func_1()` are also unchanged.
The values in the local copy of `master` in `func_2()` are

```
master.cust_no   = 7766
master.status    = M
master.cust_name = LLL News
```

Line 23 Shows three lines assigning values to the `tran` structure in `main()`. The structure pointer operator, `->`, is used to access the members of the structure. See line 17 for the discussion of the structure pointer operator.

After these statements the values in `tran` in `main()` are

```
tran.cust_no   = 6633
tran.status    = Q
tran.cust_name = MMM Bike
```

There is no local copy of `tran` in `func_2()`.

Lines 24 and 25 The call to `func_3()`, which shows that the use of pointers does not change after the first level of call. `main()` used `&tran` to call `func_1()`. From `func_1()` down, `tran` is used without the address operator or the pointer operator.

Line 26 Returns control to `func_1()`. Since `func_2()` has no return value (`void` is the return value data type in the prototype), `return` is used alone.

Line 27 Shows there is no change in the parameter list in the function header from the first function down.

Calling Functions Using Members of Structures

It is also necessary at times to call a function using a member of a structure. The calling function, where the structure is defined, uses structure syntax to pass individual members to the called function. The called function, however, knows nothing about the structure. All it knows is that individual data elements are being passed. There is no structure syntax in the called function.

In the called function the handling of parameters is the same as it is for elementary data items, strings, and arrays. If pointers are used in the function header, they are used in the body of the function. All the same rules apply.

Example

```
/*                  parm_3.c                10/05/94                        */
#include <stdio.h>
#include <string.h>                    /* 1  for strcpy() prototype         */

typedef struct                         /* 2  create structure template      */
{
   long  cust_no;
   char  status;
   char  cust_name [31];
   int   rec_count [8];

} CUST_REC;                            /* 3  template/typedef name          */

void func_1 ( long    cust_no,         /* 4  func_1 prototype               */
              char  *status,
              char   cust_name [],
              int    rec_count [] );

main()
{
   CUST_REC mast = { 0 };              /* 5  declare & initialize mast      */

   mast.cust_no  = 2244;              /* 6  assign initial values          */
   mast.status   = 'C';
   strcpy (mast.cust_name, "AAA Auto" );
   mast.rec_count [3] = 33;

   func_1 ( mast.cust_no,             /* 7  pass a copy of mast.cust_no    */
            &mast.status,             /* 8  pass address of mast.status    */
            mast.cust_name,           /* 9  pass address of mast.cust_name */
            mast.rec_count );         /* 10 pass address of structure array */

   return (0);                        /* 11 return "success" to O/S        */
}
/******************************* end of main() *******************************/
void func_1 ( long    cust_no,         /* 12 func_1 function header          */
              char  *status,
              char   cust_name [],
              int    rec_count [] )
```

```
{
   cust_no = 9988;                       /* 13 put 9988 in local copy of cust_no   */
   *status = 'F';                        /* 14 update structure in main()          */
   strcpy (cust_name, "CCC Bank" );      /* 15 update structure in main()          */
   rec_count [3] += 55;                  /* 16 update array in struct in main()     */

   return;                               /* 17 return to main()                    */
}
/********************************** end of func_1() **********************************/
```

Comments on Example

Line 1   The file `string.h` contains the function prototype for `strcpy()`, which is used later in the progam. Including the prototype allows ANSI C to compare the parameter list you send to the function with the parameter list in the prototype. This reduces errors.

Line 2   Creates a template, or record definition, for a structure used later in the program. This structure template contains a long integer field, a single-character field, a string, and an array of integers.

Line 3   Gives the template, or `typedef`, its name. This structure will be invoked whenever the name CUST_REC is used as the data type in a data declaration.

Line 4   Begins the function prototype for `func_1()`, which will be called by `main()`. This function is expecting individual data elements, which will be supplied from a structure. The function does not know or care about the structure.

   `cust_no` is the only by-value parameter in the call parameters. `*status` is explicitly a by-reference parameter because it is a pointer. `cust_name` is a string and `rec_count` is an array, and both are, by definition, passed by reference.

Line 5   Invokes the CUST_REC structure template, calls it `mast`, and initializes it to zeroes.

Line 6   Begins four lines of assigning values to the members of the `mast` structure. These are done in the usual manner, with the structure name qualifying the member name. `mast.rec_count [3]` uses the fourth occurrence of the `rec_count` array, which is a member of the `mast` structure. It is the fourth occurrence because subscripts in C start from zero.

Lines 7–10   The call to `func_1()`. Member names of the structure are qualified by the structure name, `mast`. When there is an explicit use of passing by reference, the address operator precedes the structure name, as in `&mast.status`. Both the string and the array are passed by their names, without brackets. Neither can be passed by value.

Line 11   Returns control to the operating system with a return value of zero. Zero is generally considered as successful.

Line 12   Begins the function header for `func_1()`. It matches the function prototype and declares only elementary data elements, since that is how they appear to the function. `*status` is passed as a pointer and is therefore explicitly by reference. Because `cust_name` is a string (a character array) and `rec_count` is an integer array, they are implicitly passed by reference.

Line 13 Puts a value of 9988 in the copy of cust_no, which is local to func_1(). The original mast.cust_no in main() is not affected. Structure member syntax is not used in this function.

Line 14 Updates mast.status in main(). This looks like an ordinary updating of a parameter's content in the calling function, which it is. The only quirk is that the *calling* function uses structure member syntax to pass the parameter, and the *called* function sees the parameter as an elementary data element.

Line 15 Copies a value into mast.cust_name in main(). Strings are always passed by reference, even if they are defined inside a structure. There is no local copy of cust_name.

Line 16 Adds 55 to mast.rec_count [3]. As with strings, arrays are always passed by reference, even if they are defined inside a structure.

Line 17 Returns control to main(). Since the function prototype declares the return value data type to be void, return is used without a value.

Summary of Rules for Passing Parameters

Passing Parameters from the Function Where Parameters Are Defined

1. To pass a number, a single character, or a structure as a parameter that *can* be changed, pass the *address* of the parameter:

    ```
    func_1 ( &integer_1 );
    ```

2. To pass a number, a single character, or a structure as a parameter that *cannot* be changed, pass the *name* of the parameter:

    ```
    func_1 ( integer_1 );
    ```

3. To pass a string (it *always* can be changed), pass the *name* of the string:

    ```
    func_1 ( string_1 );
    ```

    Strings can only be passed by reference, and the compiler knows that the name of the string means the address of the beginning of the string.

    Strings are arrays (see the next item), but they are so commonly considered a separate data type that they merit separate mention.

4. To pass an array (it *always* can be changed), pass the *name* of the array:

    ```
    func_1 ( sales_total );
    ```

Arrays can only be passed by reference, and the compiler knows that the name of the array means the address of the beginning of the array.

Receiving and Using Parameters in a Called Function

1. No address operators (&) are used in the function prototype or the function header.
2. A numeric or single-character parameter being passed by reference must have the pointer declaration (*) in front of its name when it is declared (defined) in the function prototype and the function header.
3. Arrays and strings have the array or string name along with empty brackets in the function prototype and function header. Arrays and strings are always passed by reference and without pointer syntax.
4. If a parameter has a pointer symbol in its declaration, keep using the asterisk when you want to refer to the contents of the parameter.

Passing Parameters from One Called Function to Another Called Function

1. If you are passing a parameter that you received as a pointer, pass the name without the asterisk. Remember that *data_name refers to the data in the calling function, and data_name is the address of that data.
2. If you are passing a parameter that is defined in the current function, follow the rules in the first section.

Run-Time Parameters

It is common to pass one or more values to a program when it begins execution. These are usually called *run-time parameters*, and they supply values for variables that influence the execution of the program.

Run-time parameters in COBOL are typically passed in one of two ways: They come from the EXEC job control statement, or they are retrieved from a file or partitioned data set. The first method is similar to how C handles run-time parameters.

When you want to pass parameters from the EXEC job control statement to a main program at run time, you create a LINKAGE SECTION in the main program with an 01 group item, often called PARM-FIELDS. The first element in PARM-FIELDS is a two-byte binary field that contains a count of the number of bytes passed from the EXEC statement. If no parameters are passed, the byte count is zero.

A main COBOL program with run-time parameters has a PROCEDURE DIVISION USING

PARM-FIELDS statement. Once the program begins, the parameter fields are available to the program. Byte count is checked to see if parameters were passed.

The method in C for passing variables to a program at run time is similar. The main() function has two predefined parameters that allow passing data to a main() function. The compiler does not care what you call them. By convention they are called argc and argv. Since there are literally millions of lines of C code which use this convention, it should be followed.

The first variable, argc, stands for argument (parameter) *count*. argc is an integer that contains the number of parameters passed to the program. The second variable, argv, stands for argument (parameter) *values*. argv is an array (table) of parameters that were passed. They come in as character strings. Any parameter that is a number or single-character field will have to be converted from a string. This is shown in the example program below.

Run-time parameters for C programs are either typed in at the operating system command prompt or placed in a script immediately following the program execution statement. The general form is

```
C:> program_name parm_1 parm_2 ...
```

where C:> represents the operating system prompt, program_name is the name of the program, and parm_1, parm_2, and so on are the values for the run-time parameters. C assumes a space separates parameter values.

Run-time parameters.

C Keyword/Symbol/Function		
	argc	(parameter count)
	argv	(parameter values)

argc and argv are parameters for the main() function when you want to supply execution time parameters. When you type the name of the executable at the command prompt and supply run-time parameters, the parameters are placed in an array of strings, one string per parameter.

argc contains the count of parameters, and argv is an array of the parameter values that were submitted. The parameters can be used directly from the array, but they are usually extracted from the argv array and placed in data elements defined in the program.

Syntax

```
main ( int   argc,
       char *argv [] )
```

Sample

```
main ( int   argc,
       char *argv [] )
```

COBOL Equivalent

```
PROCEDURE DIVISION USING PARM-FIELDS.
```

This sample does not show the chief difference between C and COBOL run-time parameters. In COBOL the run time parameters are available when the first instruction of the program executes. In C you must retrieve the parameters from the array pointed at by `argv` before you can use them. See the following "Discussion" and "Example" sections.

Include File

None. `argc` and `argv` are built into the compiler.

See Also

`atoi()`	— convert a character string to `int` (integer)
`atol()`	— convert a character string to `long` (long integer)
`atof()`	— convert a character string to `double` (decimal number)
`gets()`	— get a string of characters from the terminal
`scanf()`	— extract numbers, characters, or strings from terminal input
`strcpy()`	— copy a literal or string to another string

Parameter Definitions

`int argc`

Integer field that contains the number of parameters submitted.

`char *argv []`

`*argv` is a pointer, as indicated by the asterisk in front of it. A pointer refers to data that can be changed and is defined somewhere else, usually in another function.

Return Value

Does not apply to `argc/argv`.

Scope

Used in `main()` functions only.

Anatomy

```
main ( int argc, char *argv [] )
```
_____
                    |
         Required (if used)

`main`

The name of the function that will begin executing when the program starts. There is one and only one `main()` function in an executable program.

```
int argc
```
The data type (`int`) and parameter name (`argc`) of the first parameter in `main()`. It contains the count of the number of parameters submitted at execution time.

```
char *argv []
```
The data type (`char ... []` indicates a character array) and parameter name (`*argv`) of the second parameter in `main()`. `*argv` is a parameter (pointer) referring to an array of parameter values the user supplied at run time. Memory for this array is in system memory rather than program memory.

The way to read this line is to say that "`*argv` is a parameter that is an array of strings." `*argv` is a pointer/parameter, and `char []` is a character array. There is no number between the brackets because the array is defined somewhere else.

Discussion

`argc` is the number of parameters actually submitted at execution time. There are two unusual things about `argc`:

- It starts counting from 1.
- It always has a value that is 1 greater than the number of user parameters submitted. If two parameter values are submitted, `argc` will have a value of 3.

Most counting in C starts from zero, because most counts are offsets, or the distance from the beginning of something. `argc` is not an offset but a count, so it begins at 1.

`argc` always has a value of at least 1, because the first argument (parameter) is always reserved by the compiler, usually for the program name. In business systems, this parameter is seldom used. Most programs know what their own names are.

The following table shows the relationship between `argc`, `argv` offsets, and `argv` values:

argc count	argv offset	argv value
1	[0]	Program name
2	[1]	First user parameter
3	[2]	Second user parameter
...	...	...
n	[n – 1]	Last user parameter

`argc` should be checked by the program at start-up to see if the correct number of parameters has been submitted. See the example program below.

`argv` is an array that contains all supplied execution time parameters. They are read in as strings. Numbers and single-character fields can be supplied as parameters, but you will need to convert them from strings. This is also shown in the example program.

Philosophy of Execution Time Parameters in COBOL and C

Production jobs in COBOL shops generally run overnight, with parameters submitted hours earlier. COBOL programs check parameter values for existence and reasonableness and halt the job if the parameters do not pass inspection. Depending on how critical the job is, a programmer may get a phone call in the middle of the night, or the job may be looked at the next day.

In C shops, production jobs can operate this way, but there is another category of C production jobs which is not common in COBOL shops: programs that "talk" to the user. In the C world, it is common for the user to submit production jobs or reports for immediate execution. In turn, C programs may prompt the user for parameters.

The example program below shows the basic method of accepting parameters if the correct number was submitted and prompting for them otherwise. This is both the most simple and the most common method.

A more elaborate technique is to accept parameters or prompt for them, as below, but follow that by a loop which allows the user to change any parameter. At the bottom of the loop is a question: "Are all parameters OK?" If the answer is yes, the program breaks out of the loop. If not, the loop executes again, showing parameters and allowing the user to change them. This technique is not commonly used because, although it is very polite, it is also elaborate. It is easy to code 50 to 100 lines to accomplish and is therefore seldom done.

The technique shown in this example program is usually acceptable.

Example

```
/*              argc.c                    10/15/94                */
#include <stdio.h>
#include <string.h>                 /* 1  for strcpy() prototype   */
#include <stdlib.h>                 /* 2  for atoi() and atof()    */

char    run_option;                 /* 3  parameter destinations   */
char    as_of_date [11];
double  percent;
int     dept_no;

main (int    argc,                  /* 4  main() with parameters   */
      char *argv [] )
{
   if ( argc == 5 )                 /* 5  if count == expected     */
   {
      strcpy (as_of_date, argv [1] );    /* 6  argv to string            */
      dept_no    = atoi ( argv [2] );    /* 7  argv to int               */
      percent    = atof ( argv [3] );    /* 8  argv to double            */
      run_option = *argv [4];            /* 9  argv to single character  */
   }
   else
   {
      printf ("Enter date as mm/dd/yy \n");   /* 10  prompt and get date */
```

```
    gets (as_of_date);

    printf ("Enter Dept number \n");        /* 11 prompt and get dept_no      */
    scanf ("%d", &dept_no );
    fflush (stdin);

    printf ("Enter percent \n");            /* 12 prompt and get percent      */
    scanf ("%lf", &percent );
    fflush (stdin);

    printf ("Enter run option \n");         /* 13 prompt and get run_option   */
    scanf ("%c", &run_option );
    fflush (stdin);
}
/* rest of program goes here */

    return (0);                             /* 14 return "success" to O/S     */
}
```

Comments on Example

Line 1 The function prototype for strcpy() is contained in the file string.h. strcpy() is used later in the program. Including the prototype allows ANSI C to compare the parameter list you send to the function with the parameter list in the prototype. This reduces errors.

Line 2 The function prototypes for atoi() and atof() are contained in the file stdlib.h.

Line 3 Begins the declaration of the four data elements that will receive parameter values. The program will move argv values to these elements if they are supplied on the command line when the program is invoked. Otherwise, the program will prompt the user for values and populate these fields with the keyboard responses.

Line 4 Shows the function header for main() when there are run-time parameters. Parameter data types and parameter names are declared. These are the parameters that deliver the user-supplied parameters.

Line 5 Checks the number of parameters supplied. The program is expecting four user parameters, so it must check argc for a value of 5. Remember that the first parameter is supplied by the operating system and is the program name.

Line 6 Uses strcpy() to copy the contents of argv [1] into as_of_date.

Line 7 Converts the second parameter argv [2] to an int by calling atoi(). If you wanted to convert it to a long, you would call atol() and assign the return value to a data element declared as a long.

Line 8 Converts the third parameter argv [3] to a double by calling atof().

Line 9 Converts argv [4] to a single character. The fourth parameter is expected to be a single letter. This syntax is unlike anything else in this book, but it is still pointer syntax.

`*argv [4]` refers to the contents of `argv [4]` (which is defined as a string). Pointer syntax is used to get "contents of" because `argv [4]` is treated as a single character rather than as a string. (Since `argv [4]` is a string, it would seem that `argv [4,0]` should access the first character, but this does not work.)

Only the first character in `argv [4]` will be picked up by this statement, because it assigns the contents of `argv [4]` to a single-character field. If you enter two or more characters, only the first one will be placed in `run_option`. The other characters are still in `argv [4]`, but they are not copied.

For all other data types you treat `argv [n]` as a string and perform a string conversion. This is another case I do not try to remember. I just come back to this example when I need to get a single character from the command line.

Line 10 Begins the code that executes when an incorrect number of parameters is entered. Each parameter will be requested and then retrieved from keyboard input. This line prompts for the date and then uses `gets()` to put the reponse in `as_of_date`.

Line 11 Begins three statements which get a value for `dept_no`. There is a prompt for department number followed by a call to `scanf()` to get the response, convert it to an `int`, and put it in `dept_no`. `scanf()` needs an address for the destination of the item, which is why it uses `&dept_no`.

The `scanf()` statement is followed by the `fflush (stdin)` call. Remember that for a numeric field `scanf()` discards leading non-numeric characters, but leaves any trailing ones in the keyboard buffer. The Enter key character is a trailing non-numeric character which is still in the keyboard buffer after the `scanf()` call. It is good practice to always code a call to `fflush (stdin)` after each use of `scanf()`. It leaves the keyboard buffer empty for following statements.

Line 12 Is similar to line 11, except that this `scanf()` converts the response to a `double`. Again, the address operator is used. If your computer has a four-byte machine word you can probably use `%f` instead of `%lf`. The `scanf()` is followed by `fflush (stdin)` to clear out the keyboard buffer.

Line 13 Prompts for and gets a run option. Since the format specifier for `scanf()` is for a single character `%c`, the first character in the keyboard buffer is taken and placed in `run_option`. This is the case where the previous `fflush (stdin)` ensures correct results. If the preceding `fflush()` call were not there, this `scanf()` would fetch the Enter key character from the keyboard buffer (from the previous `scanf()` call) and place it in `run_option`. This error can take a while to figure out. If you always code `fflush (stdin)` after each call to `scanf()` your results will be what you expect.

Line 14 Returns a zero to the operating system, which will be interpreted as success.

Summary

This chapter examined functions that work like COBOL subprograms, with emphasis on how to pass and use parameters. We saw that one file can contain more than one function and that multiple files can be compiled and linked together. However, only one `main()` function can exist in an executable.

Scope of data indicates which parts of a program can access a given data element. C has three levels of scope: program global data, file global data, and local function data. Program global data should generally be avoided because of problems with inadvertent data corruption. File global data is acceptable for medium and small batch programs where all functions are in one file. Defining data local to a function offers the most protection and is the recommended choice.

Calling functions in C is similar to calling subprograms in COBOL, but without the `CALL` and `USING` reserved words. C allows functions to change parameter data (pass-by-reference), the default in COBOL. C also allows a copy of a parameter to be passed (pass-by-value), so the original field in the calling function is protected. You can't do this in traditional COBOL, but you can do it in COBOL II with the `BY CONTENT` reserved words.

Pass-by-value is the default in C and has no special punctuation. Pass-by-reference is the exception and requires the address operator `&` in front of the parameter name when calling the function. The parameter in the called function also has special punctuation, the pointer operator `*`. When you see pointers in a function header or a function prototype, that means the function can change the contents of the data element in the calling function.

Unfortunately, these rules do not apply to arrays, which include character strings, arrays of numbers, and arrays of structures. Arrays can only be passed by reference, so the called function can always update the array (or string) in the calling function.

Called functions can pass a value back to the calling function with a return value. Return value is passed with the `return` keyword, followed by a value, program constant, or expression. In business systems this is generally used to indicate the success or failure of the function, such as `return (SUCCESS)`.

Three example programs provide a dictionary of common types of parameter passing in C. Each program consists of a `main()` function and one to three levels of calls. The first program shows how to pass numbers, single character fields, and arrays (character and numeric). Numbers and single character fields can be passed by-reference or passed by-value. Both numeric arrays and character arrays (strings) can only be passed by-reference.

The second program shows how to pass structures, by-reference and by-value. It shows how the structure pointer operator is used to access members of a passed-by-reference structure. The third example declares a structure and then passes members of the structure to a function. The called function does not know that a structure is involved: all it sees are individual data elements.

C, like COBOL, allows programs to receive parameters at run time. C's method is not as simple as COBOL's, but it is relatively straightforward. Parameters are held in an area of system memory in two variables called `argc` and `argv []`. The `argc` variable has the count of how many parameters were passed. The parameter values are stored in an array of strings named `argv []`. You transfer the values to your variables with `strcpy()`, `atoi()`, `scanf()`, and so on.

CHAPTER 12

Table Handling

Introduction

Tables are called arrays in C. Array handling in C is similar to table handling in COBOL. Following a definition of arrays, this chapter compares tables and arrays, along with subscripts and indexes. We examine array definition for both one-dimensional and multidimensional arrays. Array initialization is discussed, along with default initialization.

This chapter also shows how C handles memory for arrays. Array memory can be allocated at compile time or dynamically allocated at run time. Linked lists—a method for using dynamically allocated memory—are discussed. We talk about how to use existing linked list routines instead of writing them. Dynamic memory allocation and release are also described.

What is an Array?

An array is a related set of occurrences of a data element or a group of data elements that you want to process in a tabular form. You can access array elements individually by their subscripts. They are stored contiguously in memory. An array element *occurs* some number of times.

The simplest array has one repeating element and is said to be one dimensional. More dimensions can be created. These additional dimensions define repeating groups within repeating groups. This kind of array is called multidimensional.

One of the fundamental differences between C arrays and COBOL tables is that subscripts in C always begin at 0. Unlike COBOL, where the count and the subscript always agree, in C the subscript is always one less than the count. This takes some getting used to.

For a simple array example, the following statement declares a one-dimensional array of a set of five numbers of the data type `int`:

```
int  rec_count [5];
```

Using C subscript notation, you can assign some values to the elements of the array:

```
rec_count [0] = 17;
rec_count [1] = 8;
rec_count [2] = 44;
rec_count [3] = 21;
rec_count [4] = 65;
```

Assuming the size of an `int` is two bytes and the location of the first element, `rec_count [0]`, is at machine address `1000`, memory for this array looks like the following:

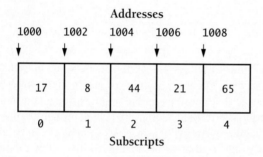

This concept is extended when you add another dimension to an array. For a two-dimensional array, visualize the data being organized by rows and columns. A two-dimensional array has two subscripts: The first refers to the row and the second refers to the column. Continuing the example, you can define a two-dimensional array for `rec_count` as follows:

```
int  rec_count [2] [5];
```

Again, using C subscript notation, you can assign values to the elements of the array, using both subscripts:

```
rec_count [0] [0] = 17;
rec_count [0] [1] = 8;
rec_count [0] [2] = 44;
rec_count [0] [3] = 21;
rec_count [0] [4] = 65;
```

```
rec_count [1] [0] = 55;
rec_count [1] [1] = 12;
rec_count [1] [2] = 9;
rec_count [1] [3] = 33;
rec_count [1] [4] = 15;
```

In production programs you would be more likely to use data values for the subscripts rather than hard-coding them as shown here.

Continuing to assume an int is two bytes and that the array starts at address 1000, here is what it would look like in memory:

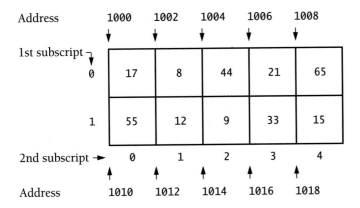

This two-dimensional array in C is arranged in memory the same way as a two-dimensional table is in COBOL. The big difference is that C subscripts start from zero. There are also some differences in subscript notation, but they are minor.

Tables in COBOL

Tables in COBOL are the workhorses of total keeping. The most common use of them is to keep one or more dimensions of totals for update or report programs. Traditional COBOL allows tables to have up to three dimensions, or levels. This is generally sufficient, as well as being about as many levels as most people can understand. COBOL II allows up to seven levels.

COBOL tables can use subscripts or indexes. Subscripts are ordinary integer data items. Indexes are actually machine registers and are not defined by the programmer as items in the DATA DIVISION. Subscripts can be changed by arithmetic statements. Index values can only be changed by PERFORM, SET, and SEARCH statements. An index can be used as a relative index, as in IND-1 + 2. COBOL II allows relative subscripting, which you cannot do in traditional COBOL.

COBOL II supports relative subscripting, which means that a COBOL II subscript is a kind of combination subscript and index. This is similar to a C subscript (as discussed below).

COBOL has a very handy SEARCH statement, which will go through a table to find a match. C, unfortunately, has nothing like this.

Arrays in C

Tables in C are called arrays. C puts no real limit on the number of dimensions an array can have, but you should still be bound by what people can comprehend, which means three or fewer levels. Declarations of arrays in C are simpler but less descriptive than in COBOL. C has subscripts but no indexes. C subscripts can be used for relative subscripting, however, which is similar to COBOL II subscripts.

C can also process arrays using pointers. Pointer syntax for array handling is more complicated and less obvious than subscript syntax and is therefore not discussed here. Everything you need to do for business problems can be done cleanly by using subscripts.

Subscript Notation

Subscripts in C are placed inside brackets rather than parentheses. Multiple subscript values in COBOL are all placed inside one set of parentheses. In C each subscript value is placed inside its own set of brackets.

COBOL

C

```
ADD TRAN-AMT TO YTD-TOTAL (DEPT, DIV).     ytd_total [dept] [div] += tran_amt;
MOVE 0 TO TOTAL-AMT (GRAND, MID, DET).     total_amt [grand] [mid] [det] = 0.0;
IF TRAN-CNT (MONTH, DAY) > 0 ...           if (tran_cnt [month] [day] > 0 ) ...
```

Subscripts in C must be declared as integer values, typically int or long. Some compilers will complain if you use long as a subscript. This can turn into a de facto limit of 32,767 occurrences in an array if int is defined as two bytes. Check your local compiler.

Relative Subscripting

As previously mentioned, C allows relative subscripting. For example, the following statement compares the current value of dept_no to the value one occurrence earlier in the array:

```
if ( dept_no [i - 1] == dept_no [i] )
```

Offset Versus Count

The biggest difference between C arrays and COBOL tables is that the first occurrence of any element in an array in C has a subscript value of zero. C uses offsets rather than counting occurrences from 1. An offset is the number of occurrences from the beginning of the array. The first element in an array has an offset of zero; thus, the first element's subscript value is zero. Obviously, this is different from COBOL, and it will take you a while to get used to it.

Most for statements in C start from zero, because that is the first element in the array:

```
for ( i = 0; i < MAX_TOTALS; i++ )
{
   ...
   total_amt += dept_amt [i];
}
```

The use of offsets means that the maximum subscript value is always one less than the count of occurrences. This leads to the common for statement construct that starts at zero and executes while the subscript is less than the maximum number of occurrences:

```
#include <stdio.h>
#define MAX_TOTALS 10
main()
{
   double dept_amt [MAX_TOTALS];
   int  i;

   for ( i = 0; i < MAX_TOTALS; i++ )
   {
      dept_amt [i] = 0.0;
   }
   return (0);
}
```

MAX_TOTALS is set up as a constant integer. All references to the array maximum use MAX_TOTALS. If the programmer later needs to change the size of the array, only one line has to be changed. The for statement then goes through the array, starting with offset 0. When i is incremented to 9, i is still less than MAX_TOTALS, so the for will execute for offset 9, or occurrence 10. The next time i is incremented, its value becomes 10. The while-true condition of the for statement is then not true: i is not less than MAX_TOTALS. The for statement terminates.

To make array processing straightforward, you should.

- Use #define to define a program constant for the array size
- Code for statements as for (i = 0; i < MAX; i++)

Subscript 0 and Subscript 1

The normal value for the first subscript in an array in C is 0. Most for statements are coded to begin from 0 and to continue while the subscript is less than the maximum number of occurrences in the array.

Although you may want to pad all arrays so processing starts at subscript 1, there are really only two cases where this is appropriate: for date-based arrays and for arrays that use data as subscripts. (The first is really a subset of the second.)

In date-based arrays an occurrence holds data for a month of the year. In such cases you want to be able to use the numeric value of a month as a subscript rather than constantly having to subtract 1 from the month to get the subscript. For these arrays you typically pad the array by declaring 13 occurrences for months and then using month as a subscript for values 1 through 12. Zero is simply not used as a subscript value.

The other case that calls for padding an array occurs when something like a department number from the data is used to maintain an array of totals. Few organzations have a department number of zero. You also pad the array by making the maximum number of occurrences one larger than the number of departments and ignoring department zero.

Arrays that are internal to programs should start at zero. For instance, a report or roll-up program that has three sets of totals should define the array as occurring three times and use subscripts 0, 1, and 2, as this example shows:

```
#define   DETAIL     0
#define   SUB        1
#define   GRAND      2

#define   MAX_TOTALS 3
int       i;
double    sales_total [MAX_TOTALS] = { 0 };
```

After defining subscript values and the maximum occurrences as program constants, the body of the program can just use DETAIL, SUB, and GRAND as subscripts. Any for statement needed to process the whole array reads something like

```
for ( i = 0; i < MAX_TOTALS; i++ )
{
   printf ("Sales total = %f \n", sales_total [i] );
}
```

Here's a summary of the most important points in C subscripting:

- Use program constants for totals and array maximums.
- Use a subscript such as i to get the data out.
- Use zero-based subscripting most of the time.

Memory Contents at Run Time

Some C compilers cause programs, when they start, to initialize memory to zeroes for every data item that is not assigned an initial value. *This is not guaranteed*, however.

Since C does not guarantee initialization to zero you should take care of it. Array initialization in C is simpler than in COBOL, even considering the INITIALIZE statement. C numeric data types, int, long, double, and so on all have the same bit configuration for a value of zero: All bits are set to zero. In addition, an empty string has this same bit configuration. This contrasts with the (IBM) mainframe world where numeric display numbers, packed numbers, and binary numbers all have different bit configurations for a value of zero.

Given that all data types have the same value for zero, all you need to do is assign a zero value when declaring the array (or any other data element). Assigning the three characters { 0 } as an initial value causes any array, structure, or array of structures to be filled with zeroes. Here are a few examples:

```
int     rec_count   [5]      = { 0 };
double  sales_total [10] [8] = { 0 };

typedef struct
{
    long    cust_no;
    char    cust_name       [31];
    double  current_bal;
} CUST_REC;

CUST_REC  master [100] = { 0 };
```

These examples show a simple method to initialize arrays at compile time. No loops are required to set values to zeroes. This is equivalent to INITIALIZE in COBOL II.

Running Off the End of an Array

We have all done it in COBOL, and we will all do it in C. Neither compiler does anything to prevent you from creating or using a subscript value greater than the upper limit of the array. Some languages do prevent you from clobbering memory with an out-of-bounds subscript, but C and COBOL are not among them. The effect in C is the same as it is in COBOL—unpredictable results—but they usually include the program blowing up.

Defining Arrays in C

To declare (define) an array in C, you give the data type and the data element name, followed by one or more pairs of brackets enclosing a number of occurrences.

Each level is defined by a pair of square brackets with an integer or an integer constant name between them. The integer value defines the number of occurrences at that level.

Syntax

```
data_type array_element [level_1_occurs] [level_2_occurs] ... [level_n_occurs] ;
```

Samples

```
long    month_count      [12];
double  sales_total_amt  [5] [12] [10];
char    last_name        [31];
long    dept_total_cnt   [MAX_DEPTS];
```

Scope

Any valid data type can be used in an array, including structures or any other programmer-defined data type.

Anatomy

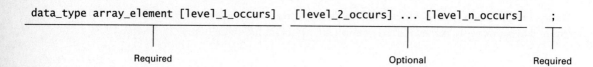

```
data_type array_element [level_1_occurs]    [level_2_occurs] ... [level_n_occurs]    ;
```

Required	Optional	Required

`data_type`

Any of the data types of C: `char`, `int`, `long`, `double`, a structure, and so on.

`array_element`

The name of the data element that occurs. Any valid C data element name is acceptable.

`[level_1_occurs]`

An integer or integer constant that defines how many times `array_element` occurs at the first level. At least one set of square brackets with an integer or constant name in between them is required to define an array.

`[level_2_occurs] ... [level_n_occurs]`

Required for arrays that have more than one dimension. Each additional dimension requires another pair of brackets with a number or occurrences or a constant name.

`;`

A semicolon ends array definitions.

Discussion

Arrays in C are inverted compared to COBOL tables. In COBOL you begin with the group item, and at each lower level you declare a number of occurrences. Each lower level can include some data elements.

C does not handle the group item concept as cleanly as COBOL does. Anytime you refer to a structure member in C, you must qualify the elementary item name with the structure name, as in `pay_rec.ytd_gross_amt`. This is true even if `ytd_gross_amt` is unique in the program. Often people simply declare all the elements of a table as elementary items so they can be referred to without qualification. Later in the chapter the sections called "One-Dimensional Array Definition" and "Structure Array Definition" show examples of both methods.

The most common name for subscripts in C is `i`. For one-dimensional arrays this is not confusing. However, when arrays become multidimensional, more descriptive names are needed:

```
for ( dept = 1; dept < MAX_DEPTS; dept++ )
{
  . . .
  for ( div = 1; div < MAX_DIVISIONS; div++ )
  {
     total_amt += expense_amt [dept] [div] ;
  }
}
```

One-Dimensional Array Definition

Use one-dimensional arrays to handle single series data, such as monthly or weekly totals. C arrays are defined differently than COBOL tables, but their use is essentially identical.

Syntax

```
data_type array_element [level_1_occurs] ;
```

Samples

C	COBOL Equivalent	
`int    week;`	`01 WEEK`	`PIC 99.`

```
                                   01 EMPLOYEE-PAY-HISTORY.
                                      05 WEEKLY-DATA                 OCCURS 52.
double gross_pay_amt        [53];        10 GROSS-PAY-AMT            PIC S9(5)V99.
double fica_amt             [53];        10 FICA-AMT                 PIC S9(5)V99.
double fed_withholding_amt  [53];        10 FED-WITHHOLDING-AMT      PIC S9(5)V99.
double state_withholding_amt [53];       10 STATE-WITHHOLDING-AMT    PIC S9(5)V99.
double net_pay_amt          [53];        10 NET-PAY-AMT              PIC S9(5)V99.
```

Discussion

The sample above shows a one-dimensional array (table), with several elements, written in both C and COBOL. In C level numbers are not used, so the subscript name is the only real indicator of what's going on in the array. Notice that the C code uses 53 for the number of occurrences. This assumes that the week variable has a range of 1 through 52 and we want to use it directly. In such a case you declare the array to have one more occurrence than the largest count. The first occurrence of the array is simply not used.

A more likely implementation of these totals is shown here:

```
#define MAX_WEEKS 53

int     week;

double  gross_pay_amt           [MAX_WEEKS];
double  fica_amt                [MAX_WEEKS];
double  fed_withholding_amt     [MAX_WEEKS];
double  state_withholding_amt   [MAX_WEEKS];
double  net_pay_amt             [MAX_WEEKS];
```

The program constant `MAX_WEEKS` allows the maximum size to be coded once only. It also allows the use of the constant name in `for` statements.

Both samples above show the total fields declared as elementary items rather than as members of a structure. Declaring them inside a structure would be more like COBOL programming; this is not done often because once the totals are declared inside a structure, the data names must always be qualified by the structure name, even if the data name is unique. Many programmers justly consider this to be a pain in the neck. An example of declaring the totals inside a structure is found on page 387.

Multidimensional Array Definition

Multidimensional arrays operate similarly in COBOL and C. Definition is slightly different in C, but the use is essentially the same.

The following sample shows a three-dimensional array. If you want to create a two-dimensional array, you code one less set of brackets. If you want a four-dimensional array, you code one more set of brackets. After you code the first dimension, you just add more brackets and subscripts for multiple dimensions. Make sure you understand what all the dimensions are doing and that you can explain it to someone else.

Syntax

```
data_type array_element [level_1_occurs] [level_2_occurs] [level_3_occurs] ;
```

Sample

C	COBOL Equivalent
`int  company;`	`01  COMPANY                    PIC 99.`
`int  division;`	`01  DIVISION                   PIC 99.`
`int  location;`	`01  LOCATION                   PIC 99.`
	`01  REPORT-TOTALS-TABLE.`
	`    05  COMPANY-TOTALS         OCCURS 5.`
	`        10  DIVISION-TOTALS    OCCURS 12.`
	`            15  LOCATION-TOTALS OCCURS 8.`
`double  sales_total [5] [12] [8];`	`                20  SALES-TOTAL PIC S9(8)V99.`
`double  tax_total   [5] [12] [8];`	`                20  TAX-TOTAL   PIC S9(8)V99.`
`double  net_total   [5] [12] [8];`	`                20  NET-TOTAL   PIC S9(8)V99.`
`double  labor_total [5] [12] [8];`	`                20  LABOR-TOTAL PIC S9(8)V99.`

Discussion

The sample above shows how to declare a set of totals with three dimensions and thus three subscripts. The C sample looks backward compared to COBOL: It has the elementary item named first followed by the occurrence numbers in brackets, and there are no names for the levels.

C is not oriented to group items the way COBOL is. C does have the structure construct, which lets you put a set of elementary items together into a group item or record. A structure can be created to bundle the elements in an array, but it is common in C to declare an array for each low-level item, as shown above. A member in a structure always requires qualification and is therefore more trouble to deal with. In the section called "Structure Array Definition" you will see this sample restated using a structure.

The COBOL example could have additional elements in the 01, 05, and 10 levels, such as names or other data. In COBOL you simply add elements at the appropriate level, but in C, you must use nested structure arrays. This process is even more of a pain in the neck than putting totals into a structure array. Fortunately, there is not much need for this in business systems. COBOL's handling of the group item concept is cleaner than C's.

Character Array (String) Definition

A string in C is defined as a one-dimensional array of characters, which is a lower level of looking at them than in COBOL. However, in C the same name can be used to refer to the whole string or, with an added subscript, to get to individual characters within the string. String definition is discussed in detail in Chapter 3, "Defining Data in C." This section is a refresher and a prelude to the next section on arrays of strings.

Syntax

```
char data_name [xx];
```

Samples

C	COBOL Equivalent
`char last_name [31];`	`01 LAST-NAME PIC X(30).`
`char month_name [10];`	`01 MONTH-NAME PIC X(9).`
`char run_date [11];`	`01 RUN-DATE PIC X(10).`

Discussion

C handles strings differently than COBOL does. In COBOL a string (defined as an alphanumeric field of two or more characters) is elemental; usually you do not need to worry about the individual characters in the field. C treats an alphanumeric as an array of characters. Further, C frequently accesses both the whole array and the individual characters.

When you want to do something with a whole string, such as `last_name`, you use `last_name` without brackets. This is what you do in functions like `strcpy()` and `printf()`. The name of the array is actually the *address* of the first element in the array. An example of this usage is

```
char last_name [31];
...
printf ("Last name: %s ", last_name);
```

When you want to reference an individual character (an occurrence in the array), you use the subscripted array name with the subscript value of the character you want. For example, to capitalize the first letter of a department name, you code

```
char dept_name [21];
...
dept_name [0] = toupper dept_name [0];
```

When you want to use part of the array from a given offset to the end of the array (string), you use the address operator, **&**, the array name, and the subscript value of where to begin, as in **&run_date [6]**. Remember that C subscripts begin at 0. This technique is used with **strcpy()**, **printf()**, and so on. An example is

```
char run_date [11] = "05/18/1994";
char pr_year  [5];
...
strcpy (pr_year, &run_date [6] );
```

COBOL does not consider **LAST-NAME** as defined in the sample above to be a table. C *does* consider **last_name** as defined in the sample above to be an array. The sample shows that what we call a string in C is actually an array of characters: one byte times an occurrence number (plus one byte for the null terminator).

C allows an entire array to be referenced by the name of the element *without* any brackets. This is how **last_name** gets used as a whole.

String Array Definition

COBOL alphanumeric tables—that is, tables of strings—have to be treated as two-dimensional arrays in C, because strings in C are themselves considered one-dimensional arrays. To get an array of strings, you must define a two-dimensional array.

Syntax

```
char  data_name [occurrences] [characters];
```

Samples

```
char  month_name [13] [10];
char  line_title [25] [81];
char  day_name   [7]  [10];
```

Discussion

Although arrays of strings are defined as two-dimensional arrays, they are usually used as though they were one-dimensional arrays. This means that a single subscript is used to retrieve a string. For further discussion, see the "Comments on the Example" section below.

Example

```
C                              COBOL

int  month;                    01 MONTH        PIC 99.

char month_name [13] [10] =
{                              01 MONTH-NAME-TABLE.
   "Month 0   ",
   "January   ",                  05 FILLER    PIC X(9) VALUE 'JANUARY   '.
   "February  ",                  05 FILLER    PIC X(9) VALUE 'FEBRUARY  '.
   "March     ",                  05 FILLER    PIC X(9) VALUE 'MARCH     '.
   "April     ",                  05 FILLER    PIC X(9) VALUE 'APRIL     '.
   "May       ",                  05 FILLER    PIC X(9) VALUE 'MAY       '.
   "June      ",                  05 FILLER    PIC X(9) VALUE 'JUNE      '.
   "July      ",                  05 FILLER    PIC X(9) VALUE 'JULY      '.
   "August    ",                  05 FILLER    PIC X(9) VALUE 'AUGUST    '.
   "September",                    05 FILLER    PIC X(9) VALUE 'SEPTEMBER'.
   "October   ",                  05 FILLER    PIC X(9) VALUE 'OCTOBER   '.
   "November  ",                  05 FILLER    PIC X(9) VALUE 'NOVEMBER  '.
   "December  " ◄───              05 FILLER    PIC X(9) VALUE 'DECEMBER  '.
} ;                            01 FILLER REDEFINES MONTH-NAME-TABLE.
                                 05 MONTH-NAME OCCURS 12
                                       PIC X(9).
```

No comma at the end

Comments on the Example

month_name is read as 13 occurrences of 10 characters each. The C version of the month array has "Month 0", because C subscripts start from 0, and you want to use the numeric value of a month as a subscript. To do this, you need to pad the array. A simple for statement using this array reads as follows:

```
for ( month = 1; month < 13; month++ )
{
   printf ("Month: %d Name: %s \n",
      month,
      month_name [month] );
}
```

Notice that when you use month_name you use only one subscript. String arrays are schizophrenic. The first subscript picks up the whole string. In a string array you use both subscripts only when you want to access an individual character. For example, to specify the first letter of a month in the month array above, you code

```
month_name [month] [0]
```

Also note that the literals are 9 characters and the definition shows 10. This allows for the null terminator at the end of each month_name, which the compiler inserts. If you make the definition 9 characters, there will be no null terminator and `month_name` will be one long string.

Structure Array Definition

When you want to bring totals together in a group item, you can define the totals in a structure and then define an array using that structure. You can also create an array for records by defining a record in a structure and then defining an array for that structure. Structure definition is covered in Chapter 3, "Defining Data in C."

Syntax

```
struct
{
   data_type data_name;
   data_type data_name;
   ...
   data_type data_name;
} struct_name [level_1_occurs] [level_2_occurs] ... [level_n_occurs];
```

Sample

```
C                          COBOL Equivalent
int  company;              01  COMPANY  PIC 99.
int  division;             01  DIVISION PIC 99.
int  location;             01  LOCATION PIC 99.

                           01  REPORT-TOTALS-TABLE.
                               05 COMPANY-TOTALS              OCCURS 5.
struct                            10 DIVISION-TOTALS          OCCURS 12.
{                                    15 LOCATION-TOTALS       OCCURS 8.
   double  sales_total;                 20 SALES-TOTAL    PIC S9(8)V99.
   double  tax_total;                   20 TAX-TOTAL      PIC S9(8)V99.
   double  net_total;                   20 NET-TOTAL      PIC S9(8)V99.
   double  labor_total;                 20 LABOR-TOTAL    PIC S9(8)V99.
}
report_total [5] [12] [8] ;
```

Discussion

The sample above shows how to use a structure to declare a set of totals with three dimensions. The C sample still looks cryptic compared to the COBOL sample, but it offers more control than declaring each total as an occurrence:

```
double   sales_total       [5] [12] [8];
double   tax_total         [5] [12] [8];
double   net_sales_total   [5] [12] [8];
double   labor_total       [5] [12] [8];
```

The difference in treatment between the structure elements and individually declared elements is structure name qualification and placement of the subscript brackets, as this sample shows:

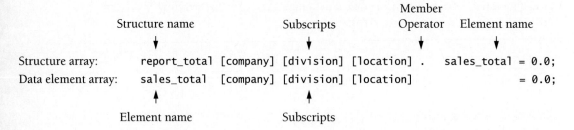

Subscripts follow the structure name, not the data element name. This is not what you expect, coming from COBOL. On the other hand, the compiler generates an error if you place the subscripts after the data element name. The error is caught early.

Although it causes a little more typing, you can put totals into a structure and keep them together. You can obviously make the structure name shorter so you do less typing, but do not make it so short that it becomes incomprehensible.

Initializing Arrays

Arrays can be initialized in three ways:

- By default (at compile time).
- By assigning values at compile time.
- By assigning values at run-time.

Default Initialization

If you do nothing to create initial values for an array (or any other data you declare), you will get whatever the compiler chooses as default values. The two basic choices for compilers are zeroes and garbage. Zeroes are fine. All C numeric types have the same bit configuration for zero (all bytes zero). A zero in the first position of a string data item is a null, which means the string has zero length and is therefore empty.

Garbage is another matter altogether. While many compilers default to initial zeroes, this is not guaranteed. If your compiler initializes arrays (and other memory) to zeroes, you won't have problems with default initialization unless you port your software to a compiler that does not initialize to zeroes. Then your programs won't work correctly or won't work at all.

The conclusion is that sooner or later default initialization will be bad for your programs' health. Don't let it happen by default.

Initialization at Compile Time

Initialization at compile time is the safe way to guarantee that your arrays have valid values at start-up. Initialization for nonzero values is slightly different for each of the following types of arrays:

- Arrays of numbers
- Arrays of strings
- Arrays of structures

Initialization of each array type is discussed below.

Initializing Arrays of Numbers at Compile Time

Syntax

```
data_type data_name [occurs] = { value_1 , value_2 , ... value_n } ;
```

Numeric Examples

```
double num_array     [6]          = { 50.3, 13.3, 45.0, 6.8, .74, 0.0 } ;
int     days_in_month [13]        = { 0, 31, 28, 31, 30, 31, 30, 31, 31, 30, 31, 30, 31 } ;
double dept_amt      [21]         = { 0 } ;
double expense_amt   [5] [3] [12] = { 0 } ;
```

Discussion

The first two numeric examples above show how to assign a series of values to a numeric array: You use a pair of braces and separate the values by commas. The last two samples show the simple method to assign zeroes for arrays of numbers of any numeric type:

```
int month_count [12] = { 0 } ;
                         ↑   ↑
                      Braces required
```

In business systems there is seldom a requirement to initialize arrays of numbers to anything other than zeroes. On most compilers = { 0 } ; should initialize an entire numeric array. If your compiler does not allow this, and you do not want to depend on default initialization, you will have to write a for loop to initialize the array. See the section called "Initialization by Assigning Values at Run Time" on page 392.

Initializing Arrays of Strings at Compile Time

Syntax

```
char  data_name [occurrences] [characters] =
{
   "value 0",
   "value 1",
   ...
   "value n"        ← Notice there is no comma at the end
} ;
```

String Example

```
char  day_name [8] [10] =
{
   "Day 0     ",
   "Sunday    ",
   "Monday    ",
   "Tuesday   ",
   "Wednesday",
   "Thursday  ",
   "Friday    ",
   "Saturday  "       ← Notice there is no comma at the end
} ;
```

Discussion

String arrays must be defined as two-dimensional arrays, since C considers strings themselves to be one-dimensional arrays. Although you define a string array as two dimensional, you initialize it as though it were one dimensional:

1. Use an opening brace after the assignment operator (equal sign).

2. Put each string in double quotes.

3. Put a comma after each string, *except the last one.*

4. End with a closing brace and a semicolon.

Don't forget to make the number in the second bracket of the definition, [characters], one character larger than the largest string literal. This reserves one byte for the string terminator, which the compiler inserts. If you use a number that is the same size as the largest literal, you get one long string instead of an array of strings.

Initializing Arrays of Structures at Compile Time

Syntax

```
struct
{
    data_type     member_name;
    ...
    data_type     member_name;
}
structure_name [occurs] =
    {
        value_1, value_2, ... value_n,    /* first occurrence values */
        ...
        value_1, value_2, ... value_n     /* "nth" occurrence values */
    } ;
```

Samples

```
struct
{
    char      description [21];
    long      pay_grade;
    double    hourly_rate;
}
job [3] =
    {
        "Technical Writer   ", 34, 17.50,
        "Programmer/Analyst", 42, 18.00,
        "Manager            ", 45, 75.25    ← Notice there is no comma at the end
    } ;
```

The following is an alternate for the sample above:

```
struct
{
    char      description [21];
    long      pay_grade;
    double    hourly_rate;
}
job [3] = { 0 };
```

Discussion

Compile-time initial values for structure arrays are straightforward. After [occurs], you put an assignment operator, =, followed by values in braces. Put values in row data order: fields for the first row, fields for the second row, and so on. For legibility, put each row's values on a separate line, as shown in the samples above. The compiler doesn't care if it is legible, but people do.

Initialization by Assigning Values at Run Time

When you have a table of packed numbers in COBOL, your only choice for initializing numbers is to do it at run time. In C it's your last resort; you initialize at run time only when you can't at compile time. If your compiler won't let you use one of the methods shown in the samples above, or you need some value other than zero in the array, use the `for` statement to loop through the array and assign values:

```c
#define MAX_DIV    7
#define MAX_DEPT   12
#define MAX_LOCN   50

int div;
int dept;
int location;

double  sales_amt [MAX_DIV] [MAX_DEPT] [MAX_LOCN] ;
...

for (div = 0; div < MAX_DIV; div++ )
{
   for ( dept = 0; dept < MAX_DEPT; dept++ )
   {
      for (location = 0; location < MAX_LOCN; location++ )
      {
         sales_amt [div] [dept] [location] = 0.0;
      }
   }
}
```

Memory for Arrays

In COBOL a table is allocated a fixed amount of memory at compile time. In C an array can be allocated a fixed amount of memory at compile time, or an array can be allocated a fixed amount of memory that is determined at run time, or an array can be created as a linked list of dynamically allocated memory at run time.

Allocating a Fixed Amount of Memory at Compile Time

In both COBOL and C the most common practice is to allocate a fixed amount of memory at compile time. All of the examples in this chapter to this point have allocated memory at compile time. When you code a data name and an occurrence value, memory is allocated at compile time:

```c
int  dept_count [12];       /* allocates 12 times size of int */
```

This method works fine, as long as you know at compile time what the largest number of occurrences will be. It is what you've been doing in COBOL for years.

Allocating a Fixed Amount of Memory at Run Time

C allows dynamic allocation of memory to a program while it is running; this is not possible in COBOL. You use two library routines to do this: `calloc()` and `free()`. `calloc()` allocates an amount of memory that you specify. `calloc()` returns a pointer to a block of memory, all of which has been initialized to zeroes.[1]

If you don't know at compile time what size an array needs to be, but you will know at run-time, use `calloc()` to allocate memory for the array. Once you allocate memory with `calloc()`, you must return the memory to the operating system by using a call to `free()`, which returns memory previously allocated by `calloc()`. Sources for the size of the array can be a read from a file, a retrieval from a database, or a run-time parameter.

Usually you either know at compile time what size the array should be or you have an unknown number of occurrences to deal with at run time. Finding out at run time how many occurrences there are usually means two passes of the data, which is usually not acceptable. The solution for this case is to use linked list library routines, which are discussed in the next section.

`calloc()` and `free()` are discussed in more detail later in this chapter.

Linked Lists: Allocating a Variable Amount of Memory at Run Time

When you need to put records in an array but you won't know how many records until run time, use a linked list library. A linked list library is a set of routines that dynamically allocate memory and maintain a list (array). A typical linked list library will have a dozen or more functions, including functions to define a list; insert, retrieve (next or previous), update, and delete elements; sort a list; release memory to the operating system; and others. The following is a typical sequence of function calls;

1. Call a "define list" function.
2. For each record read from database or file, call an "insert item" function.
3. Process the list using a "get item" function.
4. Release memory allocated to the list by calling a "delete list" function.

Each time you need to add a member to the array, you call a function and pass it the data to store. The linked list function dynamically allocates memory and creates forward and

---

[1]Another memory allocation routine, `malloc()`, allocates memory but does not initialize it; you get whatever garbage is in memory. `calloc()` and `malloc()` work the same way except for initialization. Since `malloc()` cannot be relied on for initialized memory, it will not be discussed further in this book.

backward pointers so you can go forward or backward through the list. You don't have to deal with these pointers; they are internal to the linked list functions.

When you are finished using a list, you call one of the linked list library routines to return the list's memory to the operating system.

To get a flavor of how a linked list library works, we will look at four common functions that define a list, insert an item into a list, get an item from a list, and delete a list. A good linked list library should be as simple to use as the following calls:

```
status = define_list  ( &list_num, list_type);
status = insert_item   ( list_num, &element, element_size );
status = get_item      ( list_num, which_item, &element);
status = delete_list   ( list_num );
```

Here are the parameter definitions, followed by a short discussion of the functions themselves.

status

Tells whether the function call succeeded or failed.

list_num

Identifies each linked list used in the program. A program can use several linked lists, each with a different list number. The linked list function assigns the numbers. For example, to use three linked lists in one program, you create three variables to hold the respective list numbers.

list_type

Chooses between a chain list and a circle list. A typical linked list has two pointers for each member of the list. The *forward pointer* points to the next member in the list, and the *backward pointer* points to the previous member in the list.

In a chain list the last member points *forward* to NULL and the first member points *backward* to NULL. In a circle list the last member points forward to the first member and the first member points backward to the last member. Chain lists are more common because of the usual requirement to know when you are at the bottom or top of a list.

The two diagrams below illustrate the differences between chain lists and circle lists.

Chain List

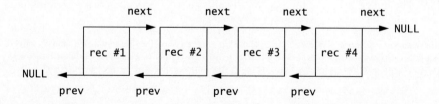

At the end of the list, the next pointer points to NULL. If your current list member is record 4, when you call the function to retrieve the list for the next record, it returns NULL. This tells you that you have reached the end of the list. Likewise, if your current list member is record 1, the prev (previous) pointer points to NULL. If you request the previous list member, you will get NULL in status. You have reached the beginning of the list.

Circle List.

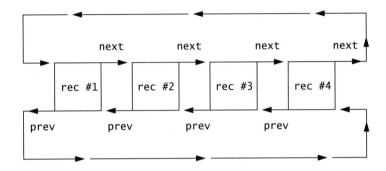

If you define a list as a circle, the retrieve function never returns NULL. If your current list member is record 4 and you request the next record, record 1 is returned. If you are positioned at record 1 and request the previous record, record 4 is returned. There is not much need for this kind of list in business processing.

element

The name of whatever element/structure/record you choose to put in the linked list. Typically it would be a structure name.

element_size

Tells the linked list function how many bytes it needs in order to store element. This value is usually supplied by using sizeof (structure_name).

which_item

Typically, a set of constants defined by #defines in the linked list library, such as FIRST, LAST, NEXT, PREV, and so on. This parameter tells the linked list function either where to put a new element or which existing one to retrieve.

Here's what typical linked list functions would do:

status = define_list (&list_num, list_type)

Tells the linked list library that you want to create a linked list. status tells you whether the function succeeded. If it was successful, define_list() passes back an identifying number for the list, list_num. list_type specifies whether the list is a circle or a chain. Typically you would want a chain so you would know when you reached the end.

```
status = insert_item (list_num, &element, element_size)
```

Puts a record or structure into the linked list. Again, `status` tells you whether the call succeeded. `list_num` identifies the list you want to add to. `&element` is the address of the structure you want to insert. `element_size` tells it how large the structure or record is. There might also be a parameter that gives explicit instruction about where to insert the structure: FIRST, LAST, NEXT, PREV, and so on. It depends on the list package. `insert_item()` creates and maintains pointers to link the new element to the previous element and to the next element. You don't have to worry about the pointers.

```
status = get_item (list_num, which_item, &element)
```

Gets data from the list. `status` tells you whether the call succeeded. `list_num` tells the function which list to read from. `which_item` is a parameter with values like FIRST, LAST, NEXT, PREV. `&element` is the address of the structure where you want the list data to be placed.

```
status = delete_list (list_num)
```

Returns memory associated with the linked list to the operating system. You call this when you are finished with the data in the list. `status` tells you whether the call succeeded. `list_num` tells the function which list to delete. `delete_list()` uses `free()` to release memory. It is important to call this function for large or long-running programs to avoid running out of memory.

Don't Write a Linked List

Using a linked list library means that you do not have to manage memory. You just call a linked list function. It takes care of memory allocation, forward and backward pointers, and releasing memory. This is a lot simpler than working it all out yourself. There are literally hundreds, if not thousands, of linked list routines available in C. People have been writing them for more than 15 years, so there is no need for another one. Buy one, or download one.

The point of using a linked list library is to create an array or list of data at run time without having to deal with memory management. The clean solution is to use a package that handles memory management.

Writing a linked list routine does not solve a business problem; it solves a data handling problem that has already been solved in C, literally, thousands of times. Again, buy one or download one; don't write the 10,000th linked list routine.

Allocate memory at run time.

C Keyword/Symbol/Function	`calloc()`

`calloc()` allocates a specified amount of memory for an array while a program is running. Memory allocated by `calloc()` remains allocated until a call to `free()` is made or the program terminates. Memory is *not* released when a called function returns control to a calling function.

Syntax

```
data_type *array_name;
array_name = calloc ( occurrences, size_of_occurrence ) ;
```

Samples

1. To allocate memory for an array of `doubles`:
   ```
   double  *dept_amt;
   int      dept_count;
   /* some code which determines a value for dept_count */
   dept_amt = calloc ( dept_count, sizeof (double);
   ```

2. To allocate memory for an array of CUST_REC structures:
   ```
   CUST_REC *mast_in;
   int       cust_rec_count;
   /* some code which determines a value for cust_rec_count */
   mast_in = calloc ( cust_rec_count, sizeof (CUST_REC) ) ;
   ```

> **NOTE:** `sizeof` is used on the *data type* of the pointer, not the pointer name.

Include File

`include <stdlib.h>`   (contains function prototype for `calloc()`)

See Also

`free()`   — return allocated memory to the operating system

Parameter Definitions

`data_type *array_name`

A pointer that receives the address of the allocated block of memory when `calloc()` is successful. It contains NULL if `calloc()` is not successful. It can be any data type. `*array_name` is defined with the pointer operator, `*`, but after it's defined you just use the name.

occurrences;

The number of elements, records, or rows you want in the array. occurrences is typically defined as an int or unsigned int, and the value is supplied at run time. (If you know the value at compile time, you don't need to use calloc().)

The compiler uses a system constant variable called size_t to determine the maximum value for occurrences. It is a data type defined in stdlib.h. Definition of size_t is usually as an unsigned int. On a two-byte-word machine, an unsigned int can have a maximum value of 65,535. On a four-byte-word machine, the maximum value is 4,294,967,295.

size_of_occurrence;

The size of one element, record, or row in the array for which memory is being allocated. The value is limited by the maximum value for size_t. It is typically supplied by using the sizeof keyword with the data type of the element or structure template name for which you're allocating memory.

Return Value

calloc() returns a pointer of type void. A void pointer is one that will take the characteristics of whatever data type it is assigned to. In sample 1 the return value becomes a pointer to an array of doubles. In sample 2 the return value becomes a pointer to an array of CUST_RECs.

Scope

Can be used to allocate memory for an array of any data type, including programmer defined ones such as structures.

Direction

Works from right to left.

Anatomy

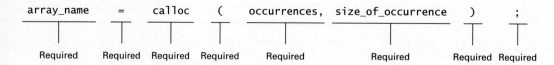

array_name

The name of the pointer that receives the return value of calloc().

Recall that a pointer is like a parameter in COBOL: It is a name that refers to an element or array defined outside the current function. In the samples above, one pointer refers to one or more occurrences of a double, and the other pointer refers to one or more occurrences of a structure type called CUST_REC.

You define a data element as a pointer (by placing an asterisk in front of the name) and thereafter just use the name. A block of memory is allocated at run time and outside the function. The pointer is a parameter that allows you to use memory which was not allocated at compile time.

=

The assignment operator that moves the return value of calloc() into array_name.

calloc

The name of the function that dynamically allocates memory to a function.

occurrences

The name of the data element that says how many elements, records, or rows to allocate. This would typically only be available at run time; otherwise, you would allocate memory at compile time.

size_of_occurrence

The size of one of the elements, records, or rows to be allocated. This is typically supplied by using the sizeof keyword with the data name of the element or structure for which memory is being allocated.

;

A semicolon ends all calls to functions.

Discussion

calloc() should not be used often in business data processing. The correct use of calloc() is to allocate a contiguous area of memory for a fixed-size array when two conditions are met:

1. You don't know at compile time how many occurrences there will be.
2. You can find out in a simple and cheap way at run time how many occurrences there are.

If you have to pass the data once to find out how large an array to allocate and then pass the data again to process it, you should use a linked list library and pass the data only once. The linked list functions will manage the memory. Business application programs should not manage memory allocations unless they are simple. It is not cost effective when the major portion of the life-cycle cost of software is programmer time.

Once you allocate memory with calloc(), you are then responsible for returning the memory to the operating system. Returning memory to the operating system is done in one of three ways: a call to free() is made, which returns memory previously allocated by calloc(); the program finishes, which returns all memory to the operating system; or the program blows up, which also returns all memory to the operating system.

Programs will blow up if enough calls to `calloc()` are made without matching calls to `free()`. This is commonly called memory leakage, but a more accurate term would be memory accrual: You keep allocating memory to your program until there's none left in the system. This is when the program crashes (and thus frees memory). This is a way to blow up programs that you don't have in COBOL.

For the average batch program, matching calls to `calloc()` and `free()` is not a problem, since the average batch program runs for a while and then finishes, thus returning all its memory. It becomes a problem in systems where programs, on-line or batch, run a long time. The logic error that allocates memory but does not deallocate memory takes a while to "eat" the system. If this error exists in a program and the program runs long enough, it will crash. Depending on the application, this can be a serious problem.

If you call `calloc()`, you then become responsible for returning allocated memory. In many cases this is straightforward, but if there is complex logic you may not correctly match every call to `calloc()` with a call to `free()`. `calloc()` and `free()` provide a new way, not available in COBOL, to make programs fail.

The example program that follows the next section on `free()` shows the use of both `calloc()` and `free()`.

Common Errors

1. Program blows up because it ran out of memory.

   If you don't check the return value from the call to `calloc()`, you will not catch the fact that your program did not get the memory requested. If you use the array as though you do have the memory, the program will blow up at some point. Always check the return value from a call to `calloc()`.

2. Strange results from the array allocated by `calloc()`, or the program blows up.

   If you pass the pointer name instead of the data type that it refers to, you will probably allocate less memory than you intend. The following code allocates memory correctly:

```
double *dept_amt;
int    dept_count;                        Data type
...                                          ↓
dept_amt = calloc ( dept_count, sizeof (double) ;
```

   The following code allocates memory incorrectly:

```
double *dept_amt;
int    dept_count;                        Pointer name
...                                          ↓
dept_amt = calloc ( dept_count, sizeof (dept_amt) ;
```

When you use `calloc()`, you must use the *data type* of the pointer in the `sizeof()` expression, not the pointer name. The pointer itself is a parameter that refers (points) to some data. The pointer is not the data. A pointer is the size of a machine word, an `int`, two or four bytes. A `double` is typically eight bytes. When you use the pointer name instead of the data type of the array, you allocate a short array unless you are allocating an array of `ints`. This means you will overrun memory when you use the array. Results are unpredictable.

If you allocate multiple arrays and use pointer names instead of data types, the arrays can overlap when you use them. This leads to unpredictable results.

Example

The example program follows the section on `free()`.

Return allocated memory to the operating system.

C Keyword/Symbol/Function	`free()`

`free()` returns to the operating system the memory previously allocated by a call to `calloc()`. Use the same pointer name for `free()` as you used for `calloc()`.

Syntax

```
free ( array_name ) ;
```

Samples

```
double *dept_amt;
free ( dept_amt );

CUST_REC *mast_in;
free ( mast_in ) ;
```

Include File

`#include <stdlib.h>`   (contains function prototype for `free()`)

See Also

`calloc()`   — allocate an area of memory to a program

Parameter Definitions

`data_type *array_name`
   The same pointer used in the call to `calloc()`.

Return Value

free() does not have a return value. It is assumed to work.

Scope

Used on any data type which worked with calloc().

Direction

Works from left to right.

Anatomy

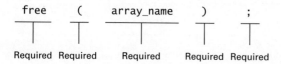

free

The name of the function that returns previously allocated memory to the operating system.

array_name

The name of the pointer used in the call to calloc().

;

A semicolon ends all calls to functions.

Discussion

free() should be called for each call to calloc(). Once you begin to allocate memory while your program is running, you must also return memory when you are finished with it.

Memory allocated with calloc() is *not* released when a function exits, unless that function is main(). There is nothing automatic about returning memory to the system except when the program finishes or blows up. So if you use calloc(), you also need to use free().

Common Error

Calling free() for memory already freed or never allocated.

This may or may not be a visible error. Some compilers ignore a call to free() that passes a pointer that has already been freed. Other compilers produce unpredictable results. Match the call to free() to the appropriate call to calloc().

Example

```
/*                      calloc.c & free()              10/08/94                    */
#include <stdio.h>
#include <stdlib.h>                               /* 1 for calloc() prototype       */
typedef struct                                    /* 2 define structure type CUST_REC */
{
   long    cust_no;
   char    cust_name    [31];
   double  current_bal;
} CUST_REC;

main()
{
   double   *dept_amt;                            /* 3 pointer for dept_amt array    */
   CUST_REC *mast_in;                             /* 4 pointer for CUST_REC array    */

   int      cust_cnt;
   int      num_depts;
   int      i;

   printf ("Enter number of departments: " );
   scanf ("%d", &num_depts);                      /* 5 get nbr of depts              */
   dept_amt = calloc (num_depts, sizeof (double) );  /* 6 allocate memory            */
   if (dept_amt == NULL)                          /* 7 check status                  */
   {
      printf ("calloc() failed for dept_amt\n" );
      return (-1);
   }

   for ( i = 0; i < num_depts; i++ )              /* 8 load array                    */
   {
      dept_amt [i] = i * 10.0;                     /* 9 array syntax                  */
   }

   for ( i = 0; i < num_depts; i++ )              /* 10 display array                */
   {
      printf ("calloc: i = %d  dept_amt = %lf\n",
         i,
         dept_amt [i] );                          /* 11 array syntax                 */
   }

   printf ("Enter number of customers: " );
   scanf ("%d", &cust_cnt);                       /* 12 get nbr of custs             */
   mast_in = calloc ( cust_cnt, sizeof (CUST_REC) );  /* 13 allocate memory          */
                                                  /* for struct array               */
```

```
if (mast_in == NULL)                        /* 14 check status          */
{
   printf ("calloc() failed for mast_in \n" );
   return (-1);
}

for ( i = 0; i < cust_cnt; i++ )            /* 15 load array            */
{
   mast_in [i].current_bal = i * 10.0;      /* 16 array syntax          */
}
for ( i = 0; i < cust_cnt; i++ )            /* 17 display array         */
{
   printf ("calloc: i = %d  current_bal = %lf\n",
      i,
      mast_in [i].current_bal );            /* 18 array syntax          */
}

free (mast_in );                            /* 19 release memory        */
free (dept_amt );                           /* 20 release memory        */

return (0);
}
```

Comments on the Example

Line 1   The function prototype for calloc() is contained in the file stdlib.h. Including the prototype allows ANSI C to compare the parameter list you send to the function with the parameter list in the prototype. This reduces errors.

Line 2   Uses typedef to define a template for a structure for a customer record. No memory is allocated when typedef is used to define a template.

Line 3   Defines *dept_amt as a pointer (parameter) that will refer to an array of doubles. debt_amt is used as an array, but no brackets ([n]) appear here because calloc() returns the address of the beginning of the array. After the call to calloc(), brackets are used to manipulate the array.

Line 4   Invokes the CUST_REC template and defines *mast_in as a pointer (parameter) that will refer to an array of CUST_REC data. CUST_REC defines the layout and size, and mast_in is the name used for the structure array. As in line 3, no brackets are used because calloc() returns the address of the beginning of the array. Pointer syntax here means that the memory will be allocated outside this function.

Line 5   Gets a number to use for the number of occurrences of the array of dept_amt. Production programs would not get the number this way. Presumably there would be a function call, a read from a flat file or database, or a run-time parameter to provide the number of occurrences.

Line 6   Allocates memory for the dept_amt array by calling calloc(). It is an array of doubles. The compiler figures out the actual byte count based on the product of `num_depts` and the size of the `double` data type. Notice that `sizeof` is used on the *data type* the pointer refers to, not the pointer name. The compiler allocates the memory and places the address of the beginning of the memory in the `dept_amt` pointer. If `calloc()` is successful, you can treat `dept_amt` as an array and not worry about pointers and addresses. The array will then be treated the same as if it had been allocated at compile time.

Line 7   Checks the status of the `calloc()` call. If `calloc()` cannot get all the memory requested in the call, it returns `NULL` (no address). This is a fatal error. When `calloc()` is successful it returns the address of the beginning of the array.

Line 8   Shows a simple load of an array which uses memory allocated by `calloc()`. This demonstrates that after the `calloc()` call, you treat the array the same as if you had defined it at compile time.

Line 9   Uses standard array syntax on an array that uses memory allocated by `calloc()`. The statement multiplies the current subscript value by `10.0` in order to put something into the array for this example.

Line 10   Displays the array with the same `for` statement that loaded the array.

Line 11   Shows a `printf()` statement that uses standard array syntax to put a value on the screen. The output will look like:

```
calloc: i = 0      dept_amt = 0.000000
calloc: i = 1      dept_amt = 10.000000
calloc: i = 2      dept_amt = 20.000000
calloc: i = 3      dept_amt = 30.000000
calloc: i = 4      dept_amt = 40.000000
etc.
```

Lines 12–18   Show the same use of `calloc()` to create an array for a structure. There are only two differences between an element array and a structure array. One is that with structures you must always qualify the member name. The other difference is that subscripts follow the *structure* name, not the *element* name:

```
mast_in [i].current_bal = 0.0     /* correct syntax */
mast_in.current_bal [i] = 0.0     /* compile error */
```

Line 12   Again prompts the user for some number of occurrences to use for an array. Presumably, production programs will be more rigorous than this.

Line 13   Calls `calloc()` for the `mast_in` array of CUST_REC records. Notice, again, that `sizeof` is used with the data type of the pointer, not the pointer itself.

   The only real difference between this call to `calloc()` and the one on line 6 is the data type used with `sizeof`. Line 6 uses `double` and line 13 uses the structure `typedef` name, CUST_REC.

Line 14   Performs the status check for the `calloc()` call. If you don't get the memory, there is no point in continuing.

Line 15   Is a simple `for` statement used to put some values into the array.

Line 16 Uses standard structure array syntax to place a value in one member of one occurrence of a structure in an array. This syntax is the same whether the array memory is allocated at compile time or run time.

The statement multiplies the current subscript value times `10.0` to put some nonzero values into the array.

Line 17 Uses the same for statement as line 15.

Line 18 Shows standard structure array syntax supplying a value to `printf()`. The output will look like:

```
calloc: i = 0     current_bal = 0.000000
calloc: i = 1     current_bal = 10.000000
calloc: i = 2     current_bal = 20.000000
calloc: i = 3     current_bal = 30.000000
etc.
```

Line 19 Releases memory assigned to the `dept_amt` array. There's essentially nothing to it.

Line 20 Releases memory assigned to the `mast_in` array.

Summary

Arrays in C generally work the same way as tables in COBOL. C does not have indexes, but C subscripts can be used like relative indexes (i + 2). COBOL II subscripts can be used this way too. C subscripts begin at zero, rather than at 1. This is because they indicate the offset from zero, rather than the count of the element. As in COBOL, there is nothing in C to prevent you from running off the end of an array.

Array declaration in C is simpler and less powerful than in COBOL. An array in C is created by placing square brackets and an occurrence number after the data element declaration. There is no concept of level numbers as in COBOL. A multidimensional array simply has multiple sets of square brackets with occurrence numbers following the data element.

You have to declare a structure in order to get an array similar to a typical COBOL table. COBOL table element names do not require qualification if they are unique in the program, but every element declared in a C structure must be qualified when used.

Arrays of strings in C must be two-dimensional, since strings themselves are one-dimensional character arrays. When you want to refer to one of the strings in the array you use a single subscript.

Occasionally you may want to pad an array in C in order to use a data value as a subscript, due to the fact that C subscripts begin at zero. An example is an array of totals by month. By declaring the array to have 13 occurrences you can use the numeric value of a month as a subscript.

If you do not initialize an array (or any other variable) in C you run the risk of having garbage values in the array when the program starts. Default initialization by the compiler should not be relied on since ANSI C does not require it. Different compilers do different things. You can initialize arrays at compile time by using an initialization expression of = { 0 }. This sets the entire array to binary zeroes, which is a valid zero value for all numeric types in C. It is also a valid "null string" value for character strings. If you must initialize an array at run time, use a for loop.

C allows a program to allocate memory to itself while it is running, which you cannot do in COBOL. This is done through the calloc() function. It allows you to avoid hard-coding an array size at compile time. This only makes sense if you can find out cheaply at run time what size the array should be. When you are finished with the memory you need to release it with the free() function.

If you cannot size an array at compile time and cannot size it cheaply at run time, use a linked list library package to handle the array. Do not write one. The linked list package will take care of allocating memory and maintaining forward and backward pointers so you can go through a list (array) in either direction. There are dozens of these packages available commercially or as shareware.

CHAPTER 13

C Standards for a Business Environment

Introduction

This chapter addresses two basic questions: What constitutes a reasonable set of standards for business data processing (regardless of language), and what constitutes a short set of C programming standards for a business data processing environment?

The standards presented here are available from the computer bulletin board of Addison-Wesley on the Internet. This Internet bulletin board is accessible through America Online, CompuServe, Genie, Prodigy and other on-line services. They are also available on diskette for a nominal fee. See the coupon at the back of the book.

The standards exist in three formats: Microsoft Word, WordPerfect, and ASCII text. You can download a file and use the text as a starting point for your own set of standards.

Why Have Standards?

The purpose of standards is to produce programs that

- Have a consistent look across projects
- Are well structured
- Are easy to read
- Will compile cleanly under ANSI C

Generating programs with a consistent appearance aids a data processing shop in two ways. First, it is significantly easier to read other people's programs when there is a common style. Second, when programs have a common style, code sharing is much easier and more common.

An efficient program is one that is easily understood by a person who did not write it. Since the cost of programmers' time is now the major cost component in both development and maintenance of software systems, it is the programmers' time that needs to be efficiently managed. Machine resources are a minor consideration 98 percent of the time.

As Ed Yourdon and Larry Constantine said many years ago in their book *Structured Design*, you won't really know which parts of a system have to be optimized until after you start to run it. What you should do is produce a clear structured analysis, a clear structured design, and clear structured programs. Test the system for correctness, and then look at optimization. When you finally optimize, only then are your standards a secondary consideration. The point is to produce well-structured, readable code for the whole system and deviate from the standards only when it is necessary, after you have discovered what needs to be optimized.

How Large Should a Standards Document Be?

Your standards document should be small enough to be held together with a paper clip—small enough that people will be able to remember most of the standards. If your standards document requires a three-ring binder to hold it, the standards will become "shelfware." The standards section of this chapter has fewer than 50 items. Using only the standards in this chapter will produce programs that look remarkably alike stylistically—and that is the goal.

The problem with a large standards document is that there are too many standards to remember. If your goal is to have standards that will be used, less is more.

Who Should Develop Standards and How?

This is a trick question. If you want standards to be followed, they must be developed by programmers. Use this chapter as a guide, not a gospel. It is not necessary to agree with every item in this chapter. What is necessary is to create a small and consistent set of standards.

The process of developing standards is, in fact, more important than the standards themselves. Standards only work if people follow them. People follow them only under two conditions: consensus and coercion. Consensus is much more desirable than coercion, but a different kind of effort is necessary to achieve it. Decree does not create consensus. Discussion, argument, discussion, argument, and more discussion must go on to reach consensus, or at least a reasonable approximation of it. People must be heard if they are to feel involved.

In a small shop it is both possible and necessary to have everyone involved. The most interesting standards meetings I ever attended were in a 10-person shop at The American University in the late 1970s. We met in a carpeted room that had lots of pillows on the floor and no chairs or tables. We sat in a circle and took our shoes off. The manager, Wally Knapp, let the discussion run itself, except for the relatively few times when a consensus did not emerge. He would then choose one of the alternatives and we would move on.

In a large shop it is simply not possible for 200 or 2000 people to sit in a circle with their shoes off and discuss standards. What should happen is that representatives from various groups get together and go through the development exercise (preferably sitting in a circle with their shoes off).

For a standards document to be successful, it must be developed in the most public way possible. This definitely includes circulating drafts from the *beginning* of the process to everyone who will be affected by the standards. It also means holding town meetings so that people who have not been in the small discussions can stand and be heard.

The sure way to have standards that will be ignored is to have them appear for the first time, in final form, in everyone's mailboxes. Programmers will yawn and ignore standards created this way, and with good reason.

Who Should Enforce Standards and How?

Standards are most effectively enforced by the people who developed them, using structured walkthroughs of programs. If programmers have been involved in the development of standards, they will have a stake in maintaining them. If standards have been issued by decree, there will be nominal compliance, at best.

A structured walkthrough of a program by peers is the only real way to verify both the logic of the program and its conformance to standards. These are equally important goals.

For greatest success, a walkthrough must be held after clean compile and *before any testing*. The later in the development process a walkthrough is conducted, the more resistance to change there will be. This is true for both logic and style. The longer a programmer works on a program, the more she or he becomes psychologically identified with it, and the harder it is to change the program. If you have a walkthrough before testing, there is no presumption that the program already works. It is much easier to deal with changes at this point than later.

If you have already had a structured walkthrough of analysis documents and of the program design, chances are the program will be reasonably clean.

In my experience program walkthroughs are most successful when there are three people involved: the programmer and two other developers. Two other people are enough to provide a fresh look at a program and are few enough that walkthroughs themselves don't become a drag on staff time.

Portability

Portability means the ability to move (port) a system from one hardware or software platform to another. One of the big raps against COBOL historically has been that each vendor endowed its version of the language with extended features, which gave its version of COBOL more capability. The problem was that each vendor, including IBM, created a set of extensions that would not compile on another vendor's machine. This effectively locked in a lot of hardware choices, which was the vendors' idea. Customer choice was not on the menu.

Prior to the development of the ANSI C standard, portability of C programs was one of the biggest lies in the business. The C language as defined by Kernighan and Ritchie was so loose that, even without language extensions, the same program could give different results on different compilers. It was a hacker's dream and a professional's nightmare.

The situation has improved significantly with the ANSI C standard. The primary consideration comes if you are moving to a computer with a smaller machine word. Two factors to be considered are memory and the size of `int`. Smaller machines imply less memory, and this could involve rewriting some routines that use large amounts of memory. The possibility of this is small, but not zero.

A larger problem is that of `int`. `int` is typically given the size of the machine word of the operating system for which a compiler is written. If a machine word is two bytes, as it is on many PCs, `int` will be a two-byte item with a range of approximately ±32,767. Most workstations (Sun, HP, and so on) have a four-byte word, giving a four-byte `int`. A four-byte `int` has a range of approximately ±2 billion. Moving to a machine with a two-byte `int` can easily create problems of overflow. The programs will compile cleanly. They may or may not run correctly. This is the case for considering banning `int`. If you always use `long`, you are guaranteed four bytes.

References

Here are some books that are pertinent to the topic of standards, style, and walkthroughs:

Psychology of Computer Programming, by Gerald Weinberg (New York: Van Nostrand Reinhold, 1975).
This book is a classic and should be required reading for every developer and manager in the business. Weinberg covers the whole range of system development from the human point of view. He also discusses walkthroughs. Each chapter ends with two sets of questions: one for programmers and one for managers. The book is still in print over 20 years after it was written.

C Elements of Style, by Steve Oualline (San Mateo, CA: M & T Publishing, 1992).
This 200-page book is about program style and thus about programming standards. It offers stimulating reading and discussion. Oualline is not afraid to point out dumb design choices in popular operating systems and packages.

Structured Walkthroughs, by Edward Yourdon (Englewood Cliffs, NJ: Prentice Hall, 1989). A whole book on structured walkthroughs. It may give you more than you want to know, but it is a thorough discussion. I think he calls for too many people in a walkthrough, but read the book and decide for yourself.

A Proposed Set of C Standards for a Business Environment

Here is a set of standards that is small enough to be held together with a paper clip. Again, it is not important that you agree with everything here. What is important is that your shop develop a coherent, consistent, and reasonably small set of standards.

Program Organization

The following list shows the order of items in programs. Items in this list, plus others, are discussed in the following pages.

Programs shall be organized in this form:

1. Source code header file
2. Include files
3. Program constant fields (`const` and `#define`)
4. Function prototypes
5. File global structures (`static`)
6. File global variables (`static`)
7. File pointer declarations
8. `main()` or other function header
9. Local structures in alphabetical order
10. Local element variables in alphabetical order, one per line
11. Instructions

Repeat as required for other functions

Global data elements are prohibited, except for items such as error numbers and statuses that apply to multiple programs. Put these kinds of things in separate include files that are included by all programs in an application. Do not routinely create global data items in your programs.

The next few sections cover the parts of a C program that precede the instructions. These are discussed and shown with conforming and non-conforming examples. Following that are standards which apply to the formatting and use of instructions.

Source Code Header File

At the beginning of each file, put a comment block like this one:

```
/*
Program name         : File name goes here
Version              : This should be supplied by the source code
                       control package
Author               : Author's name
Date written         : mm/dd/yy
System name          : system name
Users                : users' names
Function             : short description of the work performed
Programming language : ANSI C
Logic                : short description of the logic
Inputs               : files/database tables/etc.
Outputs              : files/database tables/etc.
*/
```

This almost looks like the beginning of a COBOL program, doesn't it? Your source code control package should provide the ability to make some substitutions, such as version number, into this header when you check in a file. Put some substitution tokens in the header, and let the source code manager manage them.

Include Files

- Do not contain any path names, absolute or symbolic.
- Are not nested beyond one level. Public domain or purchased libraries are excepted.
- A nested include file is an `#include` statement inside an include file. With multiple levels of nesting, you can spend a lot of time trying to find variables. You are better off having several include files in the program.

#define Statements

- Used to create program constants.
- `#define` names are all uppercase.

Conforming Example

```
#define PAGE_LENGTH 66
```

Nonconforming Example: Lowercase Name

```
#define page_length 66
```

- Using #define to create a program constant is the only way in ANSI C to use a constant to specify the number of occurrences in an array.

Conforming Example

```
#define  MAX_RECS 100
double   expense_amt [MAX_RECS];
```

Another use of #define is to create a macro, which is a piece of code that is expanded by the preprocessor. Macros are an efficiency throwback to an era of eight-bit machines that ran slowly. Macros ran faster than called functions. Their liability lies in the fact that they expand and can thus create incorrect code that can be difficult to track down. Their alleged speedier execution is insignificant in today's hardware environment. These days your programs will spend the majority of their time waiting for a database package to finish a query or an update.

   #define will not be used to create macros. Macros are banned because they are subject to too many side effects when they are expanded.

Program Constant Fields

- const names are all uppercase

Conforming Example

```
const int PAGE_LENGTH = 66;
```

Nonconforming Example: Lowercase Name

```
const int page_length = 66;
```

const fields have a small advantage over #define fields in that the data type of the assigned value will be checked against the data type of the field. However, const fields cannot be used in array definitions, which is a real disadvantage:

```
const int MAX_RECS = 100;
double expense_amt [MAX_RECS];     /* compile error */
```

The net result is that const does not have much to offer in ANSI C. It is much more useful in C++ (see Chapter 14, "C++, or What's That OOP on Your Tie?").

typedef Statements

- Will not be used in programs to create new data types, except for structure templates.

Conforming Example

```
typedef struct
{
   long   cust_no;
   char   status;
   char   cust_name [31];
} CUST_REC;
```

Nonconforming Example: typedef Used to Create New Types

```
typedef int     COUNT;
typedef double  MONEY;
```

The problem with typedef is that if everyone starts creating his or her own data types, the result is a proliferation of data types. This gets confusing, especially when there are multiple types for the same thing.

The solution is to create types for the shop as a whole. This means putting them in an include file that can be used by any program that needs those data types. This will keep the number of data types under control.

Function Prototypes

- Not required by the ANSI compiler, but they are so beneficial that they must be part of any C standard. Function prototypes are used by the compiler to check parameter lists for function calls and the parameter list of the function header.
- Use descriptive parameter names along with the parameter data types.
- Put each parameter on a separate line, after the first one.
- Line up types and parameter names.

Conforming Example

```
int get_price ( double    *price,
                int       year_month,
                char []   price_name );
```

Nonconforming Example: Parameters Not Aligned

```
int get_price ( double *price, int year_month, char [] price_name );
```

Nonconforming Example: No Parameter Data Names

```
int get_price ( double *, int , char [] );
```

Nonconforming Example: No Parameters

```
int get_price ();
```

Function prototypes are the single largest improvement of ANSI C over traditional C. Used to their fullest, they will save you more time than any other single thing you can do in a program.

Notice that the last nonconforming example has no data types for parameters. Unfortunately, this will compile cleanly in ANSI C, and it will result in no parameter checking. The "no parameter" prototype will not compile in C++.

Program Variables

- Define only one per line. This makes the code easier to read.
- Keep variables in alphabetical order. This makes them easier to find when someone inevitably has to print the program and read it *on paper* (this does happen).
- Line up variable names and line up assignment equal signs. It improves readability.

Conforming Example

```
char    current_date  [25];
char    date          [12];
int     db_status           = 0;
int     i                   = 0;
int     key_count;
```

Nonconforming Example: Multiple Declarations on a Line

```
char current_date [25], date [12];
int db_status = 0, i, key_count;
```

Sooner or later, someone will have to print the program and read it. Make it easy on that person. Many people who do not have a background in COBOL find alignment of brackets and initial assignments hard to read. People with a COBOL background find meandering brackets and assignments hard to read. Duke it out.

Structures

- Either defined as templates through **typedef** or created as one-time occurrences, but not both in the same definition. Tag names are not used.

- Structure names that declare memory (not `typedef`) are all lowercase and use underscores.

Conforming Example

```
typedef struct
{
   long   cust_no;
   char   status;
   char   cust_name [31];
} CUST_REC;

CUST_REC master;    ← Uses typedef name only
CUST_REC tran;      ← Uses typedef name only
```

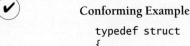

Nonconforming Example: Tag Name Used

```
struct CUST_REC
{
   long   cust_no;
   char   status;
   char   cust_name [31];
};

struct CUST_REC master;    ← require struct keyword + tag name
struct CUST_REC tran;      ← requires struct keyword + tag name
```

If you use `typedef`, you do not need to repeat the keyword `struct` when you declare a structure of that type.

Structure `typedef` Names

- All uppercase and use underscores when there is more than one word.

Conforming Example

```
typedef struct
{
   ...
} CUST_REC;
```

Nonconforming Example: Lowercase typedef name

```
typedef struct
{
   .. .
} cust_rec;
```

Using uppercase makes the created structure data types stand out.

Data Names

- All lowercase and use underscores when there is more than one word.
- Do not use hidden variables. A hidden variable is a local variable (*not* a parameter) with the same name as another variable in the function that called it. When two variables with the same name are used, it becomes a matter of context to tell which is being used. Integers used for subscripts are exempt from this requirement. (Parameters generally *should* have the same names as in the calling program because the data referred to is the same.)
- Choose meaningful names. ANSI C allows up to 31 characters for data names: use them.

Conforming Example

```
char    current_date    [25];
char    date            [12];
int     db_status              = 0;
char    run_date        [12];
```

Nonconforming Example: Mixed Case/No Underscores

```
char    Current_Date    [25];
char    Date            [12];
int     DbStatus               = 0;
char    rundate         [12];
```

The reason for using only lowercase is given in Chapter 3, "Defining Data in C." There are plenty of packages and libraries that do not conform to this standard, but that is no reason to perpetuate a poor practice.

Function Names

- All lowercase and use underscores when there is more than one word. The only exceptions are library functions written by others.
- Use the same standard for function names as for data names.

Conforming Example

```
int load_non_prem_link_list()
int get_bullet_list()
```

Nonconforming Example: Mixed Case/No Underscores

```
int LoadNonPremLinkList()
int getbulletlist()
```

Comments

- Use one of three styles:

  1. Put comment on a single line when it will fit on one line.

     ```
     /* discounts require special handling */
     if (disc_ind == 'Y')
     {
         check_discount_schedule();
     }
     ```

  2. Put comment after and on the same line as a statement.

     ```
     int page_number;     /* this is the page number */
     ```

  3. If the comment won't fit on a single line, use the following format for multiple lines:

     ```
     /*
     Allocate and initialize the LOGINREC structure to be
     used to open a connection to Server
     */
     if (login() != SUCCEED)
     {
         fprintf (errfile, "Unable to log in to Server\n");
         return (FAIL);
     }
     ```

- Pick a few comment styles and stick with them.
- If code is dead, remove it rather than commenting it out. Your source code control package has all the history.

Functions

- Start each function on a new page.
- Within a file, put functions in alphabetical order by function name.
- Alternatively, put numbers in front of function names and keep them in numerical order. Remember to precede them with a letter so the function name will compile.

  ```
  a1000_initialize();      /* will compile   */
  1000_initialize();       /* will NOT compile   */
  ```

Function Documentation

- Put a set of comments at the beginning of each function after `main()` to describe the function and the return value.

Conforming Example

```
/*
DESCRIPTION:
  This function loads a security's data into a structure that is
  then used to calculate payments.
RETURN VALUE:
  - status: whether the function succeeded or failed.
*/
int get_security_data (int      security_id,
                       SEC_REC *curr_rec )
```

You may notice that parameter documentation is missing from this item. The problem in program documentation is to create enough to tell someone what is going on, but not so much that the comments cannot be maintained (parameter lists tend not to be maintained).

Precedence of Operators

- Use parentheses instead of relying on C's 21 levels of precedence.

Conforming Example

```
result = ((a + (b * c)) / d) - f;
```

Nonconforming Example: No Parentheses

```
result = a + b * c / d - f;
```

It is risky in any language to try to remember what the precedence rules are. Using parentheses makes your intent clear.

One Statement per Line

- Put a maximum of one statement on a line.

Conforming Example

```
a = 0;
b = 0;
c = 0;
```

Nonconforming Example: Multiple Statements on a Line

```
a = 0, b = 0, c = 0;
```

This, again, is an issue of readability. Make your programs easy to read.

Indentation

- Indent three spaces per level.
- Every time there is a new level of logic, indent three spaces.
- Setting tabs to 3 won't work because most printers believe that a tab means 8 characters. Hold your thumb on the space bar.

Conforming Example

```
while (get_db_rec (rec_id) == SUCCEED )
{
   if (first_time_flag == 'Y')
   {
      first_time_flag = 'N';
      strcpy (prev_table_name, table_name );
      if (a2100_print_keys() != SUCCEED)
      {
         return (FAIL);
      }
   }
}
```

Indentation of four spaces is certainly acceptable. A two-space indentation does not create enough of a visual break. Eight spaces are too many: it leads either to wrapping lines or to choosing data names which are too short in order to fit them on a line. Choose a number and stick to it.

Line Length

- Use a line length of 80 or 90. Use the lesser of what will print on one line or show up on one line on the screen.
- Avoid line wraps (some print utilities truncate lines instead of wrapping them).
- Break up a statement if it won't fit.

Conforming Example

```
fprintf ( out_file, "GL100          GL EOM RUN      "
                    "Date: %10s        Page: %3d \n",
     run_date,
     page_no );
```

Nonconforming Example: Line Wrap

```
        fprintf ( out_file, "GL100      GL EOM RUN    Date: %10s
     Page: %3d \n", run_date, page_no );
```

The conforming example above shows a continuation of a literal and the alignment of parameters.

White Space Between Lines

- Be liberal with blank lines.

Conforming Example

```
if (in_file == NULL)
{
    printf ( "Could not open %s.\n", in_file_dsn );
    return (1);
}

out_file = fopen ( out_file_dsn, "w" );

if (out_file == NULL)
{
    printf ( "Could not open %s.\n", out_file_dsn );
    return (1);
}
```

Nonconforming Example: No Blank Lines

```
if (in_file == NULL)
{
    printf ( "Could not open %s.\n", in_file_dsn );
    return (1);
}
out_file = fopen ( out_file_dsn, "w" );
if (out_file == NULL)
{
    printf ( "Could not open %s.\n", out_file_dsn );
    return (1);
}
```

White space adds to readability by making statements stand out. The nonconforming example above is far from the worst possible case.

White Space Within a Line

- Separate each word on a line with a space.
- Put a space before and after all symbol operators (except ++ and --).
- Put a space before the first left parenthesis on a line.
- Increment/decrement operators are used by themselves and are put on a separate line (except when used in a `for` statement).

Conforming Example

```
if ( in_file == NULL)
{
    printf ( "Could not open %s.\n", in_file_dsn );
    return (1);
}
out_file = fopen ( out_file_dsn, "w" );
if (out_file == NULL)
{
    printf ( "Could not open %s.\n", out_file_dsn );
    return (1);
}
```

Nonconforming Example: No Spaces Within a Line

```
if(in_file==NULL)
{
    printf("Could not open %s.\n",in_file_dsn);
    return(1);
}
out_file=fopen(out_file_dsn,"w");
if(out_file==NULL)
{
    printf("Could not open %s.\n",out_file_dsn);
    return(1);
}
```

Again, white space adds to readability. The nonconforming example above will compile, but that is not sufficient. Programs must be readable.

Increment/Decrement Operator

- Must follow the variable it increments or decrements.

Conforming Example

```
for ( i = 0; i < ARRAY_SIZE; i++ )
```

Nonconforming Example: Operator Does Not Follow Variable

```
for ( i = 0; i < ARRAY_SIZE; ++i )
```

> **NOTE:** You can change "follow the variable" to precede the variable. It does not really matter as long as it is used in a consistent manner.

- The increment/decrement operators are not combined with other statements, except in the `for` statement. This is for simplicity and accuracy. Increment/decrement operators are capable of a lot of mischief when used in complex statements.

Conforming Example

```
rec_count++;
printf ("Results: %d %d Rec: %d\n", a, b, rec_count );
```

Nonconforming Example: Increment Embedded in a Statement

```
printf ("Results: %d %d Rec: %d\n", a, b, rec_count++ );
```

Nonconforming Example: Multiple Increment/Decrement

```
i = ++i + i--;
```

This is an issue of simplicity. It is not important whether the operator precedes or follows the data element it is modifying, as long as it is not combined with other operations. Pick one method and stick with it.

if Statements

- Braces are always used in both the `if` and the `else` blocks. Line the braces up under the `if` or `else`.

Conforming Example

```
if ( match_ind != 'Y' )
{
    mis_match_count++;
    trouble_ahead = 'N';
}
```

Nonconforming Example: No Braces

```
if ( match_ind != 'Y' )
    mis_match_count++;
    trouble_ahead = 'Y';
```

- A maximum of *one function call per condition* within an if statement.

Conforming examples

```
if (strcmp (prev_dept_name, dept_name ) == 0 )
{
    dept_rec_count++;
}
if (strcmp (dept_name, "ACCT" )  == 0  ||
    strcmp (dept_name, "SALES" ) == 0    )
{
    continue;
}
```

Nonconforming example

```
if (abs (gets()) > 100 )
{
    printf ("Value must be <= 100 \n" );
}
```

One function call *per condition* in an if statement allows multiple function calls in one if statement, as the second conforming example shows. The nonconforming example shows one function using another function's return value, all within one if statement. This is avoidable complexity.

- A maximum of one *assignment statement per condition* within an if statement.

Conforming Example

```
if ( (status = get_database_rec (cust_no) ) == SUCCESS )
{
    cust_rec_count++;
}
```

Assigning a result of a call as part of a condition is somewhat more complicated than the previous conforming example. This statement can easily be separated into a call to the function followed by a check of the status. Do not make an `if` statement more complicated than this one.

- Case statements for strings line up under the `if`.

Conforming Example

```
if (strcmp (code, "DEB") == 0 )
{
    get_debentures ();
}
else if (strcmp (code, "STN") == 0 )
{
    get_short_term_notes ();
}
else if (strcmp (code, "ZC") == 0 )
{
    get_zero_coupon ();
}
```

Nonconforming Example: String Case Continually Indented

```
if (strcmp (code, "DEB") == 0)
{
   get_debentures ();
}
else if (strcmp (code, "STN") == 0 )
   {
     get_short_term_notes ();
   }
   else if (strcmp (code, "ZC") == 0 )
      {
        get_zero_coupon ();
      }
```

The primary issue in `if` statements is the use of braces. Braces make `if` statements obvious instead of relying on the compiler to execute only the first statement after `if` or `else`. Braces also make maintenance easier. The limit of one function call and one assignment per `if` keeps the code readable. The case statement for strings is one where multiple tests are made on the same variable, which is what `switch` does. This is not what a typical nested `if` does, and therefore the case `if` statement lines up the same way `switch` does (see next item).

`switch` Statements

- Have a `break` statement in every case.
- Always have a `default` case.
- Have braces line up under the `switch` keyword.

Conforming Example

```
switch ( step_number )
{
   case 1:
      strcpy (step_name, "PAY" );
      break;

   case 2:
      strcpy (step_name, "REC" );
      break;

   case 3:
      strcpy (step_name, "SUM" );
      break;

   default:
      strcpy (step_name, "???" );
}
```

Nonconforming Example: No Break and No Default

```
switch ( step_number )
{
   case 1:
      strcpy (step_name, "PAY" );

   case 2:
      strcpy (step_name, "REC" );

   case 3:
      strcpy (step_name, "SUM" );
}
```

Formatting for switch/case is the same as in for, while, functions, and nonnested if statements. Be consistent. Requiring break and default makes the code more robust.

for Statements

- Always use braces, even if there is only one statement to execute in the loop.
- Braces line up under the for.
- Always have an initialization expression, a while-true expression, and an increment/decrement expression.

Conforming Example

```
for ( i = 0; i < 10; i++ )
{
   sales_amt += 100.0;

   dept_tot [i] = sales_amt;
}
```

Nonconforming Example: No Initialization Expression

```
for ( ; i < 10; i++ )
{
    sales_amt += 100.0;
    dept_tot [i] = sales_amt;
}
```

Nonconforming Example: No Braces

```
for ( i = 0; i < 10; i++ )
    sales_amt += 100.0;              ← Only statement in the loop

    dept_tot [i] = sales_amt;    ← Not executed in the loop
```

Nonconforming Example: Braces Not Aligned

```
for ( i = 0; i < 10; i++ ){
    sales_amt += 100.0;

    dept_tot [i] = sales_amt;
}
```

Braces are required to avoid the problem of the for executing only the first statement after the for. They are aligned for readability and consistency.

- When a for statement is used to move to a point in an array to set a subscript, put no statements in the loop, and do not put a semicolon at the end of the line where the for occurs.

Conforming Example

```
for ( i = 0; formatted_num [i] != PERIOD; i++ )
{
    ;      /* nothing happens */
}
```

Nonconforming Example: Semicolon at the End of Line

```
for ( i = 0; formatted_num [i] != PERIOD; i++ );
```

Both statements above set the subscript i to the value where a period is first found in formatted_num. The conforming example makes it obvious that nothing is happening in the loop. The nonconforming example leaves you wondering if the semicolon at the end is a typo.

Parameters

- Use no more than five per function. This is a guideline, not a requirement.
- If there are more than five, consider putting related ones together in a structure.

Program Global Variables

- Declared above `main()` without the `static` qualifier and are redeclared in other files with the `extern` qualifier.
- Do not use them for variables specific to one program. Instead use, parameters.
- There will probably be some global variables in any medium-to-large business application for exception trapping and error handling. These few global variables should be put in an include file which the programs then include.

`while` Statements

- Always use braces, even if there is only one statement to execute in the loop.
- Braces line up under the `while`.

Conforming Example

```
while ( i < 10 )
{
    sales_amt += 100.0;
    dept_tot [i] = sales_amt;

    i++;
}
```

Nonconforming Example: No Braces

```
while ( i < 10 )
    sales_amt += 100.0;         ← Only Statement in loop
    dept_tot [i] = sales_amt;   ← Not executed in loop
    i++;                        ← Not executed in loop
```

`printf()` and `fprintf()` Statements

- Use one or more `printf()` or `fprintf()` calls per line or record of output.
- Use the ANSI C literal continuation method. This ends the first line of the literal with double quotes and resumes the literal on the next line with double quotes. White space between the second and third quotes is ignored. See the conforming example that follows.
- If the `printf()` or `fprintf()` statement won't fit on one line, indent parameters three characters on the lines following `printf()` or `fprintf()`.

Conforming Example   ✔

```
fprintf ( out_file, "GL100          GL EOM RUN          "
                    "Date: %10s      Page: %3d \n ",

    run_date,
    page_no );
```

Nonconforming Example: Line Wrapping, No Parameter Indenting   ⚠

```
        fprintf ( out_file, "GL100          GL EOM RUN   Date: %10s
    Page: %3d \n", run_date, page_no );
```

Make the program readable.

Banned Items, Constructs, and Techniques

What set of standards would be complete without a list of banned keywords and techniques? Use this list for starters and amend as necessary.

1. Use of `goto` is banned. Do not `goto`. Do not collect $200.

   Do not use `goto`. Ever. Use `continue`, `break`, or `return` as appropriate.

2. Use of `int` is banned.

   This should be good for some discussion, especially in light of the portability consideration.

3. Use of string compare side effect is banned.

   Conforming Example   ✔

   ```
   if (strcmp (prod_code, "BSL") == 0 )
   {
       ...
   }
   ```

   Nonconforming Example: Say What?   ⚠

   ```
   if ( !strcmp (prod_code, "BSL") )
   {
       ...
   }
   ```

This requires a double take, at least, to understand it. The statement also uses negative logic to test equality. Why spend time trying to figure it out? Keep things simple.

4. `float` data type is banned.

   It is an anachronism (read: memory saver) that all too easily loses significant digits. Use `double`.

5. Structure tag names are banned. Use `typedef`.

   Conforming Example

   ```
   typedef struct
   {
       long    cust_no;
       char    status;
       char    cust_name   [31];
   }   CUST_REC;

   CUST_REC master;   ← typedef name + data name
   CUST_REC tran;     ← typedef name + data name
   ...
   ```

   Nonconforming Example: Tag Name

   ```
   struct CUST_REC
   {
       long    cust_no;
       char    status;
       char    cust_name   [31];
   };

   struct CUST_REC master;   ← struct keyword + tag name + data name
   struct CUST_REC tran;     ← struct keyword + tag name + data name
   ```

   Using `typedef` does not require reiteration of the `struct` keyword when using the template. Also, tag name error messages from the compiler can be hard to understand.

6. Warning messages from the compiler must be eliminated.

   It's a warning for a reason. Fix it. Don't cause the next programmer to have to decide if the program is broken or not.

7. Macros are banned.

   Macros are often a source of errors when they are expanded because the preprocessor does not know C. The expanded code does not appear in your listing and errors can be difficult to find. The machine efficiency gained is small and the error potential is large.

Summary

The purpose of programming standards is to reduce development and maintenance costs by creating programs which are well-structured, easy to read, and have a consistent look across projects. Code sharing and re-use is easier if all programs have a common style. Program efficiency needs to be defined in terms of ease of comprehension and ease of change in programs, since programmer time is now the major cost component in system life cycles.

A set of standards should err on the side of being too small rather than being too large. Standards are more likely to be used if they can be remembered. Standards should be developed by programmers, since they have to live with them. Structured walkthroughs are a tool that can speed the development process while assuring conformance to standards. Many errors can be caught during a walkthrough. Walkthroughs should be conducted by developers and should be used on analysis documents, design documents, and programs.

The standards presented in this chapter should not be taken as gospel. They should be a starting point for discussion. The text of this set of standards is available free on the Internet or for a nominal fee for a diskette (see the coupon at the back of the book).

CHAPTER 14

C++, or What's That OOP on Your Tie?

Introduction

The purpose of this chapter is to provide a broad picture of C++. Of course, it is impossible to teach the language in only a few pages, so with significant simplification and some omission, this chapter outlines the most important ideas and principles of C++.

C++ was originally developed by Bjarne Stroustrup of AT&T Bell Laboratories. The name C++ (pronounced "C plus plus") represents the letter (and language) C with the increment operator ++. It conveys that the C language is the basis of and has been incremented (extended) in C++. In the simplest sense C++ is the C language with 16 additional keywords (ANSI C has 32). You could either look at this as only 16 new keywords or as a 50 percent increase in keywords.

In fact, C++ has considerable extra capability compared to C. Most of this extra capability is a result of the object-oriented programming (OOP) capacities of C++. At the same time, existing C programs will compile without errors in C++ if they have full and correct function prototypes.

References

After reading this chapter you may want to learn more about C++. Here are three books I have found useful:

C++ For C Programmers, by Ira Pohl (Redwood City, CA: Benjamin/Cummings Publishing Co., 1994).

Pohl uses the same approach as this book, teaching a new language based on one the reader already knows. The first chapter covers the whole language, and subsequent chapters expand those topics. The examples are good although not business oriented.

C++ and the OOP Paradigm, by Bindu R. Rao (New York, NY: McGraw-Hill, 1993).
This book is unusual for two reasons: The author seems to have developed real systems in C++, and the examples use business problems. It has a nice combination of theoretical and practical considerations. At under 200 pages, it won't crush you.

The C++ Programming Language, *Second Edition*, by Bjarne Stroustrup (Reading, MA: Addison-Wesley, 1991).
This is the definitive work, written by the creator of the language. While this is not a teaching book, it is still interesting for a variety of reasons: It covers the language, contains the official reference manual, gives some history of developments of the language, and has chapters on system development, design of C++ programs, and design of libraries.

C++ as a Better C

There are two reasons to use C++ instead of C: you can use C++ as a better C compiler, and you can move into object-oriented programming. Using C++ as a better C compiler gives you immediate gains, while object-oriented programming gives long-term gains. The immediate gains are significant and relatively painless to obtain: It is perfectly acceptable to move to C++ while still writing what are essentially C programs. OOP takes a while to figure out, but that should not stop you from moving to C++.

For the C programmer fresh from COBOL, C++ offers a compiler that is much tighter than that of C. It improves the chances that a compiled program might actually run the first time, which is a common assumption in COBOL but not in C.

In addition to the advantages of a tighter compiler, C++ offers the advantages of the extensions to C, primarily object-oriented programming. OOP can be exotic, but it does offer some concrete, simple, and valuable constructs for business data processing. In C++ an object is an occurrence or instance of a class. A class is a data element or a data structure *along with the functions that maintain it*, as illustrated here:

Class: Data definition bound with associated functions

```
employee
data
definition
```

```
employee
functions
that operate
on employee
data
```

This combination of data and associated functions is called encapsulation. The only way to manipulate class data is through calls to its functions. This also means that only a small set of functions must be examined when code changes are made.

So what do classes do for you in a business system? The benefits are numerous, but two examples come quickly to mind: the `string` and `bcd` classes.

You use the string class to create character strings. The `string` class has functions to copy and concatenate data. These functions are usually specifically written so that memory does not get overwritten when you copy strings. They typically either use the size of the destination string to control how many characters are moved or dynamically enlarge the destination string. What a concept! String classes exist in books, commercially available libraries, and shareware libraries. You don't have to write a string class.

Both C and C++ handle numbers with decimal values awkwardly through floating point numbers. The basic problem is representing fractional decimal values in binary arithmetic. COBOL solves this problem through binary-coded decimal (BCD) arithmetic. The COBOL compiler turns all numbers in a computation into integers first, does computations, and then turns the result back into a number with a decimal fraction. The C++ compiler cannot do this, but widely available C++ libraries have BCD classes that can. These classes give you the ability to specify the number of decimal places for a number. They also provide all relevant arithmetic functions and round results according to the business rounding rule.

These two examples show that, using classes, C++ offers solutions to generic business problems. These kinds of classes can add a lot to a project, but even more value is obtained by designing application-specific classes. This is the heart of C++. A detailed discussion of it is beyond the scope of this book, but the second half of the chapter provides a brief overview, beginning with the section called "Beyond C: C++ as an Object-Oriented Programming Language."

The following sections discuss aspects of C++ that are improvements on their equivalents in C.

Tighter Compiler

Type checking is more extensive than in ANSI C. C++ does not assume that mixing data types is intentional. COBOL is a strongly typed language, and so is C++. This catches many errors at compile time. Errors are much easier to find and fix at compile time than when you are hovering over the warm remains of a program that recently died.

Also, the messages from the C++ compiler are much better than those from the average C compiler. They are more specific, and you can understand most of them the first time you see them.

Reduced Need for the Preprocessor

Recall that the preprocessor acts first in a compile. It looks for lines that begin with #, such as #include, and then acts according to the preprocessor directive. The C preprocessor is a potential source of problems for a system, primarily due to the use of macros. A macro is a #define statement with code and variables that performs some work. When you invoke a macro in a program, it looks like a function call. For instance, isalpha() and other class test functions are typically implemented as macros. The macro expands during compiling and does not show the expanded code.

The problem with macros is that they are prone to unwanted side effects that occur during their expansion because the preprocessor does not understand C syntax. They are so problematic that this book does not discuss how to write them.

The original reason for macros was to eliminate the overhead associated with a function call. Instead of making a function call, a macro causes code to be inserted directly in the program. If you are writing an operating system, this kind of micro-efficiency can be justified. For the average business system it is an invitation to trouble.

One of the goals in developing C++ was to decrease the need for the preprocessor. C++ solves the macro problem with a new keyword, inline. The inline keyword operates approximately the same way as a macro, except that it is subject to all the syntax checking and type checking of C++. This eliminates the unwanted side effects of macros. It is still a rare case in business data processing that this kind of micro-efficiency is required. Function calls are seldom the bottleneck in application performance.

The need for symbolic constants declared by #define has been superceded by the const keyword. C++ allows const integer data elements to be used to declare array sizes, which ANSI C does not. This capability means that #define constants need not be used in C++ programs. C++ can perform type checking on program constants when they are declared using const.

Example

```
const int MAX_RECS = 100;
double expense_amt [MAX_RECS];      // legal in C++
```

The `#include` preprocessor directive is unchanged in C++.

More Convenient Comment Symbol

C++ has a new comment symbol, //, which is available in addition to the old familiar /* and */ symbols. The C++ comment begins with // and ends at the end of the line.

Its utility comes from two features: You don't have to type anything to end the comment, and you can nest // comments within /* */ comments. ANSI C does not allow nested comments.

Examples

```
gl_amt = get_abs_val (tran_amt);        // make sure it's positive

// this is a single line C++ comment

// this is a
// multiple line
// C++ comment

/*
   This is a standard
   multi-line C comment
// with an embedded C++ comment
   which the compiler
   does not object to
*/
```

Prototypes with Teeth

Function prototypes were first introduced in C++ and then made their way into ANSI C. The problem in ANSI C is that it is possible to subvert prototype checking.

If you pass a short or long parameter list and you have fully defined prototypes, ANSI C will generate an error during the compile, forcing you to fix it. However, if you define the return value, but no parameters, ANSI C will let you pass a mismatched parameter list. In certain cases an ANSI C compiler will issue a warning, but not an error, if a program lacks function prototypes.

C++ shows no mercy in function prototypes. You must define function prototypes with both the type for the return value and the parameter list with data types, such as

```
double compute_fica_tax (long    soc_sec_no,
                         double gross_pay,
                         double ytd_fica_gross );
```

In the function header and in all calls to the function, you must match the number of parameters in the function prototype. However, you can get away with having different data types in your function header and call list. C++ will convert them or coerce them, if possible, to the data types of the prototype so that a correct set of data is passed.

Recall that converting a data type means going to another data type with a larger maximum value. Coercing is going to another data type with a smaller maximum value. Going to the larger data type will not result in a loss of data. Going to a smaller data type *can* result in a loss of data.

As with ANSI C, about the only conversions that the C++ compiler won't perform are string-to-number and vice versa. Either of those mismatches will generate a compile error. However, most C++ compilers generate a warning message if you pass a parameter that does not match the data type in the function prototype. Pay attention to these warnings.

Superior Call Parameter Handling

From a COBOL programmer's perspective (and many a C programmer's, too), the biggest improvement of C++ over C is in the handling of call parameters. Dealing with parameters in C is a confusing thicket of using the address operator, then using the pointer operator, then not using the pointer operator if you're passing that parameter again. And don't forget the structure pointer operator.

Parameters that a function can change are defined as *reference parameters*, which means the called function has direct access to the data in the calling function. According to the academics, C does not truly pass parameters by reference. True passing of parameters by reference does not require turning them into pointers. C++ allows parameters to be passed by reference without the use of pointers.

C++ adds two options to parameter syntax. One is the reference parameter symbol, **&**, which indicates a parameter's value can be changed by the called function. It is the same symbol used in C as the address operator, but it is placed at the *end* of the parameter data type and it has different handling. It still indicates the address of the data item being passed, but pointer syntax is not required either in the function header or in the function.

The other addition is the use of `const` as a parameter modifier in function prototypes and function headers. A parameter with the `const` modifier is one whose value cannot be changed by the called function. It is called a *constant* parameter. Both by-reference and by-value parameters can be made constant. If `const` is combined with a by-reference parameter, a copy of the data is not generated, and the parameter cannot be changed. This is called a *constant reference* parameter. This can be useful where large structures are being passed. The old call-by-value (pass a copy of the parameter) method is still available.

> **NOTE:** You may find `const` used in function headers in some ANSI C compilers. Its use is allowed, but const does not prevent the called function from changing the data in the calling function in C.

The net effect of these changes is that you no longer need to use pointers for most situations involving calling and called functions. Whether a parameter is being passed by reference or by value is declared in the function prototype and the function header, not in the call statement. Both the call statement and the called function simply refer to the parameters by name, without pointer operators. This is a major improvement in consistency, not to mention comprehensibility.

Examples

Here is a short comparison of function prototypes, function calls, and parameter use in both C++ and C.

```
         C++                                ANSI C

         Function Prototypes

1. void func_1 (      int    num_1,    void func_1 ( int num_1,
2.                     int&   num_2,                  int *num_2 );
3.              (const int    num_3 );      No equivalent

         Function Calls

4. func_1 (num_1,                      func_1 ( num_1,
5.         num_2,                                &num_2 );
6.         num_3 );                          No equivalent

         Parameter Use (within func_1())

7. num_1 = 7;                          num_1 = 7;
8. num_2 = 100;                        *num_2 = 100;
9. num_2 = num_3;                         No equivalent
10. num_3 = 25;   // compile error        No equivalent
```

Comments on the Example

Line 1 Displays the call-by-value syntax in a function prototype, which is the same in both C++ and ANSI C. Coding the parameter's data type and name with no modifiers causes a parameter to be passed by value. This means that a copy of the value of the field in the calling function will be passed to the called function. The called function can modify the parameter, but the effect is local: the original field in the calling function is unchanged.

Line 2 Shows call-by-reference syntax in C++ and in C. Note that in C++ the address operator, &, *follows* the data type of the parameter. In both C++ and ANSI C the address of num_2 in the calling function is being passed. If num_2 is changed by the called function, it is changed in the calling function. This is the way COBOL parameters work by default.

Line 3 Defines a constant parameter in C++. C cannot do this. A constant parameter is one that the called function cannot change. In this case a copy of the data is passed. If a statement in the called function tries to alter the value of a constant parameter, it generates a compile error.

This capability is quite useful. If the design shows that a parameter is to be read but not changed, you can define it as a constant parameter. This ensures that a programmer writing a called function can't be fooled into thinking a parameter can be changed. If you pass by value, as in line 1, the called function can change the local copy of the parameter but not the original in the calling function. This seldom makes sense and is prevented by coding parameters const.

Another valuable use of constant parameters is to pass arrays (such as character strings) that cannot be changed. Passed arrays (including strings) are always vulnerable to change in C. In C++ you can pass them as constants, so they cannot be changed. The following is a function prototype for a function that is passed a string called last_name and an array of ints called rec_count. Specifying const prevents the called function from changing them.

```
void func_1 ( const char last_name [],
              ( const int  rec_count [] );
```

As a bonus, no copy is made of the array or string. The address of the array/string is passed implicitly and the called function cannot change the contents of the string or of the array.

Lines 4–6   Exhibit a function call to each function. Notice that the C++ call looks like a COBOL subprogram call: It just uses parameter names. If you want to know how the parameters can be used, look in the function prototype. The ANSI C call is a combination of parameter names and parameter attributes.

Line 6 shows a constant parameter in C++. You cannot pass such a parameter in C.

This call uses the same parameter names as in the function prototype. In C++, as in C, the names do not have to be the same. As an aid to comprehension, however, they generally should be.

Lines 7–9   Show that in a C++ function, using parameters is the same as in COBOL. Just use the parameter names and let the function prototype determine whether you're dealing with a local copy (call by value), a field in the calling function that can be updated (call by reference), or a field in the calling function that *cannot* be updated (constant or constant reference). Notice that there is no pointer operator in the C++ statement on line 8. In fact, most C++ functions need few or no pointers.

Line 9 shows that a constant parameter can be used in a function, as long as it's not the object of an assignment statement.

Line 10   Demonstrates that C++ does not allow a constant parameter to be changed. Any constant parameter or constant reference parameter on the receiving end of an assignment statement will generate a compile error.

Consistency in Parameter Use

Because you no longer have to use pointer operators in C++ to deal with parameters that can be changed, parameter use and passing are consistent. A parameter that can be changed is defined in both the function prototype and the function header with the address operator, &, *following* its data type. The calling function uses parameter data names in the call (no addresses), and the called function uses parameter data names (no pointers) in its statements—just like COBOL.

Another plus in C++ is that there is no difference in syntax in call parameters between the first and second levels of calls for by-reference parameters. In C the first-level call statement uses the address operator, &, for a reference parameter. The called function then uses the pointer operator, *, when it uses the parameter. When that called function calls yet another function and passes that parameter, it uses the pointer name without the asterisk in order to continue to pass the address of the field from the first calling function. From the second level call down, the protocol does not change again. This mishmash of punctuation can be eliminated in C++ for most parameters. Passing addresses and pointers still has use in C++, but for ordinary parameter passing, the pass-by-reference method in C++ is clearly easier to use.

New I/O Functions

Most I/O functions in C have both a variable number and variable kinds of arguments. `printf()`, `fprintf()`, `scanf()`, `sscanf()` all allow a variable number of parameters of various types in a call. While this is convenient for the programmer, it also has its dangers. Because of the variable argument list, type checking of parameters is not done for these functions. One of the classic mistakes in `printf()` is a mismatch between the formatting symbol and the data type of the argument:

```
char   middle_init;
...
printf ("Middle initial is %s", middle_init );
```

The `printf()` is looking for a string, but it is being passed a single-character field, which does not match the format specifer `%s`. Depending on your compiler, this generates either unpredictable results or an abnormal termination. Seldom, if ever, is a compile warning issued.

A major theme in C++ is strong typing, which means having the compiler evaluate the data types of all data elements used with operators and function calls. When the C++ compiler detects an inappropriate data type in an operation or function call, it issues a compile error. COBOL is a strongly typed language and has always done this. It's still a relatively new concept in the C world.

To extend the concept of strong typing to input/output operations, C++ offers a whole new set of I/O functions. The good news is that when you use the C++ I/O functions, your code will be checked for appropriate data types at compile time. The bad news is that the output function can be even more awkward for formatting than `printf()`. And it still does not put commas in numbers. On the other hand, the input and output functions have been built in such a way that it is trivial in object-oriented programming both to use them and to extend them.

The terminology for I/O functions in C++ is slightly different from that in C, although the meanings are essentially the same. The terms *standard output stream* and *standard input stream* are used. These are equivalent to stdin and stdout. They still default to the screen and the keyboard, respectively. The include file for these I/O function prototypes is iostream.h.

cout and cin are two of the new I/O functions. cout stands for character output, and cin stands for character input. cout supercedes printf(), while cin supercedes gets(), getchar(), and scanf(). All C I/O library functions are still available. Here is an example of the new functions:

```
cout << "Enter a social security number: \n" ;
cin >> soc_sec_no;
```

The cout statement displays "Enter a social security number:" on the screen. The cin statement takes the keyboard input, converts it from character input, and puts it in soc_sec_no.

These new functions have nonfunction syntax: no parentheses. The << (output operator) and >> (insertion operator) symbols have been redefined in the context of cin and cout to eliminate parentheses. Using more familiar (though illegal) syntax, we could recode the above into

```
cout ("Enter a social security number: \n" );
cin (soc_sec_no );
```

This is helpful to visualize how it works, but the two statements above will not compile in C++.

cout and cin have been designed to take one parameter at a time. This allows type checking and thus early error detection. The reason for the redefinition of parentheses as << and >> is notational convenience. It allows what appear to be multiple parameters to be passed to cout

```
cout << "Social security number is: " << soc_sec_no << endl ;
```

Each << becomes another call to cout. Each parameter must be preceded by <<. The last parameter, endl, is actually a function being passed to cout. The endl function inserts a line feed in the stream and flushes the buffer. The output stream is usually defined as the screen. Flushing ensures that all characters are displayed.

cout: The Output Function cout was designed to supercede printf(), though printf() is still available. Only one parameter per call is passed to cout. This allows parameter checking, which makes cout safer than printf(). However, the other side of the trade for type checking is that cout can be harder to read than printf():

```
cout << "Social security number is: " << soc_sec_no << endl ;
printf ("Social security number is: %d \n", soc_sec_no );
```

It gets harder when there are multiple substitutions to be made:

```
cout << "Name: "            printf ("Name: %s %c %s Social security number: %d \n",
     << first_name              first_name,
     << " "                     middle_init,
     << middle_init             last_name,
     << " "                     soc_sec_no );
     << last_name
     << "Social security number: "
     << soc_sec_no
     << endl ;
```

One virtue of `printf()` is that it does let you see the whole literal. It is hard to believe that one could consider `printf()` readable, but compared to `cout` it can be. Type checking does not come cheaply in the I/O area.

Since `cout` does not use format specifiers like `%-20s` or `%8.2f` to format output, there must be some other method. There is a set of function calls for formatting, which can be placed in the list of parameters passed to cout:

```
cout << setw (11) << setprecision (8) << "GL Amt: " << gl_amt << endl;
```

Which equates to

```
printf ("GL Amt: %11.2f \n", gl_amt );
```

`setw()` sets the width for the item to print, and `setprecision()` sets the number of significant digits that will be shown.

If you think this is a lot of work for little benefit, many C++ programmers agree with you. It is common to use `sprintf()` to format a string of output and then submit a single, formatted string to `cout`.

Because `cout` can be awkward to use and hard to read, many people do not like to use it for formatting. However, `cout` is used extensively for writing characters to the stream. The common use, however, is to format a string with `sprintf()` and then pass that string to `cout`.

cin: The Input Function The other I/O function, `cin`, supercedes `gets()`, `getchar()`, and `scanf()`. `cin` is simpler and safer to use than these functions. It is superior in both function and ease of use and is therefore used often, although the C library functions are still available. Here's a sample, with equivalent C code:

```
C++:                          C:

main()                        main()
{                             {
   char dept [21];               char dept [21];
   char run_code;                char run_code;
   long soc_sec_no;              long soc_sec_no;

   cout << "Enter dept" ;        printf ("Enter dept" );
   cin >> dept;                  gets (dept);
```

```
    cout << "Enter Run Code:";        printf ("Enter Run Code:" );
    cin >> run_code;                  run_code = getchar();

    cout << "Enter Soc Sec #";        printf ("Enter Soc Sec #" );
    cin >> soc_sec_no;                scanf ("%ld", &soc_sec_no );
}                                 }
```

As you can see, cin is simpler than using the three different functions required in C. The compiler figures out what data conversion is necessary and generates the code to do it, which is how it should be. You also don't have to worry about leftover characters in stdin, as you do with scanf().

C++ as a Better C: Summary

With the possible exception of cout, C++ offers real advantages over C. The rigorous enforcement of function prototypes offers the greatest benefit. This significantly reduces errors in programs. Parameter passing in C++ is clearly superior to C, with a simpler call-by-reference method, the ability to make parameters constant, the ability to pass a constant parameter by reference, and the ability to protect strings and arrays when passing them.

One of the goals in designing C++ was to make it possible to integrate C++ programs with existing C programs. This, in fact, has happened. You can start moving to C++ using an existing environment of C code. You can call C functions directly from C++ functions.

While the capabilities and techniques of C++ shown thus far are significant improvements over C, we have only scratched the surface of C++. You won't exploit the real power of the language, however, until you go beyond C to object-oriented programming.

Beyond C: C++ as an Object-Oriented Programming Language

C++ was invented by Bjarne Stroustrup at AT&T Bell Laboratories in the early 1980s. He was working on telephone network simulations that, because of performance considerations, could not be reasonably modeled in Simula67, a simulation language. Stroustrup extended C by adding the concept of class.

In its simplest form, a *class* consists of a programmer-defined data type along with functions that operate on the data type. In C++ the standard C data types are supplied, along with the operators and functions that work on them. For instance, there is the data type int, which is an integer. It is operated on by +, −, *, /, abs(), and so on.

An object is an instance of a class type. If int is a class, then in this declaration

```
    int   record_count;
```

record_count is an object of class int.

One example of a class in C++ is a data type called bcd, for binary coded decimal. bcd is a common class in commercial C++ libraries. This data type allows the programmer to declare a numeric variable with a specified number of decimal places, which is not possible if you use a double. In addition to creating the data type, the creators of this class also write code that performs the operations necessary to use this data type. Operations such as +, −, *, and / are defined *within* the context of the bcd class. Once the class is created, the use of it is straightforward: bcd numbers can be used like any other numbers.

The concept of class may seem like a relatively minor extension of C, but it is a fundamental step in the evolution of computer problem solving from being procedure oriented to being data oriented.

Traditional procedural languages such as Fortran, COBOL, and C emphasize algorithms; data is raw material for processing. Many early implementations in these languages also became infamous for their spaghetti code. Uncontrolled go to statements coupled with global memory variables combined to create defective programs. Fortran and COBOL are susceptible to the spaghetti code syndrome. Fortran and C are susceptible to global memory problems.

Modular programming and structured programming were developed in the 1970s to try to bring order out of this chaos. These methods were still primarily procedure oriented: the procedure is here and the data is there. Any data needed by the procedure is read or passed to it, unless it is global data. Then it just floats around, waiting to be corrupted.

During these years modules were created that began to combine data with the code to maintain it. An example would be a code validation and maintenance routine that hid the data from other programs. Codes could be validated, added, or deleted only by calling this routine. Direct access to the codes was not allowed. This was the beginning of object-oriented programming, but it lacked one of the significant features of OOP: it was a custom solution, not a generic one.

Class: A Data Type Plus the Code That Manipulates It

One of the points of object-oriented programming is to provide a framework for generic solutions where a data type (data element, structure, or record) is created along with the functions and operators necessary to maintain it. Once this new class (data definition *plus* functions and operators that work on the data) has been created, it can be invoked over and over again in programs and used with new occurrences of the same type of data. Each time it is invoked, an object is created. Each object automatically comes with the functions and operators defined for that class. Classes look and operate like data types defined by the language.

The class/object paradigm gives programmers and designers the ability to add data types along with related operators and functions that then operate similarly or identically to data types native to the language.

The term *user-defined type* is used often in C++ discussions. In this sense, *user* means programmer or designer. (From a system programmer's point of view, application programmers and designers are users). Each class that is created is a user-defined type. The term *abstract data type* is also used, but it seems much less meaningful than user-defined type. Computer languages are already abstract.

A properly designed class has a data component and a comprehensive set of operations (functions and operators) that manipulate it. The idea is to make user-defined types behave like native types. A native type is one that is part of the language. For instance, C and C++ have the data type `int`, which is an integer. `int` requires a specified amount of memory to be stored. In addition, there is a set of operations that can be performed using `int`, such as =, ==, !=, and so on. `int` is a class: it has a particular data type definition and a set of operators and functions that can operate on it. `int` is a native class because it is defined in the language.

User-defined classes in C++ allow us to extend the language by creating new types. One obvious type that needs to be added is `string`. Character arrays are a relatively painful construct in C and C++. A COBOL programmer has a hard time understanding why alphanumerics are so much trouble in C. In COBOL, alphanumerics are simple, and they can be copied and compared using the same reserved words that are used for numbers.

One of the early classes developed in C++ by Stroustrup and his colleagues was called `string`. It takes character arrays and hides them in the `string` class. It allows string variables to be copied and compared using the same keywords and symbol operators as numbers. (One could ask why the developers of C++ didn't just put `string` into the language as a native type.)

`string` is a class. It is a user-defined data type and it has a set of operators and functions that operate on it. To use the `string` class, you merely specify it as the data type when declaring a variable. For example, this line declares a variable called `last_name` of type string, which is a class:

```
string  last_name;
```

`last_name` is an object, or an instance of class `string`.

We don't really know (or need to know) what the internal representation of `string` is, although it's likely to be a character array. What is interesting about a `string` class is the set of operators and functions defined with it. For instance, most implementations of the `string` class allow the following:

```
string  last_name;
string  first_name;
string  mailing_name;
...
mailing_name = first_name + last_name;  // now we're getting somewhere
```

The variables are declared with the data type `string`. This makes them objects of the class `string`. In the statement creating `mailing_name`, both = and + have been redefined inside the `string` class to work with character strings. This is called *operator overloading*, something you can do within a class in C++. (Operator overloading is discussed later in this chapter.) The result of creating the `string` class this way is that the `string` type now looks like part of the C++ language. This is the point of user-defined data types: to create new data types that are extensions of the language.

Class Libraries: Buy Them, Don't Write Them

Class libraries, like linked list libraries, can be tempting to write. However, the problem with class libraries is the same as with linked list libraries. Other people have been writing them for a long time and have tested them thoroughly. They have a three- to ten-year head start on writing what is often nontrivial code. There is a variety of both commercial and shareware C++ libraries available that offer many different classes in a ready-to-go form. You get cheaper and more accurate results when you use a class library that has already been tested by hundreds of other people's applications.

Encapsulation: Wrapping Code Around Data

Encapsulation means surrounding a soft gooey core of data with a hard outer shell of protective code. The idea is that the only way to get to the data is through the class functions and operators that have been defined to manipulate it. The intent is to package the code that maintains the data *with* the data. It also reduces inadvertent corruption of data by reducing access to it.

Typically, data definition and function prototypes for a class are placed in a header (include) file, and the functions and operators are placed in a C++ source file. Using the `string` class as an example, the header file is called `strng.h` and the source file is called `strng.cpp`. These names are chosen in order to distinguish them from `string.h` which has prototypes for `strcpy()`, `strcmp()`, and so on.

The functions for the class are put in a file called `strng.cpp`. The `strng.cpp` file is compiled with the `strng.h` file to create an object module, `strng.obj` or `strng.o`, depending on the compiler. The `strng.obj` file is then linked into a library file with a name you give it, say, `classlib.lib` or `classlib.a` (the suffix depends on the compiler). This completes the creation of the `string` class. The next step is to get it into a program.

A program using the `string` class must include `strng.h` in order to pick up the data definition and the function prototypes for manipulating string objects. The program then uses the string objects along with functions and operators that have been defined for class `string`. When the program is linked, it picks up the library object module where `string.obj` was placed, `classlib.lib`. This brings in the code for the class functions.

Public and Private Members of a Class

One of the central concepts of classes is that there are public members and private members. A member can be data or a function. Data definition for the class and internal manipulation functions for the class are placed in the private area of the class. No program you write can either directly access the private data or directly call the private functions of a class. This is how the data is protected.

On the other hand, any program you write can call the public functions of a class. The public functions are the interface to the world outside the class. You create, manipulate, and destroy objects of a class by using the public functions of that class. Most of the work in developing a class is designing and writing the public functions that other programs will use to manipulate objects belonging to the class.

Allocating and Releasing Memory: Constructors and Destructors

Another aspect of objects and classes is memory management. A class often has functions to take care of memory allocation and memory release for an object of the class. Memory may or may not be dynamically allocated, depending on the class. Functions that allocate memory are called *constructors*, and functions that release memory are called *destructors*.

Constructors, written as public functions in the class code, allocate memory when an object is created. As a user of the class, all you do is declare a variable to be of some class type. Your declaration is an implicit call to a constructor. You do not have to do anything additional in your program.

On the other hand, destructors must be explicitly called by your program. The class does not know when you are finished with an object. For objects that are not dynamically allocated, you do nothing. The memory is released when the program is finished.

Constructors and destructors are not shown in the following examples in order to keep the examples simple.

A Program That Uses the `string` Class

The following example program *uses* the `string` class, rather than creates it, because it is easier to use a class than to develop a class. Using a class is like using a structure. Developing a class involves a few new concepts. So, let us proceed by looking at the more familiar parts first.

This short program declares two variables (objects) to be of a type, `string`, which is a class. The program then assigns initial values to the two objects by calling an assignment function defined as part of the class `string`. Then it prints the objects by calling a print function which is defined as part of the class `string`.

We are using a primitive implementation of a string class. Just about any commercially available library with a string class will provide a complete and robust implementation. This example program omits operator overloading, constructors, and destructors in order to keep the program simple.

Example

```
//              main_str.cpp                      10/13/94

#include <iostream.h>            // 1   for C++ I/O library
#include "strng.h"               // 2   for string class definition

main()
{
    string first_name;          // 3   declare first_name as string
    string last_name;           // 4   declare last_name as string

    cout << "Test string class" << endl;  // 5   C++ equivalent of printf()

    first_name.assign ("Scott" );         // 6   use string assign function
    last_name.assign ("Amundsen" );       // 7   ditto

    first_name.print();         // 8   use string print function
    last_name.print();          // 9   ditto

    return (0);                 // 10  return to O/S
}
```

Comments on Example

The preceding program shows a simple example of how a class is used. It is reasonable to think of a class as a structure definition with functions which are specific to it. The syntax for using class functions looks like structure member syntax. And in fact, the functions are members of the class.

Line 1   Includes the C++ I/O header file, `iostream.h`. It is used for prototypes for `cout` and `cin`, the C++ basic functions for stream output and input. By default (as in C), stream output is to the screen and stream input is from the keyboard.

Line 2   Includes the header file for the `string` class, `strng.h`. It contains the data definition for the `string` class and the function prototypes for functions that operate on data elements that are declared as `string`. The `strng.h` file name omits the vowel in order to distinguish it from the C and C++ include file `string.h`, which contains function prototypes for `strcpy()`, `strcmp()`, and so on.

Line 3   Declares a data element named `first_name` to be of data type `string`, which is a user- (programmer-) defined type. Its implementation details are hidden. All you need to know is that you can define character strings as `string` and get a set of functions that will manipulate them. Notice also that a size is not declared. The `string` class takes care of it.

   Use of `string` as a data type is similar to using a `typedef` name to invoke a structure template. The difference is that in C++ you get not only a data type but also a set of operators and functions to use on it.

Line 4 Declares a data element named `last_name` to be of data type `string`. Its attributes are identical to those of `first_name`.

Line 5 Uses `cout` to display "`Test string class`" on the screen. Passing `endl` to `cout` causes a line feed to occur and the buffer to be flushed.

Line 6 Shows the use of a function that has been defined within a class. `assign()` is a function that is part of the `string` class. Invoking a function of a class is similar to using a member of a structure: the function name must be qualified. `first_name.assign()` tells the compiler to execute the `assign()` function using the object `first_name`. The compiler figures out that `first_name` belongs to the `string` class and therefore uses the `assign()` function in that class. One parameter is passed, a string literal.

In terms of writing code for a string class, this is the simplest way to assign a value to `first_name`. It is not the most elegant way. In a full string class implementation, the assignment operator, =, would be overloaded so that this line would look like

```
first_name = "Scott";
```

More details on operator overloading are discussed in the section called "Ad Hoc Polymorphism" later in this chapter.

Line 7 Assigns "Amundsen" to `last_name`. As above, the compiler relates the object, `last_name`, to the class `string` and uses the `assign()` function in that class.

Line 8 Invokes the `print()` function for the object `last_name`, which is a member of class `string`. The compiler finds the function based on the class of the object.

`print()` has no parameters and no return value, so we assume it just prints the object, `first_name` in this case. The `print()` function is examined further in the next "Example" section.

Line 9 Performs the same operation on another object in the string class, `last_name`. Comments from line 8 apply.

Line 10 Returns control to the operating system with a value of zero. The `return` statement works the same way in C++ as in C.

Header File for the `string` Class

Now we will go a bit deeper into detail and look at how to create a class. Recall that a class is typically packaged as two files: a header file and a function file. The reason for this is to separate definitions from functions so that the definitions in `strng.h` can be available to both the class function code, `strng.cpp`, and any client function, such as `main_str.cpp` where the class is used.

`strng.h` will be included in any source file where the string class will be used. It is also included in `strng.cpp`.

In this example, new keywords and operators in C++ are underlined. As in the previous example, no operator overloading, constructors, or destructors are used in order to keep the program simple.

Example

```
//                    strng.h                        10/13/94

const int LENGTH = 255;                // 1 set length for string
class string                           // 2 begin class declaration
{
    private:                           // 3 restricted access
        char a_string [LENGTH];        // 4 define the string
        int  str_length;               // 5 define length field

    public:                            // 6 public access
        void assign (const char other_string [] );   // 7 function prototypes
        int  length ();
        void print ();
};                                     // 8 end class declaration
```

Comments on Example

Defining a class involves a minimum of three new keywords: `class`, `private`, and `public`. The keyword `class` declares that a new data type and associated functions are being defined. `private` tells the compiler that whatever is defined in that section is not accessible to users of the class. This means that the private data elements cannot be used directly by your program, and the private functions cannot be called directly by your program. Data definitions are placed in the private section so that definition and manipulation of data remain localized to the class itself. `public` defines the interface to the class data via function prototypes of the functions that can manipulate the data.

Line 1   Defines a length that will be used whenever an object of the class `string` is declared. A production-quality string class would not hard-code a length. It would dynamically allocate memory based on the size of the declaration. We are implementing `string` as fixed-length in order to focus on the basic mechanisms of creating a class.

Line 2   Begins the class declaration by use of the keyword `class`. The name of this class will be `string`.

Line 3   One of the new keywords, `private`. The private section of a class is used to create the data definition. It also includes any functions that operate on the data in a way that the class designer wishes to keep private. The point is to hide internal definitions and functions so that users or clients (programmers) cannot make assumptions about how the class works. The way the class works is defined in the public part of the class (beginning on line 6), which is all anyone needs to know in order to use the class.

Line 4   The first data definition for the `string` class. Data definitions are typically placed in the private section. The field `a_string` is defined as a character array. It is allocated 255 bytes, the size of `LENGTH`.

Note also that a data element defined as `const` in C++ can be used to declare an array size. This doesn't work in C.

Line 5   Defines a length field for the array. The length field can be used to ensure that memory is not overwritten. This kind of protection is present in complete and robust `string` classes available in commercial libraries.

Line 6   Uses another new keyword, `public`, to begin the public part of the class definition. The public section contains the function prototypes that constitute the user (programmer) interface to the class. It typically does not have any data definitions.

Line 7   The first of three function prototypes for the `string` class. They are `assign()`, `length()`, and `print()`. By definition the data in an object (an instance of the class) is available to the functions defined for that class.

Many of the functions defined for a class will have no parameters, as here with `length()` and `print()`. This is because these functions do something with the object data and don't need any other data; the object data is local to the class functions.

`assign()` has a parameter, which is a character `string` (or literal) that will be assigned (copied) into the named `string` object. The prototype shows the parameter as `const`, which means that it can't be changed by the `assign()` function. `assign()` is invoked in `main_str.cpp` on line 6 as follows:

```
first_name.assign ("Scott" );
```

The keyword `const` is underlined as new because it is active when coded in a function prototype in C++. You can code `const` in a function prototype in ANSI C, but it won't prevent a parameter from being changed by a called function. In C++ `const` prevents parameters from being changed.

Line 8   Shows the closing brace and the semicolon that ends the declaration part of the class definition. The other part of the class definition is the `strng.cpp` file, which contains the code for the functions named in the prototypes.

Function File for the `string` Class

Now that we have data definitions and function prototypes for the `string` class, we need to flesh out the functions that do the work on string data. There is a little new syntax here, but otherwise these look like standard C functions. Although we are packaging the header file (`strng.h`) separately from the function file, `strng.h` and `strng.cpp` get compiled together into a single object module that goes into a library. Programs that use the `string` class include the `strng.h` file in the compile and include the library object module in the link.

As in the previous example, new keywords and operators in C++ are underlined, and no operator overloading, constructors, or destructors are used in order to keep the program simple.

Example

```
//                      strng.cpp                          10/13/94
#include <iostream.h>
#include <string.h>
#include "strng.h"

void string::assign (const char other_string [] )        // 1 assign function
{
   strcpy (a_string, other_string );                     // 2 copy a string
   str_length = strlen (a_string);                       // 3 get the length
}
int string::length()                                     // 4 "get length" function
{
   return (str_length);
}
void string::print()                                     // 5 print function
{
   cout << a_string << endl;
}
```

Comments on Example

Line 1   The function header for the `assign()` function in class `string`. If you remove `string::` from this line, it looks like an ordinary C++ function header. The syntax `class_name::` is called the *scope resolution operator*. It can be thought of as the class qualifier operator, similar to the structure member operator. The structure member operator ties a member name to a particular structure, and the class qualifier operator ties a function name to a class.

`tran.cust_id`	Means `cust_id` is in the structure named `tran`
`string::assign()`	Means define `assign()` function in the class named `string`
`first_name.assign()`	Means call `assign()` function in the class to which `first_name` belongs

As we saw in `main_str.cpp`, the `assign()` function must be used in conjunction with the object name. The compiler resolves which `assign()` function to call based on the class to which `first_name` and `last_name` belong. You could define 10, 20, or 100 classes to have an `assign()` function. The scope resolution operator ties a function name to a particular class.

What this does is allow designers to use the same name for functions that perform the same kinds of duties in different classes. If there were 20 classes that had an `assign()` function, good design would dictate that each `assign()` function behave outwardly like the others. This is necessary to create predictability and true extensibility. It also prevents name proliferation.

Line 2   Shows the use of `strcpy()` to implement the `assign()` function. The field `a_string` is defined in the private part of the `string` class definition in `strng.h`, which is included by this file. The field is available, even though you don't see it here.

C library functions are available for use within classes.

Line 3 Calls `strlen()` to get the new length of `a_string`. In a full implementation of a string class, `str_length` would be used to prevent corrupting memory by copying a longer string into a shorter one.

The `assign()` function uses `strlen()` to get the length of a string object. In your application programs you cannot use `strlen()` directly on a `string` (or any other) object. Once you define a data element as an object (member) of a class, you can manipulate it only by using class functions. This is probably the most shocking thing in object-oriented programming: you can declare data elements that are then *not* accessible except through class functions. Once a class, always a class.

Line 4 Begins the function named `length()` within the `string` class. It returns the length of `a_string`. Again, `string::` is the qualifier of the function `length()`.

This function is the one you call when you want to know the length of a `string` object.

Line 5 Shows a universal class function, `print()`. It is often called `printon()`. Every class needs the ability to display its contents. This example of a string class uses `cout` to display the contents of `a_string`, which is the only significant data item in a string class.

In more complex classes, for instance where a record type or database table is defined, the `print()` function formats and displays multiple fields.

In the statement

```
cout << a_string << endl;
```

`endl` is the C++ I/O function that inserts a line feed and flushes the buffer.

You may be wondering if this is worth the effort. The answer is yes. In a robust string class definition you can't overwrite memory, and you can use the operators =, +, ==, and != instead of `strcpy()`, `strcat()`, and `strcmp()`, plus other features. There is overhead in the beginning when creating classes, but the payoff continues for a long time.

Class Summary

A class is the marrying of structures and functions. C++ is a real departure from C, and from every other procedural language, because the data in a class can be accessed only by functions that are defined for the class. This reflects both encapsulation and object orientation. It is a different way of designing and programming computer systems with the promise of higher-quality systems and higher productivity.

Higher quality results from stronger type checking and superior enforcement of modularity. The productivity gains come from being required to put all the relevant functions in the same place as the data definition. You can't reuse code if you can't find it, and the way classes work you can always find the code. You are much more likely to use existing functions for classes because their definitions are in the same place as the data structure definitions.

The class concept itself is extensible. Once you have defined a class, you can use it as a base for other classes. This brings us to the next topic.

Inheritance: The Path to Code Reuse

Inheritance is a method of creating new classes based on existing classes. It is one of the key concepts in object-oriented programming. The existing class is called the *base class*, and the new class is called a *derived class*. An existing class can be used by more than one derived class. A derived class can also be derived from a previously derived class.

This generates a hierarchy of classes. At the root is a generic class with rudimentary data elements and rudimentary functions. As derived classes are added, they add attributes and behavior (functions) that are more specialized than the classes from which they are derived.

In a payroll system, one of the base classes would be an `employee` class. The `employee` class would contain the basic data for an employee and the functions that maintain employee data. Two derived classes which come to mind are `full_time` and `part_time`, which have some data and functional attributes that are common to both and some other data and functional attributes that are different from each other. The common data and common functions reside in the base class.

The new classes, `full_time` and `part_time`, would be based on the `employee` class. They would inherit both the common data definition and the common functions of the `employee` class. By inheriting the attributes of the base class, the derived classes (`full_time` and `part_time`) can use existing functions and data definitions without having to write overlapping ones for the new classes.

Here is a diagram showing how derived classes use and extend the base class. This is true for both data and functions.

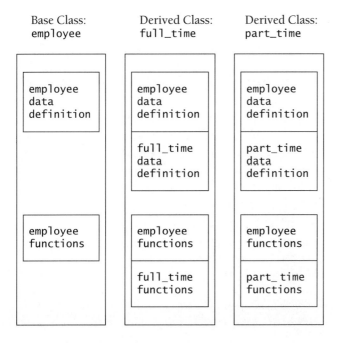

The `full_time` class inherits both the data definition of `employee` and the functions that go with it. Additionally, new data elements specific to the `full_time` class are defined in its data portion, and new functions specific to the `full_time` class are defined in its function portion. Similarly, new data elements and functions are defined for the `part_time` class.

Inheritance promotes reusability of code, one of the main precepts of OOP. Reuse is a result of a derived class inheriting both the data definition and the functions of the base class.

Polymorphism: How a Function Can Be in Two Places at Once

Derived from Greek roots, *polymorphism* means having multiple forms. In the context of C++, polymorphism refers to being able to use the same function name or operator symbol on different operands or classes. This concept is already implemented in both the C and C++ compilers, for example, with arithmetic operators.

Different code is invoked by the divide operator, /, depending on the data types of the operands. If both operands are integers, integer division is performed. If either operand is a floating point number, floating point division is performed. This concept is extended to a considerable degree in C++.

The following kinds of polymorphism are available in C++ (listed in order from the specific to the abstract):

Ad hoc polymorphism

The same function or operator can be invoked with different parameters or operands. The compiler determines which function or operator is being invoked based on the parameters or operands. The function or operator is bound (chosen) at compile time.

Inclusion polymorphism

Functions are created with the same names for different derived classes, and the functions are set up so that the choice of which one to execute is made at run time (late binding). This is accomplished through a technique called virtual functions. It replaces `switch/case` statements, which parse data at run time and then call functions based on data type. Virtual functions handle a whole `switch/case` statement block with a single line of code and do not have to be maintained when a new data type is introduced.

Parametric polymorphism

This is the most abstract form of polymorphism. In inclusion polymorphism the base class is known at compile time and the particular derived class function is chosen at run time. In parametric polymorphism one of the parameters is what the base type is. This results in two decisions being made at run time: what the base class is, and which derived class (and function) is being called.

Given its complexity, parametric polymorphism is beyond the scope of this book. However, the following sections offer some useful information about ad hoc polymorphism and inclusion polymorphism.

Ad Hoc Polymorphism: Operator Overloading

The fact that the division operator does different things depending on the operands is called operator overloading. In C++ you can write a function that will overload, or redefine, an operator *within a class*. Unfortunately, perhaps, operator overloading can be done only inside a class. That is, although you can't redefine the addition operator for the compiler as a whole, you can redefine it inside a class.

This presents the opportunity, for instance, to overload several operators in the `string` class so that `string` can be handled like numeric and single-character data types. Consider the following code:

```
string first_name;
string last_name;
string mailing_name;
...
mailing_name = first_name + last_name;
```

The + operator in the `string` class has been overloaded and now means concatenate two strings. The assignment operator, =, has also been overloaded to work with strings. Overloading is done within the `string` class and is then available to every object defined with the `string` data type.

In the `string` class definition code, a function must be written for each operator to be overloaded. The + operator gets overloaded in a function that invokes `strcat()`, and the = operator gets overloaded in a function that invokes `strcpy()`. The result is you can use operators on strings instead of functions.

Further, in a robust implementation of the `string` class, corrupting memory is prevented either by using the size of the destination item to control how many characters to copy, or by dynamically expanding the destination field.

It is important to note that the design of overloaded operators should make them work the same way that native operators do. Thus = should always mean assign, and + should always mean add. Proper extensibility of the language means making new types behave like existing ones. Predictability is part of extensibility.

Ad Hoc Polymorphism: Function Overloading

Another powerful feature of C++ is the ability to have more than one function with the same name. Traditional language link editors allow only one occurrence of a function name or program name in a library or executable. This can be a real limitation, as in the case of absolute number functions in C, of which there are three: abs(), labs(), and fabs().

Life would be simpler if there were just one routine, abs(), that would accept multiple kinds of input. Through function overloading C++ provides a tool to do this. C++ allows multiple functions to have the same name as long as the data types of their parameter lists are different. Return values cannot be used as a distinguishing characteristic.

To eliminate the abs()/labs()/fabs() thicket, we can write two new abs() functions. Their prototypes look like this:

```
long   abs ( long   some_num );
double abs ( double some_num );
```

The first abs() function above takes a long integer as an input parameter and returns its absolute value as a long. The second abs() takes a double as an input parameter and returns its absolute value as a double.

How does the compiler figure out which abs() to call? By the *signature* of the parameters. The signature is the set of data types in the parameter list. In this example there is only one parameter, but the principle holds for multiple parameters. As long as the list of parameter data types is unique, C++ will accept the function as a valid variant of the common function name. The determination of which function to call is made at compile time, based on matching the parameter data types.

Here is how these new abs() functions would be used:

```
long   input_rec_count;
long   edited_rec_count;
double gl_amt;
...
edited_rec_count = abs (input_rec_count );
gl_amt           = abs (gl_amt );
```

The source code for the two new abs() functions is

```
long abs ( long  some_num )
{
   long a_long;

   a_long = labs (some_num );
   return (a_long );
}

double abs ( double some_num )
{
   double a_double;

   a_double = fabs (some_num );
   return (a_double);
}
```

The signature for the first function is a single parameter of type long. The signature for the second function is a single parameter of type double. When you call abs() and pass it a data element that is a `long`, the first function is called. When you call it with a `double`, the second function is called. The compiler takes care of which one to call.

Notice that these functions do call `labs()` and `fabs()`, but we have buried them forever inside alternate versions of `abs()`.

This example shows function overloading done outside the scope of classes. These new `abs()` functions are not restricted to use within a class. If these functions are put in a library, they are directly available to all programs that use that library.

Another type of function overloading in C++ is overloaded functions *within* a class. These operate the same way as described above. Multiple functions with the same name are allowed in a class if the signatures (parameter data types) are unique. The difference is in scope. Function overloading defined in the code that defines a class is available only within that class. Recall that class functions are invoked by the syntax of `object_name.function_name()`. This syntax indicates that the function is part of the class that `object_name` belongs to.

Inclusion Polymorphism: Function Overloading Across Derived Classes

Inclusion polymorphism is another method of using the same function name for multiple functions within a set of classes derived from the same base class. It is a way to replace `switch/case` statements with a single function call through the use of *virtual functions*. Instead of parsing a data element to figure out which kind of data you're dealing with (and thus what function to call), you call a single function that has been defined (with the same name) for each derived class.

The determination of which function actually gets executed is made at run time (late binding) and is based on the class of the object. Conceptually, it works the same way as a `switch/case` statement, except that each `case` block is a separate function.

One common requirement in production systems is that each class have a function to print its contents. For derived classes that means printing both the base class (common) data and the data unique to the derived class. Let us continue the example of the base class of employee and derived classes of `full_time` and `part_time`. A traditional method for fulfilling this requirement is to embed the employee type ('F' for `full_time`, 'P' for `part_time`, and so on) in an employee data structure and to set up a `switch/case` statement that calls the appropriate print function based on which kind of employee is found. The problem with this is that it introduces a maintenance requirement everywhere such a `switch/case` occurs: if a new employee type is created, all those `switch/case` statements have to be changed.

In an object-oriented approach, `employee` becomes a base class and `full_time` and `part_time` become derived classes, as we saw earlier. For printing we then use a technique called virtual functions. A *virtual function* has different versions (with the same name) for different derived classes. Which version gets executed is determined at run time.

The virtual function is defined in a base class and defined again in each derived class. The virtual function in the base class is an empty shell that gets overridden by the same-named functions in the derived classes. The virtual functions in the derived classes have real code in them. The C++ keyword `virtual` is used when defining the function in the base class and is optional when defining functions of the same name in derived classes.

Each object in a derived class that uses a virtual function has a two-byte or four-byte class identifier inserted by the compiler in the data area of the object. At run time the class identifier field in the object is used to figure out which function is to be called.

Example

```
/* traditional case statement using emp_type from "employee_rec" structure */
switch emp_type
{
   case 'F':
     print_full_time (employee_rec);
     break;
   case 'P':
     print_part_time (employee_rec);
     break;
   case 'T':
     print_temporary (employee_rec);
     break;

   ...

   default:
     print_unknown (employee_rec);
}

// print using a virtual function
employee_rec->print();
```

The last statement in this example uses the structure pointer operator, ->, to point to a function named `print()`. For purposes of discussion, assume that `employee_rec` is the base class data and that there is a `print()` function for each class derived from `employee`. The pointer points to a part of `employee_rec` where the derived class identifier can be found. This causes the `print()` function for that class to be executed.

This single statement replaces a `switch/case` statement block. In fact, there would still be multiple `print()` functions, one in each derived class (`full_time`, `part_time`, `temporary`, and so on). But they are all given the same name, `print()`, and the `print()` function in the base class, `employee`, is defined as a virtual function.

The payoff of this technique comes when a new derived class is added. Since there are no `switch/case` statements, there is no hunt through thousands of lines of code to find all of them. The new derived class is defined and a `print()` function is written for it. Existing programs that call the virtual `print()` function for classes derived from `employee` need to be recompiled, but that process has many fewer errors than changing (or not changing) `switch/case` statements throughout a system.

Persistence and the Problem of C++

In the best of all possible object-oriented worlds, at the end of a program's execution everything goes away: the program, the allocated memory, and the data. In the real world this occurs in video games, and, to a lesser extent in communications networks. The majority of us have to deal with data that outlives the program's execution. This quality is called persistence. After you have created all these wonderful classes and objects, how do you save them at the end of the program?

The problem is that, as of this writing, there are few or no object-oriented database packages on the market. Of those that exist, few, if any, offer a seamless interface to C++. In practice this means that an object-oriented system design effort winds up marrying objects in memory to records or tables in a non-object-oriented database. It is something of a shotgun wedding.

What happens is that a whole layer of code gets created in C++ to read and update the underlying database. The class design effort typically winds up creating data definitions that correspond to tables or record types in a database. The resulting database design doesn't look that different from a database design coming out of a structured analysis and design effort. This is primarily because the relational database package has more influence on the database design than does the object-oriented analysis and design, since the data must ultimately reside in the database.

In terms of effort required and what the resulting code looks like, C++ database interface functions do not look much different from ones created in C. The C++ interface translates database data to objects and vice versa. In a fully implemented object-oriented environment, retrieving and storing data would not require a whole separate layer. This layer is still a traditional procedural interface.

That's the bad news. The good news is that there are now third party packages which take care of this problem. These packages maintain a direct interface to popular database packages while supplying the programmer with an object-oriented interface. Buy one rather than build one.

Summary

The concept of modularity is extended in object-oriented programming. In structured techniques, modularity means designing the procedure code into modules with well-defined interfaces and operations. Data is passed in, and data is returned: Data is considered separately from the procedure. In the object-oriented approach, the data is bound to the procedures and vice versa. Once you begin to define data in a class, the only way you can do anything with it is to use the functions that are defined as part of that class.

This is an inversion of our traditional approach to data processing. In the object-oriented approach the data is truly on top, and the functions are defined in relation to the data. There are several advantages to this:

- When used correctly, this approach produces programs that are more compact, easier to understand, and easier to work on. Modularity is enforced by the class concept.

- Data can be more tightly controlled because access to it is restricted to functions defined within the class.

- The amount of code developed in an object-oriented approach can be significantly reduced. In a typical data processing environment, almost everytime someone wants to access data in a file or database, another section of read code is written. But if that data is defined in a class, it can be gotten only from a function in the class. So instead of writing a function, you write a call to a function.

Better systems can be developed using an object-oriented approach. The data will be less prone to corruption, and there can be much more reuse of code, which should lead to reduced development costs. However, it is a completely different way of thinking about the problem. You cannot write object-oriented programs using a structured analysis and design. You need an object-oriented analysis and design.

In an object-oriented design, you design classes. A class is a combination of a data structure and the code that maintains it. In a structured approach the database is typically designed before the programs. As programs are designed, they are married to the data structure, often after it is too late to make major changes to that structure. In an object-oriented approach this marriage occurs very early. It's a fair statement to say that an object-oriented approach is an arranged marriage between child data and child procedures, followed by their growing up together.

C++ as an object-oriented language is not just another language; it is a completely different approach to solving data processing problems. In reality it takes about a year to get comfortable with C++ and the object-oriented approach. The fact is that COBOL programmers, C programmers, Fortran programmers, and Pascal programmers are all in the same boat.

We work in an industry that is continually reinventing itself. It is necessary for everyone in the business who wants to advance to be involved in continuing education. If you want to avoid becoming stuck in the backwaters of the business, you have to withstand the nuisance, if not the pain, of continuing to learn new techniques and approaches.

If you're reading this, you have taken the largest step in the process, which is accepting the requirement to keep learning. It is painful to give up the comfort and mastery of known languages and techniques and to become ignorant in new areas. The consolations are that your experience does work for you and that everyone in the business faces the same challenge.

Come on, jump in! The water's not *that* cold!

riverrun

Official ANSI C Keyword List

C is a very compact language, or so they say. ANSI C has the following 32 keywords (reserved words). Keywords in C are always in lowercase. As in COBOL, you cannot create variables that use these names.

auto	int
break	long
case	register
char	return
const	short
continue	signed
default	sizeof
do	static
double	struct
else	switch
enum	typedef
extern	union
float	unsigned
for	void
goto	volatile
if	while

Most of these keywords are discussed in this book. Keywords seldom used in business data processing are not discussed.

Actual C Keyword List

You can't do anything with 32 keywords. The C language actually has four classes of keywords/symbols/function names that are necessary to get real programs to run real applications.

1. Keywords

   See the previous page.

2. Preprocessor directives

   Hardly any program is written without at least one `#include` statement. The `#include` directive is a vital part of the language. The next most popular directive is `#define`, which is the only way to create all-purpose program constants in C.

3. Symbol operators (which act like keywords)

   C has more symbol operators (about 37) than keywords. Many of these are "verbs" that are keywords in other languages. Philosophizing aside, symbol operators are in effect keywords.

4. Reserved function names

   You may have noticed that the list of official C keywords does not contain the words *read* or *write*. The reason is that these and many other features are implemented through function calls. A set of standard functions comes with the compiler. This is called the C library. You can't do any real work without using these functions, which in fact are part of the C language. The conservative list contains about 50.

Lists of the symbol operators and the common business function names are given below.

Symbol Operators

Symbol	Meaning
->	Pointer to structure member
.	Structure member (used as a prefix)
!	Not (it has to appear somewhere in the language)
-	Subtraction/one's complement/unary minus (negate)
++	Increment (add one to)
--	Decrement (subtract one from)
(type)	Cast (forced type conversion)
*	Pointer/multiplication
/	Division
%	Remainder
+	Addition
<<	Shift bits left*
>>	Shift bits right*
<	Less than
<=	Less than or equal to
>	Greater than
>=	Greater than or equal to
==	Equality
!=	Inequality
&	Bitwise AND*
^	Bitwise exclusive OR (XOR)*
|	Bitwise inclusive OR*
&&	Logical AND
||	Logical OR
?:	Conditional expression*
=	Assignment (move/copy)
*=	Multiply and assign result to left operand
/=	Divide and assign result to left operand
%=	Get remainder and assign result to left operand
+=	Add and assign result to left operand
&=	Do a bitwise AND and assign result to left operand*
|=	Do a bitwise inclusive OR and assign result to left operand*
^=	Do a bitwise exclusive OR and assign result to left operand*
-=	Subtract and assign result to left operand
<<=	Shift bits left and assign result to left operand*
>>=	Shift bits right and assign result to left operand*
,	Comma

*Seldom used in business; not discussed in this book.

C Library Functions Commonly Used in Business Data Processing

C libraries that come with compilers can have 100 or more library functions. The following list includes those commonly used in business data processing, and they are all discussed in this book.

Function Name	Meaning
abs()	Get the absolute integer value of an integer (int)
atof()	Convert a string to a floating point number (double)
atoi()	Convert a string to an integer (int)
atol()	Convert a string to a long integer (long)
exit()	Stop the program (stop run)
fabs()	Get the absolute value of a double (floating point)
fclose()	Close a sequential file
fgetc()	Get one character from a file
fgets()	Get a string from a file
fopen()	Open a sequential file
fprintf()	Format and write to a file
getchar()	Get one character from the terminal
gets()	Get a string from the terminal
is___()	Class test (evaluate one character for alpha, digit, and so on)
labs()	Get the absolute value of a long integer (long)
printf()	Format and print on the terminal
return()	Go back to the calling function
scanf()	Read and format numbers and characters from the terminal
sprintf()	Move and format numbers and characters into a string
sscanf()	Get and format fields from a string
strcat()	Concatenate one string or literal with another string
strcmp()	Compare two strings
strcpy()	String copy
strlen()	Find the length of a string
strncpy()	String copy the first n characters
tolower()	Convert one character to lowercase
toupper()	Convert one character to uppercase

Many of these functions do things that reserved words do in COBOL. To reduce the potential for confusion, it is a good idea not to create data names that are the same as or close to function names. This is easy, since function names generally are based on verbs and data names are generally based on nouns.

APPENDIX C

ASCII Character Codes

In the IBM mainframe world, the EBCDIC coding scheme is used to assign a bit pattern for characters. The PC and workstation worlds use the ASCII character set. There are 128 values in the ASCII set, with values from 0 through 127 decimal, or 0 through 7F hexadecimal.

Values 0 through 1F hexadecimal and the value 7F hexadecimal are non-printable. Most of these are not used often in business programs.

Control (non-printable) ASCII Characters

Dec	Hex		Description	Dec	Hex		Description
00	00	NUL	Null character	16	10	DLE	Data line escape
01	01	SOH	Start of heading	17	11	DC1	Device control 1 (XON)
02	02	STX	Start of text	18	12	DC1	Device control 2 (tape)
03	03	ETX	End of text	19	13	DC1	Device control 3 (XOFF)
04	04	EOT	End of transmission	20	14	DC1	Device control 4
05	05	ENQ	Enquiry	21	15	NAK	Negative acknowledge
06	06	ACK	Acknowledge	22	16	SYN	Synchronous idle
07	07	BELL	Bell (sound)	23	17	ETB	End of trans block
08	08	BS	Backspace	24	18	CAN	Cancel
09	09	HT	Horizontal tab	25	19	EM	End of Medium
10	0A	LF	Line feed	26	1A	SUB	Substitute
11	0B	VT	Vertical tab	27	1B	ESC	Escape
12	0C	FF	Form feed	28	1C	FS	File separator
13	0D	CR	Carriage return	29	1D	GS	Group separator
14	0E	SO	Shift out	30	1E	RS	Record separator
15	0F	SI	Shift in	31	1F	US	Unit separator
				127	7F	DEL	Delete (rub out)

Graphic (Printable) ASCII Characters

Dec	Hex	Char	Dec	Hex	Char	Dec	Hex	Char	Dec	Hex	Char	Dec	Hex	Char	Dec	Hex	Char
32	20	space	48	30	0	64	40	@	80	50	P	96	60	`	112	70	p
33	21	!	49	31	1	65	41	A	81	51	Q	97	61	a	113	71	q
34	22	"	50	32	2	66	42	B	82	52	R	98	62	b	114	72	r
35	23	#	51	33	3	67	43	C	83	53	S	99	63	c	115	73	s
36	24	$	52	34	4	68	44	D	84	54	T	100	64	d	116	74	t
37	25	%	53	35	5	69	45	E	85	55	U	101	65	e	117	75	u
38	26	&	54	36	6	70	46	F	86	56	V	102	66	f	118	76	v
39	27	'	55	37	7	71	47	G	87	57	W	103	67	g	119	77	w
40	28	(	56	38	8	72	48	H	88	58	X	104	68	h	120	78	x
41	29	)	57	39	9	73	49	I	89	59	Y	105	69	i	121	79	y
42	2A	*	58	3A	:	74	4A	J	90	5A	Z	106	6A	j	122	7A	z
43	2B	+	59	3B	;	75	4B	K	91	5B	[	107	6B	k	123	7B	{
44	2C	,	60	3C	<	76	4C	L	92	5C	\	108	6C	l	124	7C	|
45	2D	–	61	3D	=	77	4D	M	93	5D	]	109	6D	m	125	7D	}
46	2E	.	62	3E	>	78	4E	N	94	5E	^	110	6E	n	126	7E	
47	2F	/	63	3F	?	79	4F	O	95	5F	_	111	6F	o			

NOTE: Decimal 96/Hex 60 is the back quote. Single quote is decimal 39/Hex 27.

APPENDIX D

Powers of 2

The table on the next page shows powers of two in decimal and hexadecimal, along with negative powers of 2 for decimal fractions.

n	2^n	hex 2^n	2^{-n} (base 10)
0	1	1	1.0
1	2	2	.5
2	4	4	.25
3	8	8	.125
4	16	10	.062 5
5	32	20	.031 25
6	64	40	.015 625
7	128	80	.007 812 5
8	256	100	.003 906 25
9	512	200	.001 953 125
10	1,024	400	.000 976 562 5
11	2,048	800	.000 488 281 25
12	4,096	1000	.000 244 140 625
13	8,192	2000	.000 122 070 312 5
14	16,384	4000	.000 061 035 156 25
15	32,768	8000	.000 030 517 578 125
16	65,536	1 0000	.000 015 258 789 062 5
17	131,072	2 0000	.000 007 629 394 531 25
18	262,144	4 0000	.000 003 814 697 265 625
19	524,288	8 0000	.000 001 907 348 632 812 5
20	1,048,576	10 0000	.000 000 953 674 316 406 25
21	2,097,152	20 0000	.000 000 476 837 158 203 125
22	4,194,304	40 0000	.000 000 238 418 579 101 562 5
23	8,388,608	80 0000	.000 000 119 209 289 550 781 25
24	16,777,216	100 0000	.000 000 059 604 644 775 390 625
25	33,554,432	200 0000	.000 000 029 802 322 387 695 312 5
26	67,108,864	400 0000	.000 000 014 901 161 193 847 656 25
27	134,217,728	800 0000	.000 000 007 450 580 596 923 828 125
28	268,435,456	1000 0000	.000 000 003 725 290 298 461 914 062 5
29	536,870,912	2000 0000	.000 000 001 862 645 149 230 957 031 25
30	1,073,741,824	4000 0000	.000 000 000 931 322 574 615 478 515 625
31	2,147,483,648	8000 0000	.000 000 000 465 661 287 307 739 257 812 5

APPENDIX **E**

Precedence and Associativity of Operators

Every compiler has rules for precedence and associativity of operators. The compiler must decide which operators go with which data elements or expressions. One of your goals as a programmer is to give the compiler minimum choices in this area. As a rule, you want tell the compiler what to associate with what, rather than letting it decide. The problem with letting the compiler decide is that no one remembers the hierarchy of precedence and the direction of associativity for all the operators.

The simple solution is to use parentheses to force the compiler to evaluate an expression the way you intend. If you let the compiler choose, there will inevitably be expressions that it evaluates in a different order than you intended. Use parentheses.

Operator	Use	Associativity
()	Function call	Left to right
[]	Array element	
->	Pointer to structure member	
.	Member of structure	
!	Logical negation	Right to left
~	One's complement	
++	Increment	
--	Decrement	
-	Unary minus	
+	Unary plus	

Operator	Use	Associativity
(*data type*) * & `sizeof`	Cast to a different data type Pointer Address Size of an object	
* / %	Multiplication Division Remainder	Left to right
+ −	Addition Subtraction	Left to right
<< >>	Left shift Right shift	Left to right
< <= > >+	Less than Less than or equal to Greater than Greater than or equal to	Left to right
== !=	Equality Inequality	Left to right
&	Bitwise AND	Left to right
∧	Bitwise XOR	Left to right
&&	Logical AND	Left to right
||	Logical OR	Left to right
?:	Conditional expression	Right to left
= *= /= %= += &= |= ∧= −= <<= >>=	Assignment Compound assignment	Right to left

APPENDIX F

Business Utility Programs

This appendix contains four routines I have found useful for solving business data processing problems in C. All of them use a number defined as double, the data type of choice when using decimal numbers in business sytems. The following routines round a double, truncate a double, format a double with commas and two decimal places, and format a double as an integer with commas, respectively.

```
round()
truncate()
dollar_comma()
double_comma()
```

These functions are available free on-line through the Benjamin/Cummings bulletin board on the Internet. They are also available on diskette, along with all the program examples in this book, for a nominal charge. See Appendix H and the coupon in the back of the book.

round() is a business rounding routine that always rounds 5 up. If your users like 5 to always round up (mine do), use this routine. The IEEE rounding method embedded in printf(), fprintf(), and sprintf() will round 5 down in certain cases. If you want your program to produce the same results as a $4.99 calculator, use this function.

truncate() truncates a double at a specified number of decimal places. This is not often needed, but again, printf(), fprintf(), and sprintf() do not always produce the desired result. This is due to the fact that they always round according to the IEEE specification, even when you use them to truncate.

If you have a report writer that can handle all of your reports, you do not need the next two functions, dollar_comma() and double_comma(). Most projects seem to have a handful of reports that the report writer cannot handle. In these cases you must write a C report program. `dollar_comma()` is a formatting function that is passed a `double` and a width. It returns a formatted character string, right-justified, with commas and two decimal places. If the number is negative, parentheses are placed around the number. `double_comma()` formats a `double` as an integer, puts commas in the string, and places parentheses around the number if it is negative.

These functions have been written with a goal of simplicity. They can be written in fewer lines, but the shorter they are, the harder they are to understand. Additional comments are given before each program.

round() : A Business Rounding Routine

When you call `round()`, you pass the address of a number that is defined as `double` and a number of decimal places to round it to. Assume `expense_amt` contains `133.445032`, and you want to round it to two decimal places, you call `round()` as follows:

```
round (&expense_amt, 2);
```

`round()` moves the number to the left of the decimal place by multiplying it by 10 raised to the number of decimal places you specify. In the above example `expense_amt` is multiplied by 100, or 10^2, giving an intermediate result of `13,344.5032`. Then .5 is added, which causes the last integer digit to go up if the first decimal digit is 5 or more. The number then becomes `13,345.0032`. The `modf()` function is then called to extract the integer portion of the `double`. It places `13,345` in a separate field. We then divide this number by the multiplier, 100, which gives us a rounded result of `133.45`.

Negative numbers are rounded according to their absolute values and are restored to negative at the end.

The functions `pow()` and `modf()` are not discussed in this book because they are seldom used in business data processing. Once you bury them in the `round()` and `truncate()` functions, you will probably never call them again.

```
/*                  round.c                10/22/94                    */
#include <math.h>
#include <stdio.h>

void round (double *num,
            int    round_to_digits)
{
   double integer_part;
   double multiplier;
   double save_num;
   double temp_double;

   save_num = *num;                         /* save sign for later      */

   *num = fabs (*num);                      /* use positive value       */
```

```
   multiplier = pow ( 10.0, round_to_digits);    /* get multiplier to shift        */
                                                  /* number to the left             */

   temp_double = (*num * multiplier);             /* shift number left of decimal pt */
   temp_double = (temp_double + 0.5);             /* add 0.5 to round up             */
   modf (temp_double, &integer_part);             /* truncate result to integer part */
   *num = (integer_part / multiplier);            /* shift number back to the right  */

   if (save_num < 0.0)                            /* reapply sign, if necessary      */
   {
      *num *= -1.0;
   }
   return;
}
```

truncate(): A Business Truncation Routine

Truncating numbers is not often required in business systems, but it does occasionally surface as a requirement. As mentioned before, printf(), fprintf(), and sprintf() only round numbers and always round according to the IEEE rounding specification. They will not always truncate numbers correctly.

The call to truncate() is the same as for round():

```
       truncate (&expense_amt, 2);
```

The only difference between round() and truncate() is that truncate() does not add .5 to the number after it has been moved to the left of the decimal place.

```
/*                 truncate.c                    10/22/94                          */
#include <math.h>
#include <stdio.h>

void truncate (double *num,
               int    truncate_digits)
{
   double  integer_part;
   double  multiplier;
   double  save_num;
   double  temp_double;

   save_num = *num;                               /* save sign for later             */
   *num = fabs (*num);                            /* use positive value              */

   multiplier = pow ( 10.0, truncate_digits );    /* get multiplier to shift         */
                                                  /* number to the left              */
   temp_double = (*num * multiplier);             /* shift number left of decimal pt */
```

```
    modf (temp_double, &integer_part);        /* truncate result to integer part  */
    *num = (integer_part / multiplier);       /* shift number back to the right    */

    if (save_num < 0.0)                        /* reapply sign, if necessary        */
    {
        *num *= -1.0;
    }
    return;
}
```

`dollar_comma()`: Format a double as Dollars with Commas

One of C's continuing irritations is not putting commas in numbers. After five digits hardly anyone can tell what the magnitude of the number is. Report writer packages take care of this for you. A problem arises, however, if the report writer cannot reasonably handle certain reports. At that point you generally write a C report program and then have to deal with commas in numbers.

The `dollar_comma()` function was written to take care of that problem in numbers that are dollars. `double_comma()` (discussed in the next section) handles numbers you want to display as integers.

You call `dollar_comma()` with a number and a width you want for the display. The formatted result is returned as a character string in return value. `dollar_comma()` is not as fancy as COBOL PICTURE clause symbols. It does not float symbols over as COBOL does. It does suppress leading zeroes, right-justifies the result, and places parentheses around the number if it is negative.

Returning the result as a string in the return value is not typical of the examples in this book, but it does allow a compact use of the function. The call to `dollar_comma()` is typically placed as a parameter in an `fprintf()` call, as follows:

```
    fprintf (out_file, "%s", dollar_comma (16, expense_amt) );
```

This call passes a width of 16 and a field called `expense_amt`, which is defined as a `double`. The call to `dollar_comma()` will be replaced by its return value, a string 16 characters long. This string is then sent to `out_file` by the `fprintf()` call.

The function uses `sprintf()` to get the `double` into a character string so that commas, a decimal point, and parentheses can be inserted. If you have not rounded the number before you call `dollar_comma()`, `sprintf()` will round it for you. You may not like the result, however.

`dollar_comma()` allows the width parameter to be between 6 and 24, inclusive. It will tell you if the width is out of range or if the number cannot be formatted in the width supplied.

Some popular widths, resulting formatting, and maximums are shown below:

Width	Formatting	Maximum
12 produces	(ZZZ,ZZZ.99)	999 thousand
16 produces	(ZZZ,ZZZ,ZZZ.99)	999 million
20 produces	(ZZZ,ZZZ,ZZZ,ZZZ.99)	999 billion

```
        Sample Results:

                              Result
                            1         2
        Width    Number    12345678901234567890

        10       123.45            123.45
        10      -123.45         (  123.45)
        16      -123.45         (       123.45)
        12       123456.78       123,456.78
        16       1234567.78      1,234,567.78
```

```c
/*              dollar_comma()      doll_cma.c      10/22/94              */
#include <stdio.h>
#include <stdlib.h>
#include <ctype.h>

#define COMMA ','
#define SPACE ' '
#define MINUS '-'

char *dollar_comma (int    width,
                    double num_to_format)
{

static char edited_amt   [101];

    char alpha_amt   [51];
    int  digit_count      = 0;
    char filler      [3]  = "  ";
    int  i                = 0;
    int  j                = 0;
  if (width < 6 || width > 24)
  {
    sprintf (edited_amt, "Width must be between 6 and 24, inclusive."
                       "Width supplied was %d\n\n",
        width );

    return (edited_amt);
  }
```

```
if      (width ==  6) sprintf (alpha_amt, "%5.2f",  num_to_format);
else if (width ==  7) sprintf (alpha_amt, "%6.2f",  num_to_format);
else if (width ==  8) sprintf (alpha_amt, "%7.2f",  num_to_format);
else if (width ==  9) sprintf (alpha_amt, "%8.2f",  num_to_format);
else if (width == 10) sprintf (alpha_amt, "%9.2f",  num_to_format);
else if (width == 11) sprintf (alpha_amt, "%10.2f", num_to_format);
else if (width == 12) sprintf (alpha_amt, "%11.2f", num_to_format);
else if (width == 13) sprintf (alpha_amt, "%12.2f", num_to_format);
else if (width == 14) sprintf (alpha_amt, "%13.2f", num_to_format);
else if (width == 15) sprintf (alpha_amt, "%14.2f", num_to_format);
else if (width == 16) sprintf (alpha_amt, "%15.2f", num_to_format);
else if (width == 17) sprintf (alpha_amt, "%16.2f", num_to_format);
else if (width == 18) sprintf (alpha_amt, "%17.2f", num_to_format);
else if (width == 19) sprintf (alpha_amt, "%18.2f", num_to_format);
else if (width == 20) sprintf (alpha_amt, "%19.2f", num_to_format);
else if (width == 21) sprintf (alpha_amt, "%20.2f", num_to_format);
else if (width == 22) sprintf (alpha_amt, "%21.2f", num_to_format);
else if (width == 23) sprintf (alpha_amt, "%22.2f", num_to_format);
else                  sprintf (alpha_amt, "%23.2f", num_to_format);

/* Clear out the receiving field. Large size is to allow space for message. */

sprintf (edited_amt, "%100s", filler );

/* set end of formatted string to allow for a right parenthesis */

edited_amt [width] = '\0';

/* move the two decimal places and the period to the output field */

edited_amt [width - 2] = alpha_amt [width - 2];
edited_amt [width - 3] = alpha_amt [width - 3];
edited_amt [width - 4] = alpha_amt [width - 4];

/* move in the integer part of the number, from right to left */

for ( i = width - 5, j = width - 5, digit_count = 0;
      i >= 0;
      i--, j-- )
{
   edited_amt [j] = alpha_amt [i];

   digit_count++;

   if (digit_count % 3   == 0      &&
       alpha_amt [i - 1] != SPACE &&
       alpha_amt [i - 1] != MINUS    )
   {
      j--;
      edited_amt [j] = COMMA;
   }
```

```
    /* replace negative sign with a space */
    if (edited_amt [j] == MINUS )
    {
       edited_amt [j] = SPACE;
    }
}

/*
if the first character is a digit or a comma, the width parameter was not large enough
*/
if (isdigit (edited_amt [0] )  ||  edited_amt [0] == COMMA )
{
    sprintf (edited_amt, "Width not large enough - allow for parentheses. "
                    "Width = %d  number = %.2f.\n\n",
       width,
       num_to_format );
    return  (edited_amt);
}

/* put on parentheses if the number is negative */
if (num_to_format < 0.0 )
{
    edited_amt [0]          = '(';
    edited_amt [width - 1 ] = ')';
}

return (edited_amt );
}
```

double_comma() : Format a double as an Integer with Commas

This function is essentially the same as dollar_comma() without the two decimal places. It formats the integer part of a double with commas, right-justified, and with parentheses if the number is negative.

Usage is as follows:

```
fprintf (outfile, "%s", double_comma (13, ytd_sales) );
```

This function also uses sprintf() to get the double into a character string. If you have not rounded the number before you call double_comma(), sprintf() rounds it for you.

double_comma() allows the width parameter to be between 5 and 24, inclusive. It tells you if the width is out of range or if the number cannot be formatted in the width supplied.

Some popular widths, resulting formatting, and maximums are shown below:

Width	Formatting	Maximum
9 produces	(ZZZ,ZZZ)	999 thousand
13 produces	(ZZZ,ZZZ,ZZZ)	999 million
17 produces	(ZZZ,ZZZ,ZZZ,ZZZ)	999 billion

```
Sample Results:
```

		Result	
		1 2	
Width	Number	12345678901234567890	
10	123.45	123	
10	–123.45	(123)	
12	123456.78	123,457	← Notice sprintf() rounding
16	–123.45	(123)	
16	1234567.78	1,234,568	← Notice sprintf() rounding

```c
/*                  double_comma          dbl_cma.c      10/22/94      */
#include <stdio.h>
#include <stdlib.h>
#include <ctype.h>

#define COMMA ','
#define MINUS '-'
#define SPACE ' '

char *double_comma (int    width,
                    double num_to_format)
{
static  char edited_amt  [101];

        char alpha_amt   [51];
        int  digit_count      = 0;
        char filler      [3]  = " ";
        int  i = 0;
        int  j = 0;

        if (width < 5 || width > 24)
   {
      sprintf (edited_amt, "Width must be between 5 and 24. "
                           "Width supplied was %d\n\n",
         width );
      return (edited_amt);
   }
```

```
if        (width ==  5) sprintf (alpha_amt, "%4.0f",  num_to_format);
else if (width ==  6) sprintf (alpha_amt, "%5.0f",  num_to_format);
else if (width ==  7) sprintf (alpha_amt, "%6.0f",  num_to_format);
else if (width ==  8) sprintf (alpha_amt, "%7.0f",  num_to_format);
else if (width ==  9) sprintf (alpha_amt, "%8.0f",  num_to_format);
else if (width == 10) sprintf (alpha_amt, "%9.0f",  num_to_format);
else if (width == 11) sprintf (alpha_amt, "%10.0f", num_to_format);
else if (width == 12) sprintf (alpha_amt, "%11.0f", num_to_format);
else if (width == 13) sprintf (alpha_amt, "%12.0f", num_to_format);
else if (width == 14) sprintf (alpha_amt, "%13.0f", num_to_format);
else if (width == 15) sprintf (alpha_amt, "%14.0f", num_to_format);
else if (width == 16) sprintf (alpha_amt, "%15.0f", num_to_format);
else if (width == 17) sprintf (alpha_amt, "%16.0f", num_to_format);
else if (width == 18) sprintf (alpha_amt, "%17.0f", num_to_format);
else if (width == 19) sprintf (alpha_amt, "%18.0f", num_to_format);
else if (width == 20) sprintf (alpha_amt, "%19.0f", num_to_format);
else if (width == 21) sprintf (alpha_amt, "%20.0f", num_to_format);
else if (width == 22) sprintf (alpha_amt, "%21.0f", num_to_format);
else if (width == 23) sprintf (alpha_amt, "%22.0f", num_to_format);
else                  sprintf (alpha_amt, "%23.0f", num_to_format);

/* Clear out the receiving field. Large space is to allow space for message. */
sprintf (edited_amt, "%100s", filler );
/* set formatted string width to allow for right parenthesis */
edited_amt [width]    = '\0';
/* move the number in from right to left in order to right justify */
for ( i = width − 2, j = width − 2, digit_count = 0;
      i >= 0;
      i--, j-- )
{
   edited_amt [j] = alpha_amt [i];
   digit_count++;
   if (digit_count % 3   == 0     &&
       alpha_amt [i - 1] != SPACE &&
       alpha_amt [i - 1] != MINUS    )
   {
     j--;
     edited_amt [j] = COMMA;
   }
   /* replace negative sign with a space*/
   if (edited_amt [j] == MINUS)
   {
     edited_amt [j] = SPACE;
   }
}
```

```
    /*
    if the first character is a digit or a comma, the width parameter was
    not large enough
    */

    if (isdigit (edited_amt [0] ) || edited_amt [0] == COMMA )
    {
       sprintf (edited_amt, "Width not large enough – allow for parentheses. "
                            "Width = %d  number = %.0f.\n\n",
          width,
          num_to_format );

       return  (edited_amt);
    }

    /* put on parentheses if the number is negative and less than zero */

    if (num_to_format < -0.0 )
    {
       edited_amt [0]           = '(';
       edited_amt [width – 1 ] = ')';
    }

    return (edited_amt );
}
```

COBOL to C Cross-Reference

This appendix is a COBOL to C cross-reference, alphabetized by COBOL reserved words.

Many COBOL reserved words do not have a corresponding keyword, symbol operator, or function in C. Most of these can be placed in one of the following groups:

1. COBOL program documentation keywords, such as IDENTIFICATION DIVISION. C has none of these.

2. COBOL FILE CONTROL and FILE SECTION keywords. C has much less structure than COBOL does with regard to file handling. In C you use only the equivalents of an FD, an OPEN, and a READ.

3. COBOL Report Writer. C has nothing like it, and neither does COBOL II.

Most of these COBOL reserved words have been omitted from the following list. Aside from these, most of COBOL translates to C and vice versa. One of the surprises in writing this book has been the realization that almost all the COBOL statements that do the real work have a counterpart in C. The C equivalents may be keywords, symbol operators, or function calls, but they are practically all there.

COBOL symbols and special numbers follow the reserved words.

Keywords

COBOL Reserved Word	C Keyword/Symbol/Function/Explanation	Chapter

ACCEPT	`getchar()`
	`gets()`
	`scanf()`
	These C functions accept input from the terminal.
		5
		5
		5

ADD		
ADD...GIVING	+ (plus symbol) C does not have an ADD keyword. C adds the way COBOL does with the COMPUTE statement, or it adds the way COBOL does with the ADD...TO statement.	8
ADD...TO	+= ADD...TO (without the GIVING clause) puts the result in the first operand. C has the same construct in the += operator.	8
ADD CORRESPONDING	N/A I don't think there's anything like this in any other language.	
ADVANCING	`\n` (line feed) or `\f` (form feed) Advancing is handled within the C `fprintf()` function.	5
AFTER	N/A Whether the printer advances before or after the intended print line depends on whether the `\n` or `\f` characters precede or follow the print line in the `fprintf()` control string.	6
ALPHABETIC	`isalpha()` See IF *data-name* ALPHABETIC.	9
ALTER...GO TO	N/A Most COBOL shops haven't allowed this one for years anyway.	
AND	&& The C language is heavy with punctuation. The double ampersand means AND.	9
AT END	EOF EOF is a global data value that comes with the compiler. It is used to sense end-of-file in the `fgetc()` function.	6
BEFORE	N/A Whether the printer advances before or after the intended print line depends on whether the `\n` or `\f` characters precede or follow the print line in the `fprintf()` control string.	6

COBOL Reserved Word	C Keyword/Symbol/Function/Explanation	Chapter
BLANK WHEN ZERO	N/A C will always print at least one zero.	
CALL...USING parm-1, parm-2	function_name (parm_1, parm_2) C recognizes calls by finding a function name and optional parameters. There is no call reserved word.	11
CLOSE *file-name*	fclose (*file_name*) This is exactly the same operation. In C it is performed through a function call.	6
COMPUTATIONAL	int long These give the same internal representation, a signed binary number, as in COBOL. The difference is that in C you don't choose the number of digits. It is set by the compiler.	3
COMPUTATIONAL-1	float Short-precision floating point items in C are usually four bytes, as they are in COBOL. float should not be used in business because it only maintains six significant digits. Use double.	3
COMPUTATIONAL-2	double Long-precision floating point items in C are usually eight bytes (double the float). double is the data type to use in C for any number with decimal places.	3
COMPUTATIONAL-3	N/A There are no packed decimal numbers in C. You'll have to find some other ways to blow up your programs. Not to worry. Use double for decimal numbers.	3
COMPUTE	Implied In C, most arithmetic statements are coded like COBOL COMPUTE statements, but without the COMPUTE reserved word. (The other C arithmetic statements are structured like the ADD...TO statement, without the GIVING clause.)	8
CONSOLE	stdout The standard output device in C is usually the terminal from which the program is run. Things you display with printf() on stdout will appear on the terminal where the program is run.	5
COPY (NO LIST)	#include "*file_name*" #include is similar to the COBOL COPY statement. In C #include is typically used to bring in common definitions and function prototypes.	2
DATA DIVISION	N/A This is implicit in C rather than explicit as it is in COBOL. Data item definition is found in files prior to the instructions.	

COBOL Reserved Word	C Keyword/Symbol/Function/Explanation	Chapter
DATA RECORD(S) IS/ARE	N/A C is less rigorous and more flexible about file handling. In C you usually read or write strings (alphanumerics) from or to the file. It's up to you to keep it straight.	
DESCENDING KEY (sort)	N/A C has no commands for sorting.	
DESCENDING KEY (table)	N/A C does not have language support for internal sorted tables. In a C business data processing environment, you should be using a database package and a report writer package. These reduce the need for program table handling.	
DISPLAY	printf() The printf() function typically displays on the terminal from which the program was run.	5
DIVIDE...BY	/ C is usually coded to do division the way COBOL does with the COMPUTE statement.	8
DIVIDE...INTO (without GIVING)	/= DIVIDE...INTO (without the GIVING clause) puts the result in the first operand. C has the same construct in the /= operator.	8
END-IF	} C uses paired braces to delimit each part of an if statement.	9
END-PERFORM	} C also uses paired braces to delimit the for and while statements, which are equivalent to certain forms of PERFORM.	10
ENTRY...USING	function_name (parm_1, parm_2) Entry is used in COBOL to allow multiple entry points in one program. C accomplishes this by allowing multiple functions to exist in one file.	11
EQUAL TO	== C uses the double equal sign to test for equality. The single equal sign in C is an assign statement; it's equivalent to a MOVE statement.	9
EVALUATE	switch/case The C equivalent is not as powerful as EVALUATE. The switch/case construct is used to take different actions based on the value of an integer or single character variable.	9
EXAMINE...REPLACING	N/A C has no equivalent of this handy statement. You must write your own loop to search and replace.	

COBOL Reserved Word	C Keyword/Symbol/Function/Explanation	Chapter
EXHIBIT	`printf()` The `printf()` function displays things on the standard output device, `stdout`, which is usually a terminal.	5
EXIT	`return (value` or `expression)` C's equivalent of the EXIT statement has the bonus of optionally returning a value. This value can be an execution status or a computed value from the routine.	10
FD *file-name*	`FILE *file_name` C condenses the COBOL FILE-CONTROL and FILE SECTION code to a single statement. The C FILE definition is analogous to the COBOL FD. They both define an address for the program to use for reading and writing files.	6
FILLER	N/A C does not have an official "ignore this data name" data name. Create your own, and call it `filler`.	6
GO TO...	`goto` There is no justification in a business environment for using the C `goto` statement. There are other statements that can get you out of loops, such as `continue` and `break`.	10
GO TO. . .DEPENDING ON	N/A This construct is superceded by EVALUATE in COBOL II. C handles this construct with the `switch` and `case` keywords.	9
GOBACK	`return ( value` or `expression )` With the C `return` statement, you can return a status code or computation result to a calling function without having to make it a parameter. This is more powerful than RETURN-CODE.	10
GREATER THAN	`>`	9
GREATER THAN EQUAL	`>=` C has no keywords for these, but it does use the same symbols as COBOL.	
HIGH-VALUE(S)	N/A There are no figurative constants in C and there is no universal program constant for this.	
IF	`if` Every language has one.	9
IF *data-name* ALPHABETIC	`isalpha()` The COBOL class test applies to all the characters in the field. The C class test only works on one character at a time.	9

COBOL Reserved Word	C Keyword/Symbol/Function/Explanation	Chapter
IF *data-name* NUMERIC	`isdigit()` The COBOL class test applies to all the characters in the field. The C class test only works on one character at a time.	9
INDEXED BY	N/A C does not have language support for internal sorted tables. In a C business data processing environment, you should be using a database package and a report writer package. These reduce the need for program table handling.	
INITIALIZE	`= { 0 }` The C assignment shown puts all binary zeroes (LOW-VALUES) in a group item (structure) or data element. In C, all numeric types have the same bit configuration for zero. Also, a character string in C is empty if the first character contains binary zeroes. INITIALIZE is more powerful.	3, 12
JUSTIFIED RIGHT	N/A In C everything is right justified unless you tell it otherwise. See the discussion in the section on `printf()` in Chapter 5.	
LESS THAN	`<`	9
LESS THAN EQUAL	`<=` C has no keyword for these, but it uses the same symbols as COBOL.	

LINKAGE SECTION	`function_name ( int    parm_1,`
	`                double parm_2 )`
	In C you define parameters being received immediately after the function name. It's equivalent to the LINKAGE SECTION combined with the PROCEDURE DIVISION.
		11

LOW-VALUE(S)	`0` (zero) or NULL Zero in C is the same as LOW-VALUES. All numeric types in C have the same bit configuration for zero, which is binary zeroes.	3
MOVE	`=` (assignment, not equality) `strcpy()` (string copy) When moving a numeric or a single character data item in C, you assign it: `num_a = num_b;` The equal sign in C is always an active operator, just like it is in the COBOL COMPUTE statement. Equality tests are done with a double equal sign (==).	7

COBOL Reserved Word	C Keyword/Symbol/Function/Explanation	Chapter
MOVE CORRESPONDING	N/A C doesn't have anything like this. Some people would say it's a good thing.	
MULTIPLY	* (multiplication operator) C does not have a MULTIPLY keyword, only the symbol. Multiply operations in C are done in the form of COBOL COMPUTE statements without the COMPUTE reserved word.	8
MULTIPLY...BY	*= MULTIPLY...BY (without the GIVING clause) puts the result in the first operand. C has the same construct in the *= operator.	8
NEXT SENTENCE	; The semicolon ends C statements. If you code one on a line by itself in an if statement, it will do nothing, and control will pass to the next statement, just as in NEXT SENTENCE.	9
NOT	! C uses a symbol operator for NOT. There is no keyword.	9
NOTE	/* */ /* begins a comment in C, and */ ends one. Comments can begin and end in any column of any line. C is much more flexible about comments than COBOL.	2
NUMERIC	isdigit() See IF data-name NUMERIC.	9
OCCURS n TIMES	long state_totals [50]; The brackets enclose a number that represents the number of times the data item will occur. Table definition in C is somewhat different than in COBOL, but use of tables and subscripts is similar.	12
OCCURS n TIMES DEPENDING ON	N/A The COBOL OCCURS DEPENDING ON is used to set up binary searches. C does not have a binary search capability in the language.	
ON integer-1	N/A C has no equivalent of this handy COBOL construct.	
ON SIZE ERROR	N/A C provides no mechanism for detecting resulting numbers being larger than the defined field can hold. C just corrupts the number, and it is often hard to figure out what happened.	
OPEN INPUT/OUTPUT file-name	fopen (file_name, access) In C you call a function to open a file and pass it the file name you defined in the C equivalent of the FD. Access is	6

COBOL Reserved Word	C Keyword/Symbol/Function/Explanation	Chapter
	"r" for read/input, "w" for write/output, or "a" for write/append.	
OPEN I-O *file-name*	N/A C does not support VSAM type files that you read from and write to at the same time.	
PERFORM *procedure-name*	function_name() C programs can be structured so that functions work exactly like COBOL paragraphs. C functions can also be made to work like subprograms.	10, 11
PERFORM... UNTIL...	while (*expression*) In COBOL II the in-line PERFORM UNTIL is quite similar to the while statement. while is an in-line loop.	10
PERFORM... VARYING... FROM... BY... UNTIL...	for (from; while; varying) The for statement in C is the equivalent of the COBOL II in-line PERFORM VARYING statement. Where COBOL says PERFORM UNTIL, C says perform *while*.	10
PICTURE	Included within data type C has a limited vocabulary for data element definition compared to COBOL. In C the data type of the data item determines the storage size. For numeric data types you only get to say whether it's an integer or a floating point number and whether it's a small one or a large one.	3
PICTURE clause symbols	%s, %f, %d, and so on C uses format specifiers such as the ones shown to format fields within the control string of a printf(), fprintf(), or sprintf() statement.	5, 6, 7
PROCEDURE DIVISION	main() PROCEDURE DIVISION is where the statements begin for the main program. The main() function declaration in C is where the statements begin for the main function.	1
PROCEDURE DIVISION USING parm-1, parm-2	function_name (int parm_1, double parm_2) The function header in C is equivalent to a combination of LINKAGE SECTION and PROCEDURE DIVISION USING in COBOL.	11
PROCEDURE DIVISION USING parm-fields	main (int argc, char *argv) To pass parameters at run time, C uses parameters in the main() function header. argc is the count of parameters and argv refers to an array (table) of parameter values.	11
READ	fgetc () (read a character) fgets () (read a string of characters)	6

COBOL Reserved Word	C Keyword/Symbol/Function/Explanation	Chapter
	`fread ()` (read a structure) Reading files in C is more work than reading files in COBOL. Since C has a weak orientation to fixed-field, fixed-length records, you often read a file one field at a time or read one record at a time and then extract the fields. Fixed-length-record processing can be done with `fread()` and `fwrite()`.	
READY TRACE	N/A (usually) Most C compilers have little or no debug or trace support. However, some C compilers and many C development environment packages do have extensive debug and trace facilities. Every shop should have either a compiler or a development package with the debug facility.	
RECORD	`struct` C uses structures to group data elements or groups of data elements. Structures do not have explicit level numbers.	3
REDEFINES	`union` `union` is analogous to **REDEFINES** of group items. `union` allows a redefinition of a structure, which is the C equivalent of a COBOL group item. C does not allow redefinition of an elementary item. `union` is so seldom used in business data processing that it is not discussed in this book.	
REMAINDER	`%` COBOL can give you the remainder as a by-product of a divide operation. In C there is a remainder operator—%, the percent sign. You have to code a separate remainder statement if you want to capture the remainder of a division.	8
RESET TRACE	see READY TRACE	

RETURN-CODE	`exit (status)`
	`return (value` or `expression)`
	COBOL allows you to return a numeric return code to the operating system. C has a more powerful facility.
	
	`exit (status)` returns control to the operating system with a numeric value in the status expression.
	
	`return (value` or `expression)` returns control to the calling function or to the operating system if called from `main()`. The value or expression can be numbers, a single character, or a string of characters, depending on how it's designed.
		10

COBOL Reserved Word	C Keyword/Symbol/Function/Explanation	Chapter
ROUNDED	N/A C has no equivalent to this handy statement. You have to code your own rounding routine or use the `round()` function given in Appendix F.	8
SEARCH (sequential)	N/A C has no keyword equivalent to **SEARCH**. However, in a C business data processing environment, you should be using a database package and a report writer package. These reduce the need for program table searching.	
SEARCH ALL (binary)	N/A Same as above.	
SELECT *file-name*	N/A All of COBOL's **FILE-CONTROL** and **FILE SECTION** statements boil down to the C equivalent of the COBOL **FD**, which is **FILE**.	6
SET...DOWN BY	`-=` **SET DOWN BY** can only be used on indexes. In C there are only subscripts. The `-=` (minus equal) operator in C is equivalent to the **SET DOWN BY** statement and can be used more widely.	8
SET...TO	`=` **SET** is equivalent to a COBOL **MOVE** statement and so is the C assignment operator, the equal sign.	7
SET...UP BY	`+=` **SET UP BY** is used on indexes. In C there are only subscripts. The `+=` operator in C can be used more widely than the **SET UP BY** statement.	8
SORT *sort-file-name*	N/A C has no commands for sorting.	
SPACE	` ' ' ` C has no figurative constants. You have to use literals or program constants (`#define`).	2
SPECIAL-NAMES	N/A You cannot rename things like `stdin`, the **SYSIN** equivalent, and `stdout`, the **CONSOLE** equivalent, within a C program. In C it is done outside the program.	
STOP RUN	`exit (status)` In C the `exit()` statement terminates the program. You can also return a status to the operating system with the `exit()` statement. IBM COBOL does this with the register **RETURN-CODE**.	10

COBOL Reserved Word	C Keyword/Symbol/Function/Explanation	Chapter
STRING	strcat() sprintf() C does not have a direct equivalent of the COBOL STRING statement. strcat() concatenates one string field onto another. sprintf() allows you to create an output field made up of literals, substituted numbers, and substituted characters.	7
SUBTRACT	– C does not have a SUBTRACT keyword, only the minus symbol. Subtraction operations in C are done in the form of COBOL COMPUTE statements without the COMPUTE reserved word.	8
SUBTRACT...FROM	–= SUBTRACT...FROM (without the GIVING clause) puts the result in the first operand. C has the same construct in the –= operator.	8
SUBTRACT CORRESPONDING	N/A This does not compute in C, just as ADD CORRESPONDING does not.	
TRANSFORM	N/A C does not support this function. You have to do it yourself with a for loop.	
UNSTRING	sscanf() sscanf() is somewhat equivalent to UNSTRING, except that you have to know the detailed layout of the field. UNSTRING just has to know what the delimiters are.	6
USAGE IS	This is implicitly generated by the data type. In the PICTURE clause, USAGE tells the compiler the internal storage format. In C the data type (char, long, double, and so on) defines what the internal storage format will be.	3
VALUE(S) IS/ARE	int record_count = 0; char file_name [10] = "AC100.out"; In C, when you define a data item, you can give it an initial value by using the equal sign, which is called the assignment statement in C. In COBOL the VALUE clause is also an assignment statement.	3
WRITE record-name	fprintf() (write a formatted string) fwrite() (write a structure) Writing files is more work in C than in COBOL. Most of the time you write a set of characters or fields at a time using fprintf(). Writing fixed-length records is supported by the fwrite() function.	6
ZERO	0 or NULL C has no keyword for zero, but it does have the program constant NULL.	

Symbols and Special Numbers

COBOL Symbol	C Symbol Operator/Explanation	Chapter
. (period)	; (semicolon) C uses the semicolon to end most, but not all, statements. C also uses the period. It has the same function as the **OF** word in COBOL; qualification of a data name within a group item (COBOL) or a structure (C). See the section on structures in Chapter 3.	1
< (less than) <= (less than or equal)	< (less than) <= (less than or equal) It's the same in C.	9
() in arithmetic expressions: `COMPUTE A = (B + C) * D.`	`a = (b + c) * d;` You use parentheses the same way in C for clarity and/or precedence in arithmetic expressions.	8

() in **IF** statements:
`IF  A = B AND`
`   ( C = D OR E = F )`
	`if (a == b &&`
	`    (c == d || e == f))`
	Use the parentheses to guarantee that the **OR** will be evaluated correctly. Notice also that C has a required pair of parentheses around the whole set of conditional statements.
		9

() in PICTURE clauses: `LAST-NAME PIC X(30)`	`last_name [31];` In C, brackets are used to give the size of alphanumeric items (called strings in C). Numeric item size depends on the data type you choose (`int`, `long`, `double`); you don't get to specify how many digits.	3

() with subscripts and indexes:
`MOVE 0 TO SALES`
`    (MONTH).`
	`sales [month] = 0`
	Brackets are used in C for subscripting the same way parentheses are in COBOL. C only has subscripts.
		12

+ (plus symbol)	+ (plus symbol) Usage is the same in both languages.	8
$ (currency in **PIC** clause)	N/A C doesn't handle money as well as COBOL. You have to put your own dollar sign on the print line, and C will not float it over to the first nonzero digit.	
* (multiplication)	* (multiplication) It works the same way.	8
* (comment)	`/*  */` (slash-star, star-slash) Slash-star begins a comment in C, and star-slash ends one. Comments can begin and end in any column of any line. C is much more flexible about comments.	2

COBOL Symbol	C Symbol Operator/Explanation	Chapter
** (exponentiation)	`pow(number, power_to_raise_it_to)` The `pow()` function takes a number and raises it to the power specified. It is seldom used in business applications.	
– (hyphen)	`_` (underscore) C uses underscores as connectors in data names and function names. The hyphen is always interpreted as a minus sign.	1
– (minus sign)	– (minus sign) A minus sign always means negative or subtract in C.	8
/ (divided by)	/ (divided by) It's the same in both languages.	8
> (greater than) >= (greater than or equal)	> (greater than) >= (greater than or equal) It's the same in C.	9
= (in IF statements)	== C uses the double equal sign to test for equality. This is an endless source of misery. You will inevitably wrongly use the single equal sign for an equality test, and the intended comparison will not occur.	9
= (in COMPUTE statements)	= The single equal sign in C is an assign statement, as it is in the COBOL COMPUTE statement. (Take the result of the calculation and place it in the field to the left of the = sign). In C it's always equivalent to a COBOL MOVE statement.	8
01	`struct` C does have a concept of levels of data in a structure, which is a rough equivalent to a COBOL group item. However, the levels in the C structure are implicit rather than explicit as in COBOL.	3

77	`char`
	`int`
	`long`
	`float`
	`double`
	77s can't be subdefined, and neither can any of these C language data definition types.
		3

88	N/A 88 level items in COBOL are tied to a specific data item and represent a name for a particular value. C doesn't have a facility to do this, although you can define names with values with the `#define` statement.	

Obtaining Code for Examples, Business Utility Programs, and Standards

All the program examples in the book, the business utility functions in Appendix F, and the programming standards from Chapter 13 are available free on-line through the Internet or for a nominal charge by phone or mail. Each program example in the book has its file name within the comment on the first line.

Free Through the Internet

All of the files are available at no charge via **FTP** (File Transfer Protocol) over the Internet from Addison-Wesley Publishing Co. The two basic methods of accessing the Internet are directly through a command line prompt or indirectly through a screen interface from an Internet service provider or an on-line service. If you are using a command line prompt, issue the command:

```
ftp.aw.com
```

and log in as anonymous. Use your e-mail address as your password. Once logged in, change to the directory for Gearing by typing:

```
cd cseng/authors/gearing/c4cobol
```

Before retrieving source code or standards, it is a good idea to look at the readme file to see how the files are organized. The command:

```
get README.gea
```

will retrieve this file. Quit FTP to log off and read the file. (Although the README.gea file can be read on-line, it is polite not to tie up the login for reading.) Then log back on when you are ready to download.

You can also get a listing of available filenames using either the dir command or ls command. These commands require no arguments.

FTP and file extraction can be complicated. Instructions vary depending on your system: DOS, OS/2, Windows, and Macintosh all work a little differently. If you are new to using FTP, you may want to consult your local network guru.

Supplements are also available from this book's page on our **World Wide Web** server. Point your browser to:

```
http://www.aw.com/cseng/authors/gearing/c4cobol/c4cobol.html
```

You may also view pages for all of our Computer Science and Engineering books at:

```
http://www.aw.com.cseng/
```

Using On-Line Services

In 1994 on-line services such as America Online, Compu-Serve, Prodigy, and others began to offer connections to the Internet. If you use an on-line service, you probably have access to the Internet. The interface will be different for each vendor, but they all offer fairly obvious methods. Follow the steps outlined above for connecting to the Addison-Wesley site. Changing directories, viewing files, and retrieving files will typically be accomplished by highlighting choices with a mouse. If you have a problem, the on-line service provider should be able to help.

Code by Mail

A diskette containing all the available files is available by mail at a nominal charge. It is available only on a 3.5-inch diskette; the diskette is formatted for use on DOS, Windows, and OS/2 only; other formats are not available.

Within the USA

By *credit card*, in the USA, call 1-800-447-2226. Ask for the program code diskette to accompany the book, *C For COBOL Programmers, A Business Approach*, by Jim Gearing. Reference Product ISBN 0-8053-1662-0. The price is $10.75, plus shipping, handling, and state and city sales taxes. Visa, MasterCard, and American Express are accepted.

By *check*, in the USA, fill out the coupon located at the back of the book. The price is $10.75, (shipping and handling is included), plus state and city sales taxes.

In Canada

In Canada contact:

>   Addison-Wesley Publishers Ltd.
>   P.O. Box 580
>   26 Prince Andrews Place
>   Don Mills, Ontario, CANADA M3C 2T8
>   Phone 416-447-5101, Fax 416-443-0948

Ask for the program code diskette to accompany the book, *C For COBOL Programmers, A Business Approach*, by Jim Gearing. Reference Product ISBN 0-8053-1662-0.

International Orders

Outside Canada and the USA, contact:

>   Addison-Wesley Publishing Company
>   International Publishing Company
>   Jacob Way
>   Reading, Massachusetts 01867
>   Phone 617-944-3700 ext. 2405
>   Telex 989572 ADWES UD
>   Fax 617-942-2829

Ask for the program code diskette to accompany the book, *C For COBOL Programmers, A Business Approach*, by Jim Gearing. Reference Product ISBN 0-8053-1662-0.

Obtaining Code and Standards by Mail

A diskette containing the example programs from this book, the business utility functions, and the programming standards from Chapter 13 is also available by mail. These files may be obtained from other sources as well, as indicated in Appendix H in the book.

To obtain a 3.5-inch diskette (suitable for DOS, Windows, and OS/2), and pay by check, use the coupon below. Make a copy of this page, fill in the required information, and send it, along with your check made out to Addison-Wesley, to the address below. Please include state sales tax with your order. Shipping and handling are included for orders prepaid by check.

Offer available in the United States only.

Please send me the source code diskette to accompany the book *C For COBOL Programmers, A Business Approach*, by Jim Gearing.

Product ISBN 0-8053-1662-0

    Diskette Price: $10.75

    Your State Sales Tax: _____

    Check Total: _____

Make check payable to: *Addison-Wesley*.

Ship to:

    Name   _____

    Street/Box _____

    City   _____

    State   _____

    Zip Code _____

Allow 2–3 weeks from receipt of coupon for delivery.

Mail this form to:

    Addison-Wesley Publishing Company, Inc.
    Jacob Way
    Reading, Massachusetts
    01867

Index